PIETY AND PUBLIC FUNDING

Politics and Culture in Modern America

Series Editors: Margot Canaday, Glenda Gilmore, Michael Kazin, and Thomas J. Sugrue

Volumes in the series narrate and analyze political and social change in the broadest dimensions from 1865 to the present, including ideas about the ways people have sought and wielded power in the public sphere and the language and institutions of politics at all levels—local, national, and transnational. The series is motivated by a desire to reverse the fragmentation of modern U.S. history and to encourage synthetic perspectives on social movements and the state, on gender, race, and labor, and on intellectual history and popular culture.

PIETY AND PUBLIC FUNDING

EVANGELICALS AND THE STATE
IN MODERN AMERICA

AXEL R. SCHÄFER

PENN

UNIVERSITY OF PENNSYLVANIA PRESS

PHILADELPHIA

Published by
University of Pennsylvania Press
Philadelphia, Pennsylvania 19104-4112
www.upenn.edu/pennpress

Printed in the United States of America on acid-free paper
10 9 8 7 6 5 4 3 2 1

Library of Congress Cataloging-in-Publication Data
Schäfer, Axel R.
 Piety and public funding : evangelicals and the state in
modern America / Axel R. Schäfer.—1st ed.
  p. cm.
 Includes bibliographical references and index.
 ISBN 978-0-8122-4411-3 (hardcover : alk. paper)
 1. Faith-based human services—Political aspects—United
States—History—20th century. 2. Public-private sector
cooperation—Political aspects—United States—History—20th
century. 3.Church and state—United States—History—20th
century. 4. Religion and politics—United States—History—
20th century. 5. Evangelicalism—United States—History—
20th century. I. Title. II. Series: Politics and culture in modern
America
HV530.S29   2012
(PU)5189315   2011046741

CONTENTS

INTRODUCTION

HOW EVANGELICALS LEARNED TO STOP WORRYING AND LOVE THE STATE

I n the past seven decades a remarkable transformation has taken place in the United States in the relationship between the federal government and religious charitable organizations in general, and between the state and evangelical agencies in particular. During the 1930s and 1940s, New Deal social programs largely excluded religious charities from receiving federal funds; the Supreme Court renewed the nation's commitment to the separation of church and state; and evangelicals assailed Catholic efforts to obtain public aid. By the first decade of the twenty-first century, however, the scene looked very different. Policy makers from both parties lauded the role of religious organizations in a system of government-subsidized social provision; the Supreme Court had largely upheld public funding of sectarian agencies; and evangelical charities were prominent beneficiaries of federal aid funneled through policies such as the "Charitable Choice" provision of Bill Clinton's 1996 welfare reforms and the George W. Bush administration's "Faith-Based Initiative."

At the heart of this transformation in church-state relations was the co-alescence of two seminal political developments in post–World War II American history: the dramatic growth of the national security and welfare state on the one hand, and the resurgence of evangelical religion on the other. Eager to ensure a stable socioeconomic climate and to safeguard America's global role, postwar policy makers sought to mobilize the administrative and spiritual resources of religious agencies for their political aims. "Subsidiarist" social policies made billions of dollars of public funds available to religiously affili-ated hospitals, nursing homes, educational institutions, and social services. At the same time, government support for religious international aid agen-cies and various efforts to fund missionary work helped integrate sectarian groups into the foreign policy framework.

Meanwhile, white conservative Protestantism also underwent a historic change as a new generation of evangelicals entered the political and sociocultural arena. Indeed, since 1945 the loosely organized evangelical movement has become the largest single religious faction in the United States and now forms one of the most strongly Republican groups in the religious spectrum. Driven by their opposition to both prewar fundamentalism and theological liberalism, and spurred by a desire for cultural respectability and transdenominational coalition building, postwar neo-evangelicals renewed their commitment to social and political activism. Among the themes that dominated debates within the movement and shaped its emergent political ideology was the relationship between church and state in general and the public funding of religious agencies in particular.

The growing ideological and administrative ties between the federal government and evangelical agencies since World War II, and the gradual revision of traditional evangelical attitudes toward the state, are the main subjects of this book. It asks questions such as: How did white evangelical and fundamentalist Christianity, in line with other religious groups, become a constituent part of the networks between public and nongovernmental agencies that underlay Cold War state building? In what ways did this provide evangelicals with opportunities to reassert their spiritual mission and open up new access to the corridors of political power? And how did the emerging links between conservative Protestantism and the Cold War state shape the movement's right-wing political mobilization? In offering answers to these questions, the book views the growth of the state and the resurgence of evangelical Protestantism not just as simultaneous or reactive processes, but as interdependent in ways that have been little understood. In the process it revises some entrenched analytical concepts in the study of both conservative religion and state building.

*   *   *

Historians of public policy have long recognized the important role played by business, nonprofits, think tanks, professional organizations, and similar societal entities in shaping and implementing American social and foreign policy. In a liberal polity marked by the separation of powers, checks and balances, and an ideology of limited government and free enterprise, mobilizing society in the name of the "national interest" generally relies more upon government incentives than state authority. Networks between the state and nongovernmental actors thus frequently form the "corporatist" or "associationalist" bedrock of U.S. public policy.[1] This applies in particular to the period of state expansion since World War II.

Although religion-based agencies fully shared in the postwar public-nonprofit networks, the institutional and bureaucratic ties between religious organizations and government have received little systematic attention in Cold War research.[2] Indeed, as political scientist Stephen Monsma has noted, granting tax dollars to sectarian organizations remains "one of the best kept secrets in the United States."[3] What is more, among the least recognized features of Cold War social and foreign policy is in fact one of the most intriguing aspects of the postwar funding networks: they involved not only mainline Protestant, Jewish, and Catholic organizations, but also white evangelicals. Though conservative Protestants had traditionally been the most outspoken opponents of closer funding ties between church and state, the ideological and institutional needs of the Cold War state, in conjunction with the political awakening of evangelicalism, laid the foundation for new political and financial links between the two.

Within the existing research matrix on state-nonprofit networks few analysts have probed the growing interrelationship between state building and white conservative Protestantism in the latter part of the twentieth century.[4] Social policy historians have discussed the postwar welfare state without paying much attention to religious charities in general and evangelical providers in particular; foreign policy experts have analyzed the relationship between conservative Protestants and the state in ideological, rather than bureaucratic and institutional terms; and social scientists generally associated the expansion of governmental functions with the advancement of secularization under the conditions of modern industrial society. Similarly, the vast literature on the Christian Right largely attributes the resurgence of postwar conservative Protestantism to internal resource mobilization outside of state institutions. Having argued that evangelicals mobilized politically primarily via the "backlash," most research has focused on how a pietistic and largely apolitical religious group hostile to the liberal state was jolted back into the political realm while reacting against the expanding power of government.

The analysis of the links between modern conservative Protestantism and the postwar state is hampered further by definitional and empirical problems. Evangelicalism is a multilayered, decentralized movement that consists of a wide variety of religious organizations and charitable corporations with divergent policies toward public funding. It includes traditional denominations, freestanding megachurches, parachurch organizations, alternative forms of worship, and interdenominational bodies. At the same time, the variety of different funding arrangements on multiple governmental levels, and the assumption that religious bodies were not eligible for public funds, complicates any measuring of the role of sectarian providers in publicly funded sectarian social service provision.[5] As a result, exasperated scholars and statisticians of nonprofits and social policy often find the system largely unmonitorable. "In almost every policy sphere," political scientist Lester Salamon concludes, "federal operations now involve a complex collage of widely assorted tools mobilizing a diverse collection of different types of actors to perform a host of different roles in frequently confusing combinations."[6] Similarly, historian Bruce Nichols, in his study of government assistance to religious foreign aid and refugee agencies, found only "fragmentary information." State Department records were often inaccessible and agencies kept spotty records or did not make them available to researchers. Moreover, official records frequently did not contain information on grants or contracts issued to voluntary agencies through local embassies, and refugee allocations frequently came from different sources in government.[7] These empirical limitations continue to proscribe the systematic study of church-state funding ties. The "virtual exclusion of religious bodies and activities from the research agendas," the authors of the chapter on voluntary, nonprofit and religious entities of the 2006 edition of *Historical Statistics of the United States* note, "have long posed formidable obstacles to gathering and analyzing credible statistics on these organizations." In turn, this precluded them from "offering much more than a hint of these activities" in their contribution to the edition. They blamed "definitional murkiness," the deeply flawed statistical understanding of American religion, and the haphazard and selective attention of federal agencies for this oversight.[8]

Viewing postwar evangelicalism and the Cold War state either as unrelated or in terms of a simple action/response scenario is also indicative of a deeper conceptual limitation of much historical scholarship on religion and politics. It arguably constitutes an aspect of what religious historian Jon Butler has called the "religion problem" of modern American historiography. The tendency to ignore the continued salience of theological traditions and their long-term pragmatic engagement with the secular realm, he maintains, has resulted in a lack of convincing historical explanations for phenomena such as the rise of the New Christian Right.[9] Indeed, only recently have scholars even suggested that evangelical organizational and political mobilization was linked to the dynamics of state building. Hugh Heclo and Wilfred M. McClay, for example, view the way organized structures of religion and government impinge on each other and on society as crucial for understanding the relationship between religion and politics. Robert Fogel maintains that the mobilization of evangelical Christians since World War II grew out of the welfare state's successful income transfer combined with its failure to solve the "moral crisis." And Robert Wuthnow emphasizes that evangelicals frequently combine active participation in national politics with intense involvement with charities in their local congregations.[10]

This study seeks to contribute to this growing body of literature. It does not offer an exhaustive account of the public funding for evangelical organizations, nor does it provide a systematic analysis of aid-to-religion policies as part of the range of fiscal instruments of the Cold War state. Instead, the book analyzes the evangelical debates about a variety of direct and indirect subsidies for religious colleges and universities, hospitals, social service providers, and international relief agencies—institutions that were regarded as essential to Cold War preparedness and became major beneficiaries of federal largesse. It asks about the institutional and ideological structures that enabled insurgent political movements to assert their voice in public policy, and explores how the movement internally negotiated the tension between an antistatist identity and the institutional integration into the Cold War state. It discusses the significance of these processes for the organizational and political resurgence of conservative Protestants. And it examines the larger meaning of these processes for both religion and state building.

By connecting conservative religion and Cold War public policy, the book suggests four main arguments that offer revisions to established scholarly interpretations. First, it challenges the notion that the expansion of the state and the growth of white evangelicalism were either antagonistic or unrelated processes, and that social policies promoted a liberal, secular state hostile to conservative Protestantism. In contrast to both the self-image of most evangelicals and the views of many academic observers, the features of the Cold War state and the internal dynamics of the evangelical resurgence involved the two sides in a process of mutual construction and legitimation. Rather than being marginalized, evangelicals mirrored the experience of other religious groups in being brought into the orbit of the Cold War state. In turn, conservative Protestants gradually parted with their traditional insistence on the separation of church and state. Instead of refusing public aid to religion outright, they made access to funds and the preservation of their faith-based practices within a system of state subsidies the linchpin of their new attitude. Indeed, their emerging political ideology was less indicative of the rejection of state building than of an effort to reconcile moral and social conservatism with imperatives of economic growth, global power, and consumer culture.

Second, the study suggests that Cold War anticommunism and evangelical involvement with Lyndon Johnson's Great Society were key factors in this transformation. White conservative Protestantism's strong commitment to fighting the "red menace" ushered in a new relationship between evangelicals and the expanding national security state. In particular, foreign aid funding engineered new organizational ties between religious activists, government, and policy elites. As the merger of military and humanitarian goals blurred the line between relief work and missionary activism, evangelical aid agencies became newly interested in taking government funds. While foreign aid helped make evangelicals a constituent part of the public-private networks that underlay the Cold War expansion of the "garrison state," the War on Poverty in the 1960s laid the foundation for the participation of evangelical social service providers in the welfare state. Although evangelicals frequently pilloried the policies of the Johnson administration as symbols of moral decline and government intrusiveness, they benefited from the particular way in which the Great Society increased public aid for religious hospitals, educational institutions, and welfare agencies. Likewise, the government practice of tolerating faith-based approaches despite antisectarian clauses in many laws allowed evangelical charities to participate fully in the public-nonprofit partnership without having to compromise their religious missions. While the War on Poverty created the structural conditions that integrated evangelical providers, however, it failed to make evangelicals part of an effective electoral coalition in support of a broad-based system of social provision. Instead, it nurtured both an attachment among evangelicals to its underlying policy trajectories and a deep resentment against its alleged moral failures. In other words, the Great Society enabled evangelicals to partake in the expansion of public funding on the basis of a sense of political and normative alienation.

Third, the findings show that this "antistatist statism" was an important factor in establishing the internal dominance of the Right within the evangelical movement. In the aftermath of the Civil Rights movement and the anti-Vietnam War protests, conservative evangelicals effectively blended the rhetoric of limited government with the increasingly savvy use of the funding instrumentalities offered by the state. Meanwhile, a resurgent evangelical Left renewed its commitment to a separationist and pacifist stance on the basis of a critique of the corruptibility of secular institutions and the military-industrial complex. During the divisive debates in the 1970s over issues such as biblical inerrancy, civil religion, and social involvement, conservatives used the Cold War nexus between church and state to spell out a coherent theo-ideological position, engage in partisan political networking, and marginalize left-wing and liberal adversaries. This suggests that the right-wing political alignment of evangelicals was rooted less in a natural affinity between religious and secular conservatism than in internal movement dynamics in the context of interacting with Cold War public policy.

This underscores the study's final contention, namely, that the political mobilization and broader popular appeal of evangelicalism since the 1970s was not primarily the result of a "culture war" against liberal state building. Instead, a mixture of symbiosis and antagonism was at the core of the relationship between the state and resurgent evangelicalism. By combining vociferous antistatism and entrepreneurial individualism with staunch support for the national security state, corporate capitalism, and public aid for religious agencies, the New Christian Right helped perpetuate the established growth-oriented, moralistic, and race and gender-coded pattern of state building, which the turmoil of the 1960s and 1970s had challenged but not changed. Seen from this perspective, the "politics of morality" was not primarily a noneconomic critique of state building, but another manifestation of an economic rationale built into the structures of state provision. In their "economic" New Deal incarnation, welfare state structures had benefited a white, industrial, and unionized workforce while preserving race, gender, and class divides. In their neoconservative "cultural" incarnation, they benefited a white, male, postindustrial electorate that sought to reassert patriarchal authority, maintain women as an unpaid workforce of care-providers, and preserve an underpaid pool of casual labor. This appealed to an electorate particularly in the South and the West of the country that, in relocating to the regions' new technocratic suburbias, had benefited from federal deficit spending, the military buildup, and the social service expansions of the Cold War era, but felt besieged by economic, race, and gender challenges in a deindustrialized, postsegregationist, and postpatriarchal setting. In other words, while the political basis of Cold War liberalism collapsed in the upheavals of the 1970s, the Right provided an ideology of state building for the post-1960s age in which the close relationship between church and state was crucial.

*   *   *

The six chapters of the book weave together research from the fields of social policy, foreign relations, social movement mobilization, the sociology of

religion, and church-state relations. Combining a comprehensive review of
the secondary literature with an analysis of newly accessible archival materials, the book focuses on white conservative Protestants organized in the
National Association of Evangelicals (NAE). Chapter 1 questions the "influential metanarrative in American social policy history" that either sees religion in general as irrelevant in the development of the modern welfare state
or argues that state building sidelined the spiritual dimension of religious
organizations.[11] It examines how Cold War public policy created a legal and
political climate that encouraged closer ties between religious entities and
the federal government. Caught between the need for expanded administrative capacities in the pursuit of Cold War objectives and the imperative to
preserve an image of limited government, planners nurtured state-nonprofit
networks as the administrative core of public policy. They devised a structure that combined centralized revenue gathering and policy planning at the
federal level with the transfer of policy implementation to nongovernmental
actors. Although commonly associated with the conservative backlash of the
1990s, the devolution and privatization of social services, as Peter Dobkin
Hall has noted, "actually describes the fundamental dynamic of American
government over the past half-century."[12]

Scholars have used terms such as the "allocative state" and "third-party
government" to provide a name for this extensive reliance of the state on
nongovernmental providers. However, the term "subsidiarity" best captures
the process of reducing the federal government from a direct provider to a
funding agency. Derived from Catholic social thought, the term combines
conceptually the devolution of functions to lower levels; the notion that mediating structures are superior to government bodies; and the definition of
social problems in terms of rehabilitative intervention. Merging national security and welfarist components, subsidiarist policies made federal monies
available to private businesses and nonprofit organizations in areas such as
higher education, defense-related and medical research, hospital building,
social services, foreign aid, urban renewal, and community development.

Cold War subsidiarity fundamentally reshaped church-state relations. In
seeking to mobilize society in the fight against communism, policy makers
drew upon both the ideological and the organizational resources of sectarian organizations. On the one hand, they tied national security to a renewed
commitment to traditional religion by depicting the Cold War as a patriotic
battle against an enemy who not only needed to be defeated militarily, but also
spiritually and culturally. Efforts to address the "spiritual illiteracy" of military

recruits and the dissemination of religious materials via government channels legitimated Christian belief as a publicly subsidized interpretive frame for understanding America's new global role. On the other hand, policy makers could also hardly ignore the administrative capacities of religious charities, which constitute about 40 percent of the nonprofit sector organizations. The provision of vast federal funding streams created new ties between the state and religious educational, health care, social service, and foreign aid organizations. Although government support for religious charities was no novelty in American history, wartime and Cold War challenges nurtured this relationship to an unprecedented extent long before the conservative resurgence and the George W. Bush administration. As Monsma has pointed out, the "two characteristics of nonprofit service organizations—their receipt of large amounts of government funds and the religious nature of many of them—overlap."[13]

In response to this large-scale expansion of government support, public aid to church-related institutions came under increasing legal scrutiny. Despite the particular challenges posed by constitutional law, however, the main Supreme Court decisions did not fundamentally contest the public funding of many religious agencies. Except in the areas of primary and secondary education, the Court largely condoned government programs funneling funds to religious charities. What is more, the simultaneous efforts by the Court to limit infringements on religion under the free exercise clause created more leeway for the assertion of the spiritual mission of sectarian organizations.[14] Meanwhile, many church leaders increasingly voiced fears about closer ties to the state. Once again, however, this did not seriously hamper the growth of public funding streams to religious agencies. Indeed, subsidiarity largely assuaged qualms among religious groups about the dangers posed by a "church-state combine." While the state drew upon the resources of religious entities, it also shielded their organizational autonomy and sanctioned their faith-based practices. Although government programs often prohibited public support for sectarian practices, the enforcement regime frequently condoned them. Cold War public policies thus opened up new opportunities for religious groups to position themselves organizationally and discursively in the foreign policy and social welfare arenas. They provided them with new access to political networks, means for expanding their missionary activities, and support in building up their charities. Although critics of liberal public policies kept touting the third sector as an alternative to the welfare state, the reality was a growing dependence on government aid.

This Cold War-induced convergence between church and state ushered in a sea change in the attitudes of religious groups toward public funding. Many religious charities became more sanguine about entering into financial arrangements with the government. While Catholic agencies had tended to be the prime beneficiaries of public funding streams, all of the main denominational groups eventually participated in postwar subsidiarity. In turn, intradenominational debates shifted away from the question of either rejecting or accepting funding. Instead, they focused on lobbying for more secure safeguards for the spiritual mission of religious agencies than those provided by benign neglect, indirect support, and the bureaucratic laxities of devolution.

Chapter 2 shifts the focus toward the particular dynamics of the evangelical awakening in the context of Cold War state building. As the world evangelicals re-engaged with was increasingly characterized by the growing power of government, church-state and public funding issues emerged as key themes in intradenominational debates. Although significant elements in the movement had traditionally insisted on the strict separation of church and state, constructing a new relationship with the state became part and parcel of postwar neo-evangelical efforts to establish a "third force" in the fold distinct from both fundamentalism and theological liberalism. Preserving an antistatist identity while simultaneously promoting closer ties with state structures, the new church-state attitude was a constituent element in the larger postwar repositioning of evangelicalism between religious piety and growing worldliness, theological orthodoxy and ecumenism, and moral traditionalism and modernity. The NAE's Office of Public Affairs (OPA) in particular showcases the gradual shift from separationism toward public policy engagement, as well as the quandaries neo-evangelicals faced in the context of their postwar re-engagement with the Cold War state. The OPA emerged in the postwar decades as the main clearinghouse for the organization's new political activism in both the foreign and social policy arenas. In this capacity it engaged in activities ranging from securing visas for missionaries to participating in congressional hearings. It ran training seminars, eased political contacts, and lobbied for political appointees. In short it positioned itself as the NAE coordinating body for placing evangelicals in government and advancing specific legislation.

The neo-evangelical efforts to revitalize the movement's relationship with the state cannot be interpreted in isolation from the contradictory framework of Cold War public policy. On the one hand, postwar growth-oriented policies, including tax breaks, full employment programs, educational investment, and funding for the military-industrial complex had engineered the remarkable socioeconomic success story of postwar evangelicalism, particularly in the South and West. By the 1960s, evangelicals were an increasingly modern, affluent, upwardly mobile group ready to enjoy the benefits of their economic fortunes. They frequently identified with the technocratic suburban setting of the Sunbelt and became largely supportive of the government investment that had undergirded economic expansion. On the other hand, however, although many evangelicals benefited from the deficit spending and social service expansions of the Cold War state, they cultivated a suburban warrior mentality that frequently depicted the federal government as a mortal enemy. Indeed, the policies that made growth and consumption the primary objective in response to social problems and global challenges delimited the liberal welfare state. Growth policies "naturalized" the consumerist axioms of acquisitive materialism, competitive achievement, and hedonistic self-indulgence. The government-subsidized, military-related prosperity thus ironically reaffirmed the antistatist and hyper-individualistic dimension of the southern and western mind.

This tension was exacerbated by another built-in contradiction that both sanctioned state intervention and inhibited the development of a system of comprehensive social provision. While postwar growth-orientation promoted the normative parameters of consumer capitalism, social policies upheld the moral codes of nineteenth-century producer-class ideology cherished by evangelicals. Indeed, welfare was traditionally locked into a moralistic, punitive, and rehabilitative construction of poverty that located the origins of deprivation in behavioral deficiencies and cultural pathology. Viewing welfare as a gratuity, this focus on character issues in antipoverty policies used concepts of moral self-control and economic independence to legitimate strong discretionary elements in the welfare system, reinforce gender discriminations, and racialize provision. In the context of 1950s anticommunism, and of the growing economic, race, and gender challenges of the 1960s, evangelicals denounced the forces that sought socioeconomic equality and the redistribution of income, yet reawakened their identification with this moralistic dimension of public policy. Together, these conflicts and tensions formed the intellectual and ideological backdrop for the evangelicals' emergence as a constituency that was simultaneously superpatriotic and separationist, consumerist and morally traditionalist, and antistatist and government-subsidized.

The middle chapters explore in more detail how the interplay of the subsidiarist state and the evangelical awakening transformed the relationship between conservative Protestants and the federal government. As Chapter

3 explains, the foreign policy arena exemplifies the dramatic shift that was taking place. Anticommunism in particular eased the evangelical transition from a traditional insistence on limited government toward the embrace of expanded federal power. As one speaker at the NAE's 1963 church-state conference put it, "the evangelical Christian will be quick to acknowledge his obligation to the defense needs of his country in a world threatened by militant, scientific and atheistic communism."[15] Reducing religion to a weapon in the Cold War arsenal, evangelicals increasingly offered uncritical support and moral sanction for the large-scale expansion of the "garrison state" and the buildup of the domestic surveillance and security apparatus. Despite their strong pacifist traditions and uneasiness about free markets, they positioned their creed as a civil religion that sanctified America's new global military role and affirmed the soundness of the liberal capitalist order. Likewise, their growing engagement with the military amplified their statist stance.

While this shift from pietistic patriotism to nationalistic statism helped integrate conservative Protestants into the liberal anticommunist foreign policy consensus and anointed America's global interests, evangelicals were nonetheless eager to preserve an insurgent identity. They were staunchly unilateralist, if not isolationist. They opposed the recognition of Red China and ridiculed the UN and "world government." They attacked the alleged Catholic infiltration of the U.S. foreign aid program and adhered to apocalyptic visions of impending global warfare. They used anticommunism as a means of infusing prophetic and millennial themes into the public policy discourse. And they retained strong anti-Semitic sentiments despite their outright support for the state of Israel.

Despite this ambivalent stance, however, the federal government's efforts to strengthen the anticommunist training of army recruits, its support for the military chaplaincy and evangelization campaigns, and its promotion of church building on military sites were decisive factors in furthering the influence of conservative Protestants. The Eisenhower administration in particular cultivated ties with evangelicals and provided protective cover for their growing missionary activities. In addition, foreign aid was a prime example of the way in which government imperatives brought evangelical players into the public policy framework. A popular area of cooperation between church and state, international relief produced an array of new bureaucratic ties and personnel interchanges. Incipient networks and funding ties in the 1950s and 1960s, such as the NAE World Relief Commission's (WRC) participation in the surplus food and ocean freight reimbursement programs, laid the foundation for the expansion of government funding for evangelical organizations in the 1970s, particularly in conjunction with the post-Vietnam War withdrawal of more liberal agencies. Due to their strong anticommunist provenance, evangelicals were often much less concerned about taking federal funds and being identified with government goals than many mainstream Protestants and secularists, who feared becoming tools of American foreign policy. By the 1990s, conservative Protestants were among the largest international aid providers taking advantage of public funding opportunities.

Although evangelical relief agencies outwardly retained a strong separationist identity, their growing identification with U.S. foreign policy goals—together with denominational competition and the absence of effective restrictions on evangelizing abroad—provided a sufficiently strong incentive to change their antistatist ideology. Despite government attempts to separate secular from religious activities, evangelical foreign aid organizations were allowed to link food distribution to proselytizing. Likewise, United States Agency for International Development (USAID) funds were used to support evangelical schools, hospitals, and scholarships abroad, even though conservative Protestant organizations led the field in restrictive hiring and demanding religious commitment. In turn, discussions within evangelicalism about federal foreign aid programs concentrated on preserving the link between service and faith, rather than on concerns about government growth.

Remarkably, the social policy arena reveals a similar picture, as Chapter 4 shows. The NAE's consistent opposition to "parochiaid" and its vociferous campaign against Catholic efforts to obtain public support indicated that, when it came to welfare policies, conservative Protestants were traditionally strongly antistatist. At the same time, however, evangelical nonprofits increasingly benefited from social policy subsidiarity. In particular, Southern Baptist hospitals, a wide range of evangelical colleges, and Salvation Army social services became major participants in federal funding streams. The Great Society programs so frequently maligned by the Christian Right provided further access to government funding while preserving the independence and spiritual mission of faith-based agencies. Expanded federal support for education offered large-scale aid to evangelical institutions and promoted the transformation of church-state attitudes. Likewise, health and welfare policies implemented under the auspices of the War on Poverty, such as Medicaid, Medicare, and Head Start, softened evangelicals' oppositional stance toward subsidiarity. As the child care debate highlighted in the chapter reveals, the NAE gradually abandoned the rejection of federal funding in favor of fighting constraints on religious providers partaking in public subsidies.

Efforts in the 1960s to clarify and reaffirm separationist doctrine in light of the growing tension between ideology and reality ironically ended up moving the evangelical debate further away from stark warnings about the looming threat of a church-state combine. In the end, the discussion within the movement was no longer mainly about the size of government, but about which funding and delivery arrangements to privilege. As Catholics became the beneficiary of social service contracts, denominational competition subtly shifted the evangelical discourse from a critique of the dangers of public aid toward demands for equal access to government programs; disquiet about rampant secularism paved the way for calls for "moral government" to protect the spiritual mission of religious agencies under public funding arrangements; and growing concerns about financial shortfalls meant that many church administrators were less concerned with state subsidies than with limiting government regulation *within* a system of public aid. Indeed, the rhetoric of separationism was less indicative of the rigid rejection of government funds than of the desire to retain ideological purity and organizational autonomy at a time when public funding for religious agencies was rapidly becoming the norm. At the same time, Supreme Court decisions, in generating renewed evangelical fears about unbridled atheism, revived evangelical interest in utilizing the instrumentalities of government for the promotion of Christian morality. The school prayer and bible reading decisions, for example, informed a new willingness to lobby for public support for sectarian education. This culminated in the NAE's embrace of the voucher system by the late 1980s and set the stage for its later support of Charitable Choice and the Faith-Based Initiative.

In the 1970s and 1980s, the seminal shift within the evangelical movement from separationism to supporting public aid shaped the political mobilization patterns of conservative Protestants. As Chapter 5 explains, it became an important part of the internal movement conflicts and purges that culminated in the dominance of the New Christian Right. Although scholarship usually attributes the sidelining of evangelical liberals and the Left to the widely publicized controversies over biblical inerrancy, the conflicts that raged in the 1970s over church-state separation and the public funding of religion were equally relevant in this process. When the evangelical movement entered the political stage with renewed vigor in the 1960s and 1970s, a new generation of college-trained liberal and left-wing leaders called for a revived commitment to fighting poverty, oppression, and injustice. Politicized in the context of the social and political upheaval of the 1960s and the Vietnam War, they established links with the Civil Rights movement, the New Left, and even the counterculture.

The evangelical Left condemned the failure of mainstream evangelicals to focus on the gospel, their undue emphasis on civil religion, and the complicity of the church in militarism and racism. This caused serious rifts in a grouping where opinions ranged from strict pacifism to biblical support for military expansion. What was clear to many conservatives within the movement was that making evangelicals an effective voting bloc within the resurgent Republican party required the marginalization of these left-leaning and liberal impulses. In this "internal backlash," however, the newly politicized generation of right-wing evangelicals did not return to the separationist church-state position of prewar fundamentalism or even 1950s neo-evangelicalism. Instead of simply rejecting the liberal state, as many analysts have suggested, the Right in fact offered more antistatist rhetoric, but amounted to a more statist movement.

The two main pillars of the Right's public policy agenda—morality politics and subsidiarity—illustrate how conservative evangelicalism derived political and cultural resonance from fusing insurgent rhetoric with the affirmation of "big government." On the one hand, conservatives used moral issues to mobilize against a secular trajectory in government that gradually removed chapel attendance, bible readings, school prayer, and Christian holiday observances from public institutions. They denounced the liberal state as colluding in the moral iniquities anathema to evangelicals, including homosexuality, abortion rights, drug use, and pregnancy out of wedlock. On the other hand, this emphasis on moral issues depicted secularism, rather than the growth of government, as the main enemy. Conservatives exaggerated the "culture war" scenario of advancing secularization and moral permissiveness as a way of shifting the evangelical discourse away from the insistence on church-state separation.

Similarly, the Right's push for subsidiarist policies, particularly tuition vouchers and child care grants, simultaneously carried forward the basic structures of postwar state building and preserved a separationist self-image. By the 1960s, the NAE, the embodiment of mainstream evangelicalism, was floundering in part because of its failure to set up an effective coordinating body for social action comparable to Catholic Charities USA or the Southern Baptist Convention's Christian Life Commission. At the same time, the organization had given birth to powerful affiliates and commissions, such as the WRC, National Religious Broadcasters, and Evangelical Foreign Missions Association. Largely dominated by conservatives, many of these parachurch organizations participated actively in public funding arrangements. In particular, organizations that had received significant impulses from the social action resurgence of the 1960s, such as Prison Fellowship Ministries, combined a softened stance toward public funding, a drift to the Right, and an appeal to disillusioned left-wing evangelicals.

By the 1970s, NAE attacks on public aid had largely ceased, and the organization had turned away from its traditional close cooperation with separationist groups. In particular, it had severed its ties with Protestants and Other Americans United for the Separation of Church and State (POAU) and its successor organization, Americans United (AU). Meanwhile, these former allies continued to issue scathing critiques of any form of public funding for religious agencies. By the same token, many liberal and left-leaning evangelical groups, such as Sojourners, preserved the antistatist and separationist legacy, attacking the military-industrial complex and consumer capitalism from a position of self-imposed communitarian separatism.

Intensifying both the process of integration into the structures of the Cold War state and the image of insurgency not only cemented the conservatives' dominance within the evangelical movement. It also helped the movement's right wing to engineer ties with secular conservatism. Unencumbered by both the evangelical Left and the traditional separationist wings of the movement, conservatives were in a stronger position to engage in partisan political networking. Once again, not only morality politics but also subsidiarity became a cornerstone of this process. Although the Republican party's adoption of the politics of morality was vital in the partisan mobilization of conservative Protestants, the new evangelical view of the state was equally important in building coalitions. In the 1970s and 1980s, a new generation of partisan NAE leaders actively used church-state issues to infuse a subsidiarist evangelical policy agenda into the Republican party.

The partisan realignments of the 1980s have turned evangelicals into one of the most committed Republican groups in the religious spectrum. This raises the question how the evangelical transformation described in the previous chapters fits into the broader resurgence of conservatism and its relationship to Cold War public policies. The Conclusion maintains that evangelicals indeed mirrored the statist and subsidiarist turns of the broader postwar conservative movement. In the decades after World War II the institutional arrangements, normative directions, and political dynamics that underlay Cold War liberalism, rather than alienating conservatives, furthered their integration into consensus politics. They sidelined conservatism's traditional fears of "big government" while enabling it to retain its antistatist credentials. While anticommunism was key to the conservative embrace of the national security state and the military-industrial complex, growth policies and subsidiarity helped stimulate a conservative corporate and nonprofit infrastructure, particularly in the burgeoning South and West. Cold War liberalism thus both generated an attachment to the state and nurtured the institutions and ideologies that opposed it.

As the economic and cultural crises in the 1960s and 1970s exposed the electoral fragilities of consensus liberalism, however, a new generation of conservatives made their voice heard. Their culture and ideas revolved around libertarian antistatism, the uncritical embrace of private economic power, and social conservatism. They issued an uncompromising call for deregulation, retrenchment, and restoration of market forces. Neoconservatism faced a dilemma, however. The crisis in the aftermath of the 1960s had simultaneously revealed the political weakness of Cold War liberalism and the structural strength of the Cold War state. Though liberal policies had failed to lay the political foundations for sustaining a unitary and generalized welfare state electorally, they had nonetheless engineered broad-based popular support for government spending, particularly in the Sunbelt constituencies of the New Right.

Therefore, the key to mobilizing this electorate, and to the broader cultural resonance of the New Right, was not relentless opposition to "big government" but the ability to calibrate effectively between an antistatist rhetoric and support for the basic structures of state building. This is where the conservative evangelicals left their imprint. While they continued to assail the federal government, they combined fiery antistatist rhetoric, entrepreneurial individualism, and moral traditionalism with staunch support for large-scale military spending, the social security state, and public funding for nongovernmental social service organizations. In short, conservative evangelicalism and its new church-state stance mediated between neoconservatives' market fundamentalism and postwar conservatives' acceptance of the liberal state.

Resurgent conservatism thus constituted not so much an alternative to the ideology and institutions of Cold War liberalism than an appropriation of the established parameters of liberal state building. The conservative calls for limited government, devolution, and morality politics need to be understood as specific ways in which the movement related to the state and sustained its basic structures in the post-1960s era. They provided a space for backlash sentiments and the deep resentments against the alleged moral failures of the liberal welfare state. At the same time, they advanced an ideological amalgam of growth politics, subsidiarity, and punitive welfarism that constituted the core of "big government conservatism."

The two main pieces of legislation promoting public funding of religious agencies since the end of the Cold War exemplified these processes. First, Charitable Choice and the Faith-Based Initiative, rather than representing a paradigm shift, "simply affirmed the centrality of religious providers in the construction of the postwar welfare state" as part of a long-term social policy consensus.[16] They showed that government funding of religious organizations was both a staple feature of Democratic administrations after the end of World War II and formed the basis upon which conservatives embraced the expansion of the state.

Second, the two measures completed the integration of evangelical agencies into the orbit of subsidiarity. Charitable Choice prohibits discrimination against religious providers in the contracting process and tolerates the display of religious symbols where government services are provided. Meanwhile, the Faith-Based Initiative allows churches and congregations to enter into direct contractual relationships with the government. The novelty of these programs lay in the fact that they provided the legal basis for the overt embrace of religious content in social policy, which had been tolerated in the previous decades but had remained on shaky legal ground. Both measures thus responded to long-term evangelical demands to loosen restrictions on religious agencies and preserve the distinctive spiritual dimension of religious providers.

Finally, the measures highlight how subsidiarity converted the self-declared guardians of separationism into advocates of public funding. They not only reflect the general growth in church support for collaboration between religious and governmental organizations but, by strengthening the ties between evangelicals and the state, helped expand the political basis for post-1960s state building. Evangelical leaders continued to voice a deep distrust of the state, link the effectiveness of welfare policy to the spiritualization of social service, and depict charitable and private service providers as alternatives to public institutions. At the same time, however, they realized that subsidiarity protected the organizational and normative autonomy of sectarian providers and confined the role of the state to that of paymaster. In turn, their political ideology fused demands for religious provision with calls for government subsidies.

*   *   *

Before entering into the details of this study, I would like to add a caveat. Although this book focuses on white conservative Protestants, subsidiarity is frequently embraced by many African American evangelicals and by liberal and progressive third-sector organizations of all kinds. The Right has neither a monopoly on funding, nor is the policy of devolving welfare delivery to state-supported philanthropic and private organizations bound to benefit only conservative organizations. What I am suggesting is that conservatives have become shrewd pursuers of their own interests in this arena. Subsidiarity as constructed by liberal state building has allowed them to combine being drawn into the orbit of the Cold War state with retaining an antistatist stance and pursuing a morally conservative agenda. In this sense the structures of subsidiarity perpetuate established patterns of normative and social control embedded in the welfare state. At the same time, however, the race, class, and gender divides built into state provision are not hermetically sealed. They do leave room for subversion and social transformation. Hence, subsidiarity has also been used by liberal and left-wing organizations to build up a movement infrastructure. As a system, it can be equally beneficial to socially progressive organizations, if only because it helps undermine the centralized and rationalized systems of social provision that impose powerful structures of subordination.

In the following chapters I have alluded to this, but exploring it further would require writing a different book. It suffices to say that the Right only negotiates and mediates the inherent contradictions of state building in new and effective ways, but does not transcend them. Thus, the ability of the New Christian Right to deflect traditional lower-middle-class resentment against corporate America, to reduce morality to a narrow culture war agenda, and to cover up the fact that capitalism itself undermined the traditional values cherished by the petty-bourgeois classes, should not distract from the prospect of new movements finding "moral inspiration in the popular radicalism of the past."[17] Indeed, as Barbara Ehrenreich astutely noted, American capitalism would in fact be threatened by a *genuine* resurgence of the traditional values of self-denial and deferred gratification.[18]

CHAPTER 1

THE COLD WAR STATE AND RELIGIOUS AGENCIES

I n a remarkable display of cross-partisan consensus transcending the clamor of the so-called culture war, politicians from both major parties frequently tout the capacity of religious organizations to address the abiding problems of poverty and social deprivation in the United States. George H. W. Bush's "Thousand Points of Light," Bill Clinton's "Charitable Choice," and George W. Bush's "Faith-Based Initiative" all seek to increase the involvement of sectarian agencies in public social welfare provision. Both conservatives enamored of "tough love" and liberals keen to encourage grassroots activism lavish praise on the personalized care and selfless commitment ascribed to religious nonprofits. As the 2008 election swept Barack Obama into the White House, increasing federal aid to religious agencies was one of the few policy legacies of the previous administration the incoming president wholeheartedly embraced.

This broad-based agreement raises the question whether the Faith-Based Initiative and similar policies need to be understood as the culmination of a long-term pattern of public funding for religious agencies, rather than as unique breaches—associated with the conservative backlash—in the wall of separation between church and state. Indeed, close funding ties between the federal government and religious agencies are neither a novelty in the history of American public policy, nor did they commonly run afoul of First Amendment limitations. Particularly in the decades after World War II, federal aid for religious organizations underwent a dramatic expansion without raising serious constitutional concerns. The war years and the Cold War not only revived religious images of the "redeemer nation" that provided religious groups with new opportunities to reassert their spiritual mission and access to the corridors of political power. It also ushered in new bureaucratic and financial ties between church and state. In turn, federal aid to religious agencies became part and parcel of the large-scale expansion of the public-nongovernmental networks that constituted one of the fundamental dynamics of the "subsidiarist" state and consensus liberalism.

The Rise of the Subsidiarist State

In the aftermath of the war neither a return to the limited broker state of the 1920s nor to New Deal-style economic planning and regulation was politically feasible. On the one hand, depression and war had highlighted the efficacy of interventionist policies and deficit spending in creating social stability and economic growth; the economic crisis and the experience of government-funded wartime prosperity had convinced even the most avid critics of the state that "big government" was here to stay. On the other hand, wartime prosperity based largely on extensive federal contracting with big business had generated a renewal of faith in American-style capitalism. In conjunction with the corporate capture of regulatory agencies and the rise of an anti-New Deal coalition in Congress, this had paved the way for a shift away from the emphasis on central planning, direct public control, and redistributive social welfare programs. Unlike in Europe, where the war-related collapse of former empires, physical destruction, socioeconomic decline, and communist advances led to a massive loss of confidence in the old elites, in the United States the icon of the "good war" fundamentally reaffirmed the political and socioeconomic order. Moreover, the Cold War defined as both an economic and a spiritual struggle against communism placed severe limits on progressive public policies. Though few Americans doubted the need for expanded government power in light of postwar global political realities, many eschewed the more radical demands for industrial democracy, income redistribution, and the comprehensive welfare state pioneered in the 1930s. "For us, the war did not produce a revolution in social relations so much as it restored the prosperity to which we had been accustomed," political scientist Edward Berkowitz noted. "The American government, unlike the British, owed its citizens nothing more than continuing prosperity; the private market, charity, state and local government, and voluntary associations would take care of the rest." [1]

Postwar policy makers thus faced a difficult task. They were hemmed in by the rejection of New Deal-style interventionism, the close ties between government and business, and the resurgence of deeply rooted traditions of hostility to a centralized state. At the same time, they were urged to build up federal administrative capacities in the name of national defense, international security, and economic prosperity. Their solution to this dilemma was politically ingenious. As Michael Sherry has noted, postwar policies created an institutional and ideological legacy that, while extending the size of the federal government, threw "a smokescreen of symbolic anti-statism over deepening government responsibility."[2] Unable to return to prewar notions of limited government, yet wary of a state that might be getting too big for its britches, policy makers constructed a distinctive administrative framework that neither copied the "associative state" of the 1920s nor constituted a simple extension of New Deal interventionism. Instead, 1920s-style associationalism, the expansion of the welfare state during the 1930s, and the growth of the warfare state in the 1940s combined to form the institutional and ideological bedrock of the Cold War "subsidiarist state."[3]

The key policy instrument in this effort to reconcile the conflicting impulses was the large-scale expansion of the public funding of nongovernmental organizations. While federal programs in the 1930s had largely maintained a sharp distinction between the government and the voluntary sector, this policy gradually changed in the postwar years. Rather than creating government agencies and providing public services directly, Cold War planners sought to attain social and foreign policy objectives by subsidizing and regulating nongovernmental organizations in areas such as higher education, health care, defense research, social services, and foreign aid. Landmark legislation such as the 1944 G.I. Bill, the 1946 Hill-Burton Act, and the 1967 Social Security Amendments funneled billions of dollars of federal funds to both private businesses and nonprofit organizations via tax policies, loans and loan guarantees, purchase-of-service contracts, surplus property donations, and direct cash grants. Furthermore, the sale or donation of government surplus land and military facilities to private and nonprofit organizations, and the reliance on nongovernmental providers to distribute foreign aid, established similar relationships in the national security arena. Combining centralized revenue gathering and policy planning at the federal level with the devolution of policy implementation to nongovernmental actors, Cold War planners thus linked up with the administrative capacities of a wide range of private and charitable organizations.[4]

Although many observers locate the "quiet revolution" of the emerging partnership between government and nonprofit sector in the retrenchment-driven 1980s, the welfare state was in fact "devolutionary and privatizing from its inception" in the postwar period.[5] Scholars have used a variety of terms to describe this feature of the Cold War public policy. Lester Salamon talks about "third-party government"; Peter Dobkin Hall uses the term "allocative state"; Donald Critchlow calls it the "second welfare state."[6] The term "subsidiarity," however, used in this context by Bruce Nichols, expresses most aptly the arrangement whereby important roles are left to nongovernmental institutions in serving essentially public goals. Borrowed from Catholic social thought, subsidiarity describes three interrelated components: a policy instrument that devolves functions to lower levels; an emotive concept that upholds the notion that mediating structures are less impersonal than government bodies and thus preferable; and an ideology that defines social problems in terms of rehabilitative intervention, rather than large-scale socioeconomic redistribution.[7]

In the decades after World War II, subsidiarity linked the federal government and nonprofit agencies together in ever closer networks. By 1967, federal government spending on social welfare had surpassed state and local government spending, in part due to the large-scale expansion of federal funding for nonprofit social service organizations implemented during the Great Society. In 1980, federal support to the nonprofit sector amounted to $40.4 billion. This represented about 36 percent of total federal spending in the areas of health, education, social services, community development, employment and training, foreign aid, research, and arts and culture. Together with state and local government funding, around 40 percent of public expenditure for human services in the United States supported the delivery of services by nonprofits. Nonprofit organizations were eligible participants in 564 out of 988 separate federal programs listed in the *Catalogue of Federal Domestic Assistance*.[8]

By the time Ronald Reagan was elected president, the federal government had already become the largest single source of direct and indirect revenues for nonprofits. Federal support accounted for over a third (35 percent) of total income of nonprofit service organizations, with many receiving over 70 percent of their funds from federal and state sources. Federal funds constituted on average 36 percent of the overall revenue of hospitals and health care providers, 22 percent of the income of educational and research institutions, and 55 percent of the combined funds of social service providers and foreign aid agencies. Despite some changes in the mix of federal and state support, nonprofits remained substantially dependent on public funds. As Lester Salamon concludes, "Although the sector is typically identified exclusively with its private philanthropic base, in fact government is its principal source of support."[9] This precedent remained a stable element in subsequent relations between the government and the nonprofit sector. Despite the rhetoric of limited government, budget cutting, welfare state retrenchment and devolution, the federal government maintained its status as the chief source of public policy and revenue during and after the Reagan era. Between 1985 and 1995, a period of supposed dismantling of the welfare state, nondefense discretionary spending—a significant portion of which went to nonprofits—actually increased by 25 percent.[10]

The subsidiarist policy momentum also fundamentally reshaped the relationship between religious agencies and the federal government. Cold War policy makers, driven by the outlined imperatives to devolve power to nongovernmental actors, developed close funding ties with religious charities. As a result, "Half a century of devolution and privatization have diffused the tasks of policy planning and implementation to state and municipal government and to nonprofit agencies created or subsidized by public funds—including religious bodies and universities, which, before the Second World War, were entirely supported by revenues from private sources."[11]

Religion, World War II, and the Cold War

What started the ball rolling was that the war and Cold War years offered an unexpected ideological windfall for religious groups. The wartime message—that the strength of a people in the battle against the evil of totalitarianism lay in their moral character—bolstered the religious component in American culture and society. In an atmosphere of anxiety and triumph, religion was seen simply as a good thing, and even marginal groups, such as evangelicals and fundamentalists, received friendly media coverage. While "Praise the Lord and Pass the Ammunition" became a slogan in the semantic arsenal of warfare, stories of "foxhole epiphanies" became staple dramatic components of postwar revivals. By resurrecting notions of the redeemer nation and the covenant people, wartime and postwar rhetoric hit the "mystic chords of American cultural memory."[12]

This ideological convergence between church and state during and after the war synchronized religious themes, nationalism, anticommunism, and the American way of life. It not only presented being religious as more or less the same as being patriotic, but also tied preparedness in the battle against communism to a renewed spiritual commitment to the social order and political institutions of the United States. As influential Presbyterian minister Edward L. R. Elson pointed out in a 1957 sermon to an audience that included President Eisenhower and Vice-President Nixon, the axe of the pioneer "has become America's gigantic industrial machine, and the world sees that. His gun has become America's powerful armament, and the world knows it well. His Book, by the power of the Person revealed therein, is pouring forth the light of a new spiritual rebirth, and the world must clearly see that."[13] In his view, America was a "conveyor of God's truth to the world" and was given the task to "resolutely perform this providentially bestowed role of world leader."[14]

Likewise, policy makers knew that religious belief in a just cause, a worldview based on a clear distinction between good and evil, adherence to moral principles, and strong enemy images were effective tools during the Cold War. They defined Christianity as a natural ally and were only too willing to reduce religion to a weapon in the anticommunist arsenal. FBI director J. Edgar Hoover pronounced "the spiritual firepower of the Christian Church" to be "sufficient to destroy all the Soviet man-made missiles."[15] And Dwight Eisenhower asked, "What is our battle against communism if it is not a fight against anti-God and a belief in the Almighty?" concluding that "when God comes in, communism has to go."[16]

The link between the constitutional order and Christianity, and between religiousness and patriotism, was given symbolic expression when the words "under God" were added to the Pledge of Allegiance. As William Miller irreverently noted, the pledge had "its rhythm upset but its anti-Communist spirituality improved."[17] Moreover, "In God We Trust" was adopted as a national motto on 30 July 1956. And Eisenhower, the self-declared "most intensely religious man I know," introduced annual presidential prayer breakfasts, opened cabinet meetings with a prayer, and created a new agency for coordinating religious affairs in the White House.[18] As he famously remarked in December 1952 shortly before assuming office, "our form of government has no sense unless it is founded in a deeply felt religious faith, and I don't care what it is."[19]

Meanwhile, religious groups in the 1950s were equally keen to bolster the spiritual component in American society. Many churches embraced the opportunity to counter the long-standing trend toward understanding democracy and American liberty as the result of an anticlerical Enlightenment tradition, secular values, and pragmatist ethics. They craved putting Christian moral thought back into the center as the template for understanding both the postwar totalitarian threats and the moral mission of the redeemer nation to spread American democracy.[20] As Scott Flipse concluded, "Pax Americana found wide support among religious people because religious leaders shared the goals and values of U.S. foreign policy leaders."[21]

In their quest to link national security to spiritual renewal, however, politicians and church leaders did not confine themselves to moral exhortations about strengthening the commitment to traditional religion. Eager to expand the links with voluntary organizations in pursuit of Cold War foreign and social policy objectives, policy makers naturally turned to religious charities, which even today make up four of every ten nonprofit sector organizations and account for as much as two-thirds of their donated revenues and volunteer labor force.[22] With religion as "godmother of the nonprofit sector," most nonprofit hospitals, mutual aid societies, educational institutions, social service organizations, and international relief agencies could trace their origins back to religious impulses.[23]

While the administrative capacities of religious agencies caught the eyes of Cold War planners, many religious charities, remembering the devastating financial impact of the Great Depression, relaxed their opposition to public subsidies. Eager to rebuild their institutional base after the war, expand their growing foreign relief and missionary activities, and cultivate religion's positive wartime image, even the more separationist religious organizations were willing to rethink their traditional stance. While prewar hospitals, higher education institutions, social service providers, and foreign aid agencies had largely relied upon charitable giving, postwar philanthropies reshaped their programs to take advantage of subsidiarity and worked effectively "to increase federal funding in these fields, while minimizing federal controls."[24] As Theda Skocpol has noted, "to the degree that professionally administered social services have developed in the United States, church-affiliated agencies have developed at the heart of the process, as anxious as any other agencies to have funding and support from state and national governments."[25]

This newfound mutual interest should of course not distract from the fact that the use of public funds to subsidize religious and philanthropic institutions had a long history. During the eighteenth and nineteenth centuries, state and local government supported religious education and care institutions for the poor. By the late nineteenth century the use of subsidies to voluntary institutions had become the prevailing method of financing religious institutions, turning churches into quasi-governmental bodies. Throughout

the Gilded Age and the Progressive Era, church and state were closely connected, particularly in areas such as child services.[26] Not until the war and
the postwar years, however, did the subsidiarist state come into its own as
the federal government began to dominate the field of public funding for
religious agencies. Even the large-scale expansion of state administrative capacities in the 1930s had not significantly enlarged these state-religious networks. New Deal funding was largely confined to public agencies, in part as
a reaction against the perceived failure of charities to respond to the disasters
of the Great Depression and a sense that private charities were not the most
effective way of using public funds.[27]

The Growth of Church-State Funding Ties

During and after World War II the ideological church-state convergence and
the religious nonprofit sector's newfound openness to state funding helped
establish a new organizational field between the federal government and religious groups. As a result, a wide variety of new funding streams began to
benefit a plethora of human service activities of religious charities. "Church-
related social services are openly 'sold' to government on the one hand and
on the other church programs have been supplemented by state aid," an evangelical critic of public funding complained, "It is common practice for religious social workers to accept reimbursement from government for services
rendered and for expenses incurred while retaining their employed status
with religious institutions."[28]

The mutual construction of state and religious nonprofits on the basis
of the institutional and ideological trajectories of Cold War public policy is
best observed in the areas that policy makers considered vital for sustaining national defense, creating social stability, and safeguarding international
security. These encompassed primarily foreign aid, higher education, health
care, and social services. Despite the growing significance of religious organizations in the subsidiarist funding arrangements, however, remarkably
little reliable statistical information exists on religious nonprofits and funding
ties with the government. Many studies note the problem of tracing funding information through a wide variety of unstandardized sources, including
annual reports, audits, budgetary statements, board meeting minutes, correspondence, policy statements, interviews, and on-site observations—data
that often do not separate purchase-of-service contracting from direct grants.

Likewise, data on federal support are difficult to obtain; no government-wide overview is available, and few programs maintained sufficient records to identify the scale of resources flowing to nonprofits.[29]

Moreover, defining faith-based services and organizations is "fraught with variability and ambiguity." Theological differences and varieties in state regulatory norms led to disparities in what religious groups provided. Likewise, the presence of a wide range of religious bodies, including congregations, denominations, affiliated secular agencies, and interchurch boards, resulted in different modes of supplying it. "The fact that religious entities provide services both directly through congregations and other bodies exempt from federal and state registration and reporting requirements, as well as through affiliated secular corporations—community development corporations, hospitals, schools, and social welfare agencies—further complicates matters."[30] Although the emergence of large denominational and interdenominational bodies had been the major organizational trend in religious life since the nineteenth century, the postwar period also saw a range of countervailing impulses. These included, in particular, the establishment of megachurches, the emergence of parachurch organizations (such as Habitat for Humanity and Alcoholics Anonymous), and the growth of faiths outside of Judeo-Christian traditions.[31]

As a result, snapshot information gleaned from rich but unstandardized data from a variety of sources has to suffice for tracing the main outlines of this relationship and the transformation of church-state relations under the auspices of the Cold War in the social and national security policy arenas. What is undisputed, however, is that although many nonprofit organizations may no longer be tied to their specific denominational past, 78 percent of all private colleges and universities still have a religious affiliation, one-third of all child care providers are church-based, and one-third to half of international aid providers have a clear religious base. Moreover, a large number of hospitals and many social service organizations, such as the YMCA and the Salvation Army, continue to have strong religious ties.[32]

Foreign Aid

The quintessential Cold War program—showcasing the growing cooperation between church and state in the pursuit of the shared goals of humanitarian intervention, commercial access, military support, and containment—was foreign aid. Government aid programs, beginning with the Marshall Plan, were initially launched to funnel relief into war-torn areas, but were subsequently expanded to provide aid for impoverished countries generally. In turn, foreign aid turned into a vast federal program as America's global political interests and economic power involved dealing with foreign refugee crises, drought relief, infrastructure projects, and resettlement programs. As humanitarian and national security interests merged, foreign aid appropriations not only became one of the most reliable components of the federal budget, they also significantly expanded federal support for religious relief agencies. These clearly constituted the private organizations most favored by the U.S. government in their work abroad in the aftermath of World War II. In its efforts to deliver aid, the government offered religious aid bodies reimbursement for ocean freight costs, donations of excess government property and surplus food, and direct program and institutional support grants. The "triumph of subsidiarity," in the words of Bruce Nichols, was thus firmly entrenched in the foreign aid field before the Vietnam War.[33]

As both government and religious organizations recognized the urgent need for postwar international aid and shared the desire to fight communism, church-state networks became a central feature of U.S. international aid policy. Convinced that support for church-related institutions would buttress national defense, secretary of state John Foster Dulles earmarked federal funds for religious agencies in foreign aid.[34] Similarly, the director of the United States Information Agency (USIA), George V. Allen, told the North Carolina Council of Churches in 1959 that he would like to see the churches "take over" America's foreign relations by working for peace.[35] Already in 1948, a subcommittee of the House Committee on Foreign Affairs had acknowledged that voluntary agencies that "represent in part the interest of American religious groups in their co-religionists in other countries" should be seen as "an essential counterpart of foreign assistance programs." Fourteen years later, USAID director Fowler Hamilton reported that the use of religiously affiliated institutions for foreign aid purposes "has been confirmed by legislation enacted by the Congress for every year from 1947 through the foreign aid legislation enacted this year." He also pointed out that funneling public funds into religious human aid agencies acknowledged that "missionary efforts" had for decades been the major means of expressing "the American citizen's concern for the welfare of his less fortunate fellowman in foreign lands," and that religious organizations had traditionally carried the burdens of humanitarian aid.[36]

Throughout the Cold War subsidies to voluntary sector assistance programs gradually increased, opening up new opportunities for the development of bureaucratic ties and personnel interchanges between government agencies and religious organizations. Between the 1950s and the 1980s, the Escapee Program, first implemented by the Truman administration, funneled millions to religious relief organizations helping eastern European and Soviet refugees. Likewise, the State Department's Bureau for Refugee Programs made ample use of missionary societies in the Far East. And the Cuban refugee crisis of 1960–61 ushered in new federal funding streams for resettlement work of religious agencies, culminating in the Kennedy administration's policy of extending welfare services to asylum seekers via direct assistance to voluntary agencies.[37] Churches also benefited from war claims legislation, through which enemy assets confiscated by the United States were used to fund the building of religious institutions, as happened in the Philippines under the War Claims Act of 1948 and subsequent legislation.[38]

The most common forms of government aid to religious relief agencies were donations of surplus food and the provision of ocean transportation. A key facilitator of this support was the government's Advisory Committee on Voluntary Foreign Aid (ACVFA), created in 1946. Appointed by the president, the committee had no regulatory powers, but became an important instrument of cementing the liaison between government and the voluntary sector. After submitting their programs, budgets, and audits, voluntary agencies registered with and licensed by ACVFA "received the benefits provided by the federal government then and thereafter toward their respective programs."[39] They gained access to the Department of Agriculture for surplus food allocations, the Department of Commerce for export licenses, the War Department for operations in occupied areas, the Department of Justice for political propaganda, and the State Department for passport and visa issues.

Further funding ties between federal agencies and ACVFA-registered and approved voluntary-sector organizations developed in the aftermath of the government's decision to fund ocean freight costs in 1947, to provide surplus food distribution abroad under the Agricultural Act of 1949 and the 1954 Food for Peace legislation (PL 480), and to offer international technical assistance under Truman's Point Four proposals, which later developed into the USAID program. Under Titles II and III of Food for Peace, voluntary agencies could receive surplus food stocks for overseas famine relief, emergencies, school lunches, refugee relief, and, within limits, development programs. USAID also provided funds to provide technical assistance abroad and to train foreign nationals at American colleges and universities, businesses, hospitals, and government agencies.[40]

By 1962, religiously affiliated agencies constituted more than half (24 of 46) of the organizations registered with the ACVFA, giving them access to government surplus food allocation, export licenses, and logistical help. That year's list of religious-affiliated participants in U.S. government overseas projects provides a good snapshot of the extent to which assistance was provided under congressional mandate. Screening more than 1500 current projects and 700 contracts, USAID director Fowler Hamilton reported that during fiscal year 1962, USAID had spent over $3 million to finance overseas shipments of surplus food and that roughly 70 percent of the distribution was handled by agencies with religious backgrounds, including Catholic, Jewish, evangelical and mainline Protestant agencies.[41]

While religiously affiliated institutions played only a minor role in USAID contracting for training foreigners in the United States, millions of agency money went directly to sectarian schools and colleges abroad. Among the largest and most controversial of these programs was a $3.77 million contribution to improving primary education in Colombia's Catholic-run school system, and two projects (totaling $3 million) for improving higher education in South Korea involving Presbyterian and Methodist churches and colleges. Acknowledging the centrality of religious institutions in providing humanitarian aid, health care, and education abroad, Hamilton admitted that "in some foreign countries schools and colleges, founded by missionaries or having some connection with a religious body, are the only resource through which to work."[42]

Religious agencies at times faced harsh criticism over allegations of inappropriate proselytizing. In the Far East, where the State Department Bureau for Refugee Programs made ample use of missionary societies, conflicts erupted in 1958 when Catholic Relief Services, Lutheran World Relief, and Church World Service were accused of using surplus goods to evangelize recipients in Taiwan.[43] Likewise, in the 1960s, Catholic Relief Services' handling of surplus food distribution in South Vietnam, a country where Catholics made up only about a tenth of the population, incited criticism from Buddhists and Protestants. Catholic distribution of food to 150,000 members of the South Vietnamese militia, which made provisions part of their army pay, caused particular offense. Similar cases were reported from Latin America, where selling surplus food in markets appeared to be "the characteristic outcome of the donation program." In addition, the use of foreign aid funds in USAID and the Peace Corps to subsidize missionary movements abroad raised a lot of eyebrows.[44]

Despite intermittent attempts to separate secular from religious activities, however, the distinction remained blurry. As the First Conference on Churches and Social Welfare organized in 1956 by the mainline Protestant National Council of the Churches of Christ (NCC) noted, foreign aid was not so much an area where religious organizations were seeking government support, but where government sought to employ the skills of the staff of church agencies.[45] Catholic agencies in particular were in the forefront of cooperating with government. Feeling much less restrained by traditional separationist positions than many Protestant groups, Catholic Relief Services had become the largest private aid agency in the world by the 1950s and the recipient of over 50 percent of the relief supplies from the State Department's International Cooperation Agency. For Protestant and other agencies this raised "a very practical question of survival in a field increasingly dominated by the partnership between the State Department and the Catholic church."[46] The mainline NCC in particular began to feel the pressure. In response, the 1956 church-state conference suggested that "the church should contribute personnel to an operation under government auspices, or turn over its agency to government." Though this meant "foregoing, at least for the moment, a gain in prestige," it was better than opening up "the way to a mortgage on its independence."[47] The fledgling evangelical magazine *Christianity Today*, however, was more acerbic about the changing church-state setting: "The determination of some Protestant spokesmen to dictate American foreign policy," it warned, "seems to be shaping new opportunities for direct ecclesiastical intrusion into state affairs."[48]

As the disastrous war in Vietnam led to a shake-up of the funding networks between the government and voluntary agencies, however, this established pattern of Catholic participation, mainline dithering, and evangelical opposition began to unravel. Many mainline Protestant and secular agencies, fearing that they would become pawns in the hands of American foreign policy strategists, distanced themselves from government support.[49] Nonetheless, the trauma of Vietnam did not fundamentally undermine the subsidiarist relations in the international aid arena. Instead, it pulled new players into church-state funding networks. Despite their tough separationist stance, conservative Protestant agencies, motivated by their strong anticommunist heritage, were much more comfortable with being identified with American government aid programs than mainline Protestant and secular agencies.[50] This issue is explored in more detail in Chapter 3.

It suffices to say that in the ensuing decades cooperation with government remained the norm for most religious foreign aid providers. By the

1980s, close to 70 percent of Catholic Relief Services' total agency income came from government sources, while the mainline Protestant Church World Service received 43.6 percent and Lutheran World Relief trailed with 24 percent. The respective figures for evangelical organizations were 70.7 percent for the Seventh-Day Adventists and 38.2 percent for the NAE's World Relief.[51] Of thirteen international aid and relief agencies with total revenues of over $80 million registered with the USAID in 1991, seven were religiously based; 67 percent of religious international aid agencies reported receiving public funds by the early 1990s. Although religious foreign aid agencies received less of their budget from public sources than secular organizations, the number of secular aid agencies receiving no government funds at all was significantly higher (36 percent) than the number of religious agencies (30 percent).[52]

Education, Health Care, and Social Services Prior to the 1960s

The ideological confluence of religion and politics during the war and in postwar years not only set the stage for the development of closer ties between sectarian foreign aid agencies and the federal government. In education, health, and social welfare, many postwar planners also saw religious agencies as natural allies in addressing some of the most pressing postwar concerns. These institutions received federal funds either because planners regarded them as vital to preparing the nation for the exigencies of the Cold War, as in the case of higher education, or because there had been a long-standing tradition of public subsidies, as in the case of certain social service providers, particularly children's services.

Religious higher education, in particular, was one of the main beneficiaries of federal funding. The 1944 Servicemen's Readjustment Act, better known as the G.I. Bill of Rights, funneled large amounts of federal monies into religious colleges and universities. The bill in general provided federal educational, health, disability, unemployment, and retirement benefits for sixteen million men and women who had served in the armed forces. It also expanded the Veterans Administration (VA), which facilitated low-interest loans via mortgage insurance for purchasing houses, farms, or setting up businesses for over four million veterans. In educational allocations, the bill mainly covered stipends for college tuition, classroom materials, and living expenses. It also earmarked funds for creating new colleges and universities and enlarging older ones. During the seven years of its operation, close to eight million veterans used G.I. funds to attend a variety of educational institutions. In addition to the G.I. Bill, the 1958 National Defense Education Act, passed in the aftermath of the Sputnik shock, poured money into religious institutions. Together with its various extensions, the Act provided new funds for college construction, student loans, and science teaching. Moreover, loans for dormitory construction were often obtained under laws that provided financing for public housing.[53]

These funding measures not only subsidized the operations of the religious higher education sector, they also did so without engendering large-scale administrative intrusion. By providing mainly indirect funding, support came with very few strings attached and allowed participating institutions a wide scope of administrative discretion. The G.I. Bill, for example, allowed colleges and universities to keep control over admission policies and curricula in spite of receiving public funds, as servicemen were given vouchers that could be used to apply to any school.[54]

Moreover, many religious colleges and universities benefited from urban renewal programs involving the government's powers of eminent domain and condemnation. Title I of the Housing Act of 1949 provided federal funding to cities to cover the costs of acquiring areas considered slums. The sites were then made available to private developers to construct new housing. The 1954 Housing Act made these "urban renewal" projects even more attractive to developers via Federal Housing Administration (FHA)-backed mortgages and other subsidies. Churches or religiously affiliated institutions were thus able to obtain prime inner urban sites that had been declared slums at heavily discounted prices. In the case of the Lincoln Square redevelopment plan in New York City, for example, federal and local government offered prime real estate to Fordham University, a Catholic institution, in what effectively amounted to a subsidy of $4.6 million.[55]

Even in the controversial area of federal funding for parochial schools, church-state ties continued to strengthen in the postwar period. Despite the Supreme Court's *Everson v. Board of Education* (1947) ruling that put severe restrictions on federal funding for religious primary and secondary education, a 1953 survey found that in half the states tax money subsidized bus transportation, textbooks, and auxiliary educational services for parochial school students. Aid to "federally impacted areas," meaning districts that had experienced severe overcrowding and stress on services due to new defense installations, was also gradually expanded. In effect, these funds offered an alternative federal support structure at a time when political controversies still prevented the passage of general federal aid-to-education laws.[56]

Within the complex field of federal funding for religious agencies, the issue of primary and secondary education remained the most fought over, producing the most prolific and inconsistent court rulings. As far as legislation was concerned, anti-aid provisions dating back to the "Blaine amendment" campaign in the nineteenth century continued to be the most potent impediments to federal funding. Motivated by anti-Catholic sentiment, Republican heavyweight James G. Blaine had led a crusade to add a constitutional amendment forbidding direct government aid to religious educational institutions. Though the campaign failed at the federal level, it succeeded in putting exclusions on religious funding into enabling legislation for new territories applying for statehood and into commensurate state legislation. Indeed, these restrictions remain effective in more than two-thirds of the states today.[57]

In contrast, public support for religious health care was much less controversial. Sectarian institutions received federal funds mainly under Title VI of the 1946 Public Health Service Act, better known as the Hill-Burton Hospital Survey and Construction Act. The Act made federal funds available for the construction, replacement, and remodeling of hospitals and other medical facilities, as well as for research purposes. While the original program merely provided aid for hospital construction, its 1949 expansion included funding for research, experiment, and demonstration programs. In 1954, support for construction of nursing homes was added; subsequent legislation steadily allocated more for all categories of hospital and medical aid.[58]

The expansion of this program between the late 1940s and the 1960s resulted in the progressive increase in the amount of funds received by religious organizations. A 1953 survey found that federal grants to sectarian hospitals totaled $87 million. By 1960, sectarian hospitals had received close to $330 million in Hill-Burton funds, with an average of half a million $ per institution. Of 1,608 religiously affiliated hospitals, close to 40 percent (634) received federal funding, including 41 percent of the almost 900 Catholic hospitals, almost half (49 percent) of 57 Jewish hospitals, and over a third (35 percent) of the more than 660 Protestant hospitals. Although mainline denominations accounted for the highest percentage of funding, 12 out of 40 Southern Baptist hospitals received funds amounting to roughly $6 million and averaging more than half a million dollars per hospital. In total, over half the funds allocated under the Hill-Burton Act went to the private and nonprofit sector, and of these the largest category was religious. The state's expansion of the nation's hospital infrastructure was thus to a large extent achieved by funding church institutions.[59]

Sectarian hospitals, like religious higher education facilities, were also primary beneficiaries of postwar housing policies and donations of surplus government property. Many religious entities, for example, built housing for the elderly with FHA mortgage insurance and direct government loans from the Housing and Home Finance Agency of the Community Facilities Corporation, which was made possible under the Housing Acts of 1959 and 1961. Moreover, after World War II, the federal government found itself with numerous superfluous military bases, installations, and equipment. Instead of selling them to the highest bidder, however, these assets were largely donated for welfare and educational uses. As a result, many churches received highly valuable land, buildings, and other property at a fraction of their value. In many instances, these donations created significant windfall profits for religious organizations, especially when donated land was later sold off. According to a 1964 report of the Department of Health, Education and Welfare, 41 percent of the acreage going to religious groups went to the Catholic church. Protestant organizations also did very well out of surplus government property deals. A 1962 report stated that Protestant churches received real estate and buildings with an original value of $25 million, for which they paid $133,000.[60]

In comparison to health care, federal funding of religious social services grew less rapidly. This was not because federal planners were less eager to tap into the resources of religious agencies. Quite the opposite, they regarded them as the key to addressing some of the most pressing social and moral concerns of the war and postwar years, such as juvenile delinquency, family disorder, alcohol consumption, divorce, vice, and crime.[61] However, this was an area where state and local government funding for religious charities was well established, particularly in the institutional care of delinquents, the mentally ill, child protection, and foster care. Nonetheless, the federal government was beginning to make its presence felt. A 1955 National Council of Churches survey found that 69 Protestant agencies had received over $1 million in direct public subsidies for social welfare expenditures and that 132 agencies had received over $6 million from public sources as reimbursement for services. And most of the funds the federal government spent on vocational rehabilitation went to nonprofit providers, including Goodwill Industries run by the Methodist Board of Missions.[62]

These changes came slowly, though. In the 1950s federal funds that had been restricted to staff and administration costs, and could not be used to reimburse private agencies for care services, were gradually made available to sectarian organizations. Starting with the 1962 Social Security amendments, the federal government committed itself to a larger funding role in social services by boosting the federal share paid to states for services to welfare recipients from 50 to 75 percent. Although primacy was still placed on paying public sector agencies, this effectively meant a significant increase in federal funds allocated to charities, since states often subcontracted to nonprofit providers—many of whom were religiously affiliated. This set the precedent for the future structure of social service provision.[63]

By all accounts church-state funding ties were thus firmly established prior to the key programs of the Great Society. By 1963, there were 115 separate programs in health, education, research, housing, and foreign aid in which church agencies were active participants.[64] Among religiously based hospitals, nursing homes for the aged, children's institutions, and children's services surveyed in the early 1960s, 71 percent had contractual agreements providing for government assistance. Most sectarian hospitals received large construction grants, and most sectarian welfare agencies had entered into purchase-of-service arrangements. Catholic agencies were somewhat above the average (83 percent) and Protestants somewhat below (64 percent), with Episcopalians and Lutherans receiving the most tax support. Jewish agencies were the most independent and Catholic agencies the most dependent on tax funds. Although a third (34 percent) of all agencies received less than 10 percent from public funds, 15 percent received more than half their income from public sources.[65]

The Great Society and Beyond

The Great Society significantly furthered the integration of religious organizations into the public-private funding arrangements and established new precedents for church-state funding streams. It broke through long-standing restrictions on federal funding of religious and other voluntary social services and extended the established state and local practices to the federal arena. In addition to their determination to increase federal funding, Great Society planners sought to shake up the bureaucratically complex, financially insecure, politically suspect, and often wasteful funding arrangements between charities and state and local government. They not only increased dramatically the amount of federal money funneled into nonprofit organizations, but also changed the entire system of nonprofit funding. The War on Poverty put the emphasis on direct federal-to-nonprofit allocation, circumventing traditional mediating levels of state and local bureaucracies. New federal programs, such as the Community Mental Health Centers Act (1963), the Community Action component of the 1964 Economic Opportunity Act (EOA), and the 1965 Medicaid and Medicare programs became the main carriers of the expanded public-private funding arrangement. In this context, churches emerged as major beneficiaries of government funding and became administratively involved in a wide range of federally funded social programs.[66]

In the higher education arena, federal funding reached its peak with the higher education acts of 1963 and 1965. These made an unprecedented amount of federal money available to church colleges via federal student loans, capital financing, research contracts, and subsidized construction loans.[67] "All efforts to remove church colleges were defeated," a conservative Protestant lobbyist noted with chagrin, acknowledging that the new laws gave "equal opportunity to church colleges along with public schools in getting aid for their medical and dental colleges and universities."[68] Religious colleges and universities also benefited from the programs of the Office of Economic Opportunity (OEO), such as Upward Bound, which funded college recruitment of low-income students for summer courses. In overall terms, an estimated quarter of federal expenditure on higher education and more than half (54 percent) of federal research funding in 1980 went to nonprofit higher educational and research institutions. This constituted about 14 percent of total federal funding for nongovernmental organizations and about 22 percent of the overall income for these institutions.[69] Moreover, the landmark 1965 Elementary and Secondary Education Act established a precedent for the controversial funding for parochial schools by providing indirect federal funds to students.[70]

These measures also ushered in the large-scale conversion of conservatives to public funding for private schools. They therefore established patterns of direct and indirect aid programs that shaped church-state relations beyond the heyday of the War on Poverty.[71] As Stephen Monsma concluded in the early 1990s, programs ranging from the G.I. Bill via Basic Education Opportunity Grants to work-study provisions offered regular support to religiously based higher education "without the great stirring of controversy that typically accompanies programs that would grant aid to religiously based K-12 schools." According to his survey, religiously based educational institutions received a higher percentage of government funds than secular ones. While 65 percent of colleges and universities with a strong religious identification received more than 10 percent of their income from public funds, only 53 percent of secular institutions did. Surprisingly, almost all (97 percent) of the religiously affiliated institutions examined in the study received at least some public funds. Even more astonishing was that Protestant entities, who had traditionally opposed public funding, were surpassing Catholic institutions. Twenty-five percent of mainline Protestant and 35 percent of conservative Protestant colleges and universities received more than 20 percent of their funds from public sources, as compared to 23 percent of Catholic institutions.[72]

Likewise, in the health care field the creation of Medicare and Medicaid provided large-scale funding for religiously based hospitals, mental health institutions, nursing homes, and other health care agencies, while at the same time limiting the role of the federal government to that of bill payer. Three quarters ($1.75 billion) of the annual budget of the New York Roman Catholic archdiocese, for example, came from government sources in the early 1990s, and of this amount roughly one billion "derived from federal health care programs in the form of Medicaid and Medicare payments."[73] The Great Society also expanded other related programs: 75 percent of housing for the elderly built with FHA mortgage insurance, and over half of similar projects financed by the Community Facilities Corporation under the 1959 Housing Act were provided by churches by the early 1970s. "In low-cost housing programs, the risk to the church is, again, minimal, since the government guarantees the loans and often pays the rents as well," a staunch defender of church-state separation declared. The tax-exempt profits were then often plowed back into church programs.[74] Lester Salamon has estimated that by 1980 close to half (47 percent) of federal expenditure on health and hospitals went to nonprofit providers, constituting over a third (36 percent) of their overall income. In fact, health care providers received the lion's share of federal funds for nonprofit agencies, with over 60 percent going to them and other medical providers. Despite the conservative rhetoric of "retrenchment" and cuts in means-tested and human welfare provision during the Reagan administration, federal support to the nonprofit sector shifted even more toward health care, reaching 70 percent of federal nonprofit expenditure by 1985.[75]

The most dramatic change, however, came in the area of social service funding, where the federal government had not played a prominent role until the early 1960s. Here the Great Society's transformation of the structure of nonprofit funding through direct federal-to-nonprofit allocation was most palpable as the War on Poverty helped finance congregation-based child care, antipoverty programs, and mental health centers.[76] Although the 1964 EOA barred direct subsidy of churches and stipulated that federally funded facilities should be devoid of sectarian or religious symbols and decorations, it left plenty of room for church support. In particular, Head Start, as one of the keystones of the Great Society edifice, established numerous funding relationships with congregation-based child care providers, particularly among African American churches. Funds provided through the OEO helped finance church-based antipoverty efforts, job creation schemes, migrant worker programs, and construction projects. Money given to Community Action agencies and mental health centers—as alternatives to the state social service bureaucracies and public state hospitals—funneled further funds into religious agencies.[77] "Three or four years ago it was impossible for a federal agency to give a direct grant to a religious group," OEO director Sargent Shriver remarked, "today we are giving hundreds of grants without violating the principle of separation of church and state."[78]

The landmark 1967 Social Security amendments (Title IV-A) in particular proved a watershed both in terms of the expansion of the federal role in social service funding and the reliance upon religious nonprofits. The Act transferred social service costs from the states to the federal government, vastly expanded the client population, and added new areas of service provision. It institutionalized the two cornerstones of the Great Society credo, namely the reliance upon direct federal funding of social services and the use of nonprofit providers. The legislation allowed states to finance social services with three quarters of the expenditure provided by federal funds and only one quarter from either private or state sources. Crucially, it dropped prohibitions against federal funding for voluntary agencies and specifically encouraged states to enter into purchase-of-service agreements with private providers. Most remarkably, the amendments allocated almost unlimited amounts of money to states for contracting out of social services. In turn, new federal categorical programs funneled hundreds of millions of dollars per year to nonprofit community health centers, community action agencies, Head Start programs, neighborhood health clinics, drug and alcohol treatment centers, runaway shelters, and child and adult protective services.[79]

As a result, by 1969 religious groups received an estimated $7 billion annually from the many programs of government aid available to them. "Today government regards the church as simply another agency to be used in the furtherance of its social programs," C. Stanley Lowell, associate director of POAU, bemoaned in the early 1970s, "Government hires churches just as it hires many other kinds of private agencies." His worry that this had created a revolving door between church and state, because "literally thousands of Protestant ministers and Roman Catholic priests and nuns have left their positions with the church in order to become administrators of antipoverty programs," was confirmed by a comment by Sargent Shriver. So many clergy had gone to work for his office, he noted, that "OEO now means Office of Ecclesiastical Outcasts."[80]

As the open-ended financing provided in the 1967 Social Security Act resulted in the explosive growth of federal expenditures, however, it increasingly caused fiscal planners sleepless nights. Federal grants going to service agencies alone, which amounted to $164 million in 1963, had risen to almost $1.7 billion by 1972 and were only temporarily capped at $2.5 billion in 1973. Thus, "In a short five years, a manageable, relatively minor social services program funded by the federal government had become a monster out of control."[81] To a significant extent, this large-scale increase in expenditures was due to purchase-of-service contracting of states with private agencies. Between 1971 and 1976, overall states' spending on purchased social services rose from 25 percent of social service expenditure to 49 percent, and "many state agencies relied almost exclusively on nonprofit agencies to provide service, especially new and innovative services such as community residential programs, respite care, and day treatment."[82]

Attempts in the mid-1970s to rein in spiraling costs via caps, more rigid oversight, and shifting expenditures back to the states remained largely symbolic. Although Title XX of the Social Security Act (1974) introduced some restrictions, it retained or expanded the types of funding that had benefited religiously based services. This included support for child care and family services, counseling, protective services, health care, family planning, legal services, and provision for the developmentally disabled. Under Title XX the system of federal funds remained a crucial incentive for states to buy services from private agencies. It thus continued to express the "objectives of a nexus of policy makers who were skeptical or downright hostile toward state and local public welfare bureaucracies, dedicated to expanding the scope and availability of social welfare services, and favorably disposed to nonprofit service delivery."[83] Moreover, the federal government increased expenditures in established entitlement programs, such as Social Security, Medicaid, and Medicare, which frequently involved religious nonprofit providers. In addition, state governments increasingly spent funds to purchase services from nonprofit agencies. By 1980, for example, 46 percent of Catholic Charities and 17 percent of Salvation Army income came from government sources.[84]

The close funding contacts between government and both religious and secular nonprofits in social services thus continued to thrive in the afterglow of the Great Society, reflecting the strength of the political constituencies created by public-private funding arrangements. By 1980, federal funds comprised 65 percent of total government spending on all levels of social welfare services, excluding Medicare and Medicaid, compared to 37 percent in 1960. Total federal spending rose from $1.14 billion in 1960 to $13.5 billion in 1980. By 1982, combined governmental sources funded 62 percent of mental health services, 54 percent of social services, 53 percent of legal services, 52 percent of housing and community development, 51 percent of employment, training, and income support, and half of institutional and residential care. Nonprofit agencies, as Smith and Lipsky note, had become agents of government in the expansion of the American welfare state.[85]

The election of Ronald Reagan in 1980 ushered in the first significant exercise in social welfare retrenchment and cost-cutting since World War II. The 1981 Omnibus Budget Reconciliation Act (OBRA) cut Title XX funds by 20 percent, abolished federal funding for specific programs, and replaced federal funding streams with the Social Services Block Grant (SSBG), which allowed state more discretion in funding decisions. As a result, total federal spending on social welfare services through SSBG and other grant programs dropped from $8.8 billion in 1980 to $8.1 billion in 1988, declining from 64.4 to 52.4 percent of total social welfare service expenditure. Meanwhile, the government's share of nonprofit revenue dropped from 53.5 percent in 1977 to roughly 44 percent in 1984. Particularly hard hit were programs that provided education, training, health care, income assistance, and social services to the working poor. The new laws abolished federal funding for nonprofits such as child welfare agencies, battered women shelters, and job training programs, and significantly cut funding for community action agencies and neighborhood health clinics.[86] These cuts in turn caused anger particularly among Salvation Army and Lutheran Services personnel.[87]

The welfare state retrenchment of the 1980s, however, amounted less to a reduction in social service funding streams than to a reversal of the federalizing trends of the 1960s. It restored state and local discretion in awarding welfare and severely cut benefits for poor and minority populations, but did not abolish the basic social insurance framework set up during the Great Society. While the federal share in welfare expenditures fell, state and local government frequently took over responsibility for many services that had started in the 1970s with federal monies, and increasingly spent funds to purchase services from nonprofit agencies. Although many state governments initially cut services, state spending approached or exceeded pre-block grant levels by the mid- to late 1980s as nonprofits increasingly turned to state and local government to compensate for declining federal assistance. In turn, state and local spending on social services increased from $4.8 billion in 1980 to $7.3 billion in 1988. Combined federal, state, and local government spending on social services—excluding public health insurance expenditures for programs such as Medicaid and Medicare—grew overall from $13.6 billion to $15.2 billion.[88] The subsidiarist state itself thus remained essentially intact, in part due to both congressional resistance and organized lobbying by a broad coalition of third-sector pressure groups that organized in the wake of previous expansions of welfare programs. As Peter Dobkin Hall concluded, "Privatization—out-sourcing public agency functions to private sector firms—has meant little more than giving official recognition to trends that were already long-established."[89]

The 1990 Child Care and Development Block Grant is a particularly illustrative example of subsidiarist state building continuing on the basis of the growing participation of a wide range of religious providers. Part of the George H. W. Bush administration's Omnibus Budget Reconciliation Act, the program boosted federal aid for child care along the lines of vouchers and certificates, rather than grants or contracts—intriguingly by increasing the block grant allocation under Title XX. In the House, the bill was promoted by conservative Christian Representative Charles Stenholm (D-Tex.), who called it the "child care's version of food stamps if you will—kid stamps." Stenholm made clear that the bill was designed to prevent a program that supported care "performed by *government*-trained and *government*-regulated personnel in *government*-licensed centers."[90] By devolving decision making to the states, minimizing federal regulatory intervention, and ensuring access to all types of agencies, the block grant appealed to a wide range of religious social service providers. In particular, by making certificates available for congregation-operated programs, it significantly increased their willingness to take government funds because vouchers, unlike direct grants, did not come with specific restrictions on religious practices. The block grant thus reigned in the ability of government to limit religious instruction, curtail employment discrimination on the basis of religious belief, and hamper discrimination in admission among sectarian agencies receiving public funds.[91]

Reauthorized in 1996, the block grant anticipated the features of subsequent legislation on public aid for religious providers, particularly Charitable Choice and the Faith-Based Initiative. They are discussed in more detail in the book's Conclusion. What is important to keep in mind, however, is that decades prior to these two milestones in church-state subsidiarity, reliance upon public funds in social services had become a pervasive feature among many religious groups. By the early 1990s, 65 percent of Catholic Charities U.S. revenues came from government sources, as did 75 percent of the funds of the Jewish Board of Family and Children's Services, and 92 percent of Lutheran Social Ministries' income;[92] 67 percent of Catholic and 59 percent of mainline Protestant child service agencies received over 60 percent of their income from public sources. Overall, 42 percent of child service agencies who fell into the most religious category received more than 60 percent of their funds from government.[93]

The Political Economy of Subsidiarity

Within a body politic that regularly invokes the "wall of separation between church and state," public funding for religious agencies faces a range of legal, political, and cultural constrictions. Secular critics frequently lambaste public aid as the thin end of a wedge allowing for undue religious influence in public policy, while many religionists worry that government funds impose limits on the spiritual dimension of charities. As a result, two main obstacles stood in the way of large-scale government funding for religious nonprofits. First, subsidiarity raised constitutional questions about aid to religion. Second, it clashed with traditional misgivings among many religious groups about closer ties to the state.

As it turned out, however, neither constitutional restrictions nor antiestablishmentarian sentiments seriously impinged upon the expansion and popularity of funding ties after World War II. Despite a number of landmark decisions on church-state issues, the Supreme Court neither established clear legal principles nor provided consistent rulings on government aid to religious agencies. Moreover, Court decisions that protected religious organizations under the free exercise clause created more opportunities for them to expand their spiritual mission. Likewise, subsidiarist practices allayed fears among religionists about government intrusion. Devolution, limited regulatory oversight, indirect funding streams, and the absence of effective restrictions on proselytizing militated against infringements on the organizational autonomy or religious content of religious agencies. Despite a number of highly publicized cases of government interference and a plethora of statutes prohibiting public support for sectarian practices, government funding was often indirect and came with few strings attached. Policy makers exhibited concerns with bureaucratic capacities, political expediency, and cost-effectiveness, rather than fears about breaching the First Amendment. Statutory restrictions on funding religious activities were frequently flouted and few sectarian agencies experienced any federally mandated curtailment of their practices.

What is more, contrary to critics who chide big government for destroying the charitable sector, the development of philanthropic entities in the period after the Second World War paralleled the rise of the national security and welfare state. Public funds played a crucial role in underwriting the expansion of charitable activities of religious organizations in the postwar years. This, together with the de facto bureaucratic sanctioning of sectarian practices, facilitated a seminal shift in church-state attitudes, particularly among Protestant denominations. As a result, lobbying for clearer legal safeguards, rather than the issue of rejecting or accepting funds, became the key focus of intradenominational debates.

The Supreme Court and Public Funding

In response to the significant expansion of federal funding for religious providers after World War II the practice of state aid to church-related institutions came under more intense legal scrutiny. Ironically, however, the various decisions by the Supreme Court in the postwar period, while rhetorically upholding the hallowed principle of the wall of separation between church and state and prohibiting public aid in primary and secondary education, left a vast array of government subsidies to church-based hospitals, welfare organizations, and foreign aid agencies unchallenged. In the end, these inconsistencies even provided new opportunities for the public funding of primary and secondary education.[94]

The landmark *Everson v. Board of Education* and *Lemon v. Kurzman* (1971) decisions were cases in point. The *Everson* case dealt with a New Jersey law that provided state aid for transporting children to both public and religious schools. The Court's narrow 5–4 decision was notoriously Delphic. On the one hand, the Court handed down a thundering defense of the no-aid-to-religion doctrine based on the establishment clause of the Constitution and Jefferson's adage of the "wall of separation." It asserted that public funds should not be used to finance religious primary and secondary education. On the other hand, however, the Court upheld the legality of New Jersey's public support for student transportation by arguing that the money was provided for the secular aspect of parochial schools only. Thus, the Court simultaneously announced that not a single dollar could go to religion, and authorized the state of New Jersey to pay to transport students to parochial schools.[95]

The *Everson* decision had two crucial consequences for the larger legal framework of church-state funding ties. First, by distinguishing between secular and sectarian purposes, it sanctioned public funding of religious agencies if certain criteria of "public purpose" were met. Second, by focusing exclusively on school funding, *Everson* left long-standing government subsidies to other church-controlled organizations unaffected. As a result, the decision's backing for state funding of services that supported the *public* purposes of sectarian institutions was used by other courts to uphold public aid to sectarian social welfare agencies. For example, based on *Everson* and the 1899 *Bradfield v. Roberts* decision, a spate of state court cases upheld the constitutionality of the Hill-Burton Act by distinguishing between the religious auspices of an institution and its public purpose. The 1947 Supreme Court ruling thus reinforced the remarkable contrast between the legal assertion of the separation of church and state in education and long-standing cooperative practices in health care and social provision.[96]

In 1971, public funding for religious school was at the center of another Supreme Court ruling that formulated a key legal principle governing church-state funding ties. *Lemon v. Kurzman* pulled the constitutional rug from under state programs that supplemented teacher salaries for secular subjects at religiously based schools. Many of these programs had been based on the secular-sacred distinction spelled out by the *Everson* decision. The Court's opinion, however, written by Chief Justice Warren Burger, established a new tripartite test as a guideline for the interpretation of the establishment clause and the basis for deciding the constitutionality of government aid. The famous *Lemon* test permits public funding of faith-based organizations as long as the law establishing the program has a secular purpose, neither advances nor inhibits religion, and does not foster excessive government entanglement with religion. The Court also determined that if a school receiving public money is "pervasively sectarian," state aid violates the First Amendment.

As in the *Everson* case, however, the apparently restrictive nature of the ruling did not seriously question the established funding ties between government and religious groups in areas outside of primary and secondary education. Indeed, on the same day it issued the *Lemon* decision, the Court in a separate ruling legitimated federal expenditures for building projects on religious college campuses. Its decision in *Tilton v. Richardson* (1971) upheld

48 Chapter 1

the constitutionality of the Higher Education Facilities Act of 1963, which authorized federal aid to church-related colleges and universities in the form of construction grants for facilities used for secular educational purposes. Moreover, although subsequent Court decisions defined "pervasively sectarian" more closely to cover institutional control by a religious body, religious exercise requirements, faith-based preferential admission for students, and religious conditions in hiring faculty, no consistent criteria emerged. Instead, the Court, invoking the traditional distinction between sectarian and secular purposes, continued to maintain that religiously based institutions of higher education and social welfare provision were not pervasively sectarian.[97] Even the large-scale expansion of federal funding for church-related agencies during the Great Society raised few legal eyebrows as the distinction between the fields of welfare and education in state-aid rulings continued to characterize the Court's attitude. Church-state funding during the War on Poverty, as one of its most vocal critics noted, was "remarkably elusive so far as lawsuits are concerned."[98]

Prior to the *Lemon* decision, the Supreme Court had already taken on another looming issue in church-state relations, namely, the constitutionality of tax privileges for religious entities. Traditionally, churches received the most permanent and calculable benefits from a wide range of privileges accorded to religious bodies under federal and state tax and regulatory regimes. These included tax exemptions, not having to incorporate or file tax returns, and the deductibility of donations without burden of proof. In the postwar period, these exemptions were extended to the ownership of religious property, including highly lucrative housing projects, and to profits made by commercial businesses leased back or operated by a church. C. Stanley Lowell of POAU put it bluntly: "For government to use the taxing power on behalf of the church is to join the two," he declared, "the simple tax exemption for a modest house of worship has burgeoned into virtual establishment of religion."[99]

Despite continued litigation against often cryptic and ambiguous tax rules and various probes into the constitutionality of religious exemptions, a general tendency toward easing restrictions on religiously affiliated agencies prevailed. Although the courts limited religious use exemptions strictly to places of worship, they broadened the scope of charitable use exemptions to include religious education, fellowship, recreation, mission work, and social services.[100] In its seminal 1970 *Waltz v. Tax Commission* decision, for example, the Supreme Court decided that these exemptions were not based on the traditional concept of "good deeds," which recognized that charitable activities eased the burden on taxpayers. Arguing that the "good deeds" argument would entail the imposition of accounting rules and the annual examination of church books and activities, the Court instead justified exemptions as a means of preventing "excessive entanglements" forbidden under the 1947 *Everson* decision.[101]

The *Everson, Lemon,* and *Waltz* decisions show that prior to the end of the Cold War "few objections were raised either to the massive government subsidies received by large Protestant, Catholic, and Jewish social service agencies or to the funds granted to inner city congregations that run job training, neighborhood revitalization, and other anti-poverty programs during the 1960s."[102] In *Bowen v. Kendrick* (1988) the Court once again confirmed this pattern. It upheld the constitutionality of the Adolescent Family Life Act in which Congress had authorized federal funds for programs to fight teenage pregnancies and premarital sex. In a narrow 5–4 decision, the Court defended the law on the basis of the *Lemon* test. The controversial majority opinion, written by Chief Justice William Rehnquist, argued that the law had a secular purpose, that prohibitions for funding religious purposes were implied, and that the institutions receiving funds were not pervasively sectarian. As Steven Monsma reminds us, only two Supreme Court cases, namely *Bradfield v. Roberts* in 1899 and *Bowen* in 1988, directly confronted the use of public funds for religious social service provision—and in both cases the Court upheld the practice as within the "no-aid-to-religion" interpretation.[103]

Nonetheless, the *Lemon* test did result in one crucial change to the legal framework of subsidiarity: It added to the concern with the *outcome* of public funding of religious agencies a focus on the *kinds* of public aid provided. The Court's implicit approval of government funds for religiously based higher education, for example, was largely based on the indirect nature of these funding streams. Available for use in both religious and secular institutions, these posed less of a constitutional problem than direct aid, because the funds were dispersed to eligible students, who then made their own choices.[104] Ironically, this opened up new opportunities for the public funding of primary and secondary education, which had previously been largely struck down. In the 1983 *Mueller v. Allen* decision the Court approved a Minnesota program of limited tax credits to all parents, including those who sent their children to religious schools. In its ruling, the Court distinguished between direct aid to religious schools, which conflicted with the First Amendment, and money given indirectly to these institutions through parents or students, which did not fall afoul of constitutional provisions.[105]

In the decades since the end of the Cold War, Court rulings further condoned this limited support for religious primary and secondary education. *Agostini v. Felton* (1997) broke through long-held objections to direct public funding for parochial education by allowing poor children at religious schools to receive remedial instruction from public school teachers paid with federal funds. Moreover, *Mitchell v. Helms* (2000) enabled religious schools to receive direct federal aid in the form of computers, media resources, and library materials. And *Zelman v. Simmons-Harris* (2002), in which the Court upheld the constitutionality of school vouchers despite previous opposition in *Public Education and Religious Liberty (PEARL) v. Nyquist* (1973), underscored this willingness to extend public support to sectarian schools as long as the aid flowed through individuals and was the result of their choice.[106]

Government Interference in Religious Agencies

The constitutional separation of church and state has not stood in the way of religiously affiliated institutions participating in the growing public funding streams to nongovernmental agencies. Nonetheless, other limitations had the potential to curtail severely the range and size of church-state networks in the human services infrastructure of the Cold War state. Many critics, particularly those from strict religious backgrounds, warned about the corrupting effects of cozy relations between religious charities and federal agencies.[107] They noted that many government funding programs prohibited belief-based discrimination, religious instruction, and the display of religious symbols. Direct public funding, they warned, gradually eroded the agencies' religious identity, hindered the development of religiously based approaches, led to secularization, and reduced church support for social activism. They maintained that contracting furthered dependency on government funds, limited the spiritual approach of religious organizations, and caused loss of agency autonomy. In short, they feared that "who pays the piper calls the tune."[108]

Although on the surface these fears might ring true, there are important caveats to the scenario of meddlesome government forcing nonprofits into a straitjacket with the lure of federal funds. Indeed, government funding overall created few pressures on religiously based entities to curtail or eliminate their religiously based practices. At the 1956 NCC conference on church and social welfare, delegates expressed few worries about government interference with the autonomy of church-related agencies. Instead, they were highly critical of religious agencies themselves, which continued restrictive hiring and admission practices despite receiving government funds.[109] By the early 1980s, most directors of religious agencies reported that "their worst fears about loss of autonomy had not been realized."[110] Likewise, one conservative observer admitted, many of the government-supported programs of Jews, Catholics, and mainline Protestants retained "a distinct religious flavor, often including voluntary religious activities, religious symbols, and a readiness to discuss faith matters with clients."[111]

Two aspects of the funding regime in particular cast doubt on the notion that government funding translates into more rigid controls. First, although government support for nonprofits is extensive, most of the money reaches nonprofits indirectly. The types of funding have important implications for the relationship between government and nonprofits. The most direct funding streams, such as grants, often translate into the greatest federal influence, while less direct arrangements, such as vouchers and reimbursement schemes, have significantly fewer strings attached. Considering that many nonprofits jealously guard their autonomy, it comes as no surprise that the direct route is the least used of the three forms of assistance. Similarly, the general trend since 1945 has been in the direction of voucher-type mechanisms. By 1980, only 20 percent of all federal aid to nonprofits came directly from the government via grants, loans, and contracts, whereas 53 percent was channeled through individuals with vouchers and reimbursement schemes, and another 27 percent reached nonprofits through block grants to state and local governments. Clearly, if the federal government was affecting the nonprofit sector, it was doing so indirectly.[112]

The second component of subsidiarity that questions the intrusion scenario is that the expansion of federal funding for nonprofits was in most cases accompanied by the loosening, rather than a tightening, of regulatory controls. Many observers note the high level of autonomy of private and nonprofit actors in the funding regime. Often it was the federal programs that were less restrictive than state and local equivalents. For example, reporting requirements were liberalized in the Social Service Block Grant, while state contracts were usually awarded for specific programs that allowed nonprofit agencies little leeway. Despite specific stipulations in social service legislation and a tendency toward prolific regulation, the federal government relied more on financial incentives than on direct control. It devoted less capacity to monitoring implementation than is suggested by the frequent complaints about overregulation.[113]

In effect, "benign neglect" characterized the general approach to funding religious social services after World War II. While overt violations of
antisectarian or antidiscrimination rules did at times cause unease, in most
instances government simply handed over the money with certain broad
guidelines and let religious agencies proceed at will. Neither did government restrictions clash with the emphasis on a distinctly spiritual approach
pursued by many religious agencies. Though frequently pushing for bureaucratic standardization and regulation, government agencies for the most
part quietly tolerated or condoned the autonomy of religious agencies and
their spiritual mission.[114] "Instead of a hierarchical relationship between
the federal government and its agents, therefore, what frequently exists in
practice is a far more complex bargaining relationship in which the federal
agency often has the weaker hand."[115]

The experience differed, however, depending on the type of religious entity and the directness of funding ties. Higher education was the least prob-
lematic area of church-state interaction. In this area, a large percentage of the
funds came in the form of indirect aid via the G.I. Bill, student loan programs,
or work-study funding. This type of funding was often acceptable even to
religious institutions apprehensive of government intrusion. In a survey
from the early 1990s, almost a third of religiously based colleges and universities receiving public funds had compulsory chapel services. Yet only 13
percent mentioned any problems with government at all, and just 7 percent
reported being forced to curtail their practices. Meanwhile, 91 percent of the
religiously affiliated colleges and universities receiving public funds reported
that they engaged openly, rather than subtly, in religious exercises.[116]

A somewhat different picture emerges from the survey of religious family
and child care service agencies. Here, almost a third (30 percent) reported
some problems with pressures from government. The main bone of contention was required church attendance and the presence of religious symbols.
The higher incidence of conflict in the social services arena had in part to do
with more direct funding streams and a more assertive pursuit of sectarian
goals. In foster care and family services, for example, churches often used
public funds to discriminate and serve a sectarian clientele. Nonetheless, only
11 percent of child service agencies receiving public funds in the early 1990s
reported that they were actually forced to curb these practices. Likewise, a
large majority (77 percent) reported that they openly engaged in religious
practices.[117]

Finally, government funding in the foreign aid arena has not only been generous but has often financed openly sectarian practices that ran counter to nondiscriminatory requirements. As discussed earlier, public monies supported missionary operations and personnel abroad. Churches were also aided in their proselytizing programs by serving as distributors of government goods. In turn, religious agencies were at times accused of using relief goods and surplus food to spread their sectarian message. In light of this, it comes as no surprise that around a fifth (22 percent) of the international aid agencies surveyed in the 1990s reported running into problems with government officials. Nonetheless, less than a tenth of the religiously based foreign aid agencies—versus almost a quarter (24 percent) of the secular ones—reported that government funds caused them to change their relief or development priorities to meet government wishes, and almost two-thirds (62 percent) engaged openly in religious practices. The impression given by international aid officials was that "as long as the religiously based aid agencies are not too overt or up-front with their religious practices, they can get by with a significant amount of mixing religious elements into publicly funded activities and programs."[118]

The overall lack of government interference, however was not the only factor in placating religious critics of subsidiarity. The growth of religious social service agencies as part of the large-scale expansion of government-nonprofit funding networks was equally important. As a major player in the charitable field, religious entities partook in the exponential growth of the nonprofit sector during and after the 1960s, when the federal government extended its powers at the expense of state and local agencies. As Peter Dobkin Hall put it, "one of the most significant expressions of the expansion of government was the dramatic growth of the nonprofit domain."[119] Indeed, more than two thirds of all social service nonprofits were formed after 1960.[120]

By the 1990s, the vast majority of religious agencies reported that public funding had helped them expand their services and programs. Public funds supported the growth of student numbers and the extension of campus facilities of religious colleges and universities, and enabled the vast majority of religious foreign aid agencies to expand their services. Moreover, since the 1960s retirement and nursing homes, foster care programs, shelters for battered women, pregnancy clinics, counseling centers, substance abuse programs, training for the unemployed, medical relief, and similar endeavors run by churches and affiliated organizations have mushroomed.[121] Congregation-based child care in particular grew dramatically in the postwar era, driven by the baby boom, suburban development, church expansion, and the increasing number of women entering the labor market.[122]

In the process, church-based charities often developed into more complex entities. Sharp rises in government funding for day care, homeless shelters, child protection, counseling, legal aid, family planning, community living, and the like meant that charitable agencies "were transformed from relatively small community-based organizations reliant upon private donations, volunteer labor, and in-kind assistance to much larger agencies dependent primarily on public funds."[123] Forming partnerships with government, many nonprofits thus expanded from single- to multiple-purpose operations that provided a vast array of services. These included formal education, social welfare, pastoral counseling, charitable fundraising, recreational facilities, medical care, libraries, and summer camps. As Kenneth Wald has pointed out, "several of the largest churches have become the hubs for worldwide operations, complete with the organizational complexity of a major corporation."[124] This applied in particular to the many parachurch social service agencies created since 1970, including World Concern, Food for the Hungry, Samaritan's Purse, and International Christian Aid.[125]

The Transformation of Church-State Attitudes
Among Religious Groups

These experiences with subsidiarity ushered in a string of intradenominational debates that re-examined and redefined the traditional principle of church-state separation in the decades after World War II. These efforts to formulate a new policy have received little attention from historians and other scholars, yet their significance is difficult to overestimate. As Bernard Coughlin remarked in the mid-1960s, "Realizing that the role of the state is bound to be more inclusive, religious leaders are revising their former policies of absolute separation of church and state as obsolete in today's society."[126]

Historically, religious groups had differed markedly in their positions on taking public funds. Roman Catholic and Jewish administrators largely supported government funding and saw neither subsidies nor purchase-of-service arrangements as violations of church-state separation. Both also had centralized national welfare bodies with significant influence over local agencies, particularly the National Catholic Welfare Conference, the National Conference of Catholic Charities, and the Council of Jewish Federations and Welfare Funds.[127] In the case of the National Conference of Catholic Charities, the impetus behind its formation in the early twentieth century came not only from the growing sense that consolidated charity organization and fundraising were more efficient, but also from the "growing desire among church leaders to collaborate meaningfully with government and civic organizations in social welfare activities."[128]

Meanwhile, Protestants were much more divided and rarely agreed on government funding. The decentralized nature of Protestantism meant that the National Council of Churches and the various denominational social action departments could make suggestions, but did not have policy-making authority. "Frequently the practices of two local agencies within a denomination are in conflict with each other, and both are at variance with the thinking of national administrators," Coughlin noted. He even argued that "there is closer theological kinship and a greater degree of social-philosophical unity between certain Protestant churches and the Catholic church than exists among the rest of the Protestant denominations taken together."[129] This policy indeterminacy among Protestant agencies, however, also meant that they carried on the majority of debates about a compatible church-state principle and the impact of government funding on both the ideology and governance of religious agencies. The Hill-Burton Act in particular, "perhaps more than any other in our social welfare history," ushered in "denominational agencies' examination of their policies and attitudes toward the acceptance of government assistance."[130]

Three main positions characterized the Protestant fold. First, Anabaptists and other revivalist and evangelical movements traditionally espoused an uncompromising separationism that resisted any form of church-state cooperation. They mainly feared the clandestine secularization of religious social services and their absorption into a government-run system. They also warned about the establishment of religion through the back door and the marginalization of religious social services in society.[131] In contrast, church leaders and administrators from mainline backgrounds, though at times sharing these fears, were on average less wary of closer ties to the state than their evangelical brethren. Historically, the older wing of Protestantism, primarily Lutherans and Calvinists, sought to maintain close relations to the state. Many Lutherans, for example, called for expanding government aid for institutional chapels and salaries for spiritual ministries. And the Board of Christian Social Action of the American Lutheran Church, in particular, was in the vanguard of advocating church-state cooperation in the field of education. In addition, the Methodists, though originating in a later revival, also explicitly rejected the separationism of free church Protestantism and its concept of a "secular" state. Their acceptance of Hill-Burton funds attained particular significance, since the Board of Hospitals and Homes of the Methodist Church directed more health care institutions than any other board working with the Welfare Department of the National Council of Churches. Methodists also increasingly advocated extending the principle of church-state cooperation from welfare to education, calling for Hill-Burton funding to include school construction and backing a range of other direct subsidies. Moreover, they embraced tax exemptions for church property and the chaplaincy program in the armed forces and Congress. Forming a second major group, Methodists and Lutherans, together with Episcopalians, thus ended up in the forefront of adopting policies that embraced government funding.[132]

In between these two factions was a third group. It included denominations that attempted to square the circle by combining a separationist identity with the acceptance of funds. The 169th General Assembly of the Presbyterian Church, U.S.A., for example, which was "unalterably opposed" to the use of public funds for sectarian education, at the same time encouraged its agencies to use tax funds for sectarian welfare activities. Likewise, the mainline Evangelical and Reformed Church continued to call for a rigid distinction between church and state, yet accepted Hill-Burton funds and public support for children's services and programs for the aged. This ambivalence created "two streams of influence" in which church leaders rhetorically rejected government funds and church administrators embraced them. As the growing role of the state forced the re-evaluation of ties with the government, it frequently resulted in the absence of clear restrictions on government aid, rather than in an open embrace of public funds. "Most agencies state that they have no policies about receiving or not receiving government aid," while at the same time over 60 percent of agencies surveyed in the 1960s said they received public funding and only 5 percent in practice maintained a policy of absolute separation.[133]

As the availability of public funds grew, denominational competition with Catholics, fear of financial shortfalls, and the desire for political access formed increasingly powerful incentives among reluctant Protestants to accept public aid. At the same time, however, calibrating carefully between continued rhetorical rejection of government funding and its practical embrace increasingly came to define the Protestant stance. The foreign aid field, in particular, served as a catalyst for this repositioning. As indicated earlier, Catholic agencies had been the prime beneficiaries of international relief funding, forcing other denominations "either to seek government aid or to drift to the edges on the joint public/private relief effort of the last four decades." In turn, by the 1950s many Protestant agencies had developed their own rationale—or rationalization—for taking government funds. They focused less on *whether* to take public funds than on *how much* to take—a compromise that "was somewhat academic, but it served to meet criticism from within the churches." Despite resistance from various quarters, by the 1960s a consensus had emerged that the use of federal dollars and subventions was acceptable, even necessary, in supporting religious international aid programs.[134]

The careful and circumspect policies of the NCC further exemplify this tenuous and often labored new position of the mainline Protestant churches. The 1955 Cleveland conference concluded that acceptance of Hill-Burton money was not contrary to separationism and that purchase-of-service arrangements should include sectarian organizations.[135] A year later, the First Conference on the Churches and Social Welfare affirmed that "the church and government should act together as partners" in social welfare. Although the meeting reflected the divisions among Protestants over accepting government funds, it pointed to the basic consensus that subsidies through grants to individuals were preferable to agency subsidies, and that agency autonomy needed to be ensured. Spelling out criteria of accepting government aid, the conference asserted that "we believe that the provision of needed material aids, such as food and shelter, by modern government, may well enhance the ministry of the church by leaving her free to use her resources toward spiritual objectives."[136]

Moreover, the conference proceedings lauded the cooperation between public and church welfare agencies in regard to the spiritual ministry of church. They concluded that "by means of proper integration, the whole of society can benefit from the church's spiritual vision and power without encumbering her with the great financial burden, the administrative responsibilities, and in some cases the political dependence which have engendered anti-clerical attitudes in many other societies." Finally, stressing that "often the way laws are administered is as significant as the laws themselves," the meeting encouraged church members to "serve on public boards, participate in community planning discussions of public welfare administration, and otherwise aid in the effective administration of the law."[137] These sentiments of cooperation were voiced even more forcefully during the NCC's 1957 National Conference on Policy and Strategy in Social Welfare, which included both Protestant and Catholic leaders. As Coughlin concluded, for Protestant churches especially this was "a new course and a long way from the 'absolute separation' and the 'wall of separation' language generally associated with the church-state principle."[138]

*   *   *

By the end of the 1960s Cold War subsidiarity had not only transformed church-state relations but had also ushered seminal revisions in the attitudes of religious groups toward public funding. While Catholic and Jewish church leaders and administrators traditionally regarded neither subsidies nor purchase-of-service arrangements as violations of church-state separation, Protestant groups also gradually shifted away from their traditional insistence on strict separation. However, the emergent Protestant stance remained more ambivalent than that of other denominations. The Protestant rejection of state aid did not give way to an outright embrace of subsidiarity, but to a more subtle approach that distinguished between types of public funding according to the extent to which they allegedly threatened the autonomy of religious agencies. In other words, Protestants combined the pragmatic acceptance of funding ties with a focus on how to preserve the independence and faith-based approach of religious agencies within a growing administrative state.

This entailed a new concern with the real and potential uncertainties in the legislative and administrative construction of subsidiarity. Although benign neglect and indirect funding streams provided a significant measure of independence, this meant protection by default only. Arbitrary restrictions on sectarian organizations, though rare, had the potential to "result in the serious compromise of their religious autonomy, if suddenly they were uniformly applied to all religious nonprofits receiving public funds."[139] Likewise, while the Supreme Court had imposed few limitations, its often inconsistent rulings left the door open for statutory limitations on hiring practices, religious exercises, and behavior standards. The experience of subsidiarity thus nudged mainline Protestants away from the outright debate about whether or not to accept government money. At the same time it pushed them into lobbying for more secure legal safeguards for public funding arrangements.

The dynamics of subsidiarity and the intrareligious debates about church-state relations outlined in this chapter formed the backdrop for the re-engagement of evangelicals with Cold War public policy. The next four chapters explore in detail how evangelicals, traditionally the most separationist wing in the Protestant family, repositioned themselves in this new environment between World War II and the end of the Cold War. They analyze in what ways evangelicals began to partake in the public funding arrangements engineered by Cold War foreign and social policy, how this transformed their church-state attitude, and what role this played in their partisan mobilization.

CHAPTER 2

THE EVANGELICAL REDISCOVERY
OF THE STATE

W artime exigencies and postwar global challenges not only fostered the growth of the state and promoted closer church-state cooperation, they also prompted a new generation of conservative Protestants to reengage with society and politics. Moving away from theological obscurity, cultural isolation, social withdrawal, and political marginality, they became once again vocal advocates for christianizing America and promoting Christians in government. As historian Joel Carpenter put it, "The postwar evangelical movement reached into the older denominations, the offices of Capitol Hill, the studios of Hollywood, and up the Hit Parade charts as well."[1]

While the resurgence of evangelicalism has been the subject of many studies, the role of the changing relationship between evangelicals and the state in shaping the postwar movement's theological and ideological outlook has rarely been explored in scholarship. As neo-evangelicals re-activated their broader political, social, and cultural aspirations in a world that was increasingly characterized by the growing power of government, however, they once again opened themselves up to the public policy sphere. Seeking the revival of social witness and desiring a Christian state, evangelicals carried on a new debate about political involvement and kept abreast of political issues. They invested time and effort in politically educating an evangelical elite; they cultivated contacts with government officials and agencies at the highest levels; they monitored legislative processes, lobbied on behalf of political causes, and mobilized grassroots campaigns; and their publications gave extensive coverage to questions of church and state. "This year was one of 'open-season' on church-state relations," noted NAE Office of Public Affairs (OPA) director Clyde Taylor in November 1963; "there has been more considered study of the many problems involved than we have seen in many years, and the end is not yet."[2]

This evangelical re-engagement with the state took place in the context of two seminal developments that profoundly shaped the postwar resurgence. First, it was part and parcel of the internal efforts by postwar neo-evangelicals to forge a new theological identity distinct from both separatist fundamentalism and theological liberalism. The relationship between church and state in general, and the public funding of religious agencies in particular, became key themes in the self-demarcation of neo-evangelicalism as a "third force" in American Protestantism. Indeed, the church-state debates signified a neo-evangelical position that sought to reconcile the desire to preserve separationism with the urge to overcome marginalization and acquire political influence. In redefining their relationship to the state, neo-evangelicals strove both to engage with the culture at large and to retain their subcultural identity.

Second, the evangelical repositioning was affected by the broader socioeconomic and sociocultural dynamics of wartime and postwar state building and its contradictions. Defense spending, infrastructure investment, and middle-class social benefits pumped billions of dollars into Texas, California, Florida, Arizona, and other evangelical strongholds in the South and the West. By the 1960s, conservative Protestants in parts of the region were among the prime beneficiaries of the politics of economic growth that underlay the dramatic shift in socioeconomic power from the older commercial centers of the Northeast to the thriving cities of the Sunbelt since the 1940s. While growth-oriented policies linked the nation's economic well-being to the willingness of consumers to spend, however, the welfare state had traditionally been tied to moral norms more associated with nineteenth-century producer-class ideology than with the "rehabilitation of desire" (Christopher Lasch) that formed the normative basis of consumerism.[3] Rigid behavioral requirements, morals-testing, intrusive supervision, and punitive intervention implanted in social policy demanded that the poor develop a work ethic, be self-disciplined, and overcome "dependency." And racially coded provision and gender discriminations embedded in the administrative organization and the normative content of public policy reinforced a hierarchical system of social provision.

In other words, while traditional notions of moral self-control were embedded in the producerist construction of the welfare state, growth-oriented public policies furthered a consumer capitalism that could never quite get enough of the hedonistic impulse. This tension within Cold War state building was keenly felt among those embracing a staunch moral and religious conservatism while thriving in a setting characterized by affluent white-collar suburban living based on government-subsidized industries. It lay at the core of the emerging evangelical attitude toward the Cold War state that combined antipathy toward the "permissiveness" of liberal welfarism with an embrace of growth-oriented and subsidiarist policies, and demands for punitive intervention with the cult of entrepreneurial individualism.

Placing church-state issues at the center of both the internal awakening and the sociopolitical transformation of postwar evangelicalism suggests revisions to established interpretations that locate the movement's political identity primarily in the "backlash" against the iniquities of the liberal state. As the example of the NAE shows, evangelicals became increasingly aware of the opportunities for social and political assertion afforded by the Cold War state. In gradually parting with their traditional separationism and pietist isolationism, postwar evangelicals began to pave the way for a rather different view of the state. This contrasts sharply with established interpretations that regard a clear-cut distinction between secular-liberal statism and right-wing retrenchment as the pivot of the political ideology of evangelicals in the region where the conservative resurgence began to reshape the political direction of the nation.

Church-State Issues in the Neo-Evangelical Awakening

In the decades after the end of World War II, white evangelical Protestants sought and attained a measure of sociocultural legitimacy, theological authority, internal unity, and political influence they had not experienced since the nineteenth century. At the beginning of this process stood a new generation of self-declared "neo-evangelicals" who wanted to make conservative Protestantism relevant again within mainstream culture and theology after years of self-imposed isolation. Evangelist Billy Graham, theologian Carl F. H. Henry, and Congregational minister Harold John Ockenga were among those who constituted this new cadre of "progressive fundamentalists" (Joel Carpenter) or "post-fundamentalist evangelicals" (Donald Dayton).[4] In their desire to reaffirm orthodox Protestantism's cultural and political significance in modern American society, they positioned themselves as a "third force" between fundamentalism and theological liberalism.[5]

While affirming religious orthodoxy, neo-evangelicals rejected fundamentalist theological exclusivism and its fortress mentality and sought to disentangle themselves from the prewar movement's more xenophobic and bigoted aspects. The postwar reformers, Carl Henry maintained, were turning away from the term fundamentalism "not because of any inclination to disavow traditional fundamentals of the Christian faith," but because of "its inadequate scriptural content and its current earned and unearned disrepute."[6] Advancing a platform of "cooperation without compromise," neo-evangelicalism offered a less dogmatic approach in contrast to the vilification of liberalism in the fundamentalist camp.[7]

At the same time, Henry and his wayfarers denounced liberal theology while embracing its ecumenical impulses: "Even at best liberalism reflected the invasion of a secular spirit," the theologian declared.[8] Its relativistic foundations and "anthropocentric optimism" had falsely posited the natural goodness of man and the notion of automatic progress. Painting a vivid image of the desolation, spiritual emptiness, and cataclysmic doom of the period from 1914 to 1945, Henry concluded that "the controlling ideas of modern philosophy, supposedly gleaned from the touchstone of a sound rationalism or empiricism, are not nearly as relevant to the judgment hour of western civilization as were the revelational views of man."[9] Moreover, many evangelicals were dismayed at both the growing liberal influence within the mainline denominations and a wartime government elevating the more organized mainline Protestant bodies to the status of official representatives of American Protestantism.[10]

By the end of the 1950s the neo-evangelical insurgents had made great strides in their quest. Institutionally, their efforts to establish a broad interdenominational basis, reassert the spirit of revivalism, and create new national evangelical networks had resulted in the creation of the three main pillars of neo-evangelicalism: the NAE in 1942, Fuller Theological Seminary in 1947, and the magazine *Christianity Today* in 1956. A decade after the war, evangelicals had "shed the stigma of being a religious sect and had come to enjoy a central place within the mainstream of American culture." At the same time, they had demarcated the "lines of cognitive defense" that proved crucial in establishing firm subcultural foundations.[11]

The new engagement with church-state issues was part and parcel of this dual agenda. As Leonard Sweet put it, "The liberal accommodation to culture in matters of doctrine and ethics was replicated among many evangelicals in matters of politics and economics."[12] Though indebted to pietism, premillennialism, and church-state separation, evangelicals in the postwar period felt a

growing desire to "christianize the social order" and to make their faith politically relevant. Declaring the "age of anxiety" a wake-up call for political
involvement, W. Stanford Reid, professor of history at McGill University and
editor-at-large of *Christianity Today*, urged evangelicals in 1958 to develop a
Christian position on a wide range of government issues. In his view, this included the welfare state, international relations—especially with Russia, China,
and the UN—unemployment, capital accumulation, and racial segregation.[13]
In a 1954 radio speech, the NAE's Taylor pointed out that while evangelism
should be the priority, conservative Protestants also needed to exercise their
citizenship responsibilities. Urging political involvement, he noted that the
twentieth-century Christian "has two ways open to serve His Lord and nation"
in the United States. "As a Christian citizen we can be, as was the Apostle Paul,
a TRANSFORMER by spiritual processes but we can be REFORMERS through
active Christian citizenship," he declared. "What we need across our nation is
organized Christian lay leadership to promote Evangelical action. This would
encourage evangelicals to take part in our political life and run for office." Moreover, he added, it would "supply evangelicals with information about every candidate for office in ample time before city, county, state and national elections."[14]

In Taylor's view, evangelicals not only had a duty to elect godly men; they
also had the opportunity to act upon a "dynamic conviction that will take evangelical laymen into political control of local governments." Throughout his long
career Taylor pursued this agenda in meetings with government officials and in
articles, speeches, and radio addresses. "Leaders across our land are crying for
spiritual leadership, for spiritual power and convictions. Why shouldn't we who
call ourselves by the name of Jesus Christ start now to witness everywhere, take
Christ with us everywhere and apply the power and life of Christ to every problem," he exclaimed, concluding that "if we have failed as citizens, our failure as
witnesses has been worse."[15] In the same vein, *Christianity Today* editorialized
in 1960 that "a good beginning is for each and every Protestant churchgoer to
get active in one of the 150,000 precincts and learn how politics operates so he
or she can become a factor in good government."[16]

The NAE—the main organization of the evangelical establishment between the 1940s and the 1980s—showcases the centrality of church-state
issues in the movement's postwar political awakening. Sociopolitical engagement, after all, formed one of its core concerns. Although the NAE tended to
speak for northern evangelicals and was politically conservative, it was also
representative of the broader postwar movement. By including Pentecostals
and members of the Holiness and Anabaptist traditions, it succeeded in em-

bracing a broader denominational and geographical sweep than the fundamentalist American Council of Christian Churches (ACCC). Although the Southern Baptist Convention and the Lutheran Church-Missouri Synod kept eluding the NAE, it encompassed a wide variety of backgrounds in its constituency, which consisted of entire denominations, independent congregations, and conservative factions within mainline denominations.[17]

The NAE's main organizational and ideological resources came from the Puritan-Reformed component of fundamentalism, which emphasized cultural responsibility and a desire for "Christian America." Moreover, the increasing power of the federal government had been an important impetus behind its foundation.[18] "Relations with Government" headed the list of "fields of cooperative endeavor" in a circular issued by the Temporary Committee for United Action Among Evangelicals in the early 1940s, which urged evangelical groups in the United States to develop the "corporate means of making their wishes known" via a loose association. This was followed by radio broadcasting, public relations, evangelism, preservation of the principles of separation of church and state, freedom for home and foreign missions, local cooperation, and Christian education.[19]

In the course of the next few years, the NAE set up a wide range of task-specific commissions as permanent working groups for planning, research, and policy recommendations. They indicated the main areas of neo-evangelical interest and organizational activism. The Industrial Chaplaincy Commission sought to place evangelical clerics in plants and factories. The Commission on Chaplaincy and Service to Military Personnel assisted chaplains in the military. The Commission on Evangelism organized conferences and city-wide campaigns, and sponsored the World Day of Prayer and other cooperative efforts by churches. And the Evangelical Home Missions Association focused attention on urban problems, inner city needs, hospitals, and prisons. Various other commissions, some quite short-lived, were concerned with higher education, social witness, theology, and women's fellowship.[20] Moreover, the NAE established the Evangelical Action Commission (EAC), whose role as a "policy defining body in the field of social matters" covered not only religious education, welfare, and family relations, but also "care for all matters in connection with church-State separation." It also included the implementation of NAE resolutions relating to government and outside agencies, as well as testimony before congressional committees. However, the impact of the EAC remained limited throughout its existence, in part because many of its functions were devolved to other committees.[21]

The most prominent of the NAE's task-specific commissions was the War Relief Commission (WRC), created in 1944. As the NAE's international aid agency, it was initially concerned mainly with sending clothing and medicine to refugee camps in Germany, Italy, and other European countries. Renamed World Relief Commission after the war, it was incorporated as a nonprofit subsidiary corporation of the NAE in the 1960s and gradually expanded its field of action, especially in emergency relief (Biafra, Bangladesh), long-term self-help programs (Korea), and refugee programs (Vietnam). Its tasks also included agricultural rehabilitation and development, the creation of farming cooperatives, refugee settlement and rehabilitation, reclamation, literacy programs, and children's clinics. "The commission is rather unique in its policy of always endeavoring to present the Gospel in every relief program it establishes," Clyde Taylor declared. Later renamed World Relief, it became one of the most successful foreign aid organizations.[22]

The organizational hub for most of the NAE's political activities, however, was the OPA, set up in 1943. Led by Taylor, its main function in the 1950s and 1960s was to provide services for mission agencies and chaplaincy commissions, facilitate contacts between the Pentagon and the clergy, liaise between evangelicals and the government, and serve as "watchman" on church-state issues.[23] Taylor, whose role in the political awakening was pivotal, set up the Washington office in response to the perceived need for "a service agency before government." His main objectives included working with the Federal Communications Commission (FCC) to retain equal access to airwaves, keeping "the doors open for evangelical missions through relations with both the U.S. and foreign governments," and a biblical thrust in Christian education. [24]

As a clearinghouse for all beltway-related matters, the OPA engaged in activities ranging from securing visas for missionaries to participating in congressional hearings. By organizing training seminars, facilitating political contacts, and promoting specific appointees, it became the main coordinating body for the NAE's efforts to place evangelicals in government and pushing for specific legislation. Taylor used the office, for example, to campaign against President Truman's appointment of a personal representative to the Vatican, and against the ratification of the United Nations Declaration of Human Rights by the United States. He also helped the NAE establish a representation at a variety of White House conferences. Already by 1952, Clyde Taylor saw a "steady growth of this office in general prestige and influence" and an "almost unlimited field of opportunity" in the political aspect of the NAE's activities. "We were granted an interview with the Secretary of State on less than twenty-four hours notice," he proudly declared in his mid-year report that year: "The heads of all departments are always willing to see us."[25] He confidently noted nearing retirement in 1972 that "government officials have an appreciation of agencies that esteem the government worthy of easy contact through a Washington representative."[26]

The OPA had by the early 1960s become the main center for the NAE's political work.[27] Though it rarely had more than a handful of staff members, its role in a diverse and volatile organization makes it a perfect case study of processes of intellectual transformation and political repositioning. The OPA's main foreign policy-related functions were to establish contacts with government agencies in support of foreign missions, organize campaigns against alleged abuses of Protestants by the Catholic church abroad, battle the UN and its secular agenda, and coordinate the displaced persons and international aid efforts. In addition, it monitored religious liberty issues, helped place conservative Christians in government, and kept "a close watch on legislation and the enemies of the gospel operating in government circles."[28] Its main social policy-related functions included ensuring evangelical representation at legislative hearings, aiding NAE members in protecting tax exemptions, and monitoring legislation that pushed for federal aid to church-related agencies. In particular, the OPA organized campaigns against "parochiaid," targeting Catholic attempts to obtain public support for the faith's schools. It did this in cooperation with POAU, founded in 1948 in response to the *Everson* decision upholding public financing of bus transportation to parochial schools and Truman's proposal to exchange ambassadors with the Vatican.[29]

A typical list of what "formed the grist that has kept the staff on their toes" in these years included dealing with "religious persecutions, congressional legislation, Capitol hearings, immigration problems, Social Security entanglements, and Selective Service cases."[30] The NAE's initial strategy was deceptively simple: get Christians into government and the rest will take care of itself. Indeed, theologian Carl Henry located the church's problem less in political involvement as such than in the "liberal" danger of relying on a specific legislative program. Eager to promote evangelical participation in the political process, he advocated a "transition from private to social action" and emphasized extending "God's purpose of justice and order through civil government." Linking the saving of souls in an unredeemed world to proclaiming the "moral presuppositions of a virile society," he stressed that the evangelical should be represented "in his personal convictions on the frontiers of government and in the corporate processes of society."[31]

One of the key initiatives that facilitated the closer personal and institutional contacts between evangelicals and state officials envisaged by Henry and Taylor was the OPA's "Seminar on Federal Service." Designed to prepare a fledgling evangelical political elite from Christian colleges for federal employment "where they will have an opportunity to witness for Christ and to serve their nation," the seminar series, which began in 1957, grew in popularity over the years. Its programs typically included training on government organization as well as visits to specific departments, the White House, and Capitol Hill.[32] In effect, evangelicals defined government service as a mission field. The seminars, historian Earle Cairns declared at the NAE's 1961 Conference on Church-State Issues, were part of a larger "strategy of infiltration of well-trained, devout Evangelicals into all branches of government." Cairns even compared them to the antislavery campaign in the nineteenth century.[33]

Leading figures in the NAE agreed: "We must face the fact that we must get Christians into government."[34] For Clyde Taylor this meant that evangelicals should focus their attention on the State Department, "with its great diplomatic service and its control over the movement of U.S. citizens."[35] Reporting on the 1961 seminar, which had ninety participants, he saw proof of success "in the increasing number of men and women who caught the vision through this Seminar and are now serving their country and their Lord in government work." Many of them, he added, were "overseas in Foreign Service and other government branches."[36] In fact, one of the success stories of this strategy was Taylor's own son, Clyde Donald Taylor. From working for POAU he went into the Foreign Service in the 1960s, after having been employed by the OPA in between.[37]

As these successes gradually entered the evangelical consciousness, the OPA pursued an ever more ambitious program focused on foreign policy. In his 1962 proposal of seminars for laymen and clergymen, for example, Clyde Taylor suggested including an address by a senator or congressman on "'The Strength of Our Nation' in the military, political, economic and spiritual sense," a USIA presentation, and a tour of the FBI including "something on communism, subversion and resisting the communist threat." The proposal also featured Gene Olson of the Agriculture Department on "the role of a Christian in policy formation" and the NAE's man in the Pentagon, John Broger, on "Positive Christian Action in Promoting Freedom."[38]

Similar to the foreign policy arena, training evangelicals for federal office in the educational and social policy fields was one of the central aspirations of the OPA and a core part of its strategy of infiltration. Keen to keep pace with developments in the social welfare field, Taylor hoped in 1959 to use the planned Youth for Christ Teen Convention in Washington "to widen the vision of young people in possible participation in our government."[39] Two years earlier, the NAE commissions on social action, higher education, and evangelical action had held the first seminar on federal service for educators. Its aim was "to offset the sinister forces working within our government as well as the pagans coming in from our great universities and colleges."[40] Reporting on the seminar, Taylor maintained that it had alerted evangelical educators "to the immense possibilities in government service for the graduates of our Christian colleges. In that way our young men and women can serve God and their country at the same time. Without taking their church into government they can, by their personal witness in life, take Christ into government." The seminar was "a result of an appeal by one of our government leaders to the N.A.E. to do something about the situation that government faces." Taylor complained that while the big state universities churned out highly qualified people to go into government service, they had failed to provide them with any absolutes in moral and ethical standards. The qualifier he added, however, was indicative of the larger issue at stake for evangelicals: "What is the use of fighting communism without, and totalitarianism within, when even our state universities send us men whose whole life is built on expediency and compromise."[41]

Throughout the 1960s and 1970s, the seminars continued to grow in importance and included many high-caliber speakers. The 1977 OPA report noted that the popular federal seminar for college students featured "top executives from the administration . . . and a Supreme Court Justice" and that the following year's event would be held in connection with the Washington Leadership Briefing.[42] Reports from field directors across the country were unambiguous: "This type of contact for evangelicals is most significant."[43] What is more, as these evangelical efforts to get Christians into government found fertile ground in the context of the Cold War–related transformation of church-state relations, traditional pietistic and separationist tendencies gradually fell by the wayside. While leading figures in the NAE reiterated at the church-state conference in 1961 that "benevolent separation is a necessary concept," two years later the language was much less circumspect.[44] A 1963 NAE resolution declared that, although church and state did not coincide, "neither are they properly to be considered in conflict."[45] As an evangelical career foreign officer pointed out, "All of us are constantly involved in government: student loans in college, service in the armed forces, government employment agencies, FHA mortgages, Social Security. It is no longer . . . appropriate for any American to declare that he is not interested in government."[46]

As evangelicals learned the ropes, whether in the foreign service, the social welfare bureaucracy, or on community planning boards, their desire to take Christ into government merged subtly with the urge to take the church into state affairs. Caught between the wish to preserve church-state separation and the desire to overcome their cultural marginalization, they faced a classic dilemma: "To be free from the state is to be weakened in political influence; to be institutionally united with the state is to be a mere political functionary."[47] While Bernard Coughlin thus succinctly summarized the problem, others were even more blunt. Under the circumstances of extensive government funding of services, POAU's C. Stanley Lowell noted in the early 1970s, "the church's only alternative to being controlled by government is for itself to control government."[48]

Between the mid-1940s and the early 1970s, long before the appearance of the New Christian Right on the political scene, Clyde Taylor and the OPA had thus defined the areas of evangelical public policy activism that ultimately shaped the movement's political resurgence. As evangelicals became increasingly embroiled in politics, the role of the office grew. By the mid-1970s the NAE, desiring a more visible evangelical presence in the nation's capital and a more active part in the political process, expanded both staff and functions of the OPA. Under the leadership of Robert P. Dugan, Jr., whose role is discussed in Chapter 5, the OPA became a key facilitator of closer ties to both the Republican establishment and the resurgent neofundamentalist Christian Right. Dugan expanded the political role and range of the OPA by hiring a constitutional lawyer and a legislative researcher "to provide the legal analysis and political research necessary to maintain credibility." He also began publishing political newsletters such as *NAE Washington Insight* (1979). Dugan defined the public concerns of the NAE more broadly as encompassing "religious freedom, the sanctity of human life, justice for the poor and oppressed, peacemaking, stewardship of natural resources, and the proper role of church, family, and government," noting that "biblical principles are translated into political action consistent with NAE resolutions, such as one condemning abortion on demand."[49]

In the same vein, the church-state issues first put on the agenda by post-World War II neo-evangelicals re-emerged as key themes in the post-1960s political mobilization of evangelicals. The separation of church and state "had been distorted to allow ACLU lawyers to undermine our Judeo-Christian heritage," Carl Horn of "Americans for Robertson" raged in a "confidential memorandum" to Christian leaders in 1987.[50] And Robert Dugan insisted in a letter to John R. Dellenback, president of the Christian College Coalition, that America's search for religious leadership was nowhere "more apparent than in the arena of church-state relations." Citing theologian Richard John Neuhaus, he declared "the old actors," such as the National Council of Churches "exhausted" and the new ones, including the New Christian Right, "impossible." Concluding that "mainstream evangelicals stand in an excellent position to provide America with biblical leadership," he asked Dellenback to explore "whether a coalition of evangelicals might align on certain political objectives to help shape national public policy."[51]

In essence, revisiting the church-state discussions within evangelicalism in the postwar decades counters the conventional view that social and political issues did not engage evangelicals until the 1970s and that morality regulation was the only policy issue in which they had an interest. Although morality always featured prominently, evangelicals paid much more attention to broader economic and welfare issues than just to the moral concerns that came to characterize the rise of the New Christian Right.[52] In fact, evangelicals in the 1960s still lambasted the Catholic church for being "the chief factor in opposing permissive birth-control legislation, clinics, hospital policies and medical advice," while "Protestant churches and councils have been . . . opposing the Catholic view."[53]

The Cold War State and Evangelicals

In recent years a wide range of studies have probed the significance of the decades preceding the "culture war" for evangelical politics. This research has highlighted a range of previously ignored factors in the political mobilization of conservative Protestants, including the buildup of a conservative infrastructure on the basis of think tanks and big-business funding; evangelical grassroots campaigning, church organizing, and coalition building; and the political and economic transformation of the South and the West after World War II.[54] Many of these findings point to an argument that has so far received remarkably little scholarly attention, namely, that the political resurgence of evangelicalism was less the result of a spontaneous moral outburst against the political and cultural upheaval of the 1960s than of the movement's engagement with the liberal state. Indeed, they suggest that Cold War state building, rather than its later unraveling, created the social conditions that provided new opportunities for evangelicals to assert themselves.

In his seminal book on the evangelical resurgence, economic historian Robert Fogel, for example, argued that the resurgence of moral issues in the welfare debate, which opened up opportunities for conservatives to make electoral inroads into a previously solidly Democratic constituency, should be understood as the result of postwar social policy successes, rather than their failure. In his view, evangelicals benefited from the welfare state's re-distributionist income transfer programs, expansion of educational opportunities, and reduction in health care inequality. At the same time, however, evangelicals decried the "moral failure" of the welfare state to nurture a sense of purpose, social inclusion, and a deeper meaning in life.[55]

Fogel's conclusions turn the spotlight onto two dimensions of state building that were crucial in shaping the evangelical re-engagement with church-state issues: the politics of growth and the moral construction of poverty. Understanding the way in which they framed evangelicalism's emerging church-state ideology and its participation in the subsidiarist state requires a more detailed foray into these economic and normative dimensions of public policy—since at the core of the movement's new relationship with government was not only the metamorphosis of prewar fundamentalism into postwar neo-evangelicalism, but also the simultaneous transition from the New Deal state to the Cold War state.

The Politics of Growth

In the postwar period, policy makers made economic expansion in a high-consumption capitalist economy the primary objective of government intervention. Indeed, if the experience of the Great Depression and the wartime economic boom had a legacy in common, it was the growing conviction among a broad cross-section of Americans that the self-regulating market had failed and that some measure of economic planning, government intervention, and deficit spending would be necessary to prevent economic disaster in the postwar era. Wartime prosperity, in combination with fears of a postwar economic downturn due to the collapse of war-related government contracting, turned military spending into a major economic proposition and laid the groundwork for the "military Keynesianism" of the Cold War. Postwar planners, who deemed both the maintenance of a costly international military presence and a stable domestic economy crucial for maintaining America's new role as "defender of the Free World" and "Arsenal of

Democracy," increasingly saw the Cold War military buildup in terms of both its social and economic benefits.[56] Arguing that "one of the most significant lessons of our World War II experience was that the American economy, when it operates at a level approaching full efficiency, can provide enormous resources for purposes other than civilian consumption while simultaneously providing a high standard of living," the drafters of NSC-68 maintained that massive rises in military spending would "increase the gross national product by more than the amount being absorbed for additional military and foreign assistance purposes."[57]

As postwar guns-and-butter thinking turned the expansion of the "garrison state" into a function of the "social security state," federal fiscal practices changed from an emphasis on balancing the budget to ensuring that expenditures fulfilled strategic and policy objectives.[58] Military spending, which had hovered around 15 percent of total federal outlays in 1939, frequently exceeded 40 percent in the postwar period, reaching a staggering 62 percent between 1946 and 1965. Defense spending on this scale provided employment for large numbers of soldiers and civilian personnel, and pumped billions of dollars into private businesses.[59]

This was particularly apparent in the South and the West, where evangelicalism maintained an institutional and cultural stronghold and federal investment was particularly lavish. Transformed in the 1930s by New Deal spending on social welfare and large public building projects, such as the Tennessee Valley Authority, the Bonneville Power Administration, and rural electrification, wartime and postwar defense spending ensured that the region would become a magnet for defense contractors. Infrastructure modernization and renewed investment in southern and western military capacities via subsidies and tax cuts for corporations provided employment for large numbers of soldiers and civilian personnel.[60] They turned the Sunbelt into a gunbelt. In places such as Seattle or San Diego at least 20 percent of manufacturing employment came from the military, which provided one of the main sources of income. As federal funds turned agricultural areas into sprawling metropolises, both economic activity and population grew at a breathtaking speed and created a modern-day Gold Rush. "Until the 1940s, Huntsville was an agrarian backwater with two main products: cotton and watercress," a recent report on the Alabama city recalled, "sixty years later, it has more PhDs per capita than anywhere else in the US." Chosen during World War II as the site for a large munitions factory, it evolved into a missile research center and home of the early space program.[61]

In addition, the South and West also constituted the two regions where either direct government support for or reliance on nonprofits to deliver publicly funded services was disproportionally high.[62] Postwar middle-class social benefits and generous aid programs for returning soldiers, such as housing subsidies, loans, tax breaks, and full employment policies, helped develop the region. The Federal Housing Administration and the Veterans Administration, for example, provided mortgage insurance for suburban tract developments, which "made possible the easy transfer of savings funds out of the cities of the Northeast and the Middle West and toward the new developments of the South and West."[63] Evangelicals thus benefited from the socioeconomic and sociodemographic developments spawned by the largesse of the Cold War state. As government subsidies helped shift economic power to the booming South and West, they also engineered the upward mobility, suburbanization, and numerical increase of conservative Protestants. By the 1960s, evangelicals were no longer significantly more rural, older, poorer, or less educated than the average American.[64]

The coalescence of growth-oriented policies and the military-industrial complex with southern and western revivalism formed the background for the new evangelical engagement with church-state issues in general, and the subsidiarist state in particular. Indeed, government spending translated into support for the postwar evangelical missionary surge. G.I. benefits and surplus war goods became key resources for the war-inspired efforts at world evangelization. William K. Harrison, a highly decorated evangelical World War II veteran, naval officer, and senior negotiator in the Korean War ceasefire, knew this only too well. Listing the blessings of American life for Christians he called for more social involvement and renewed missionary activism from increasing wealth.[65] Likewise, the Cold War-induced development of the South and West nurtured the growth of evangelical and fundamentalist charitable organizations. Evangelical social services grew in conjunction with both federally funded educational expansion after World War II and the membership gains of the conservative churches. Indeed, the significant increase in charitable giving in the region can largely be attributed to the rise of fundamentalist Protestantism, since evangelicals generally tended to give a larger proportion of their gifts to religious charities than members of other religious groups.[66]

This renewed social and charitable activism received a further boost from war-generated interest in the evangelical message itself. As religion emerged untainted from the war years, evangelicals used their old-time revivalism to appeal to a broad audience concerned about the spiritual and sociocultural effects of war. Widespread worries about teenage delinquency, for example—frequently attributed to the absence of father figures during the war—translated into popular support for the Youth for Christ campaigns.[67] Meanwhile, the spatial dislocation and suburbanization in the region posed a challenge that evangelicals were better able to respond to than mainline churches. Evangelicals not only relocated with their flock more easily, their forms of religious community also developed greater appeal in the mobile and fluid setting of the postwar South and West. Evangelicals had a head start in a region that had provided the setting for powerful awakenings, such as the Azuza Street revival, and was the stomping ground of evangelical icons such as Aimee Sample McPherson, Charles Fuller, and Billy Graham.[68] In a sense, postwar evangelical institution building replicated nineteenth-century patterns. As Michael O'Neill explains, "throughout the century of immigration and westward expansion, Protestantism multiplied, grew, and made its influence felt in nearly every area of American organizational life, founding colleges, social welfare agencies, and hospitals."[69]

While generating the large-scale expansion of government and transforming the economic fortunes of evangelicalism, however, the growth-oriented and subsidiarist matrix of Cold War public policy did not constitute the triumph of the progressive liberal state. Instead, the bureaucratic practices, ideological premises, and political constellations that underlay the process of mobilizing and managing the war economy left a contradictory imprint on the postwar period. While legitimating government intervention, the war at the same time undermined the prospects for the continuation of New Deal-style policies. Wartime reliance on the expertise of large corporations and the close ties between government and business in mobilizing and managing the war economy strengthened opponents of the New Deal. Military contracting had resulted in 70 percent of war contracts going to large corporations, and government profit guarantees, cost-and-fixed-fee policies, expansion financing, and the suspension of antitrust suits cemented government-business links.[70] This not only meant large profits for big military corporations, such as General Motors, Boeing, and Lockheed Martin. It also facilitated the corporate takeover of the war effort via a plethora of mobilization boards, advisory committees, and regulatory agencies staffed with personnel recruited from big business.[71]

The more the war effort relied on the administrative and organizational capacities of corporate America and was associated with the effectiveness of businessmen and state-private networks, the more New Dealers were relegated to the role of onlookers. By 1942, an anti-New Deal coalition of Republicans and southern Democrats in Congress portended the postwar rejection of New Deal interventionism by dismantling the Works Progress Administration, the Civilian Conservation Corps, the National Youth Administration, the National Resources Planning Board, and other flagship government agencies involved in long-term social planning.[72] Similarly, the failure of the Wagner-Murray-Dingell bill, which sought to place the federal government in charge of unemployment programs, workmen's compensation, and a comprehensive federal health insurance program, indicated the wartime strength of the forces of conservatism that regarded the New Deal as short-term pump priming at best and creeping socialism at worst. "The war marked a retreat from designs for government coercion of economic enterprise in favor of federal fiscal policy," Michael Sherry has noted, "the spigot of government rather than the hammer of the state's regulation would guide economic energies."[73]

Growth-oriented policies thus implicitly gave free rein to business and confined the interventionist role of government to the indirect management of the economy. By locating the key to solving social problems in economic growth and labor force participation in a high-consumption economy they sanctified market solutions and limited government, and depicted private action as inherently better than public intervention. Rather than relying on redistributive policies and direct public control, the politics of growth employed deficit spending and subsidies to private businesses and nonprofit organizations as the main instruments for achieving social and economic stability. As Sherry put it, "The common ground of fiscal policy defined the means by which government could stimulate the economy without coercing its private institutions."[74]

The policies of the Truman and Eisenhower administrations exemplified the view that the country could solve socioeconomic problems by virtue of growth, without structural changes or government control. The 1946 Employment Act, for example, a watered-down version of Truman's proposals for a full employment bill, created the Council of Economic Advisers and specified that the government should pursue employment policies that fostered and promoted the system of free enterprise. Large-scale infrastructure projects, such as river dredging, electrification, land reclamation, and dam and harbor building provided contracts for private construction companies via the Bureau of Reclamation, the Army Corps of Engineers, and a range of other agencies. Urban redevelopment underwritten by the 1949 and 1954 Housing Acts, the postwar extension of the federal highway system and, after 1956, the creation of the interstate highway system meant millions of private construction industry jobs and economic stimulation via federal subsidies and public works projects. Likewise, in the foreign policy arena, economic aid programs, such as the Marshall Plan, were in part designed to secure overseas investment climates and market access for big corporations, and to provide money to purchase American products. These policies showcased the close link between an international U.S. presence and American economic well-being, and helped ensure the global reach of American multinational firms in the aftermath of the collapse of European competitors and colonial empires.[75] As Eisenhower's secretary of defense, Charles E. Wilson, famously put it, "what's good for the country is good for General Motors, and vice versa."[76]

Similarly, the politics of growth, seen as a welfare policy instrument, privileged market solutions over public control and established the primacy of economic expansion over social solidarity. Postwar planners understood poverty and social deprivation largely as a result of insufficient economic growth and the lack of employment opportunities, rather than of the failings of market mechanisms. They designed social policies as instruments of boosting consumer spending through subsidies, tax breaks, full employment policies, and deficit spending without engaging in economic restructuring. As James Patterson has noted, "the key to progress was not welfare—that was relatively insignificant—but economic growth."[77] The various federal loan programs, for example, benefited the middle classes in their quest for suburban homes and college education. Likewise, although the federally administered Social Security system was expanded to include previously excluded groups to become America's largest generalized social welfare program in the 1950, its expansion was the exception in a climate that allowed states to control and cheapen unemployment insurance, encouraged the development of private social insurance plans, and relied upon company-based pensions negotiated by labor unions. "A feature of the years immediately following World War II was a remarkable attack on the notion of expanding and improving public services," John Kenneth Galbraith criticized in his 1958 book *The Affluent Society*: "a certain mystique was attributed to the satisfaction of privately supplied wants," which regarded all public services as a desolating burden on private production.[78]

In turn, the political climate growth-oriented and subsidiarist policies generated in the South and West in particular was at best marked by a profound ambivalence toward "big government." On the one hand, the dominance of government-subsidized extractive, military, and high-tech industry meant that economic fortunes in the South and West, including those of many evangelicals, were closely linked to Cold War spending in ways that

supplanted fears of the growing state. On the other hand, upward social mobility generated a political culture of entrepreneurialism that reinforced notions of private property, individualism, and antistatism.[79] Though affluent
due to government spending and growth-stimulating policies, many people
in the region expressed a visceral hatred of the federal government. As Lisa
McGirr has noted, government-subsidized prosperity in the "military-related
suburbs" ironically reaffirmed the faith in the entrepreneurial and antistatist
dimension of the American dream. "Notwithstanding that economic growth
took place as a result of the largesse of Uncle Sam, for many the link was indirect, since they made their fortunes in private businesses, in construction,
and as professionals serving the new communities."[80]

Of course this "antistatist statism" had been, in a sense, characteristic of
the American West all along. Throughout the nineteenth century, massive
federal investment in road building, railroad subsidies, military protection,
mail services, and the like created an economic dependency on federal investment while at the same time perpetuating an antigovernment ideology of
proprietarian individualism. Faith in free-wheeling capitalism, an entrepreneurial ethic, the cult of the autonomous individual, and the moral superior-
ity of market forces in combination with the reliance upon federal investment
thus constituted a "western model" of state building.[81]

The Moral Construction of Poverty

Postwar state building, in addition to being underpinned by growth-oriented
and subsidiarist policy instruments, also reflected an ideological construction
of poverty that both served to uphold social norms and to perpetuate race,
gender, and class divisions. In welfare policy both liberals and conservatives
mainly adhered to a "poverty knowledge" (Alice O'Connor) that located the
origins of deprivation in behavioral deviance, rather than in socioeconomic
inequality; privileged therapeutic or punitive interventionism over less deni-
grating bureaucratic entitlements; and defined welfare as a gratuity, rather
than as a social right.[82] Constructing social policies on the basis of moral categorizing and different levels of "deservingness" resulted in a segmented and
hierarchical system of social provision, which rigidly distinguished between
"assistance" and "social insurance." While the more centrally administered
and inclusive insurance programs served a largely male working- and middle-
class clientele, the administration of welfare programs was devolved to state
and local levels, and subjected a largely female and minority population to
arbitrary coverage, stigmatizing requirements, and moralistic intrusion.[83]

Morality talk, therefore, is not just part of the rhetorical arsenal of resurgent conservatism but was hard-wired into the system of social provision. Although many conservative critics of the welfare state insist on a stark contrast between their agenda of personal responsibility, voluntarism, and retrenchment on the one hand, and the "permissiveness," welfare dependency, and bureaucratism allegedly nurtured by liberal social policies on the other, both approaches are often strikingly similar. Indeed, the terminology of welfare dependency, dysfunctional families, culture of poverty, and the deficiencies of poor communities had gained scientific legitimacy within the liberal research tradition beginning with the transformation of American social theory in the late nineteenth century. These concepts became fundamental to progressive social thinking and diverted attention from economic interpretations of poverty.[84] In the words of Michael Katz, "the capture of the social science agenda by government combined with the capture of poverty research by economists to confine the scope of debate within market models of human obligation and interaction. . . . In the process, they either ignored or belittled the few alternative frames proposed."[85]

In an incisive analysis of the foundations of progressive social thought, historian Jeffrey Sklansky provides further evidence for the coalescence of progressive and conservative welfare thought. He points out that the Progressive-era focus on social interaction as the basis for value formation entailed discarding the overarching concern with the redistribution of wealth and the ownership of the means of production. Social thinkers ranging from John Dewey and Charles Horton Cooley to Simon Patten, he maintains, saw individual liberty no longer rooted in economic independence and the social contract, but in economic interdependence and social self-actualization. By the same token, however, the "social self" of progressive theory, by tying value formation to social interaction and declaring the poor deficient in the development of their social norms, defined poverty as a problem of insufficient socialization, rather than as a problem of the maldistribution of income.[86] This analysis helped channel reformist energies either into addressing the deficiencies of the poor through social work intervention and workfare policies, or in the direction of macroeconomic planning to remove barriers to employment and stimulate economic growth. In effect, linking poverty to behavioral patterns couched the traditional "moral tales" (Robert Reich) about deservingness, which had historically framed the welfare debate, in the authoritative language of the social science professional.[87] In American social work, for example, the emphasis was on disciplining and rehabilitating clients, rather than on income maintenance. In the words of William Epstein, "the literature of the social services can be read as a denial of greater spending for the basic institutions of a humane civic culture, an attempt through myth to ignore stark cultural failure, supplanting it with the fiction of cure, prevention, and rehabilitation."[88]

No matter how charitable, compassionate, and sophisticated it is, however, rehabilitative social work intervention is inherently more stigmatizing than impersonal systems of social provision based on citizenship rights. Its recourse to moral themes, by definition, denotes certain groups as morally worthy and others as morally suspect, and expands social provision on the basis of arbitrary means-testing, morals-testing, and targeted programs at the expense of generalized entitlements.[89] Rather than drawing a clear line of distinction between "liberal" and "conservative" welfare ideologies, it is therefore more appropriate to talk about different conceptions of the liberal welfare state vacillating between "hard" and "soft" paternalism (Michael Freeden). While hard paternalism indicates recourse to social control and punitive measures, soft paternalism stresses social participation, interdependence, and "social inclusion." Both, however, rely upon a "rhetoric of incapacitation," and both focus on social-relational, rather than on socioeconomic issues, while at the same time ignoring problems of commodification and social injustice.[90] Understanding poverty in these terms, Alice O'Connor has pointed out, created the "knowledge base that, however unintentionally, has opened itself to conservative interpretation" and anticipated the later right-wing critique of "permissiveness."[91] As Michael Katz ruefully noted, "no one noticed that the foundation of liberalism had crumbled, until it was too late."[92]

These normative codes that underlie the moral construction of the welfare state are intimately tied to race and gender conceptions. As Matthew Frye Jacobson reminds us, the language of republican virtues and the producer-class ideology, which propounded that work and economic self-sufficiency created moral self-determination, had historically legitimized citizenship rights for white males while denying them to women and minorities. The racial construction of nineteenth-century republicanism maintained that property in one's own labor was the basis for moral self-development and the ability to participate in political decisions. On this basis it declared excluded groups unfit for self-government owing to their economic dependence and lack of moral agency. The racially coded language of work and property, Jacobson maintains, was not an anomalous departure from the democratic ideal, but constitutive of American liberal democracy. It mediated between the contradictions inherent in a society that was both capitalist and putatively

democratic. It was integral to American political culture, which was characterized by the conflict between the needs of the capitalist economy, namely
the imperative of cheap and abundant labor, and the needs of the republic,
such as the imperative for a committed citizenry.[93]

Twentieth-century "poverty knowledge" to an extent simply mirrored
these linguistic strategies traditionally employed to exclude women and African Americans. This manifested itself institutionally in social policies that
perpetuated gendered and racialized social hierarchies and power relations.
Although women in the United States were more involved in designing the
welfare state than in Europe, they often ended up being treated worse. For
example, the early "maternalist" American welfare state in the late nineteenth
and early twentieth centuries, which included Mothers' Pensions, was designed to enable poor mothers to stay at home and take care of the children,
but was also meant to discourage welfare as an alternative to paid work. This
established a policy tradition in which welfare payments were mostly geared
toward single-parent families headed by mothers. At the same time means
tests, man-in-the-house rules, suitable-home regulations, cuts in benefits for
having illegitimate children, and threats of neglect proceedings for applying
for welfare created a punitive and oppressive climate and upheld the nuclear
family as an idealized counterimage. Although female advocates of mater-
nalism frequently used their ascribed roles as upholders of moral values to
break out of the confines of the household and enter the political arena, the
emancipatory potential of this step was mitigated by the conservative content
of their social ideology, which was often moralistic, strictly middle-class, and
designed to preserve traditional gender relations.[94]

Similarly, the racial divide inscribed into the system of social provision
segregated African Americans disproportionally into the most discretionary,
stingiest, and politically exposed programs. Racial discrimination was the
result not just of the mobilization of racist attitudes but also of the normal
workings of institutional structures, which, as Robert Lieberman maintains,
were equally powerful in defining racial hierarchies and identities. During
the New Deal, for example, agricultural, domestic, and service workers were
excluded from Social Security, leaving a larger number of African Americans
without coverage. Likewise, The G.I. Bill and racially coded housing policies in the postwar period mainly provided subsidies for the development of
homogeneous, white middle-class suburbs at the expense of both African
Americans and inner cities.[95]

The "rhetoric of incapacitation," gender discriminations, and racially

coded provision embedded in the administrative organization and normative content of social policy reinforced a hierarchical welfare system and inhibited the development of universal coverage. Its moralistic, punitive, and
rehabilitative underpinnings resulted in a "segmented welfare state." In this
arrangement, a variety of government, private, and nonprofit agencies use
bureaucratic discretion to administer a wide range of programs to different
social groups on the basis of a cultural construction of poverty that serves
to maintain social norms rather than to address problems of social deprivation. Indeed, welfare policies, as Joel Handler and Yeheskel Hasenfeld insist,
are not rational responses to objective conditions of poverty, but symbolic
answers to ideological conceptualizations of poverty. They amount less to an
attempt to find effective solutions to social problems than to a confirmation
of core social norms, such as the work ethic, established gender roles, and the
social status of donor and recipient.[96] "Poverty knowledge" is thus primarily a
form of cultural affirmation and reassurance "that poverty occurs outside or
in spite of core American values and practices, whether those are defined in
terms of capitalist markets, political democracy, self-reliance, and/or a two-
parent, white, middle-class family ideal."[97] Workfare policies, for example,
serve to perpetuate poverty as a warning to those who might be tempted to
slacken off in their work habits. The "purpose of the work requirement is not
actually to set welfare recipients to work, but to reaffirm the work ethic; to
confirm the importance of work in defining social, gender, and ethnic status;
and to legitimate the morality of low-wage work."[98]

Cold War social policy thus combined two largely contradictory ideological
elements: on the one hand support for consumerist politics of growth, which
valorized wasteful self-indulgence, immediate gratification, and conspicuous
consumption; on the other hand producerist notions of "respectability" and
"deservingness" founded upon an ethic of limits, self-discipline, and moral self-
control. Of course in many ways this tension between the normative parameters
of consumer capitalism and the traditional moral codes of nineteenth-century
producer-class ideology reflected the traditional ambiguities and contradictions of American culture. It constituted another instance of what Daniel Bell
has called the "schizoid character" of the American moralistic temper. From
the start, he argued, America had been "at one and the same time the frontier
community where 'everything goes' and the fair country of the restrictive Blue
Laws." Lawmakers imposed moral restrictions "with vehemence in areas of culture and conduct—in the censorship of books, the attacks on 'immoral art', etc.,

and in the realm of private habits; yet it was heard only sporadically regarding the depredations of business or the corruption of politics."[99]

In embracing both the old-fashioned work ethic and a new-fashioned indulgence in consumer choice, postwar evangelicals embodied a similar type of "disciplined hedonism" (Hugh Heclo).[100] In other words, while the apostles of "traditional values" of thrift, self-discipline, and self-control denounced the moral breakdown of society, the consumer capitalism they embraced could never quite get enough of "permissiveness." This dual emphasis on moralism and capitalism, however, ignored the contradiction between stable community and family life and the imperatives of consumer culture. The rhetorical defense of "family and neighborhood" could not easily be reconciled with support for unregulated business that replaced neighborhoods with shopping malls and superhighways, the corporate search for lower labor costs and higher profits that caused family breakdowns, or a hedonistic ethic that relied upon the constant creation of new demands and discontents.[101] As the socioeconomic and sociocultural forces unleashed by World War II and the postwar period increasingly exposed these tensions, evangelicals, therefore, sought to find ways of reconciling the consumerist norms of postwar capitalism with upholding traditional morality and established hierarchies. It was this effort, rather than the supposed rejection of liberal state building and the welfare state, that was at the center of their re-engagement with the state.

Two changes within the moral matrix of public policy during the Cold War further stimulated the formation of a distinctive evangelical political profile along these lines. First, in the 1950s the spiritualization of the Cold War as not only a military but also a normative and cultural battle against totalitarianism and communism, generated a new interest in moral legislation (see Chapter 3). Images invoked in popular culture suggested that fighting communism involved much more than guarding U.S. material interests and power. It meant protecting Mr. and Mrs. America and the morality of their way of life. Anticommunist propaganda emphasized what Elaine Tyler May has called "domestic containment," which tied the defense of American political, economic, and security interests to the affirmation of traditional gender roles, core social norms, and consumer culture.[102] In the context of the Cold War, evangelicals thus affirmed the moral grounding of American culture in a time of spiritual warfare without challenging consumerism and the "precarious prosperity maintained by cold war spending, highway and automobile building, sprawling suburbias, overeating, overbuying, forced premature obsolescence—always plagued by waste, unemployment, poverty, inequality, misuse of the environment, lack of public services, and the threat of annihilation" that formed the socioeconomic foundation of Cold War success.[103]

Second, efforts in the 1960s to dismantle the race and gender discriminations of the welfare state, and the administrative and legal structures that institutionalized them, catapulted evangelicals back into the public sphere (see Chapter 4). As part of the War on Poverty, a new generation of social activists and policy makers helped remove rules that effectively excluded many African Americans from Social Security, set up Medicare as a largely color-blind program, and engineered civil rights legislation that outlawed the most blatant discriminatory practices.[104] In turn, evangelicals rallied around morality politics and subsidiarity, employing them as policy instruments that would maintain women as an unpaid workforce of providers in the home and an underpaid pool of casual labor outside of it. It is, therefore, misleading to argue that moral issues detracted from economic ones, or that conservative groups were able to mobilize an electorate that objectively did not benefit from deregulation, devolution, and privatization. Instead, the moral-cultural agenda addressed the economic, race, and gender concerns of a white working and lower middle class under siege in a deindustrialized, globalized, post-1960s setting more effectively than Cold War liberalism.[105]

*   *   *

In summation, this chapter hints at a much more complex relationship between resurgent evangelicalism and Cold War state building than the simple stimulus-response scenario of the backlash argument suggests. It argues that both the desire for ideological self-assertion and the interaction with the Cold War context shaped the emerging church-state ideology of postwar evangelicalism. The rise of the welfare and national security state, in conjunction with neo-evangelical theological repositioning, institutional growth, and sociocultural transformation, had brought the NAE into closer contact with the federal government. In turn, long before the rise of the New Christian Right, evangelicals had begun to revisit their relationship with the state and to position themselves within its structures.

In taking a closer look at this process, the following chapters focus on two main dimensions. First, they emphasize the relevance of paying analytical attention to internal movement dynamics and ideology formation. They put the spotlight on the movement's attempts to square the circle between adherence to traditional separationism and the desire for political influence; the tension between limited-government sentiments and being the beneficiaries of government-generated socioeconomic improvement; and the ambivalence between promoting evangelicals in government and christianizing the social order. Despite their traditional aversion to closer ties to the state, postwar evangelicals forged a distinct "third party" identity within Protestantism in part by relocating themselves within the institutional and cognitive frame provided by Cold War foreign and social policy. Although originally designed to assert traditional evangelical attitudes against a coterie of classic enemies, including the Catholic church and the secular state bureaucracies, the various evangelical debates provide a snapshot of conservative Protestantism's growing receptiveness to the advances of the subsidiarist state. They reveal the increasing level of administrative and financial entanglement of evangelical agencies with Cold War government. In turn, the eagerness to participate in the opportunities public policy offered for spreading the gospel, rather than simply denouncing the liberal state, formed the backdrop for the organizational resurgence and political mobilization of evangelicals.

Second, the chapters place the evangelical engagement with the growing administrative state in the context of Cold War state building and its contradictions. They show that the conservative Protestant position was carefully calibrated between an antistatist message and institutional ties to the liberal order. As evangelicals forged a new church-state relationship and ideology via their growing participation in public funding arrangements, they positioned themselves as both agents and adversaries of the Cold War state. They effectively blended the rhetoric of limited government, retrenchment, and entrepreneurial individualism with the active embrace of growth-oriented, devolutionary, and moralistic policies. Seen from this perspective, subsidiarity is not a neutral policy tool that is simply used by conservative religionists in order to deliver social services. Instead, subsidiarist structures are in themselves part and parcel of a normative construction of state authority that transports specific gender, race, and class divides. In the process, evangelicals both delimited the liberal welfare state and carved out a sphere for state intervention. In the end this both stabilized and undermined Cold War state building.

CHAPTER 3

EVANGELICALS, FOREIGN POLICY, AND THE NATIONAL SECURITY STATE

Evangelicals were by no means natural supporters of the large-scale expansion of state defense capacities, despite their frequently unrivaled patriotic fervor. Indeed, the fundamentalist-modernist controversy of the 1920s had turned many conservative Protestants into strict advocates of an uncompromising church-state separationism and foreign policy isolationism.[1] World War II and the Cold War, however, brought about a metamorphosis that nudged religious conservatives into a new engagement with the state. Evangelical identification with Cold War anticommunism, in particular, facilitated the ideological convergence between church and state and provided the resurgent evangelical movement with new opportunities for political involvement. By spiritualizing the anticommunist struggle via scripturally based interpretations of American power, evangelicals called for a new level of identification of Americans with their established social order, political institutions, cultural practices, and moral norms. Moreover, Cold War administrative needs, especially in the military and foreign aid, engineered new personal and institutional ties between evangelicals, government, and political elites. These made evangelicals a constituent part of the public-private networks that underlay Cold War state building. Despite traditional misgivings about church-state ties, a strong pacifist tradition, and suspicions about civil religion, postwar engagement with the national security state eased the transition for evangelicals from their traditional insistence on separationism and limited government toward the embrace of Cold War state building in the name of national defense and global power. This culminated in the development of a distinctive evangelical foreign policy profile that was characterized by efforts to mediate between shoring up American policy and preserving a subcultural image.

From Spiritual Restoration to Civil Religion

The ideological imperatives of World War II and the Cold War both pro-moted moral-spiritual approaches in public policy and condoned closer in-stitutional cooperation between church and state. As explored in Chapter 1, Cold War defense policies and ideological anticommunism encouraged scripture-based interpretations of the American experience and the reaf-firmation of the religious origins of the United States. The depiction of the nation's struggle against the evils of totalitarianism as a spiritual battle—in which the strength of the nation lay in its moral commitment—provided resurgent evangelicalism with opportunities to regain public legitimacy and interpretive power. With the positive image of postwar religion serving as an amplifier, evangelicals reasserted previously marginalized theological con-cepts such as Armageddon, the Antichrist, and the Apocalypse by linking them to America's new global role as "defender of the Free World." Fired up by wartime patriotic fervor, eager to show the relevance of their creed, and desperate to leave behind cultural isolation and political marginality, the rest-less neo-evangelicals were keenly aware of opportunities the foreign policy field offered them. "A remarkable convergence was taking place . . . between the national public mood during World War II and the early postwar years and the aspirations of a new generation of fundamentalist and evangelical leaders," Joel Carpenter concluded.[2]

Evangelicals saw foreign policy issues primarily as conduits for establish-ing religious interpretations as relevant patterns for understanding world af-fairs and for infusing redemptive themes into a broader political and cultural discourse. By reconstructing foreign policies on the basis of biblical narra-tives, evangelical theologian Carl Henry maintained, conservative Protes-tantism could achieve both respectability and relegitimate biblically based viewpoints.[3] For a faith that had great reverence for the power of ideas, this agenda-setting function was more important than the short-term impact on policy decisions. As Henry put it, "the interpretation of the news is of grow-ing importance in the current world situation."[4]

Hence, postwar evangelicals presented their religious reading of world events as a matrix for understanding the new international role of the United States. They interpreted the emergence of America's global power as the re-sult of the nation's recovery of a "sense of destiny and purpose" derived from "the religious symbolisms of the men and women who laid the cultural foun-dations of American society." They juxtaposed this with the abandonment of traditional belief in the wake of the anticlerical Enlightenment, the rise of theism and transcendentalism, and the secular values and pragmatist ethics of liberalism.[5] In the same vein, evangelicals reconceptualized the public dedication to the Christian faith as the key to preparing the nation for the Cold War stand-off. Eliding the differences between religious and national mission, Carl Henry tied the nation's security to a renewed commitment to the Bible. Invoking the "sense of divine providence" that had once shaped an America "strong in spirit, dedicated to fulfillment of God's will," he saw the fight against communism as the basis for "sharing with the world the bold witness of faith in the Redeemer."[6]

Conflating the traditional born-again experience with the renewal of patriotic fervor was the centerpiece of this agenda. Conversion, a staple of evangelical belief, saw public confession and the individual's turn toward God as the first steps toward salvation. In connecting the born-again experience to Cold War patriotism, evangelicals extended the conversion scenario beyond the level of the individual. They not only invested a personal emotional drama with new sociopolitical relevance, but also presented it as a coherent political ideology. By positing the conversion narrative as an interpretive frame for perceiving world events, they linked religious to political liberty. They constructed a relationship between the defense of religious belief and the secular social order, and between religious aspirations and "rational self-interest" in foreign policy. In effect, they made the active embrace of the religious foundations of American society and culture the outward sign of salvation. As Billy Graham exclaimed, "If you would be a true patriot, then become a Christian. If you would be a loyal American, then become a loyal Christian."[7]

Likewise, obscure strands of millennial and prophetic thinking regained authoritative status in the policy discourse when packaged as biblical readings of world affairs. The foreign policy arena was particularly suited for this strategy, since America's postwar role was not yet fully ideologically and culturally legitimized in society, and the transition from isolationist sentiment and the fear of entangling alliances to the new postwar role of global superpower had left an interpretive vacuum. By explaining America's new role in the world in eschatological, millennial, prophetic, and apocalyptic terms, evangelicals helped fill the postwar interpretive void with religious content. While a growing number of prewar Americans had dismissed concepts such as the Antichrist, Armageddon, Judgment Day, and the Second Coming, linking these terms to the threat of totalitarian communism and nuclear warfare made them very real and palpable.[8] As historian Paul Boyer pointed out, "one cannot fully understand the American public's response to a wide range of international and domestic issues without bearing in mind that millions of men and women view world events . . . through the refracting lens of prophetic belief."[9]

While the stated goal of evangelicals had been to relegitimate religious concepts, their flag-waving patriotism in effect located spiritual renewal in the postwar exercise of America's global power. Conservative Protestants thus translated their traditional pietistic patriotism, which associated America with the redeemer nation and compared its mission to ancient Israel, into a civil religious sanctification of American-style democracy, liberal capitalism, the military buildup, and the growth of the national security state. Depicting the Cold War struggle as a "just war" and a spiritual battle between good and evil, evangelicals encouraged a new level of identification with America's socioeconomic order and political institutions. "Instead of obscuring and depreciating the American dream which has built this noble society," NAE cofounder Harold John Ockenga declared, "we ought to exalt the elements of it over against it." Viewing "freedom of ballot, freedom of the press, freedom of economic activity, and freedom of speech" as the key advantages of the West, he demanded that "firmness must be backed up by military strength and force."[10] Likewise, Lieutenant General William K. Harrison, executive director of the Evangelical Welfare Agency, directly connected religious freedom and economic affluence by noting that "no other people have had so much material wealth and strength as have United States citizens, and Christians certainly possess their share."[11]

Under the guise of fighting the totalitarian threat, evangelicals not only embraced liberal capitalism and the expansion of the garrison state, but also the punitive state. Their support for the buildup of the postwar surveillance and security apparatus helped keep public funds flowing to J. Edgar Hoover and others engaged in "flushing out" the alleged "enemy within." Depicting the Cold War as both a military and a spiritual struggle, evangelicals contributed to defining the threat not simply in terms of political treason, but also cultural subversion and moral iniquity. They largely supported Eisenhower's security-loyalty program that discriminated against homosexuals and alcoholics in the name of countering communist infiltration. They cheered when McCarthy derided the State Department, universities, and Hollywood not only as bastions of snobbery and elitism, but also of moral permissiveness. And they applauded Hoover and Strom Thurmond when they merged anti-

communism, homophobia, racism, and anti-Semitic sentiments in their vilification of the Civil Rights movement as a threat to the traditional family and
the moral fiber of the nation.[12]

In the postwar atmosphere of both triumph and anxiety, neo-evangelicals
thus promoted their worldview as America's proper ideological response to
the totalitarian threat and insisted that traditional evangelical Protestantism
was the genuine civil religion of the United States. In synchronizing religious
themes, national strength, and the American way of life, evangelicals shifted
the emphasis in the spiritual struggle from the church standing against the
forces of evil to church and state fighting side by side, with the state needing
the church to get its spiritual priorities straight, and the church needing the
state to secure its field of action. As POAU executive director Glenn Archer
exclaimed, "Protestantism stands for self-government; Protestantism stands
for democracy. Protestantism belongs to America because its principles are
American."[13]

The Dual Positioning of Postwar Evangelical Foreign Policy

In walking the fine line between spiritual restoration and civil religion, the
emergent evangelical foreign policy agenda displayed the same dynamic tension between integration into mainstream culture and preservation of a separatist identity that characterized postwar neo-evangelicalism more generally.
In effect, evangelicals developed a "baptized" foreign policy vision that both
phrased America's postwar role in biblical terms and expressed evangelical
beliefs in the terminology of Cold War liberalism. While they successfully
connected biblical interpretations to the liberal order and thus helped integrate conservative Protestants into the foreign policy consensus, they also retained a deeply apocalyptic, premillennialist, antiliberal view of world events.
In the words of Joel Carpenter, they positioned themselves as both effective
communicators of the myth of American righteousness and die-hard supporters of conservative piety.[14]

Rephrasing the traditional conversion narrative in nationalistic terms, for
example, facilitated the association of redemption with American-style democracy. At the same time, the conversionist policy discourse replaced the
foreign policy emphasis on order and stability with an emphasis on "regime
change," giving it a militant edge. Rejecting the secular order, it attributed
worldly evil to man's sinful nature and saw true world peace as the result of

divine intervention. True peace could not be achieved by accommodation and appeasement, but only by a heart-wrenching spiritual transformation. "National stability and survival depend upon enduring spiritual and moral qualities," Carl Henry declared, noting that "statesmen as well as theologians realize that the basic solution to the world crisis is theological."[15] Or, as the "two-star evangelical" William Harrison put it, "What Marx, Lenin, and Stalin needed was not simply an exposure to the 'Christian ethic' but to be 'born again.'"[16] This tension between "positive revivalism" (George Marsden) and separationism remained at the very core of a distinctive evangelical foreign policy agenda.[17] Combining prophetic internationalism and unilateralist isolationism, evangelicals focused on a limited number of primary themes in their engagement with foreign policy, namely Israel, the UN, anticommunism, and anti-Catholicism. In all four cases, the outspoken evangelical identification with Cold War foreign policy was accompanied by an equally virile adversarial stance.

Israel and the UN

The founding of the Jewish state in 1948 was a crucial catalyst for the reengagement of evangelicals with foreign policy. In parting with their traditional anti-Semitism, evangelicals combined biblical belief with support for U.S. foreign policy. In particular, they viewed the founding of the Jewish state as a sign of the impending return of the Messiah and the fulfillment of scriptural prophesies. The Bible had foretold that a power from the north would attack Israel and that the ensuing war would overshadow all previous wars. Evangelicals thus merged their support for Israel with the expectation of cataclysmic military conflict, and were particularly attuned to attempts by the Soviet Union to gain a foothold in the region. Since conservative Protestants regarded all manifestations of military conflict in the Middle East as signs of attack by the forces of evil, Israel could rely on firm evangelical backing in the 1950s.[18]

Nonetheless, traditional anti-Semitic strains remained present in neoevangelicalism. At the 1961 NAE conference on church-state relations, for example, leading figures in the organization insisted that evangelicals needed to push for a Christian amendment to the constitution and that "care is needed that we do not move into a position of simply tolerating such minority groups as atheists and Jews."[19] Likewise, neo-evangelicals did not relinquish their active pursuit of converting Jews. They also continued entertaining the notion that the Holocaust was God's punishment for the waywardness of the Jews.[20]

While the pro-Israel stance reflected a new engagement with global politics, evangelical attitudes toward the UN were indicative of the strength of unilateralist and isolationist sentiment within a group that consistently thought in a nation-state framework. This stance was theologically informed by biblical readings that ascribed particular eschatological significance to "nations" and viewed "world government" as a sign of the impending advent of the Antichrist. "There are still many who have taken all references to a coming superman, or the Antichrist, as being of spiritual and not actual interpretation," Harrison warned, "but there is developing before our eyes a philosophy that can lay the ground work for just such a development: The one-world concept, the United Nations, the frantic desire for any collective organization or arrangement to prevent war."[21] Not letting the historical specificity of the nation-state stand in the way of a good literal reading of the Bible, evangelicals regarded nations, rather than international bodies, as potential redemptive agents. This not only meant that they defined foreign policy in strictly national terms; it also led to an uncritical identification of America with the "New World Israel."[22]

Along these lines evangelicals fervently attacked the UN as fundamentally anti-Christian. Since the ideological basis of the UN was humanistic and secular, they argued, it lacked the moral foundations of the United States embedded in its "respect for law and for the rights of others . . . established upon a reverence for almighty God."[23] Giving voice to traditional isolationist sentiments, OPA director Clyde Taylor feared a "world federation of states with an international government that would of necessity, in order to procure conformity, limit our freedoms."[24] Likewise, Carl Henry maintained that international alliances needed to be grounded in shared moral and spiritual values. "Evangelicals consider alliances of nations uncommitted to transcendent justice to be as futile a foundation for future mutuality as premarital promiscuity," he declared, concluding that "as evangelical Christians see it, the vision of One World, or of United Nations, that is built on geographical representation rather than on principal agreement is as socially unpromising as is a lawless home that neglects the commandments of God."[25] In the 1950s, the NAE therefore urged evangelicals to contact their congressmen in support of the Bricker Amendment that promised to "keep our Constitution the final law in the U.S.A., not the UN Charter or some other treaty."[26] If the Amendment, sponsored by Senator John W. Bricker, a conservative Ohio Republican, had passed, it would have placed restrictions on the range and ratification of treaties and executive agreements entered into by the U.S. government.

Both the evangelicals' unwavering support for Israel and their contempt for transnational institutions have received significant scholarly attention in the past decade in the context of the George W. Bush administration's Middle Eastern policies and its open disdain for the UN in the run-up to the invasion of Iraq. This indicates that the merger of national-security oriented *Realpolitik* with a prophetic attitude not only characterized the evangelical political awakening under the impact of World War II and the Cold War, it also continues to shape the contemporary conservative foreign policy agenda.[27] Indeed, both are to this day central planks in the foreign policy platform of the New Christian Right. While both the pro-Israel stance and the rejection of the UN have been the focus of much academic debate, however, two other core components of the postwar evangelical reengagement with foreign policy have received less scholarly attention, namely anticommunism and anti-Catholicism. Both, however, were equally crucial in mobilizing evangelicals politically, facilitating new ties to the Cold War state, and in preserving an evangelical ideological and institutional subculture between the early 1940s and the mid-1970s.

Anticommunism

Even before the Bolshevik revolution, evangelicals had frequently identified Russia with the biblical Gog in the Armageddon scenario. The Cold War confrontation added to their sense that the world had entered the period of the final standoff between good and evil that, according to Scripture, preceded the Second Coming of Christ. In the eyes of many evangelicals the Cold War was not simply a conflict between two worldly powers, but a spiritual struggle of biblical proportions that could only be won through a renewed national commitment to the vision of a kingdom of God. As such, evangelicals defined communism biblically as a monolithic threat and politically as the antithesis of America. According to Billy Graham, the Cold War was the third major crisis of the nation after the revolutionary war and the Civil War, and it could only be transcended by turning to God.[28]

Evangelical biblical exegesis based on the Scofield Reference Bible meant that conservative Protestants understood communism as a false religion, rather than as simply an oppressive political system. In their view, it was part of Satan's efforts to mock God by setting up a worldly realm that mimicked divine creation. Seen from this standpoint, communism was not simply a functional, if detestable order, but a system that engendered deep inner attachments by employing similar images of a union with a higher power as those of Christianity.[29] "The false Communist appeal to a better world, to a heaven on earth . . . is an alluring and powerful motive," J. Edgar Hoover declared in *Christianity Today*. "The minds of thousands of men and women, including many in our own country, have succumbed and are today furnishing world communism the incentive, intelligence, and dynamic power to make it a master of millions of human souls." In his view, communism was a counterreligion whose threat came from its ability to "secure the full allegiance of the human heart."[30]

While communism's deceitful nature also meant that it was ultimately doomed to failure, this did not diminish the need for Christian vigilance. As Carl Henry noted, "that communism, with its terrors and suppressions, may have within it the seed of its own destruction does not mean that this much hoped for event is in the immediate offing."[31] By the same token, evangelicals often reverted to medical metaphors in framing the communist challenge. They argued that communism was a spiritual illness "associated with systematized delusions, not susceptible to rational argument."[32] Likewise, J. Edgar Hoover compared it to a malignant tumor.[33] Conversion was thus redefined as a therapeutic intervention and church leaders were cast in the role of doctors who "should appreciate the evil nature of the germ of godlessness" and should be able to "see beneath the superficial symptoms to the underlying spiritual pathology."[34]

This evangelical understanding of communism demarcated the political agenda of postwar conservative Protestantism. It resulted in two dominant attitudes in evangelical political consciousness. First, seeing communism as a perverted or false religion and a spiritual disease meant that it could be counteracted only by a collective commitment to the religious foundations of the nation via a public renewal of the Christian faith.[35] "Oh, that Christians today had the zeal that Communists have in propagating their satanic doctrines," Taylor proclaimed in 1954, "There is no reason why, revived by the Holy Spirit, we shouldn't surpass them in zeal. We have the Truth and the power of God back of us."[36] Noting that the OPA was "increasingly conscious of the race between freedom and communism," he criticized the tendency in Washington "to view this as an economic, political, and technological race, not as a spiritual race." In contrast, he argued that evangelicals had "a responsibility to make the nation aware that the struggle is, in fact, a spiritual one. In this connection our office is participating in a new effort to develop this consciousness."[37]

Second, the "deep threat" of communism engendered fears of subversion and betrayal, which meant that an effective antidote had to match the techniques and methods of the communists and employ them for the cause of Christianity. Americans needed "to fear that the defense forces of the nation will be rendered impotent by decisions of communist sympathizers in places of importance and authority," Harold John Ockenga warned.[38] Unconditional loyalty, idealism, systematic ideological indoctrination, and recourse to fundamental texts were required to counter communism, J. Edgar Hoover asserted in his many tracts for *Christianity Today*. Drawing freely on a wide variety of literary metaphors and racist stereotypes, he described Lenin as "a beady-eyed Russian" and Karl Marx as a mad scientist "busy mixing the ideological acids of this evil philosophy."[39] Likewise, presenting the "Communism Report" at the 1961 NAE staff retreat, Ron Arnold maintained that "the deceptive nature of communism must be exposed as well as the sharp spiritual conflict in this warfare." He reiterated that "NAE encourages study of Communist techniques" and that "NAE purposes to expose Red tactics to the church."[40] Under the conditions of the Cold War the more self-reflective dimension of postwar neo-evangelicalism frequently succumbed to hysteria, especially as Hoover and other conservatives found ways of conflating New Deal liberalism with communist subversion. In its most extreme form, this "church militant" mindset provided spiritual legitimacy not only for the excesses of Hoover's surveillance and intimidation apparatus, but also for the use of extreme military force. Ockenga, for example, demanded an "aggressive diplomacy" that "will maintain access to Berlin whatever come even if this means using atomic weapons."[41]

The evangelical conceptualization of communism as a spiritual challenge not only demanded patriotic rededication, however. It also called for a serious confrontation with America's own unexorcized ghosts and moral pitfalls. Never losing sight of anxiety amidst triumphalism, evangelicals saw America as besieged, remained highly critical of the corruptibility and worldliness of secular institutions, and viewed the communist threat as the result of America's own apostasy.[42] While their term for global blasphemy was communism, their name for domestic apostasy was secular liberalism. The danger of this "ideological disease," they argued, lay in its secularizing tendencies that threatened to undermine the moral fiber of the nation. As Mennonite theologian Paul Peachey noted in *Christianity Today*, "Communism, which we despise, and the secularism of the West are blood relatives."[43] It was on this basis that Carl Henry and others attacked the failure of the liberal mind to provide a proper spiritual response to the totalitarian nightmares of the twentieth century. In Henry's view, liberalism's naturalist ontology and its moral relativism could not explain evil. It was thus useless in understanding the nature of twentieth-century totalitarianism. Because of this spiritual flabbiness, he argued, liberalism threatened the spiritual and moral defenses of the West during the Cold War. In contrast, evangelicals posited their concept of patriotic conversion. In their view, only a firm belief in transcendent moral principles could fill the West's concept of freedom with the necessary meaning to make it as powerful an intellectual potion as communism.[44]

Despite this fervor, however, evangelicals were careful to wield the sword of anticommunism altogether too forcefully. Though avidly anticommunist, they were at pains to disassociate themselves from the militancy of Carl McIntire, Billy James Hargis, and other fundamentalist firebrands. Moreover, the short-lived "brown scare" during the war had impressed upon evangelicals the need to separate themselves from extreme right-wing political connections.[45] Projecting a softened image, Ron Arnold emphasized that the NAE's answer to communism was "not to stage investigations or expose Reds as such, but to have a spiritual ministry to be related to churches." At the same time, however, he warned that winning souls to Christ should not deflect from anticommunist vigilance, since "outside groups are anxious to take over the anti-communist fight."[46]

The combination of rejecting fundamentalist extremism while projecting anticommunist resolve was also crucial in cementing the political credentials of postwar evangelicalism. "The extreme right wing or hyper-anti-communists have discredited themselves with those who formulate public policy in Washington," Taylor pointed out in 1962. Although they "have a large following at the grass roots," he regarded the NAE's "more reasonable, less emotional, and thoroughly factual approach" as more effective in Washington.[47] In turn, the evangelical anticommunist crusade took on a special flavor. On the one hand, it adopted a number of high-profile foreign policy causes, such as staunch opposition to diplomatic recognition of "Red China."[48] On the other hand, it increasingly shifted the discourse away from tirades on socialism and communism toward issues of cultural subversion and moral iniquity. This became particularly apparent when the NAE renewed its anticommunist campaign in early 1960s. Reporting on NAE contacts with William Y. Elliot, dean of the Harvard University Summer School and a government advisor, Taylor wrote that "in an off the record conversation with him we have discussed the possibility of setting up an overall board to advise and direct, and to a degree screen out undesirables, in a strong anti-communist program." He noted that

Elliot was "a religious man and would like to see, in fact he insists on, using the moral basis as an approach to the whole communist program." Implying that the NAE needed to disassociate itself not only from liberals, but also from the John Birch Society and other groups on the extreme Right, Taylor criticized General Edwin Walker, a fiery anticommunist and member of the Officers' Christian Union. "Evangelicals have found it impossible to really get through to him," he noted, "He is a man who has a one track mind. They have found no matter what they ask him to talk about in their meetings he always ends up attacking communism."[49]

Likewise, by 1962 NAE executive director George Ford voiced doubts about the effectiveness of the NAE's anticommunist Freedom through Faith program: "There is a changing climate of public opinion specifically as relating to the ecumenical movement and to the threat of communism," he pointed out. In his view, anticommunism "undoubtedly has passed its peak as far as drawing attendance to rallies and response in form of contribution" was concerned and that instead the "real answer must spring from a general spiritual renewal within our country."[50]

As George Marsden, Jerome Himmelstein, and Lisa McGirr have concluded, this shift from conspiratorial, apocalyptic anticommunism to moral issues allowed conservative Protestants to move into the respectable mainstream and was a key factor in their broad-based political success.[51] It served as the inspiration for the New Right's "social issues" focus in the 1980s. By the late 1960s, both evangelicals and political conservatives had largely abandoned paranoid red-baiting in favor of antiwelfarist and antisecularist invective. The center of conservative grassroots activity, as McGirr has noted, shifted "from the anticommunist study groups and home meetings of the early 1960s" toward "new single-issue campaigns, as well as to a conservative religious awakening." Richard Nixon, Ronald Reagan, and others muted the extremist tendencies expressed in anticommunist tirades in favor of attacks on liberal "permissiveness," "welfare chiselers," "criminality," and "big government." Ranging from Nixon's "forgotten man" rhetoric to New Right attacks on liberal "professional problem-solvers and moral relativists," conservatives denounced the alleged moral breakdown of society embodied in sexual libertinism, drug abuse, abortion, and homosexuality.[52]

Anti-Catholicism

Considering the sustained efforts of the New Christian Right since the 1970s to build coalitions across denominational divides, it comes as a surprise that of all the ghosts of the fundamentalist past in postwar evangelicalism, anti-Catholicism was the one that lingered the longest. Evangelicals in the 1950s and 1960s were often more virulently anti-Catholic than anticommunist, and they rarely acknowledged any differences between Moscow and the Vatican. In fact, they often put their anticommunism in the service of fighting the much older enemy.[53] As Taylor noted in 1952, American Catholics "have been just as guilty of falsifying facts and in publishing them as have the Communists from the Kremlin."[54]

Ignoring finer differences, evangelicals conflated the threats of secular communism with what they considered to be the perverted Christianity of Catholicism. Anti-Catholic diatribes were often closely followed by evangelicals taking a swing at communism as they elided the differences between the drive toward a state church and totalitarian oppression.[55] "The largest strength of the Communist party, next to Russia and China, is in Italy, home of Vatican City," Carl Henry explained, "Only European lands on which the Reformation made a strong theological impact are today virile in their resistance to Communism."[56] In essence, evangelicals invoked traditional anti-Catholicism and anticommunism as rhetorical devices for largely the same purpose, namely, to rally their forces against the enemies of Protestantism, to affirm conversionist theology as the spiritual basis of the American political order, and to assert their claims for institutional access against the Catholic quest for public funding.[57]

The main reason for the virulence of anti-Catholic sentiment was that the Catholic challenge was ultimately closer to home than the communist threat. Even the most avid red-baiter had to admit that the incidences of communist subversion remained limited in the United States. In contrast, Catholic institutions had a real and palpable presence in American society. In particular, evangelical antipathy was fed by the wartime and postwar clash of evangelical overseas missionary activities with similar Catholic efforts. Linking revivalism at home to America's global calling to evangelize the world, neo-evangelicals had made a renewed emphasis on international mission work and global solidarity with Protestants a core part of their agenda.[58] The NAE's mission efforts constituted an important dimension of these activities. Administratively, these efforts coalesced in the OPA. Originally created mainly to assist foreign mission boards with travel documents, the Washington office soon acquired new functions as evangelical foreign missionary activities expanded rapidly during and after the war.[59]

By 1949, the OPA had an office staff of four and handled the "Washington problems" of over ninety mission boards. It not only facilitated the issuing of visas and passports by working with the Passport Division of the State Department, but was also "involved in safeguarding the rights of our American missionaries in unfavorable religious climates," preventing the deportation of evangelicals, arranging for medical help, and navigating the corridors of power in Washington.[60] In the process, Taylor declared, "One of our first discoveries was the fact that there were already in existence strong enemies of the Gospel."[61] In turn, both mission work and keeping "a close watch on legislation and the enemies of the gospel operating in government circles" dominated Taylor's work.[62] By the latter he meant primarily the Catholic church.

As the renewal of mission work brought evangelicals into conflict with Catholics, an often virulent strain of anti-Catholicism became the hallmark of the OPA's lobbying activities. Much of its legislative campaigning on the ground was directed against perceived Catholic repression abroad. In his *Watchman in Washington* reports, Taylor frequently denounced the persecution of evangelicals by Catholic regimes. In the case of Colombia, the "vicious reaction of fanatical Romanism putting government under pressure to harass Protestants" prompted him to ask for an NAE resolution "denouncing the satanic tactics whereby the Roman heirarchy [sic] and the government it dominates . . . links all Protestants with Communists in Colombia and calls for their 'suppression' meaning in general, liquidation."[63] In mentioning the evangelical campaign against the Spanish government, he described the country as "an absolute Roman Catholic dictatorship violating most God given freedoms."[64] And liberally employing anti-Catholic sentiments, his office actively intervened on behalf of evangelicals in Greece, Bolivia, Ethiopia, and Portugal.

Crucially, the OPA's successes in counteracting alleged Catholic abuses generated an awareness of the opportunities provided by working with government agencies. Taylor triumphantly noted in the mid-1950s that "after years of working with and giving full cooperation to government agencies we have seen the fruit. Men on the inside of government, knowing the stand of N.A.E. and our specific interests in religious matters, are calling and alerting us when critical matters come up." Citing the U.S. treaty with Haiti as an example, he touted the NAE's success in pushing through a religious freedom clause. "Roman pressure in Haiti had taken it out. The State Department was going along with them. We in turn alerted all the other offices in Washington who would be interested and then joined together in persuading the Senate committee to hold up the treaty ratification until corrective action could be taken."[65] In Colombia, where the Catholic government had closed a large number of Protestant schools, churches, and missions, the "excellent cooperation" between the NAE and the federal government managed to get many of the chapels reopened. When the government of Portuguese East Africa tried to close Protestant elementary schools, Taylor declared that "we know the Roman archbishop is back of it, with the government acting as his stooge. As mission boards we can do nothing. As American citizens, backed by an interested government, we believe the problem will be solved."[66]

Hence, the anti-Catholic campaigns were both a crucial means of mobilizing the evangelical constituency for the expansion of missionary activities abroad and of facilitating political re-engagement. As the OPA made legislative campaigning and networking with government agencies the focus of its activities, it generated renewed evangelical interest in foreign policy, furthered new institutional contacts with the state, and turned the fate of missionaries into a political issue. "When world matters involving foreign missions are discussed by our Department of State we are invited," Taylor proudly noted already in 1949.[67] Reporting to the evangelical constituency on "legislation bearing on the church and evangelical activity around the world," he urged his fellow believers "to influence their congressmen for the right."[68]

Letter-writing campaigns, in particular, began to be employed in order to put pressure on the federal government to lean on foreign states to desist from discriminatory practices.[69] The Colombian case, for example, formed the backdrop for thousands of letters from evangelicals to their senators and to the president. "We in turn have acquired a new respect for the influence of such letters upon our government," Taylor declared.[70] Finding that government increasingly affected the work of evangelical churches, he concluded that "as we were called upon to assist we were forced to take an informal course in government and it's [sic] complexity."[71]

As evangelicals hitched their efforts to establish new missions to pressuring government into creating a stable "investment climate" abroad, a subtle but decisive change took place in their rhetoric. Though they had few qualms about openly expressing anti-Catholic sentiments, evangelicals began to package their campaigns less in anti-Catholic invective and more in general terms as the defense of religious liberty, the rights of Protestant missionaries overseas, and the separation of church and state. Depicting religious freedom as inseparable from political freedom and democratic government, Taylor noted that "our defense is not made because they are Christians but because they are U.S. citizens and hence our government has certain basic obligations to protect and guarantee their freedoms. Usually the basis of such defense is the treaty of 'peace, friendship and navigation' signed between the countries involved."[72]

This set the stage for what became one of core campaigns of the NAE during and after the Cold War, namely the call for religious freedom treaties that included clauses guaranteeing the right to worship and to propagate the faith.[73] Indicating their growing legal and political competency, evangelicals used the religious freedom defense as a means of opposing international treaties that they regarded as potentially threatening to their missionary interests. In 1970, for example, the OPA's Floyd Robertson expressed fears that the Genocide Treaty, first submitted by Harry Truman, "could be construed to prohibit the efforts of missionaries to evangelize because this would obviously change their culture and conceivably provide 'mental harm' for the people."[74] In the ensuing years the NAE devoted significant resources to the religious freedom campaign as a way of protecting the missionary activities of evangelical Christians. By the mid-1980s, OPA director Robert Dugan noted that a conference on religious liberty had been a success as "certainly the State Department was affirmed in its new policy of considering religious liberty to be one of its criteria for evaluating human rights in nations around the world."[75] In 1998 the campaign culminated in the passage of the International Religious Freedom Act in Congress.

In the long term, phrasing evangelical interests as a religious freedom issue had another advantage. Though initially spawned by both anticommunist and anti-Catholic sentiments, the emphasis on religious liberty was crucial in enabling evangelicals to form transdenominational coalitions once rabid anti-Catholicism had yielded to a less confrontational stance, especially after the Second Vatican Council.[76] While anti-Catholicism lost its raw edge, however, it continued to surface and to demarcate postwar evangelicalism as both mainstream and militant.[77] The NAE campaign to prevent diplomatic relations with the Vatican, for example, continued well beyond the 1960 election.[78] In fact, it continued well into the 1980s. "We have battled this all the way, in keeping with a 1943 NAE resolution, reiterated ten times since," Dugan, for example, reported in 1984 when the Reagan administration appointed an ambassador to the Vatican.[79]

Political and Institutional Inroads

This combination of prophetic and eschatological with nationalistic and antiliberal strains in the evangelical foreign policy ideology significantly furthered the movement's coalition with political conservatives. The election of
Dwight Eisenhower in 1952 in particular gave evangelicals direct access to
the White House. While Truman had kept a distance, Eisenhower, largely
due to his personal friendship with Billy Graham, provided conservative
Christians both with political inroads and social status. Graham successfully
urged Eisenhower to become the first president ever to be baptized during
his term in office. He also made sure Ike became a member of an evangelical
congregation, and he gave him a copy of the fundamentalist Scofield Reference Bible, which Eisenhower apparently kept on his nightstand.[80] Declaring
that he was "a convinced, nearly fanatical protestant," Eisenhower expressed a
desire to lead the country in a spiritual renewal.[81] By the same token, Graham
did not keep his political opinions to himself when he lauded speeches by
conservative politicians or implored Eisenhower not to relent in Indochina.
He also made himself a spokesman for American interests abroad during his
missionary travels. Until well into the 1960s, military supremacy, uncompromising anticommunism, and 100 percent Americanism were the ideological
pivots of Graham's political involvement.[82]

The close personal ties between Graham and Eisenhower were part of a
general rise in religious sentiment in Washington's political circles. Cabinet
meetings generally began with a tribute to God, and one of the jokes that cir-
culated in the capital was "*damn*, we forgot the opening prayer."[83] Evangelicals
increasingly sensed that laboring in the vineyard of the beltway was beginning to pay off. Clyde Taylor concluded in 1954 that "during the past ten years
great strides have been made by evangelicals in maintaining such relations
with our government's attention. Where it involves U.S. citizens, we request
action and generally get it. Where it involves American interests, the State
Department does what it can within its legal field of action."[84] Three years later
he pointed out that "N.A.E. today is an established organization in the United
States that is being recognized by all government agencies and granted representation at every level." It was respected even though it held tenaciously to
its conservative theology "and in general to its conservative viewpoint politically."[85] Reporting in 1959 that the OPA had arranged a visit of NAE officials
with President Eisenhower to report on world conditions, Taylor pointed out
that "this visit has been made possible by the excellent liaison that we have

been able to build up between NAE and departments of the executive branch of Government."[86]

These contacts were part of an emerging network between neo-evangelicals and leading politicians and businessmen in the 1950s that shaped the foreign policy outlook of conservative Protestantism. The OPA's seminars on federal service discussed in the previous chapter played an important role in generating and strengthening these networks. They included, for example, Kansas Senator Frank Carlson, evangelical organizer Abraham Vereide, and Minnesota Representative Walter H. Judd. A "congressman, physician, missionary" who kept a "vigilant eye on the world strategy of Communism," Judd published articles in *Christianity Today* that not only featured the classic mantras on the Soviet threat and the need to keep out Red China, but also spelled out a strategy beyond a European-centered Cold War stand-off. Support for France and Britain in the Suez war, Judd argued, risked losing U.S. influence among African and Asian countries. Instead of alienating Third World peoples, he suggested that Americans should become stronger themselves in order to free others.[87]

Both Judd and Vereide were close to Eisenhower and managed to get the president's support for the 1953 "March of Freedom" organized by the NAE. Eisenhower also lent his support to International Christian Leadership (ICL), an evangelical organization led by Vereide with close ties to the NAE.[88] ICL organized breakfast, prayers, conferences, and informal meetings of politicians and bureaucrats, and set up an effective network of evangelical Christians in politics and the military. Both Judd and Carlson belonged to this group, as did Chief Justice Earl Warren, deputy secretary of defense Robert Anderson, and Missouri senator Stuart Symington. Carlson and Vereide also organized the first "presidential prayer breakfast" with 500 guests from the upper echelons in politics and business in Conrad Hilton's Mayflower Hotel. The event guaranteed evangelicals broad media coverage and public attention. During this time Graham also developed close relations with Richard Nixon and Lyndon Johnson. Among his most prominent supporters were Texas oil millionaire Sid Richardson and Virginia senator A. Willis Robertson, Pat Robertson's father.[89]

Building on networks of this kind, the NAE grew increasingly confident in its efforts to liaise with government agencies, as well as in its reliance on the State Department to provide protective cover for the growing evangelical missionary activities in Europe and Asia. For instance, the goal to spiritualize American foreign policy generated new evangelical interest in government agencies involved in cultural work abroad. The NAE actively pushed for the inclusion of religious materials in the propaganda work of the USIA. "The Voice of America and the U.S. Information Agency that represent us by propaganda overseas should be of intense interest," Taylor insisted in 1954.[90] By 1957, Carl Henry was able to report that both the USIA and the Voice of America were showing "a fairer measure of evangelical participation" and were overcoming the dominance of left-wing writers.[91] In turn, the fifteenth Annual Conference of the NAE in Buffalo adopted a resolution commending USIA and the Voice of America for "forward steps now being taken . . . in the handling of religious information."[92]

Evangelicals hailed especially the USIA's approval of Moody Institute films for international educational purposes. *The God of the Atom*, for example, lifted "the question of the use of the atom bomb beyond the elemental issue of the peaceful or destructive employments of nuclear energy to the higher principle of the spiritual purposes of the universe."[93] By 1959, Taylor could also report that the OPA "had success in getting evangelical books into the USIA libraries overseas."[94] In these efforts to get the evangelical message across, the NAE was not interested in providing a balanced view or simply using religion in general for purposes of political propaganda. Instead, it sought to promote its specific agenda. "A temperament that exalts all religions indiscriminately and blurs out genuine distinctions between religions, inevitably neglects the Hebrew-Christian heritage," Henry declared. In particular, he criticized Elton Trueblood, the chief of religious information of USIA, for his alleged deference to Islam. "Non-Christian religion is flattered and encouraged, and the tax-supported policy of the American government casts weight against the Christian witness of American foreign missionaries," Henry grumbled.[95]

During these heady days of religiopolitical convergence, a *Christianity Today* poll of Protestant clergymen showed that they favored Eisenhower 8–1 over Democratic candidate Adlai Stevenson.[96] The magazine reported a general sense of satisfaction with the direction of the country under Eisenhower. It noted that "although policy issues bore conspicuous weight" in this support, it was mainly derived from Ike's faith in God and in objective moral norms.[97] Nonetheless, the personal and intellectual links between the Eisenhower administration and evangelicals did not give conservative Protestants control over policy decisions. Despite his close ties to Graham, Ike was not overly concerned with evangelical piety. As William Miller chided, Eisenhower was "a fervent believer in a very vague religion." Indicative of his attitude was that after declaring Independence Day of 1953 a day of prayer and repentance, he took off to go fishing, play golf, and spend the evening at the bridge table.[98]

There were also no clear indications that Eisenhower's foreign policies were decisively influenced by evangelicalism. Despite the strident anticommunism, NATO's strategy of massive retaliation, and John Foster Dulles's "roll back" ideology, Eisenhower followed a reasonably moderate course. He neither believed that the Soviet Union wanted another war, nor did he consider use of the atomic bomb a realistic military option. In contrast to recurrent evangelical demands for "an aggressive spiritual-moral international policy," his foreign policy focus tended to be on collective security and containment. [99]

Although the immediate impact of evangelicalism on American foreign policy was limited, the political inroads pioneered during the Eisenhower administration were invaluable to the movement. They allowed evangelicals to learn lobbying techniques, engage in political networking, get media attention, and acquire *Herrschaftswissen*, the expertise required for exercise of power. In turn, evangelicals managed to gain influence in a number of institutions. Their involvement with the military, in particular, is one area of Cold War church-state relations scholars have recognized for its significance beyond the narrow field of religious and missionary history. While marginal in the military before World War II, evangelicals proved highly successful in their postwar infiltration campaign, as historian Ann Loveland has shown. Although relations remained fraught with tension and mutual suspicion throughout the 1950s and 1960s, the evangelicals' pro-defense orientation, superpatriotism, unfailing support for the Vietnam War, and effective proselytism earned them both influence and respect within the armed forces and from the military leadership. Moreover, as missionary impulses and Cold War defense interests came together, evangelical proselytizing became closely linked to the desire to use the "promilitary Cold War stance to gain greater influence in public policy at the national level."[100] The process of engaging with the military thus presents a classic example of the way in which the confluence of government imperatives, evangelical social awakening, and the transformation of church-state relations shaped the political ideology of conservative Protestantism. As a result, evangelicals gradually disassociated themselves from their separatist, pacifist, and antimilitarist past.

From the perspective of the state, the desire for spiritual sanctioning of the Cold War mission merged military and religious goals. As America's global power grew and the war experience reinvigorated notions of the redeemer nation, military planners increasingly regarded missionary enterprises as useful for the promotion of U.S. national interests. In turn, military logistics, surplus war materials, and government benefits helped fuel the postwar missionary expansion. "Thanks to the huge stock-pile of war materials that were left when the conflict ceased," Joel Carpenter remarked, "mission agencies were able to buy into the logistical prowess of the American war machine at bargain basement prices."[101] In the same vein, General Douglas MacArthur's support for missionary work in Japan and Korea made him a hero in the eyes of the evangelicals.[102] MacArthur "aggressively promoted Christianity in occupied Japan by facilitating extensive missionary work on the part of American religious groups and encouraging the distribution of millions of Bibles and Testaments."[103]

By the same token, the federal government pushed for the implementation of anticommunist training programs in the military, presence of military chaplains, and expanded church building on military sites as means to shore up the moral backbone of recruits. During World War II, military leaders had expressed profound uneasiness with the lack of wartime discipline. Many in the upper echelons of the military establishment blamed alcohol abuse, venereal diseases, and other related ills on the lack of moral fiber and the "spiritual illiteracy" of young soldiers. These concerns prompted the Truman administration to implement "an unprecedented religious and moral welfare program in the armed forces," which included compulsory character education, increased opportunities for religious activities, and an enhanced role for chaplains in military training. In 1951, secretary of defense George C. Marshall made moral training a requirement for young servicemen. Many of the lectures and publications in the character guidance program promoted Bible-based morality, faith, and religious worship as a necessary part of service to the "covenant nation."[104]

From the perspective of postwar evangelicals, military involvement gave them an opportunity to express their newfound social commitment, make their spiritual message politically relevant, secure political access, and outdo Catholics and mainline Protestants in the process. The initial impetus for re-engagement with the military can be traced back to the social reform impulses awakened by profound uneasiness about the debauching influences of war on the morals of young soldiers. Removed from the wholesome influences of church and family, trying to prove themselves in an all-male setting, emerging from a close shave with death, and getting drunk on victory, G.I.s—so evangelicals maintained—were vulnerable to the ravages of alcoholism, venereal disease, and licentiousness.[105] Renewed evangelical effort thus went into missionary activism among military personnel. Operating out of the OPA, the NAE's Commission on Chaplaincy and Service to Military Personnel, which started in 1943, led evangelization campaigns in the military and succeeded in converting thousands of troops. This crusade received help from denominations outside of the NAE, such as the Southern Baptist Convention, and parachurch organizations, such as the Officers' Christian Fellowship and the Navigators. Many of these postwar evangelical revivals integrated the war experience into religious rhetoric and ceremonies. Bill Bright's Campus Crusade for Christ, for example, frequently used military terms such as "enlist, advance, rally, campaign, blitz."[106]

Both government imperatives and evangelical efforts were decisive factors in establishing closer contacts between church and state and in furthering the influence of conservative Protestants. The shared commitment to the Cold War mission was, for example, the background upon which the career of one of the most influential evangelicals in the defense sector unfolded. Enjoying the support of Admiral Arthur W. Redford and Secretary of Defense Charles Wilson, evangelical John C. Broger was put in charge of implementing the Pentagon's program to fight the "spiritual illiteracy" of young soldiers. Broger, who had set up a successful evangelical radio network in Asia after World War II, was recruited by Redford for the Pentagon with the clear mission to strengthen the moral backbone of G.I.s in the struggle against communism. What added urgency to this effort were recent reports that American prisoners of war in Korea had declared they had no desire to return to the United States and would collaborate with the enemy instead.[107]

Broger occupied a strategic position in the Pentagon in the 1950s and 1960s, first as deputy director of Armed Forces Information and Education (AFIE) and later as its director. His concept of "Militant Liberty" became the basis of moral and ideological training programs in the military. Designed to show the link between Christianity and freedom, the most common theme of the numerous films and radio plays distributed by AFIE was that of the American hero defending his hometown against communist subversion. For this purpose, Broger frequently used materials produced by fundamentalist and extreme right-wing organizations, despite the fact that these groups mostly regarded as traitors not only fictitious towns but the very real federal government, the press, and America's NATO allies. The John Birch Society, for example, supplied the script for the film *Communism on the Map*. Broger also promoted ties to conservative and patriotic organizations such as the Freedoms Foundation and the American Heritage Foundation. Throughout his career Broger retained close ties to the evangelical establishment. Named "Evangelical of the Year" in 1968, Broger directed the NAE's Freedom Studies project largely centered in the OPA.[108]

Evangelicals were thus in a position to shape the content of moral training manuals in the armed forces. Meanwhile, their distinctive interpretation of world events was spread by a small but influential group of military men. Although few high-ranking officers openly declared their evangelical faith in the 1940s and 1950s, there were some prominent exceptions. The leading "Bible-reading general" was William K. Harrison. An active supporter of MacArthur's missionary zeal in postwar Japan, he was well received as a speaker at evangelical rallies. Harrison was a career officer who advanced rapidly in the army. He headed the allied delegation during the truce negotiations in Korea, and by 1954 he was commander-in-chief of the forces in the Caribbean. His career also shows that evangelicals—particularly through organizations such as the Officers' Christian Union, which had close ties with Inter-Varsity Christian Fellowship, Christian Business Men's Fellowship, and Campus Crusade for Christ—gradually gained access to the higher military ranks.[109]

Harrison, who served as president of the Officers' Christian Union for almost twenty years, not only added to the respectability of evangelicalism, but also became one of the movement's crucial sources for information and advice in defense and foreign policy matters. His views shaped the political outlook of evangelicalism in the 1950s and 1960s. In particular, he gave voice to the evangelical rejection of the UN and exemplified the movement's political support for Israel. Harrison was convinced that another world war was inevitable and firmly believed in the imminence of Armageddon and the Apocalypse. He also expected a Soviet attack in the Middle East and viewed the Cold War as a struggle against a demonic power. "The war that might ensue when the balance becomes unequal might well be a great world war of a destructive nature never before known to man," he surmised, "Right in the vortex of the conflict would be the land of Israel and the Jewish nation. The possible developments described above appear to me to have a noticeable similarity to biblical prophecies concerning the end of the age and the second advent of Christ."[110] Steeped in premillennialist fundamentalist thinking, Harrison's views thus relativized the general perception that evangelical theology was becoming more mainstream in the 1950s.

Finally, the expansion of the number and role of chaplains helped promote the influence of evangelicals in the military. The federal government sanctioned religious activities by paying for military chaplains, supporting church construction on military sites, and making chapel attendance compulsory in Army, Navy, and Air Force Academies. Chaplains were omnipresent in the program, conducting individual interviews with new recruits and delivering character education lectures. Although Baptists, Seventh-Day Adventists, and other conservative Protestant groups traditionally regarded chaplains in the armed forces as a violation of the separation of church and state, the number of evangelical chaplains increased steadily.[111] By the 1960s, Southern Baptists in particular greatly exceeded their quotas in the chaplaincy program "in which hundreds of their ministers were supported by tax funds for work that is necessarily of a sectarian character."[112]

Evangelical involvement with the military chaplaincy, however, was not without controversy. The NAE in particular initially remained circumspect. Suspicious of the military leadership, evangelicals quarreled with the ecumenical drift of the military chaplaincy and its standardized publications that deemphasized sectarian identities and allegedly promoted theological liberalism.[113] Citing cases where organizers of Bible study groups and other religious activities were punished and discharged as unfit, Clyde Taylor even saw in it the potential to destroy religious liberty. With the military discriminating against evangelicals and limiting religious exercises, the chaplaincy, he argued, led to a blurring of doctrinal distinctions and a tendency of chaplains to think of themselves as military men.[114] At the same time, evangelicals also struggled to get their message across within the military. Broger's films and materials were not terribly popular, and excessive missionary zeal earned evangelicals derisive nicknames such as "God's Gestapo" and "the Green Berets of the Christian community."[115] Throughout the 1950s and early 1960s, the NAE thus remained on the margins in the military. Instead of promoting evangelical chaplains, the OPA often intervened to get exemptions for clergy, missionaries, and seminarians who had received draft notices.[116] "No religious agency that we know of has better service when it comes to defending our young men, including seminary students and pastors, from accidental or discriminatory draft by the Selective Service System." Taylor boasted in 1957.[117]

Mounting concerns about Catholic dominance of the chaplaincy, however, in combination with improved opportunities to spread the sectarian message through other channels, generated growing support in the late 1960s for closer ties with the military within the NAE. In particular, the prospect of getting involved in counseling, moral education lessons, Bible study, religious revivals, and retreats revived evangelical interest. This also reflected the evangelicals' more secure status and concomitant willingness to adapt to the pluralistic religious context in which they operated.[118] The Vietnam War, in particular, proved to be a turning point. Though they had achieved some success by the mid-1960s, their unswerving support for the war effort helped evangelicals become the dominant religious group in the military. Harrison, for example, became an outspoken apologist for the intervention in Vietnam. By the early 1970s, the NAE's Commission on Chaplaincy and Service to Military Personnel, led by Floyd Robertson, represented 19 denominations and had 128 chaplains in service and "enjoyed the best rapport with the military in general and the Chiefs of Chaplains in particular."[119] As Ann Loveland concluded, "once regarded with indifference, disdain, or suspicion, by the mid-1970s evangelicals had attained not only membership and visibility but also respect and influence within the U.S. armed forces."[120]

Evangelicals and Foreign Aid

In addition to the growing involvement of evangelicals with the military, foreign aid highlights the way in which the confluence of government imperatives to expand administrative capacities and the resurgence of evangelicalism both shaped the national security state and transformed the antistatist ideology of conservative Protestants. Ideologically, as well as institutionally, state and evangelical international aid providers became closely entwined during the Cold War in ways that nurtured both the expansion of the federal government and the growth of religious agencies. In addition to the Seventh-Day Adventists and the Salvation Army, the NAE's World Relief Corporation (WRC) became a major player in government-funded transportation and distribution of surplus foods, hospital building, land reclamation programs, and similar endeavors.

Although the foreign aid field shows that the desires of the postwar state and of resurgent evangelicalism increasingly matched, opposition to breaching the barrier between church and state initially remained strong in conservative Protestant ranks. In the 1940s and 1950s, evangelicals feared that government foreign aid money would inhibit their desire to relate service to faith, and the NAE's preference for doctrinal commitments was at times ill suited for ecumenical cooperation, particularly with the interfaith American Council of Voluntary Agencies (ACVA).[121] Well into the 1950s, the NAE, in cooperation with POAU, remained an outspoken critic of the foreign aid program. Brandishing both separationist and anti-Catholic rhetoric, *Christianity Today* maintained in 1958 that Catholic participation in the government's foreign aid program constituted a "bold bid for power by a religious denomination" and that "ecclesiastical control of foreign aid would turn this program into a power tool of the Roman hierarchy."[122]

Even identification with Cold War foreign policy goals did little to mute the separationist fervor of evangelical scribes. *Church & State* editor C. Stanley Lowell mocked proponents of foreign aid subsidiarity by noting that "one of the oldest claims advanced for aid to church-related institutions was that such aid would buttress national defense."[123] Likewise, *Christianity Today* criticized Eisenhower, whom evangelicals generally regarded positively, for watering down the spiritual element of foreign aid.[124] Similarly, a 1956 *Christianity Today* poll showed that many evangelical ministers did not regard curtailing foreign aid and fighting communism as mutually exclusive. A majority of clergymen called for foreign aid to be reduced, and some saw it simply as a "federal giveaway." One minister asked for "a firmer stand on church-state separation" and for "a positive stand on freedom of religion wherever American money and troops are sent abroad" while demanding the cessation of foreign aid "to any church-sponsored institution at home and abroad."[125]

Wading into the debates, Carl Henry likewise invoked a plethora of classic fears and enemies. Foreign aid, he thundered, led down the garden path of big government, breached the separation of church and state, constituted an undue tax burden, delegated too much control to the UN, and had been hijacked by the Catholic church. It was driven by commercial self-interest and a desire for military strength, not spiritual service. While largely unsuccessful in shoring up international support for U.S. policy, it had served to help pro-American dictators. In his view, foreign aid was the result of "the outworn optimism of the liberal social gospel." It threatened the "socialistic substitution of government assistance for individual responsibility" and the usurpation of a field better left to private industry and voluntary efforts. Even more alarming was that it impeded missionary agencies, because foreign aid funds were used to promote education "divorced from religio-ethical commitments in global areas threatened by the aggression of naturalistic irreligion." International aid thus failed to promote the Christian principles, which in his opinion constituted the West's distinctive view of life.[126]

The NAE faced a dilemma, however. While it was reluctant to endorse government-funded activities, evangelical groups such as the Seventh-Day Adventists and the Salvation Army were willing participants in overseas aid

provision and used their international networks for the distribution of surplus food under the 1954 Food for Peace legislation. Moreover, the growing participation of Catholic and mainline Protestant agencies heightened
the NAE's anxieties. As noted in Chapter 1, Catholic Relief Services had not
only become the largest private international aid agency by the 1950s, it also
was the recipient of the majority of government relief supplies.[127] In turn,
evangelical fears grew that foreign aid money was supporting Roman Catholic institutions abroad and sanctioning discriminations against Protestants.
"Observers report that recipients think the Roman Catholic Church, not the
U.S. Government, has been the [food] donor," Henry grumbled, "In India,
bags of grain were altered to conceal the fact of American shipments."[128]

A combination of fear of Catholic control, anticommunist fervor, concerns about surreptitious secularization, financial pressures, and a growing
sense of the opportunities for faith-based practices ultimately set in motion
the process by which evangelicals ended up embracing closer church-state
ties in foreign aid. Ironically, one of the key factors in the development of
this new attitude was the contradiction inherent in evangelical attitudes to
government-funded foreign aid. While evangelicals denounced Catholic or
secular control, they recognized that government subsidies enabled sectarian groups to impose their teachings. The very fact that Catholics could use
federal aid to promote their views thus not only generated fears of Catholic
control, but also made evangelicals aware of the autonomy religious providers
had under public funding arrangements. Thus, while Carl Henry continued
to reiterate traditional separationist arguments, his initial attack on foreign
aid gradually gave way to qualified support. Setting aside previous worries
about the undue expansion of big government, he called for spiritualized foreign aid regardless of the size and role of the state. Foreign aid, he suggested,
needed to be placed "in the service of truth, morality, and the world of spirit"
in order to "exercise a permanent ministry."[129] *Christianity Today* even later
admitted that "the Point Four program has indirectly furthered some aspects
of Christian missionary effort."[130] In the same vein, WRC chairman Christian
N. Hostetter in his 1963 review of existing aid contracts calmed fears by noting that in most cases "the entire operation of the relief program rests in the
hands of the church agency."[131]

Though originally invoked to shore up the separation of church and state,
the evangelicals' continuous denunciation of Roman Catholic successes in
gaining government money gradually undermined conservative Protestantism's separationist agenda. It made evangelicals realize that opposing foreign

aid also meant they could not use public funds for their own purposes. In turn, although they retained all the trappings of traditional anti-Catholicism, conservative Protestants increasingly linked their attacks on Catholics to calls for an equivalent evangelical presence within government foreign aid programs. The issue was no longer how to preserve ideological purity by remaining independent of government funding, but how to compete with Catholics and mainline organizations for funds and influence without abandoning separationist rhetoric. By 1954, Taylor urged his fellow evangelicals to apply pressure on the State Department "to counterbalance the influence of the Roman heirarchy [sic] and other forces that constantly exert their maximum influence for their own interests regardless of the legality of their action."[132] In particular, the NAE campaign to add religious freedom clauses to foreign aid contracts showed that efforts to use government to ensure equal access gradually replaced the insistence on separationism.[133] The organization's calls for the United States to curtail aid to nations that did not guarantee religious freedom were more driven by the desire to limit the Catholic church's influence and facilitate evangelical access to foreign aid programs than by opposition to foreign aid as such.[134]

In addition, evangelical identification with the anticommunist crusade played a key role in the shift away from separationist orthodoxies and toward the participation of evangelical agencies in federal funding arrangements. Representative Walter Judd admonished *Christianity Today* readers that in the fight against communism, the main significance of religious foreign aid was not to replace government efforts, but to "give meaning to, and put heart and soul into the government programs," which "*ad*minister, but rarely do they minister."[135] The upshot was that evangelicals, who had always "openly talked of the need to relate service to faith," used the rhetoric of church and state separation no longer to impede government funding, but to shore up their spiritualized foreign aid work within the framework of a growing administrative state.[136] Indicating the new direction, even Anabaptist C. N. Hostetter declared that the main problem with church cooperation in overseas government programs was not public funding as such but a restrictive contract that "denies the church agency a satisfactory measure of selectivity in choosing candidates" and "constitutes the agency as an arm of government."[137] In short, as Bruce Nichols has pointed out, "Within the voluntary community, variations on the Catholic philosophy of subsidiarity have carried the day" and became the norm in Cold War America.[138] Despite the persistence of separationist attitudes, concerns with access and autonomy were winning out over inhibitions about taking money.

On this basis, the WRC became an avid participant in government foreign aid programs. This not only heralded the entry of the NAE into the
foreign aid field, but also mirrored the larger changes to church-state cooperation triggered by the government's desire to expand the involvement of
religious-based agencies. As the NAE's international aid agency, the WRC became involved in a wide variety of areas, including rural reclamation and development, refugee services, medical support, and educational programs. In
the 1960s, the WRC, later renamed World Relief, was incorporated as NAE-
WRC, Inc., a nonprofit subsidiary corporation with all shares owned by the
NAE. This allowed it to gain separate tax exempt status and improved its ability to qualify for government funds.[139] In 1980, Carl Henry listed the WRC
"with 30,000 related churches" among the key success stories of postwar evangelicalism, comparing it to Robert Pierce's World Vision, a highly successful
California-based evangelical aid provider that had thrived on federal grants.
Henry pointed out that the WRC, under the aegis of World Evangelical Fellowship, Evangelical Foreign Mission Association, Interdenominational Foreign Mission Association and Development Assistance Services, "has already
been sharing in the resettlement of refugees with a program that by the end
of 1981 may involve one in five NAE churches."[140]

The first sustained cooperation between the government and the NAE's
agency, then still called War Relief Commission, came as a result of a curious
convergence of evangelical complaints and government frustration. In October 1948, Clyde Taylor and another POAU member went into the office of the
Commission on Displaced Persons (CDP) "to protest that more Protestants
had not been coming in" as part of the resettlement program for former prisoners of war, camp survivors, refugees, and other displaced people across Europe. To their surprise the Commission not only shared their concern, it also
asked them to take over responsibility for the program.[141] Apparently claiming that the mainline Protestant World Alliance, the organization currently
in charge of Displaced Persons (DP) resettlement, had "miserably failed to
handle" the situation, the CDP asked the NAE to be in charge of placing 3000
European Protestant DPs within the next eight months.[142]

This was a tempting opportunity for the NAE to qualify for full recognition as an agency working on behalf of the CDP. After discussing the issue
with Taylor and a variety of church representatives, the WRC produced a
report on the situation for the NAE's Executive Committee. Presented by
WRC chairman Erling Olson, the report expressed interest in the program,
but also warned about the financial and logistical imponderables of venturing

beyond war relief work. In particular, it raised concerns over the provision that if sponsors failed to meet their obligation, the responsibility for the displaced person's care would fall back upon the WRC. Nonetheless, the report also noted that the Protestants should not falter as long as the Catholics and Jews were involved in these programs. Moreover, with the military paying for transportation and demanding that only one organization be responsible for each religious group, the NAE remained willing to participate. Reporting on the discussions in the NAE's Committee on International Cooperation, executive director R. L. Decker thus concluded that despite some concerns "the Committee feels that this is an open door for N.A.E."[143]

In the aftermath of its decision to get involved in the DP program, the NAE immediately ran into numerous problems. These included competition with bodies such as the Southern Baptist Convention and the Lutheran World Service, staff shortages, red tape, long processing times, high costs, and the need to cooperate with other religious organizations.[144] By October of 1949, however, some problems had been ironed out and the NAE's DP program was in full swing. Cooperating with the Mennonite Central Committee in Europe, the NAE had by then placed 190 DPs and sponsored an additional 300 or so. Clyde Taylor smugly reported that in a number of cases the NAE had beaten the Catholics and was able to place families "the NCWC had tried to get."[145]

Nonetheless, the program was causing him severe headaches. Though supplies and travel were paid for by the government, and relations between sponsors and DPs had been smooth, "financially the program has not been an asset."[146] However, the DP program marked the beginning of long-term working ties between evangelicals and the government in international aid and further stimulated the NAE's desire to pursue related activities. By 1957, the OPA organized monthly luncheon meetings with leaders of evangelical organizations that focused on the foreign aid program and religious influences in Washington. While Taylor admitted that "the immediate results of this are not too evident," he was confident that the meetings would be "extremely beneficial to our Washington office operation."[147] By the same token, the OPA frequently participated in State Department briefings on foreign aid described as "off-the-record conferences to alert leaders here in Washington to developments under the responsibility of the State Department and its overseas relations."[148]

By the late 1950s the WRC had established thriving administrative relationships with government agencies. Together with a range of other evan-

gelical agencies, such as the Mennonite Central Committee and the aid
organizations of the Seventh-Day Adventists, it had also become a routine
participant in the profitable foreign aid programs. As the majority of funds
available to religious groups were no longer directed at refugees, but were
provided via the surplus food program, the organization proved increasingly
willing to take government money.[149] In October 1960 WRC executive director Wendell Rockey reported that in the previous nine months his organization had shipped close to 5 million pounds of U.S. government surplus foods
with a value of almost $245,000 and had been reimbursed for ocean freight
shipment.[150] By 1966, the WRC shipped over 11 million pounds of government surplus foods valued at over $400,000 to countries such as Chile, Viet-
nam, Korea, and Burundi.[151]

The WRC program in Korea was of particular significance because it
openly combined evangelical missionary activism with ever closer contacts
with government.[152] Focusing on the Korean efforts, Rockey reported in
1961 on the "spiritual impact" of the WRC's activities. "There is gratifying
evidence that a Christian relief ministry, accompanied by an effective Christian witness, bears abundant fruitage," he noted. Among the main achievements, he listed 600,000 "tracts distributed to needy people receiving food."[153]
In 1963, the Korean program was about to receive a further boost from the
government. The WRC report pointed out that food distribution would be
expanded to include another 7,500 people and that self-help programs would
funnel aid "provided through the joint effort of the U.S. Department of Agriculture and the World Relief Commission" to recipients who would be partially paid with foodstuff. Listing overall shipments, including surplus food
valued in excess of $1.3 million, Rockey noted that "with the World Relief
Commission distributions of food and clothing, there is also given a tract,
gospel portion and many opportunities for a personal testimony."[154] Similarly,
a 1973 agenda paper of the WRC showed that recipients of government surplus food in Korea were "under the direct supervision of evangelical area
leaders. They were exposed to the Gospel in many different ways and their
compensation and reward was WRC provided surplus food, clothing, vita-
mins, materials, equipment, and so forth."[155]

As the awareness grew that foreign aid subsidiarity put few overall re-
straints on the spiritual mission of conservative Protestant agencies, the NAE
sought to retain church-state separation as the core evangelical ideology while
at the same time using it as a political tool in the competition for public funds
with other religious providers. Throughout the 1960s this duality—verging

on duplicity—characterized evangelical approaches in this area. Another example is the NAE's attitude to the Peace Corps, one of the Kennedy administration's flagship programs. Initially, the NAE was worried that the Peace Corps would infringe upon its mission and youth work overseas. The more publicly voiced concern, however, was that the Peace Corps would be taken over by the Catholic church. The NAE and POAU charged that the Catholic church was forcing out Protestants and that USAID and the Peace Corps were used to subsidize missionary movements abroad. This was allegedly the case in West Cameroon, for example, where Catholic schools were staffed with Peace Corps personnel. Firing another volley in the anti-Catholic cannonade, Taylor declared that "it seems that [the Roman Catholic Church] can't see any government funds available without wanting to get their hand in the till."[156]

Below the radar, however, the NAE was beginning to have second thoughts about attacking the Peace Corps. After a consultation with an evangelical Peace Corps staffer, Taylor and Don Gill reported disquiet about the negative reaction of evangelicals to the Peace Corps in contrast to the positive approach of the Roman Catholic Church. "They are out recruiting and as a result 50% or more of those going overseas may be Roman Catholics. So while we scream they enlist. It is very self-evident that there is only one answer to this."[157] Worried about being outdone by Catholics and mainline Protestants, the NAE changed its tune and moved from confrontation to cooperation. The Peace Corps "may have lasting value in our relations with certain other areas of the world," Taylor noted, particularly since "we have contact with certain thoroughly committed Christians in the administrative levels of the Corps."[158] Refraining from further attacks, he declared that "we have every reason to believe that there's going to be considerable latitude and opportunity for these folks to live and witness to their Christian faith even though they may not do preaching on Peace Corps mission."[159]

The NAE's reaction to the alleged Catholic misuse of foreign aid funds provides a further example of the way in which government funding first mobilized and then transformed evangelical separationist sentiments. Attacking House majority leader John William MacCormack as "the Catholic giveaway congressman from Massachusetts who generally provides the gifts to the Roman Catholic Church," the NAE in 1959 denounced a bill they feared constituted an attempt to funnel federal funds to Catholic organizations to set up churches and schools in the Philippines.[160] The association also complained that USAID money was financing the building of a Catholic university in Ecuador, and that Alliance for Progress funds provided by the Kennedy

administration in 1961 were used to support a Roman Catholic school system in Colombia that forced closure of Protestant schools and discriminated
against non-Catholics.[161] These tirades were familiar and ubiquitous.[162] At
the same time, however, a seminal change was taking place in the NAE's approach. "From another standpoint it can be seen that the improvement of the
general system of education in Colombia may pave the way for a more open
society in which the Gospel message might enjoy greater freedom," Clyde
Taylor explained, adding that "the long-range values must be weighed against
the short-term benefits and our policy must be governed accordingly."[163] Indeed, USAID funds increasingly supported evangelical schools, hospitals,
and scholarships to religiously based institutions.[164] Wendell Rockey noted
that the WRC, through its registration in Washington, had succeeded "in getting cash grants of $35,000.00 for Oriental Missionary Society for their build-
ing project in Hong Kong, and a grant of $85,000.00 for the Evangelical Free
Church towards the building of their hospital in Hong Kong."[165]

Throughout this period the NAE handled the foreign aid issue rather
gingerly, triangulating between placating its own stalwart separationists, denouncing Catholic abuses, and maximizing the financial and mission benefits
inherent in public aid. When the association drew up its church-state resolutions in the wake of its 1963 church-state conference, the statement on foreign aid was conspicuously absent. In this field there "appears to be no solid
wall of separation here between church and state," the draft proposal read. Although it warned that "certain co-operative involvements require continued
study and constant surveillance, such as the government payment of salaries
for persons in church welfare service and government gifts to welfare budgets," the proposed statement concluded that "it is permissible and may at
times become the duty of the church in foreign relief to distribute food to
those in countries where by law the preaching of the Gospel is prohibited."[166]

Similarly, the NAE reaction to an USAID statement on church subsidies
was indicative of an organization hedging its bets. Prompted by a letter from
a Baptist editor to President Kennedy in 1962, the NAE had directed its ire
against a USAID policy that had left large loopholes for funneling money
to church institutions.[167] In his subsequent announcement withdrawing the
statement, agency director Fowler Hamilton declared that "foreign assistance
funds may not be provided for the advancement of sectarian religious purposes." Rather than ending church subsidies, however, he promised to end
discrimination in aid provision. In surplus food distribution, technical training contracts, and educational and health assistance no funds would be ex-

pended "without prior assurance and built-in guarantees that there will be absolutely no discrimination on religious grounds in the matter of who will benefit," he declared.[168] The NAE leadership was rather pleased with this. Taylor, who was shown the statement's "first release, even before it was given out to the press," triumphantly reported that "the administrative ranks of the Agency for International Development are now quite conscious that church-state relations are of considerable importance, particularly when the White House raps their knuckles in a situation like this."[169]

The networks and funding ties pioneered in the 1950s and 1960s via the surplus food and ocean freight reimbursement programs laid the foundation for the expansion of government funding for evangelical foreign aid agencies in the 1970s, particularly in conjunction with the post-Vietnam refugee flow.[170] As explored earlier, this was also the time when support for the Vietnam War effort translated into evangelicals becoming the dominant religious group in the military. The growing involvement in Vietnam further softened the evangelicals' separationist stance as the WRC entered the relief effort in the region at the same time as Catholic, mainline, and evangelical peace church agencies—especially the Mennonite Central Committee—were having second thoughts about maintaining close ties to the U.S. government. While many mainline Protestant and secular agencies feared that they would become the extended arm of American foreign policy, the WRC and other evangelical agencies with strong anticommunist leanings "tended not to share the same hesitation as did many secular agencies to being identified with American government aid programs."[171]

In turn, while the NAE continued to oppose public funding of religiously based schools, hospitals, and welfare agencies, it was much more circumspect when it came to criticizing foreign aid. Its main concern here was to ensure that public funding did not place restrictions on proselytizing. What helped in this regard was that involvement in Vietnam further eased the pressure to separate mission from aid. Sources indicate that the WRC had little to fear from U.S. officials, who frequently saw tolerating evangelism as a small price to pay for having workers friendly to U.S. policies in the refugee camps. The pursuit of evangelism rarely produced any sustained criticism from within the American government. In many instances, in fact, it was not the government that interfered, but evangelical agencies themselves, as in the case of charges that Seventh-Day Adventists had promised pocket money in exchange for conversion.[172]

The involvement in Vietnam also indicated how dependent the WRC had become on government funds by the 1970s and the problems it faced replacing public sources of support when Congress largely discontinued the surplus food program. By the end of 1973 the WRC's worst fears had come true as the program had been almost completely discontinued. "For a period of years, we have been apprehensive," the Executive Committee admitted. It warned that despite efforts to raise more money from Christian sources the WRC was "far behind when it comes to balancing the overall budget" after the loss of government provisions. Urgent calls for reorganizations followed at the heels of the phase-out of the surplus food program.[173] However, the postwar replacement of charitable contributions by government funds had turned into a long-term problem shared by other voluntary organizations. Because of the widespread impression that it could largely rely upon government funds, the WRC continued to run into difficulties raising contributions from other sources.[174]

By the 1980s, government imperatives to expand administrative capacities and the resurgence of evangelicalism had cemented further the links between the state and conservative Protestantism in the foreign aid field. Over 70 percent of Seventh-Day Adventist and close to 40 percent of World Relief total agency income came from government sources.[175] Federal grants and contracts had also helped World Vision, the California-based evangelical relief agency established in 1952, become one of the largest international aid providers. In 1991, it alone received $19.3 million in contracts, grants, and other assistance. While Catholic agencies, as pointed out earlier, received the largest share of their income from public sources, conservative Protestants obtained a bigger share than their mainline brethren. Only a quarter of evangelical international aid organizations surveyed in the 1990s received no government funds at all, as opposed to one half of mainline Protestant agencies.[176]

Moreover, in the early 1990s fewer international aid agencies with a strong religious commitment reported problems with government in carrying out their religious mission than either less religious or secular organizations. Less than 10 percent indicated that government funds caused them to change their relief or development priorities to meet government wishes. Meanwhile, conservative Protestant organizations led the field among religious agencies in restrictive hiring and encouraging religious commitment. While a third of the agencies surveyed in the 1990s reported problems with government in carrying out their religious mission, there was strong evidence to suggest that these were minor conflicts and that USAID officials appreciated the moral framework of conservative Protestants. Citing a high-level official with a conservative Protestant international aid agency, Stephen Monsma concluded that "one does not get the picture of agency heads struggling and squirming to live up to their religious missions in the face of strong government opposition." Despite the persistence of separationist views, foreign aid clearly constituted a field of church-state relations where generous government funding not only had become the postwar norm, but also financed openly sectarian practices.[177]

*   *   *

In summation, the war years and America's postwar international entanglements provided a crucial impetus for the re-engagement of evangelicals with public policy and the state. Discovering foreign policy as a mission field, evangelicals channeled their renewed desire for political and cultural relevance into a dual process of relegitimizing evangelical views in the broader culture and interpreting the new global role of the United States via biblical concepts. As a result, while seeking to provide credibility for biblical prophesies and advocating patriotic conversionism, they ended up linking the domestic spiritual awakening to the exercise of America's global power. And though denouncing the iniquities and worldliness of American society, their superpatriotism spiritualized liberal capitalism and the American way of life. Moreover, particularly in presenting Christian teachings as the only effective antidote to communism, evangelicals decoupled the threat to religious freedom from the expansion of the national security state. They not only depicted traditional Protestantism as the genuine civil religion of the United States, but also sanctified the military buildup.

This, however, contrasted markedly with the isolationist tradition that had dominated evangelicalism until the 1940s. In this tradition, faith in the "redeemer nation" was balanced by separationist pietism, support for the "garrison state" by pacifism, and the embrace of American-style liberal capitalism by sentiments critical of the iniquities of the market. Seeking to reconcile these divergent impulses, evangelicals continued to preserve separationist, unilateralist, and exceptionalist positions while simultaneously sanctifying Cold War anticommunist foreign policy. They fervently attacked the UN by invoking biblical prophesies that linked the rise of the Antichrist to the emergence of world government. Their deep-seated anti-Catholicism, which rarely differentiated between Moscow and the Vatican, was at odds with the pluralistic reality of American life and only gradually gave way to the more transdenominational campaigns to promote religious liberty. Despite steadfast support for Israel, their biblical demand for the conversion of the Jews and expectation of cataclysmic warfare retained traditional anti-Semitic sentiments. And although evangelicals sought to tone down indiscriminate red-baiting, their rabid anticommunism justified some of the worst excesses of McCarthyism.

Although the immediate political influence of evangelicals was quite limited, their commitment to patriotism, anticommunism, and military strength paved the way for new contacts between religious and political circles in Washington, particularly during the Eisenhower administration. As the defense needs of the Cold War state, in conjunction with the political awakening of evangelicalism, laid the foundation for new organizational fields, funding ties developed between the two in the national security arena. The expansion of the evangelical military chaplaincy, efforts to strengthen the anticommunist and moral training of recruits, and support for NAE-led evangelization campaigns within the army were decisive factors in establishing contacts between church and state. In addition, the promotion of church building on military sites and the distribution of conservative religious materials via USIA and other government agencies furthered the influence of evangelicals. What is more, foreign aid subsidiarity strengthened the ties between government agencies and the NAE. Pioneered in the 1940s and 1950s via the DP resettlement program and surplus food distribution, World Relief and other evangelical aid organizations established thriving administrative and funding relationships with government. These expanded further in conjunction with the post-Vietnam withdrawal of more liberal agencies from government support arrangements.

These ties created not only valuable access to government, but also pioneered the re-evaluation of traditional church-state attitudes. As military and humanitarian goals came together, evangelical foreign aid organizations were allowed to link food distribution to proselytizing, and public funds were often used to finance school buildings, hospital construction, and scholarships at religiously based institutions. This absence of effective restrictions on evangelizing abroad, together with denominational competition, identification with U.S. foreign policy goals, and desire for agency growth, ushered in a change in evangelicalism's strong separationist identity. As traditional fears of breaching church-state boundaries were replaced by the desire for spiritualized foreign aid under public funding arrangements, discussions within evangelicalism concentrated on the autonomy of evangelical agencies and their equal access to foreign aid funds, rather than on concerns about big government. Moreover, as the next chapter shows, the subsidiarist links between the state and conservative Protestantism in the foreign aid arena provided the template for the gradual development of similar ties in the social policy domain.

CHAPTER 4

EVANGELICALS, SOCIAL POLICY, AND THE WELFARE STATE

The broadly supportive attitude of evangelicals toward the national security state contrasted sharply with their rhetorical hostility to the postwar welfare state. While neither the growth of defense-related government bureaucracies nor anticommunist excesses enraged the majority of evangelicals, the expansion of state social responsibilities apparently generated tremendous trepidation. Evangelicals traditionally feared that the growth of government welfare functions and funding threatened church agencies, undermined spiritual approaches to deprivation, and encouraged immoral behavior. They argued that it jeopardized the separation of church and state and benefited a self-interested liberal elite of bureaucrats and social welfare professionals. Since conservative Protestants saw spiritual conversion, rather than social engineering and material redistribution, as the main aim of social policy, they mostly regarded welfare as more properly a church function.[1] In the words of *United Evangelical Action* editor James DeForest Murch, "The NAE is critical of socialistic trends in politics and economics including the welfare state. The average evangelical senses a humanistic and materialistic philosophy [underlying] these trends. The New Testament emphasizes basically individual responsibility."[2]

Fundamentalists were even more adamant in their antistatism. Contrasting charitable giving with the alleged materialistic conception of the welfare state, the Church League of America's Edgar C. Bundy denounced government provision as a massive collectivist scheme in which "controlling elements of the U.S. government, of the monolithic National Council of churches, of the great denominations, and of powerful foundations are bound together in an unpregnable [sic] interlock." This, he concluded, showed that "where political forces move in on church affairs, the preaching of Christian doctrine of individual salvation is of necessity silenced."[3]

In taking this unequivocal antistatist rhetoric literally, research on evangelicalism has rarely questioned the hostility of conservative Protestants to the welfare state. However, while a strong antiwelfarist stance was a core element of neo-evangelical rhetoric and self-image, evidence from the Cold War decades tells a slightly different story. Indeed, religious conservatism did not necessarily translate into support for conservative economic policies, and the history of the evangelical vote shows that many evangelicals remained generally supportive of the New Deal welfare state, the politics of economic growth, and the government-subsidized military-industrial complex. Moreover, their fear of despotic government was increasingly counterbalanced by their calls for the state to take a moral stance.[4] Although Carl Henry saw government not as the appropriate mechanism for enforcing particular moral values, in opposing easy divorce, liberalized abortion, extramarital sex, and homosexuality he simultaneously believed that state intervention could help ward off violations of godly ethics.[5] In short, the tension between traditional separationism on the one hand, and support for the Cold War state and calls for a "Christian government" to be an agent of morality on the other, were more characteristic of evangelical attitudes than outright antistatism.

This ambivalence came to the fore in the movement's heated disputes about the growing public funding of religious providers. Though largely ignored in scholarship, the evangelical debates about subsidiarity were crucial in transforming church-state attitudes and facilitating a new relationship to the welfare state. They show that the very basis upon which evangelicals sought to assert their separationist stance simultaneously laid the foundation for a much softer approach to church-state funding ties. While evangelicals vociferously denounced the Catholic church for its willingness to take public funds, they gradually modeled their own approach on Catholic precedent. Although they tried to hold on to their distinctive separationism, they increasingly found themselves at odds with the secularist implications of this position, particularly in the aftermath of the school prayer and Bible reading decisions of the Supreme Court in the early 1960s. Seeking to build up their institutional infrastructure, conservative Protestant organizations on the ground increasingly partook in public funding streams notwithstanding church pronouncements that ran counter to such involvement. And although they feared the effects of increased oversight and regulation through federal agencies, evangelicals increasingly recognized that subsidiarist funding arrangements provided extensive administrative leeway and encouraged a spiritualized approach to solving social problems. What differentiated conservative Protestants from other religious groups in the end was not their refusal to accept public funds, but that they retained their separationist rhetoric and self-image in spite of closer ties to the state.

Evangelical Support for the Welfare State

Evangelical grassroots attitudes to the postwar welfare state were characterized by broad political agreement mixed with growing cultural unease. As suggested in Chapter 2, evangelicals largely embraced the basic axioms of the Cold War welfare state, including deficit spending, macroeconomic planning, and Social Security.[6] A 1956 *Christianity Today* survey of Protestant clergy, for example, revealed significant support for strengthening Social Security laws, increasing old age benefits, and curtailing military spending.[7] Likewise, in the 1960s Billy Graham backed the War on Poverty and called for "modestly expanding social awareness."[8] As Kenneth Bailey noted in his 1964 study of southern white Protestants, "a majority of the scattered comments on economic policy which now appeared in the religious press were sympathetic toward New Deal regulatory and welfare programs."[9]

Similarly, George Wallace's 1968 presidential campaign attracted a significant evangelical following with a platform that embraced Social Security increases, better health care, and the right to collective bargaining. Seeing himself as a champion of the average man against the power of wealth and privilege, Wallace and his American Independent Party eschewed economic conservatism. Jerome Himmelstein labeled his agenda a "neopopulist combination of statist economics with social conservatism."[10] *National Review* was less subtle, calling it "Country and Western Marxism."[11] Moreover, conservative denominations gradually revised traditional attitudes that considered Social Security coverage of ministers and other church employees a violation of church-state separation.[12] The result was that by 1972 an attack on Social Security unleashed a torrent of protest letters from evangelicals.[13] In effect, evangelicals had accepted "a level of government activity and involvement unknown a hundred years ago."[14]

Jimmy Carter's political stance equally illustrated that being a full-fledged evangelical did not mean being an economic or political conservative. Although in 1980 Carter lost many of the evangelical Protestant votes he had gained in 1976, a majority of evangelicals still opted for him.[15] Even disenchantment with the Carter presidency and the shift to Reagan in 1980 was not accompanied by a fundamental reorientation in the political views of many evangelicals.[16] A 1986 straw poll among *Christianity Today* readers, for example, showed that 73 percent called for more federal money to be spent on cleaning up the environment, 49 percent supported "having the federal government provide more low interest loans and subsidies to small farmers," 42 percent called for the federal government to take a stronger role in mediating racial tensions, 38 percent supported raising taxes to pay for deficit reduction, and 35 percent backed federal day-care legislation.[17]

Despite the consolidation of the Republican vote among evangelicals by 1988, George Gallup found that, although evangelicals were considerably more conservative than non-evangelicals on lifestyle matters, such as abortion, homosexuality, and school prayer, they were slightly more liberal on a range of economic issues. Seventy-four percent of non-evangelicals, but 83 percent of evangelicals, favored raising the minimum wage. Seventy-one percent of non-evangelicals, but 72 percent of evangelicals, favored increased spending on programs for the elderly. Nine percent of non-evangelicals supported cutting entitlement programs to reduce the deficit, but only 8 percent of evangelicals did. In the same vein, large minorities of evangelicals identified with causes such as environmentalism (39 percent) and civil rights (33 percent), and two-thirds supported the Equal Rights Amendment.[18]

Although evangelicals were at the tail end of a list of groups advocating government spending, still over half (52 percent) of white evangelicals—only marginally fewer than non-evangelical Protestants (54 percent)—favored increased government expenditure for various social programs, such as Social Security, health care, aid for the homeless, and help for the elderly. On replacing Social Security with a private insurance program, Catholics and white evangelicals were evenly divided. Likewise, all religious groups in the 1988 elections were more likely to vote for candidates that supported public works programs and automatic cost-of-living increases in Social Security and federal pensions. Overall, the Gallup polls revealed that non-evangelicals and the religiously unaffiliated, rather than evangelicals, were the ones who were most clearly opposed to expanded government programs.[19] As one study put it, "Even with controls, the standardized coefficients show that the orthodox are more liberal on government job provision, spending on Social Security, giving profits to workers over shareholders, and trust in organized labor."[20] In fact, Gallup's findings on the 1988 elections indicated that, as far as evangelicals were concerned, "Democratic candidates are not hurt by, and are actually helped by, relatively liberal economic programs."[21]

This attachment to New Deal policies suggests that evangelical political attitudes reflected traditional economic indicators. Surveys that connect religious orientation to socioeconomic status and political partisanship show that evangelicals, like most people with lower incomes and from less advantaged backgrounds, were more likely to support government social programs to aid the poor, favored increased social spending, and advocated the redistribution of wealth.[22] A high percentage of evangelicals (39 percent) could be found among what George Gallup calls "moralists"—mainly middle-aged, middle-income, white, suburban, and rural or small town Republicans who oppose abortion, embrace school prayer, and support social spending except when targeted at minorities. Meanwhile, only 22 percent of evangelicals are among the most pro-business and antigovernment "enterprisers." Similarly, while the percentage of white evangelicals among "1960s Democrats," who make up 8 percent of the adult population, is low (13 percent), the percentage among "New Deal Democrats" (11 percent of the adult population) is significantly higher (25 percent). The latter group often consists of blue-collar voters who support social spending but are conservative on questions of personal lifestyles.[23]

These findings suggest that in spite of the large-scale partisan realignments since the 1980s there is no clear relationship between orthodox biblical views and attitudes toward government and social welfare. In effect, evangelicals were much more economically progressive, and antistatist sentiments much less important to evangelical political identification, than is commonly assumed. Though many observers expect religious conservatives to take antistatist positions, generally only a minority in this electorate opposed government welfare efforts.[24]

The Ambiguities of Evangelical Social Thought

This subcutaneous support for the welfare state, however, clashed with the ideological dynamics of the evangelical social awakening in the postwar decades. As pointed out in Chapter 2, evangelicals sought to position themselves between prewar fundamentalism and mainline Protestantism. Their renewed forages into the welfare field constituted a crucial aspect of this desire to carve out a neo-evangelical identity. It was distinct not only from the isolationist pietism of the fundamentalists but also from the social gospel of the mainline Protestants. Carl Henry, for example, criticized in the 1950s that

fundamentalists had made the great mistake of allowing liberals and secularists to capture the social reform field for their ideology.[25] Meanwhile, Clyde
Taylor denounced the social gospel and its alleged support for the materialistic premises of the welfare state. "Men whose religion was a social gospel and
whose purpose was to transform the social order," he raged, "might well be so
deeply involved in socialism in general that they could easily be mistaken for
communists and at the very least they would give considerable consolation to
the communists who are constantly preaching state socialism."[26]

Hence, as neo-evangelicals renewed their commitment to social witness in the postwar period, they reasserted traditional social attitudes and
denounced the growth of the welfare state. They depicted church-based
charitable work as face-to-face giving based on personalized compassion and
sympathy, contrasting it with the cold, uncaring, impersonal state-run systems.[27] Their focus was on getting evangelicals to enter the political process
in pursuit of Christian and moral issues, rather than in search of social and
political transformation.[28] "We do not want the Church into politics, only its
members as U.S. citizens," OPA director Taylor explained in a radio broadcast
in 1954.[29] According to Henry, a new generation of evangelicals needed to
reclaim the field of social reform based on a program of redemptive regenera-
tion. By reconstructing social policies on the basis of individual conversion,
a focus on the family, and moral values, he maintained, evangelicalism could
achieve both respectability and infuse Christian meanings into the welfare
debate.[30]

The key objective for evangelicals, who regarded poverty as a moral
rather than a social problem, was therefore to connect biblical themes, spiritual concerns, and character issues to the policy discourse. They tended to
see welfare recipients either as trapped and dependent, or as ruthlessly calcu-
lating. Since in their view the root causes of human ills were the sinful heart
and mind, expressed either in the surrender to worldly passions or the cult
of human rationality, genuine social reform could not be effected through
the redistribution of wealth, income maintenance programs, or comprehensive bureaucratic solutions to poverty. Instead, individual moral conversion
was the sole foundation of social change. Steeped in Augustinian thought,
evangelicals emphasized the limits of human agency and the power of divine
intervention revealed in stories of sin and salvation, despair and conversion,
dependency and liberation, repentance and reformation, and awakening and
sanctification.[31]

At the center of evangelical social thought was thus the goal of creating a moral community of converted individuals. Ironically, however, this inner spiritual change was supposed to manifest itself in what amounted to the embrace of culture-specific moral norms that had developed historically, especially in the context of the confluence of nineteenth-century evangelicalism and market society. Regarding work as the cornerstone of nurturing individual moral responsibility, evangelicals located the solution to poverty in creating entrepreneurial individuals whose behavior was guided by middle-class values. Ultimately, evangelical character talk was thus an expression of the close association of bourgeois social norms of self-help, productivity, and competitive achievement, and the religious demand for self-control, personal piety, and stable community and family life.[32]

At the same time, this evangelical combination of bourgeois norms and spiritual conversion, however, contained a tension between the goal of disciplining the poor and the aim of converting and rehabilitating them. On the one hand, *agape*-driven social service is generous and caring in trying to effect conversion based on unmediated love. It believes in the basic dignity, freedom, and moral potential of the aid recipient and is marked by what Richard Hofstadter once called a "breadth of feeling" and a "shallowness of social analysis."[33] On the other hand, evangelical *caritas* and its emphasis on moral norms can be merciless in its stigmatization of those seen as wayward and undeserving. It blames the poor for their fate and for bringing moral corruption upon the community. Combining nineteenth-century laissez-faire liberalism with traditional Calvinist dispositions, this impulse seeks to discipline the pauper, impose work requirements, and regulate individual moral conduct. It sees charity more as a legal than a moral obligation, distinguishes rigidly between the deserving and undeserving poor, and regards poverty as punishment or as self-inflicted.[34] Scrupulously utilitarian, it is obsessed with the worthiness of clients and the cold calculation of benefits so that the indolent will not find relief more rewarding than work.[35]

Whether they talked about combining compassion with coercion or "honest, tough love," evangelicals in effect embraced a contradictory approach to social reform in pursuing the moral salvation of the poor while assuming their moral decrepitude. In the final analysis, the old nineteenth-century conflict between the economistic concerns of scientific philanthropy, with its emphasis on accounting methods, measurable outcomes, rationalized procedures, and cost effectiveness, and the humanitarian impulses of religious charity, which desired to relieve suffering first and ask questions later, remains one of the central features of the evangelical welfare ideology.[36]

The idea of "social rights," however, is almost completely absent in evangelical social thought. Charity, unlike grace, is not freely given. It is not a rightful entitlement, but a gift.

While on the surface operating on antiwelfarist premises, this built-in ambivalence actually resulted in a conflicted attitude toward the exercise of state power. On the one hand, belief in the ministry of the church and spiritualized approaches to poverty reinforced the doctrine of separation and limited government. "Ideally the purpose of the state is to preserve justice, not to implement benevolence; ideally, the purpose of the church is to preach the Gospel and to manifest unmerited, compassionate love," Carl Henry maintained. Dissolving "righteousness into love" and diluting "social justice into compassion," he concluded, "not only destroys the biblical view of God on the one hand but also produces the welfare state on the other."[37] As a 1966 NAE circular declared, "just because the state has elected to become more deeply involved in welfare is no justification for us to become unequally 'yoked' with the state even though we may have common objectives in some areas such as welfare and education."[38] In turn, neo-evangelicals were initially among the most outspoken critics of public funding for religious agencies. In February 1959, Henry devoted a long article in *Christianity Today* to outlining the dangers of the growing reliance of Protestant churches on federal monies.[39] Likewise, Clyde Taylor made the separationist stance and opposition to the welfare state a linchpin of evangelical identity: "It seems to us that the whole doctrine of the separation of church and state is being put under growing pressure and every effort is being made to break down this wall. Any government that is determined to take care of its citizens sooner or later will get into the area of supporting sectarian religion unless the public is very vigilant."[40]

On the other hand, however, antiwelfarist sentiments were part of a critique of the social gospel, rather than of the power of the state as such. In particular, the obsession with the moral worthiness of clients potentially legitimized punitive state intervention and approved of the state's enforcement of moral standards.[41] "Although liberal churchmen will throw their energies behind a public health program," Henry criticized, "they tend to remain silent about many of the personal vices." Arguing that to evangelicals "the best alternative to the 'welfare' state is the just state," he left the door open for the same bureaucratic intrusion evangelicals had otherwise denounced.[42]

By the same token, the emphasis on Christian government raised the question whether the state should play a role in funding the charitable service providers that would impart the moral values necessary for the poor to develop a work ethic, be self-disciplined, and overcome "dependency." Already in the late 1950s, a *Christianity Today* editorial by Carl Henry on the cozy ties between liberal philanthropic foundations and the state both described the evangelical dilemma and sketched out the changing NAE policy. Initially, the article extended the ubiquitous criticism of Catholic efforts to secure public funds to the big liberal philanthropies, particularly the Ford, Rockefeller, and Russell Sage Foundations. It raised concerns about the rise of a "new class" of administrators who switched back and forth between foundations and government. On top of this, it denounced the alleged communist infiltration of foundations, their lack of moral absolutes, their support for research critical of capitalism and Christianity, and their preference for "totalitarian thinking over against the principle of limited government." This argument, however, set the stage for a discursive shift from simple denunciations of government funding toward demands for the right *kind* of institutions as the recipients of support. In a thinly veiled reference to evangelical institutions, the editorial demanded that the "imbalance" be rectified and argued that tax exemptions should not "undermine liberties" but needed to "strengthen the moral pillars on which our free society rests." If support for foundations that "oppose radical and leftist policies and programs" had existed, Henry concluded, "the destinies of our decade might now be different." The magazine thus not only urged conservative Protestants to set up counterinstitutions, but also implicitly put government policies in charge of "the reinforcement of those evangelical spiritual (and moral) ideals . . . of the American heritage."[43]

As this dual set of tensions—between political support for New Deal-style policies and ideological opposition to the welfare state, and between separationism and the moral state—unfolded, the adoption of a consistent evangelical policy on church-state relations was becoming ever more pressing.[44] Carl Henry in particular criticized that evangelicals had "developed no Bible-based ethic impinging on the basis, method, and function of social structures and groups such as the state, labor movements and business corporations, minorities and so on."[45] He urged his fellow believers not only to spell out specific positions on church-state issues, but also to clarify whether these were "principles inherent in revealed religion," "practical inferences from such principles," or "prudential positions distinguished from such principles."[46] With pressure mounting, the NAE executive committee recommended in November 1960 Taylor's call for a special conference "to discuss our evangelical concept of separation of church and state" and to consider the issue of "State Welfare versus Church responsibility in the field of welfare."[47]

By the early 1960s the internal church-state debates thus coalesced around a number of NAE conferences. Although they covered a wide range of issues, stretching from the faltering government campaign against communism via birth control legislation to tax exemption, one subject dominated the discussions: the expansion of government funding for nonprofits and the participation of religious organizations in the subsidiarist welfare state.[48] As Henry declared, "what is at stake is more than an indictment of Roman Catholic and Protestant attraction to staggering Federal monies to church enterprises, but the necessary definition of the Protestant philosophy of social welfare and the formulation of guiding principles of application."[49] The reawakening of evangelical social concern in the context of the rise of public-private funding arrangements thus brought the issue of subsidiarity to the forefront of intrachurch discussions. As it turned out, however, what started out as an effort to reassert separationist doctrine in light of the lack of clear evangelical pronouncements and policies in regard to state funding ended up providing qualified evangelical support for the subsidiarist state.

Subsidiarity and the Transformation of Evangelical Church-State Attitudes

In February 1961 a small group of leading NAE figures met in the Hotel Continental in Washington to discuss church-state relations in light of the apparent permanence and likely expansion of government welfare services. Participants included R. L. Decker, George Ford, Donald Gill, Rufus Jones, W. S. Mooneyham, James DeForest Murch, and Clyde Taylor.[50] The meeting, which constituted "probably the most significant action of the [Evangelical Action] Commission" in that year, indicated that the NAE was seeking to define its church-state stance as part of its positioning as a third force in American Protestantism.[51] "In a republic we have even greater obligation to use our citizenship for the glory of God and the good of men," historian Earl Cairns declared. Suggesting that evangelicals use "flexible tactics" for a "limited strategy" in the process of Christianizing the social order, he noted that social action need not be divorced from the hope for Christ's return. The evangelical expectation of "a cataclysmic, supernatural cleansing of earth," he argued, both prevented "a despair which feels that nothing can be done in a perishing world" and "a false optimism which looks for the creation of utopia by human effort in the manner of the Social Gospel."[52]

Henry's contribution to the 1961 conference revealed the strength of ambivalent feelings among evangelicals regarding public funding. Rather than welcoming the opportunity to spread the gospel via state-supported church agencies, Henry warned about the possible implications of "appending of a sectarian religious witness . . . to government-subsidized welfare." Was this not "widening the expectation that welfare is a responsibility of the State rather than of voluntary contributions?," he asked, raising the specter that "advancing sectarian prestige on the edge of government expenditures" would sacrifice the religious content of welfare as such. If state provision were to expand on the basis of an inherent connection between secular welfare and Christian witness, he warned, recipients might no longer regard welfare services as a "love-gift" but as a legal obligation from the state.[53]

Despite valiant efforts the 1961 meeting failed to draft clear church-state principles in this particular area. The planned statements on tax exemption, aid to higher education, and aid to education were deferred.[54] Instead, the EAC asked the Board of Administration to authorize a broader-based conference on church-state relations. By the spring of 1963, with the Kennedy administration's social policies in full swing, the NAE organized the National Conference on Church-State Relations at Winona Lake, Indiana. Anticipating an attendance of up to 150 evangelical leaders, the conference was called "for the purpose of surveying the field of Church-State relations in the USA, reaching conclusions in each area, and drafting proposed policy consistent with our evangelical principles."[55] Held in coordination with similar meetings organized by state organizations of the NAE, the conference provided a detailed review of the historical, theological, constitutional, and practical issues involved in spelling out an official position. Moreover, it aimed to formulate consistent policies that had so far been lacking. Noting that a findings committee had been appointed to achieve an NAE policy and program, Murch saw the conference as the "most comprehensive, scholarly and definitive discussion of Church-State Relations ever held by a major evangelical body in recent years."[56]

The church-state conferences were pivotal in the wider evangelical debate about subsidiarity that shaped the movement's emergent political ideology. As public funding for religious agencies became the main focus of evangelical concern, four interrelated themes rose to the top of the agenda: the fear of Catholics taking the lion's share of new public funds; concerns about the growth of secularism; worries over the financial situation of religious agencies; and questions about the autonomy of sectarian agencies under subsidiarist funding arrangements. On all four counts postwar evangelicals started out by noisily denouncing public funding of religious agencies. In the end, however, anti-Catholicism, antisecularism, financial concerns, and the administrative experience with subsidiarity gradually softened the separationist dogma.

Anti-Catholicism

Since the 1930s and 1940s the campaign against Catholic pressure for increased public aid for religious agencies had been at the center of evangelical political activism in opposition to the growth of the welfare state.[57] In particular, the expansion of federal funding for sectarian health care, higher education, social welfare, and foreign aid in the postwar period raised anew the old specter of Roman Catholic dominance. Decrying government subsidies to Catholic churches via urban renewal and surplus property donations, Clyde Taylor concluded that "this struggle into the foreseeable future will always have anti-Roman Church overtones."[58] Linking separationist diatribes with dire warnings about the pernicious power of "Romanism" and its "planned infiltration" that threatened religious liberty and the republican order, evangelicals viewed legislation promoting public funding for religious providers as a Catholic conspiracy to effect a church-state combine.[59]

Catholic efforts to secure federal aid for parochial schools and religious hospitals, Taylor warned, pointed to "efforts of the Roman Church to promote Church-State union with the church dominant." Noting that restrictions on Bible distribution, the teaching of evolution, and the Catholic influence in elections and on city school boards had significantly weakened Protestant influence, he admonished evangelicals in 1954 to get involved politically.[60] He defined the role of the OPA accordingly in 1957: "In general, evangelicals have been alerted to the tactics and acts of the American Roman Catholic hierarchy to use every legal loophole to advance the cause of their church, whether it be by securing Hill-Burton funds to put up hospitals, the FHA to buy land, special legislation to get an 8–million dollar gift for their work in the Philippines, or raiding federal, state, and local treasuries wherever possible."[61]

Among the most astute critics of subsidiarity and leading anti-Catholic fearmongers was C. Stanley Lowell. Closely allied with the NAE through his position as associate director of POAU and editor of its monthly magazine, *Church & State*, Lowell denounced the United States for fraudulently "approaching a practical union of church and state while loudly and even earnestly proclaiming separation of the two." While churchmen thought they were obtaining benefits for their institutions, he saw a state using the church to achieve secular aims in defense and welfare policy. He charged that government disguised the true extent of this "backdoor establishment of religion" via a "strategy of deceit and circumvention." This strategy, in his view, included providing aid to individuals rather than institutions; insisting on the separation between religious and secular provision; defending devolved funding on the basis of cost efficiency; and calling on the church to aid in national defense and in the war against poverty. In this way state aid both pretended to preserve the vestiges of sectarian independence and sustained with tax funds a vast institutional spread of the church.[62]

In this "inchoate amalgam of government and religion" in the welfare field, Lowell explained, "the church abandons its innovative role and merges with the state's bureaucracy" and "the clergy become agents of the state quite as surely as police and firemen, and parish organizations become little Tammany Halls." In his view, this produced "a kind of religio-political operation for people service" where taxpayers paid not only for the service but also for the church. "They are paying for it under attractive guises and to the accompaniment of pleasant sounds," he concluded," but they are paying for it all the same."[63]

By the 1960s, as reports on "Roman Catholic infiltration of government agencies" and "staggering increases in Roman Catholic appointments to public office" multiplied, countering Catholic influence in government moved to the center of the NAE's strategy of evangelical political mobilization.[64] The campaign, however, began to shift from denouncing public funding to highlighting the discriminatory effects on evangelical Protestants of legislation pushed by Catholic, Jewish, and mainline Protestant lobbies.[65] Evoking traditional Protestant fears of the sinister activities of the Catholic church, Taylor in 1960 reported an incident where the children of a Presbyterian widower were taken away by their Catholic uncle. "We might remind ourselves that this is being done at the demand and order of the same church that is seeking to establish its control here in the United States," he declared.[66] Similarly, in his presentation at the 1963 church-state conference he pointed out cases of "flagrant religious discrimination" against Protestants in government agencies. He also painted a frightening scenario of school boards handed over to the Catholic church, parochial schools run at public expense, and Protestants forced to attend schools where Catholicism was taught. "Any Protestant starting litigation is apt to have farm buildings burned or risk other violence," he warned.[67]

The NAE's anti-Catholic campaign of political mobilization, packaged in the rhetoric of church-state separation and the defense of religious liberty, reached a fever pitch in the run-up to the 1960 elections. Together with POAU, the NAE joined the camp of militant anti-Kennedy activists. "We know that Romanists do not accept the separation of the Church and state," Carl Henry editorialized, "we know that they constantly seek tax money for their own uses."[68] After consultations with POAU, Taylor lauded the organization's program that consisted mainly of mass mailings, public rallies, church study groups, and buying advertising space, but also included producing a film designed to show "the total lack of support of separation of church and state by the Roman Catholic hierarchy." Noting that POAU was going to follow "the line that the American people will have to determine if a vote for Mr. Kennedy as President will accelerate the current drift toward Roman clerical tyranny in America," Murch and Taylor suggested that the NAE should make use of its materials. They recommended employing POAU as a front organization so that it "carried the brunt" while enabling NAE "to do a very effective piece of work." At the same time, they implored their fellow evangelicals to avoid "at all costs" personal references to Kennedy and to make the campaign "a matter of principle, a matter of separation of church and state."[69]

The terrifying predictions generated by Kennedy's election did not come true, of course, and the shrill anti-Catholic campaign tone gradually subsided in its wake. After the election *United Evangelical Action* editor Murch declared that there was a sense among Protestant leaders that Roman Catholicism "is now different in America, and that the Protestant concept of Roman Catholicism is outmoded." The issue of church-state relations, however, did not disappear. Instead, Murch argued that it was time for a new evangelical strategy. This included consistent policies on the role of religion in public schools, federal aid to parochial schools, and on evangelical colleges and hospitals. It also encompassed tax exemptions and legislation affecting the family, including divorce and birth control.[70] In the same vein, Clyde Taylor was both sanguine and vigilant when it came to working with the new administration. Although evangelicals needed to monitor Catholic efforts to get subsidies, he was hopeful about the ability to thwart these aspirations. Evangelicals had people on the inside "who understand and will help," he surmised. "The top brass has shifted, but the middle men and women (the ones who know the ropes and do the work) are still right there."[71]

Nonetheless, anti-Catholicism remained virulent in the NAE beyond the Kennedy election and the Second Vatican Council. Despite acknowledging the growing cooperation of Catholics and Protestants, evangelicals kept accusing Catholicism of being "a strange mixture of half truth and half error."[72] Fighting Catholic infiltration of government agencies and federal aid to parochial schools continued to be evangelical priorities in the aftermath of the 1960 elections. They were only matched by concerns over "drives to weaken anti-Communist activities in the U.S. Government" and "international Communism and its effects on missionary activities."[73] In one respect the pre-election fears had come true, Taylor declared: "The Church of Rome *does* try to pressure a national leader to act against both his conscience and his promise."[74] Criticizing Catholics for involving themselves "more and more in political, economic and especially the welfare matters of our government," evangelicals warned in 1966 that their adversaries' "monolithic strength and size, their political power and the penetration of government" threatened to "override any controls that the government might try to exercise over them." As more public funds were made available through Great Society legislation, Catholic agencies were "using government funds in their hospital programs, in the new poverty program established by the government (including pre-school education) and in seeking every way possible involvement with the government and government funds for their educational system."[75]

Outwardly, anti-Catholicism was thus tantamount to evangelicals affirming their commitment to church-state separation. After chronicling the "massive drive for state aid to private and parochial schools," which he viewed as "a power thrust of the bishops of the Roman Catholic Church," C. Stanley Lowell urged participants of the 1963 church-state conference to stand "steadfastly and unequivocally and unapologetically for the present construction of the First Amendment."[76] However, it was not just *Catholic* aspirations Lowell and others were up against. As subsidiarity was becoming the norm, competitive pressures on all other religious organizations to take state aid increased dramatically, and even Lowell had to acknowledge the growing appeal of the Catholic position.[77] By 1963, POAU executive director Glenn L. Archer assailed mainline Protestants for "a posture of craven and fawning accommodation toward the Roman Catholic Church, which is the greatest enemy of Church-State separation in the world."[78] And Murch noted with chagrin that "economic pressures" had "forced wide acceptance and the weakening of a consistent position" on state aid, adding that many mainline Protestants were "finding common ground with Roman Catholic social welfare agencies and beginning to speak the Church-State language of the 'new Catholicism' in dealing with the government." As a result, "all sorts of compromises with the principle of Separation of Church and State are made in order to get the huge sums which are constantly being appropriated." In their wake, the "traditional resistance of the public to direct aid to church agencies of all sorts is being psychologically weakened" and the wall of separation eroded.[79] Not mincing his words, Taylor put it more bluntly: "Their example is contagious, and Protestants and other groups are being infected."[80]

In bemoaning the effectiveness of the Catholic church and the weakness of a divided Protestantism, evangelicals implicitly recognized the successes of organized Catholicism in obtaining federal money and getting its voice heard. On this basis, anti-Catholic sentiment gradually ushered in a fundamental shift in evangelical engagement with the state. Employing a dual strategy, evangelicals on the one hand affirmed their commitment to separationism, continued to expose Catholic infringements, and denounced perceived threats to Protestant providers. On the other hand, they increasingly looked for ways of matching the effectiveness of Catholics in lobbying for and receiving public funds. As subsidizing nongovernmental agencies became ever more ubiquitous, focusing on the potential benefits of public funding gradually overshadowed concerns with preserving the separation of church and state.

Evangelicals thus simultaneously opposed Catholic policies and used them as a means for revising their own separationist doctrine. "Either Christians who love the Lord are going to take Christ into the political life of our nation or the increasing infiltration of Roman Catholic power will take our place," Taylor exclaimed.[81] Others went further. There was no clear biblical basis for strict separation of church and state, Joseph M. Dawson, a Southern Baptist and expert on church-state relations, pointed out in *Christianity Today*. Instead, separationism was a doctrine that had been developed by left-wing Puritans in a specific historical context. Dawson even argued that separationism did not stand in the way of the extension of government welfare services, including Social Security, veterans' benefits, housing, health care, education, agricultural subsidies, and controls on monopolies.[82] Moreover, he noted that nineteenth-century Protestantism had nurtured close organizational and ideological ties to government. Its rhetorical insistence on the separation of church and state originated in the anti-Catholic campaigns of the time, rather than in theological doctrine. Separationism was thus mainly a sociopolitical legitimization of Protestant dominance in response to challenges posed by the mainstreamization of Catholicism.[83]

Antisecularism

In addition to anti-Catholicism, the battle against "secular humanism" shaped the neo-evangelical revision of traditional separationism. Evangelicals viewed Western culture as locked in a struggle between worldviews based on Scripture and those based on atheistic naturalistic assumptions.[84] In presenting themselves as a force challenging the alleged dominance of the latter, however, evangelicals not only stressed the religious roots of the American political system and the links between religious and political liberty, but also increasingly concluded that "in abandoning social concern they had left the field to the secular state."[85] Calling for NAE representation at the White House Conference on Children and Youth in 1960, for example, Taylor argued that this would counter the "the whole approach to the problem" that was "humanistic and to a very large degree socialistic, or that of a welfare state."[86]

As fears of secularism became a central theme in evangelical politics, a crucial shift in evangelical attitudes to the subsidiarist welfare state occurred. Instead of attacking government as such, evangelicals decried the extent to which "the effort of agnostics, atheists, and misguided zealots who misinterpret separation of Church and State, to take all religion out of government" threatened the spiritual dimension of social policy.[87] Linking evangelicalism's assorted enemies, Taylor regarded "creeping secularism" as another facet of the communist threat and as "the other side of the question" of the Roman Catholic grab for public funds.[88] In the same vein, a statement issued by the Committee on Historical Precedent during the 1961 church-state conference noted that the "'wall of separation' does not demand irreligion or hostility to religion by the state, but is rather a friendly separation. It is evident that the founding fathers had no desire to separate the state from God, but to prohibit it from being tied to any institution of religion."[89]

The landmark 1962 and 1963 Supreme Court decisions outlawing prayer (*Engel v. Vitale*) and Bible reading in public schools (*Abington Township School District v. Schempp*) both exacerbated evangelical fears of the secularist capture of the state and further softened their traditional separationism. Although the NAE supported the narrow legal basis upon which the Supreme Court had ruled the Regent's Prayer in New York schools unconstitutional, the organization increasingly warned that "a tiny minority, made up of atheists and agnostics, is using this means to superimpose an implicit secularism upon our public institutions."[90] In his review of the court cases, NAE general director George Ford noted that the "public school yard is probably about the bloodiest battleground in this present conflict between Church and State." Although he continued to express concerns about a state religion, he no longer regarded this as the only danger in a battle that pitted "the pluralistic religious nature of the society" against the "establishment of sectarian secularism as the religion of the land."[91] Summing up the emergent direction in church-state thinking, NAE executive director R. L. Decker warned in 1963 that the "complete observance of separation of Church and State often times seem to evangelicals to be encouragements toward the development of a purely secular state."[92]

The depth of these sentiments became apparent at the NAE's Annual Convention later that year. In response to the Court's decisions, delegates passed a resolution declaring that "the resulting revolutionary changes in long-established practices are beginning to create a moral and religious vacuum in our education system in which secularism, humanism, practical atheism and amorality are beginning to take root and thrive." In their view, this threatened "the very foundations of our society and the welfare of the nation." Although the executive committee of the EAC had suggested a more limited proposal, a majority of convention delegates endorsed a campaign for a constitutional amendment that would "allow reference to, belief in, reliance upon, or invoking the aid of God, in any governmental or public document, proceeding, activity, ceremony, school or institution."[93]

This push for a Christian amendment to the Constitution became a rallying cry for evangelicals in the ensuing decades. It embodied the tension between the desire to preserve separationism and the aspiration to see a Christian state enforcing laws based on biblical morality.[94] Particularly in the wake of the Supreme Court's 1973 *Roe v. Wade* decision, the growing sense that the state was no longer supporting the laws of God revived evangelical efforts to restore volunteer prayer in public schools via new legislation and to overturn the Court's decisions via a constitutional amendment.[95] By the same token, it marked the beginning of NAE efforts to build a transdenominational coalition that culminated in the pursuit of the Religious Freedom Restoration Act passed in 1993.[96]

By the early 1970s evangelicals had clearly shifted from encouraging separation as a way of keeping secularization out toward downplaying separation as a way of getting evangelicalism in. Crucially, support for subsidiarity increasingly became part of this battle against secularism. Nolan B. Harmon, retired bishop in the United Methodist Church, suggested in *Christian-*

ity Today that public utilities offered a model for the proper structuring of church-state relations. In effect, he called for state support and regulation of churches. "Christianity has a greater share in the nation . . . than has atheism," he declared. This required a "frank acknowledgement that while church and state are and must be *organically* distinct, they are inextricably locked together in a mutual commonweal." The relationship between the two, he suggested, should be guided by the fact that "the church has an equity in the state and the state has an equity in the church."[97]

Even the most ardent defenders of a traditional stance began to temper their approach. Though continuing to warn about the breakdown of the wall of separation, Clyde Taylor condemned Supreme Court Justice William O. Douglas's call for limits on state financing of religious activities in the School Prayer decision as a sign of the pernicious influence of secularism and antireligious sentiment. In an ironic twist, this stalwart defender of separationism now rebuked Douglas for wanting to do away with chaplains in the army, the G.I. Bill's provision of tuition for denominational colleges, funding of school lunches in parochial schools, and tax exemptions.[98]

Financial Pressures and Pragmatic Considerations

Above and beyond these theological and ideological debates, federal tax and fiscal policies prompted a revision of evangelical separationist mantras. One of the key functions of the OPA throughout the postwar period was to help evangelical churches retain and clarify their tax-exempt status. At the same time, however, the NAE continued to lobby actively against extended tax exemptions for church institutions, viewing them with suspicion as yet another Catholic cabal. Taylor, for example, fought a bill to exempt Catholic institutions, mainly parochial schools, from paying federal excise taxes as an "indirect effort to get government assistance."[99] Likewise, a 1961 NAE resolution affirmed that "tax exemption for churches and religious institutions. . . . should not be construed as including the operation of secular enterprises not directly related to the function of the church or religious institution."[100]

Growing concerns about various attempts by the Internal Revenue Service (IRS) to police tax-exempt organizations more strictly in regard to their nonprofit status and their political neutrality, however, ushered in an attitudinal change. Crucially, they generated fears of secularist intrusion, rather than of the subversion of church-state separation. Worried about Kennedy campaign announcements that threatened IRS inquiries into the tax exempt status of the NAE, Taylor called for "suitable action to be taken to try and head this thing off through the Republican administration."[101] Similarly, he helped defeat attempts to tax income of missionaries abroad.[102] More than anything, however, the 1970 *Waltz v. Tax Commission* case (see Chapter 1), in which the Supreme Court tested the constitutionality of tax exemptions for churches, dramatically highlighted the transformation that had taken place within evangelical ranks. Initially, an *amicus curiae* brief drafted by counsel for Americans United for the Separation of Church and State (AU), the renamed POAU, argued that tax exemptions for churches were unconstitutional. Shortly before the case was argued, however, the organization suddenly directed counsel "not merely to refrain from submitting a brief against exemption, but to prepare and submit one supporting it." Although one can only speculate about the reasons of this complete turnaround, Leo Pfeffer has argued that "it is a reasonable guess that the clergy and lay leaders in Protestant churches recognized that Protestants too enjoyed the benefits of tax exemption."[103]

The tax exemption issue showcases the broader entanglement of evangelical charities in public funding arrangements. Keen to expand their growing relief and missionary activities in the postwar period, many evangelical agencies were tempted to use public funds, even though their churches had consistently condemned this practice. Among both Southern Baptists and NAE-affiliated evangelicals, pragmatic considerations increasingly clashed with church doctrine as rising expenditures made it harder for administrators to pursue a policy of outright rejection of government funds.[104] Warning about a "Protestant muddle in social welfare" in the late 1950s, *Christianity Today* acknowledged that evangelicals were increasingly caught up in subsidiarist arrangements and that numerous funding ties had developed despite the separationist mantras.[105] With his usual perspicacity, Carl Henry pointed out the dangers posed by the NAE constituency's inconsistencies. He warned that they would "dull the force of a consistent protest against N.C.C. concessions to a welfare state philosophy" and "establish precedents which Roman Catholicism can exploit . . . for sectarian ends." In addition, he feared that they were the thin end of a wedge. Once government subsidies were approved in principle, evangelicals would have a difficult time opposing the purchase of other welfare services from religious agencies.[106] A 1966 NAE circular put it bluntly: "Within our evangelical ranks we have seen a tendency on the part of some to take whatever they can get and hope for the best."[107]

The discussions at the 1961 NAE church-state conference reflected this reality, which Bernard Coughlin has called the "two streams of influence" prevalent in conservative Protestantism: While church leaders often spoke of the danger of relying on tax money, local agency administrators frequently accepted government funds. Thus, when it came to the question of the joint participation of church and state in welfare programs, the NAE records prosaically noted that it was "difficult to stop this kind of thing. Our World Relief Commission, our evangelical welfare agencies, our hospitals, our colleges, etc. Must ask ourselves what are the proper functions of the Church, in terms of welfare programs, etc." The answer was beginning to emerge, however. "The principle of separation of Church and State would dictate that we should oppose subsidies of religious or church organizations by government in any form," the adopted statement by one of the committees read; "however, when laws are passed which would benefit religious or church organizations it may be proper, conscience permitting, for evangelicals to accept their share of the benefits on the basis of equal justice."[108]

A similar sign of weakening in the evangelical position was apparent among Baptists. On the one hand, Southern Baptist administrators were the ones most likely to give voice to absolute separationism and to classify both purchase-of-service and subsidies as violations of the separation of church and state. On the other hand, they benefited significantly from Hill-Burton funds, the federal employment of military chaplains, and funding for foreign mission hospitals.[109] Hence, despite the fact that the Southern Baptist Convention had time and again condemned the acceptance of Hill-Burton money and other legislation providing public funding for religious agencies, close funding ties developed between Baptist institutions and the state. "Their record is by no means spotless," C. Stanley Lowell concluded. "Baptists have succumbed here and there and the Adventists found the plenitude of subsidies available for their massive hospital program more than they could resist."[110] Indeed, in his survey of 215 social service agencies that had no policy regarding the receipt of government funds, Coughlin discovered that over 60 percent received public aid. "A written policy determines action, but action also generates a policy," he noted acerbically. Although "segments of some denominations hesitate to seek or accept government funds," he concluded, these "are small and are growing smaller."[111]

What is more, the NAE's dilemma on public funding matters cannot be separated from some of the movement's organizational weaknesses. Under the conditions of subsidiarity the main funding ties developed between government and nationally organized denominations and church bodies, such as Catholic Charities USA or Lutheran Social Ministries. They also included individual conservative denominations outside the NAE that had streamlined their social service agencies, such as the Southern Presbyterians, who organized a Department of Christian Relations (1946), and the Southern Baptist Social Service Commission, the precursor of the powerful Christian Life Commission (1953). In contrast, the decentralized and fragmented nature of the NAE made it difficult to set up an effective coordinating body for evangelical welfare agencies. Evangelicals in the NAE were more likely to form freestanding social service agencies that resisted government funding.[112] In turn, they faced a twofold challenge, namely "the struggle to bureaucratize the church's structure and the struggle to preserve the purity of religious ideology while adjusting to a new pattern of relationship with government."[113]

The simultaneous efforts by the NAE to retain separationism while calling for enlarged funding streams for nongovernmental social provision need to be understood in the context of this failure—or unwillingness—to build up the required specialized bureaucracy. Neither the EAC nor the Social Action Commission (SAC) developed much organizational or political clout. The 1961 EAC report, for example, listed the lack of financial appropriation and the inability of members to dedicate sufficient time to commission work as major handicaps.[114] Financial shortfalls, lack of professionalization, and a wide range of competing evangelical agencies also hampered the work of the SAC. Here the NAE's failure to recruit the Southern Baptists was particularly palpable, as the NAE came to be seen "as another parachurch group, rather than a normative call to Christian union."[115]

By the 1970s the strains were beginning to show. Not having developed effective coordinating bodies in the 1950s and 1960s meant that thriving individual social service agencies and self-help groups dominated evangelical social action and church-state engagement. However, this also marked the beginning of a sustained campaign to promote "policies that would reallocate funds from large sectarian agencies that had traditionally benefited from government largesse to evangelical congregations that have not historically provided social services and to small religiously-tied service providers."[116] In short, as evangelicals became aware of the instrumentalities of nonprofit funding, they employed separationist doctrine no longer simply to assail the quasi-corporatist arrangements between the state and nationally organized religious and secular welfare agencies, but to legitimize shifting the funding streams toward their own decentralized "counter-institutions." As Chapters 5 and 6 show, it is this thinking that ultimately informed evangelical support for Charitable Choice and the Faith-Based Initiative.

The Features of Subsidiarity

Finally, the administrative and normative characteristics of Cold War subsidiarity furthered the integration of evangelicals into the subsidiarist welfare state. As explored in Chapter 1, although many statutes and regulations guiding public funding either explicitly excluded or put severe restrictions on religious providers, religious organizations were able to participate in the growing funding streams and suffered surprisingly little government interference. One of the main reasons for this "benign neglect" was that government support often reached nonprofits indirectly via vouchers, block grants, and reimbursement schemes. The expansion of federal funding for nonprofits along these lines was in most cases accompanied by the loosening, rather than a tightening, of regulatory controls, especially during the peak years of Lyndon Johnson's Great Society programs.

This discrepancy was not lost on evangelicals. Listing a range of federal, state, and local programs, C. Stanley Lowell noted that while "none of them mention churches as eligible recipients of the funds" and many contained "specific renunciations of aid for any program of worship or sectarian instruction," funds funneled into religiously based organizations under these schemes had encountered few challenges. The 1964 Economic Opportunity Act, for example, banned the display of religious symbols and decorations in federally funded facilities, and included a disclaimer about aid to sectarian institutions. Although it barred direct aid to churches, however, Lowell argued that "within the broad altitude of programs conceived and designed in one way or another to relieve poverty there was wide room for church subsidy."[117] By the same token, evangelicals acknowledged that government subsidies had enabled sectarian groups to impose their teachings without significant government interference. Government "hands over the money along with certain broad guidelines for its expenditure," Lowell grumbled. "The church takes it from there. If there is some crass, overt violation of the guidelines, government might react to it. But other than this, the church simply proceeds on its own and does as it wills."[118] Likewise, at the 1963 church-state conference, Clyde Taylor maintained that in taxpayer subsidized hospitals and welfare institutions "we find Roman Catholic orders given a free hand to apply Roman Catholic Canon Law to regulations."[119]

Many critics from conservative Protestant backgrounds thus increasingly recognized the potential benefits of a funding system that effectively sanctioned the faith-based approaches of church-affiliated agencies. In turn, lax regulatory controls, indirect funding, and the lack of restrictions on evangelizing were key factors in bringing conservative Protestants into the subsidiarist networks that underlay Cold War state building. "The church may as an agent administer government assistance without compromise of the principle of separation of church and state if the church's policies are not controlled or influenced thereby or vice versa," the NAE's 1964 resolution on "The Church and Welfare" read. It acknowledged that the principles of Christian social welfare involved "many facets of cooperation" and that "there appears to be no solid wall of separation here between church and state." Instead of insisting that church and state needed to inhabit separate spheres, it concluded that "separation must be maintained by clear working relationships" where "certain policies may be stipulated and agreed upon, but the choice of the personnel and total administration of the program must be the entire responsibility of the church."[120]

Taylor's 1966 assessment of Sargent Shriver's use of War on Poverty funds to channel millions of dollars directly to churches and church councils offers a glimpse of this change of heart. "The war on Poverty certainly has its merits," Taylor acknowledged. In particular, he cited OEO reports about VISTA volunteers having been assigned to churches or church councils, a grant of $7.5 million being given to a Roman Catholic diocese in Mississippi, and a further $400,000 having been granted to the North Carolina Council of Churches. Although he concluded that evangelicals "would be hard pressed to justify meeting the mission budget through the receipt of federal funds," he recognized that "our involvement is two-fold: the obvious is the use of public tax money for church promotion and expansion. The second is more subtle and may mean a moving toward 'federalized home missions'."[121] Great Society funding had thus helped calm evangelical fears that taking public funds would infringe on agency autonomy, marginalize religious content, and absorb them into a government-run system.

Surveying church-state funding ties more than two decades later, Stephen Monsma shatters the myth that the nonprofit institutions receiving public funds tended to be the ones that had watered down their religious commitment, or that public funding had forced religious agencies to become more secular. The "surprising pattern" of the religiously based institutions receiving more public funds than their secular counterparts, he concluded, was the result "not of the less religious, but the more religious institutions receiving more public funds." Hence, Catholic and conservative Protestant nonprofits in particular received significant amounts of public funds without being forced to compromise their religious mission and practices. Indeed, many of their child care agencies, international aid providers, and higher education institutions receiving public aid were "pervasively sectarian" in the sense of the Supreme Court's *Lemon* decision. Conservative Protestant organizations especially led the field among religious agencies in restrictive hiring, mandatory religious exercises, and encouragement of religious commitment, yet rarely felt under strong pressure from government to curtail or eliminate these practices. Overall, they reported few problems with restrictions in carrying out their religious mission.[122]

The Public Funding of Evangelical Agencies

While Catholics, mainline Protestants, and Jewish groups had by and large embraced public funding in the Cold War era, the real enigma is that conservative Protestant organizations, which had traditionally been the most outspoken defenders of church-state separation, did not remain at the margins of the general reshaping of church-state relations. Indeed, conservative Protestant organizations shared in this public funding arrangement and in some fields even reported larger proportions of their budgets coming from government sources than other religious providers. As explored in Chapter 1, religious higher education—and increasingly also primary and secondary education—was one of the main beneficiaries of federal support. Likewise, the state's expansion of the nation's health care infrastructure relied heavily on funneling federal monies to religious institutions, particularly via the Hill-Burton Act. The most dramatic change to church-state funding ties, however, came in the area of social service funding, where the federal government increased funding and access for congregation-based providers in both discretionary welfare and established entitlement programs. Although very little research has gone into the extent of evangelical participation in these developments, a closer look at these main areas of subsidiarity highlights the growth of funding relationships between conservative Protestants and the government and their role in the transformation of evangelical church-state attitudes.[123]

Higher Education

Throughout the 1950s and 1960s the NAE, in cooperation with POAU, frequently reiterated its rhetorical rejection to any kind of federal aid to colleges and universities and insisted that both grants and loans were unconstitutional. Keeping a close eye on legislation promoting subsidies, the NAE Executive Committee restated in 1958 that the organization was "opposed to Federal aid for education."[124] Similarly, Taylor warned in 1960 about the slippery slope of public aid that led from mere assistance to supporting religious teachings. "The whole purpose of the sectarian college is to act as an agent of the parent body, particularly in propagating its belief," he reminded his fellow Christians, "yet many of these schools are willing to take Federal aid."[125] Lowell used even more evocative language. He warned of the emergence of "a hybrid creation" that contained "the vices and weaknesses of both and the virtues of neither. . . . The church institution, as in the case of the college, becomes a quasi public institution."[126]

Fired up by these sentiments, evangelicals lobbied hard for the defeat of government aid to education. Fordham University's acquisition of a campus in New York City with the help of FHA funds earmarked for slum clearance, for example, became a cause célèbre that mobilized evangelicals on the ground. It resulted in an early example of an angry letter-writing campaign by evangelical churches, civic organizations, and individuals against Catholic institutions that benefited from federal support programs. Deploring the use of public funds, evangelical Ann Smith encouraged POAU director Glenn Archer to "take the serpent by the tail, knowing that it has no power, even if it tries to snap back and bite."[127] Similarly, in his 1961 report to the NAE Board of Administration, Taylor warned about a state proposition on the ballot in New York for an amendment that "would allow the State to guarantee up to $500,000,00 in loans to private colleges (90% of which are Roman Catholic institutions)."[128] These campaigns continued well into the 1960s. In 1964, for example, EAC chairman James DeForest Murch appeared before the House and Senate Subcommittees on Education to counter legislation that "would have channeled millions of dollars into hands of the Roman Catholic hierarchy."[129]

In the same vein, evangelicals expressed satisfaction when federal aid to education legislation was voted down in Congress. The defeat of the Pucinski Amendment to the respective education bill, Taylor reported in July 1960, "was an excellent and solid gain for our cause."[130] A year later he triumphantly informed the NAE Board of Administration that the Office of Education in the Department of Health, Education and Welfare had disallowed use of National Defense Education Act funds to support seminaries. "As a healthy byproduct of opposition to any aid to parochial schools, we find that another gap in the wall separating church and state has been closed," he reveled. Both Emory University, a Methodist institution, and mainline Protestant Union Theological Seminary in New York had previously used these funds to train individuals for the ministry.[131]

While the campaign against educational funding was a cornerstone of evangelicals' anti-Catholic political organizing, however, it also exposed the cracks in the NAE's political identity. This became apparent in 1961 when the NAE found itself in a paradoxical position: On the issue of federal aid for sectarian education it supported a Catholic president, whom it had vigorously opposed only a year earlier, against an evangelical Republican. It was "possible that we could have Rockefeller, a Baptist, in 1964 supporting aid to parochial schools, opposed to Kennedy, who would support separation of Church and State," Lowell grudgingly noted at the 1961 church-state conference.[132] Taylor concurred. In marked contrast to the hysteria in the run-up to the Kennedy election, he found it "satisfying to note that the stand of our President and of the Department of Education is the strongest we have known in conserving separation of Church and State."[133] In contrast, he criticized Republicans who had introduced plans for state tuition grants for higher education. Noting that "both Goldwater and Rockefeller are weak in their church-state declarations as was Mr. Nixon," he predicted that the issue could become a key topic in the 1964 campaign.[134]

This was indicative of the deeper dilemma for the movement. In contrast to its vocal defense of separationism and acerbic anti-Catholic campaign, significant amounts of federal funds in fact traditionally went to evangelical and fundamentalist colleges and universities via tax breaks, grants, and low-interest loans. According to an NAE-commissioned review of evangelical colleges regarding "principles and practices in response to federal aid, loans, and gifts," there were "few church-related colleges that did not have some program under Federal auspices" during World War II.[135] This pattern continued into the postwar period. Beginning with the G.I. Bill, federal support had reinvigorated fundamentalist and evangelical colleges and Bible schools, including Wheaton College and Fuller Theological Seminary, by funding the enrollment of war veterans. Especially at Wheaton, this included many students who went into mission work.[136]

By the 1950s, the NAE review pointed out, the pursuit of "urgent national goals" in the battle with the Soviet Union emphasized the strengthening of national security and the attainment of specialized technical skills. As a result of the Cold War-related federalization of responsibilities, many evangelical colleges "accepted federal aid in the form of long-term low interest rates through the HHFA for housing and National Defense Education Act loans on tuition."[137] Federal loans for Southern Baptist schools through 1962, for example, added up to $36.6 million for dormitories and $4.7 million for students even before the Great Society higher education programs made federal funds available on an unprecedented scale. The Public Health Service awarded Baptist schools over $9.1 million for research in 1959–1961, and through 1961 the National Science Foundation gave Baptist schools half a million dollars in grants. Moreover, between 1945 and 1960 roughly $3.3 million in government surplus land, buildings, and equipment came into Baptist ownership for token payments.[138] Likewise, NAE-member denominations were among the beneficiaries of surplus government donations to higher education facilities. Evangel College in Springfield, Missouri, for example, an Assemblies of God institution, "was put into business by an original gift of 58.6 acres from the site of a General Hospital declared surplus and later received an additional donation of 30 acres by the Federal Government."[139]

This was only the beginning, though. In addition to the G.I. Bill and subsequent legislation, the Great Society programs funneled millions of dollars to conservative Protestant colleges for student recruitment, administrative costs, classrooms, libraries, laboratories, teaching equipment, and dormitory construction.[140] Despite continuing to warn about "dangerous precedents" and reporting minor successes in the anti-aid campaign, Taylor increasingly had to report the failure of efforts to limit public support for religious higher education.[141] Moreover, as various laws expanding federal aid to education were debated in Congress in the early 1960s, the NAE found it increasingly difficult to pursue a consistent separationist policy. EAC chairman Murch noted with chagrin that the organization had "been handicapped, especially in the field of higher education, in formulating a position representative of the NAE" because "a large number of evangelical colleges have accepted Federal aid of various kinds."[142] The organization even found itself unable to testify in opposition to a 1962 federal aid to church colleges bill at House Subcommittee on Education hearings. Though it had vigorously rejected aid to parochial schools in previous hearings, when a modified bill granting aid to church colleges was presented, Murch conceded that "we felt we could make no consistent or valid protest because of the large number of evangelical colleges which have accepted such aid."[143] And noting that "some of our church schools are very much opposed to this aid and others are declaring themselves in favor of it if they possibly can get it," Taylor acknowledged that "interesting sides [were] being taken" on higher education.[144]

The NAE sought to clarify the evangelical position and to draft new resolutions on federal aid to education at its seminal 1963 church-state conference. At this occasion, James Forrester presented the aforementioned review of the EAC and the Education Commission, which illustrated the dilemmas of many evangelical colleges. Evangelicals, he maintained, were torn between two extremes demarcated by those who "feel that massive assistance must come from the participation of the Federal government if the colleges are to match the demand both inside and outside the country for the upgrading of our national human resources" and "those who eschew all forms of Federal aid." Though worried that greater involvement with government could compromise the transcendent purpose of Christian colleges, Forrester's analysis showed that a potent mixture of factors had weakened the separationist stance. Leading among them were identification with Cold War goals, financial pressures, awareness of the indirect nature of funding streams, and concerns about secularist intrusion.[145]

Likewise, the lack of financial support for higher education from within the movement seriously increased the allure of federal funding. Although they deplored federal aid, evangelicals rarely offered their own support for the rising costs of church-related higher education. Judged by their budgetary commitment, Forrester grumbled, evangelicals "do not believe that higher education is important to them." Crucially, he regarded foundation money and corporate giving as only a very limited alternative, since "these sources are often not committed to a specifically Christian perspective any more than is the Federal government." Although he suggested that evangelical colleges should realize the potential of beneficial tax laws to build up endowments and provide scholarships, Forrester's somber conclusion was that "in the absence of aid from private sources and church groups, many boards of small church-related colleges see the loan programs as the only available option to mediocrity or extinction."[146] In light of the availability of federal funding while church support was drying up, many evangelical colleges had few alternatives if they were to heed Carl Henry's admonition that "Christianity must not withdraw from the sphere of education, but must infuse it with new spirit and life."[147]

In short, the main issue for evangelical colleges in Forrester's view was no longer "whether they will accept some form of Federal aid, but how they can preserve their spiritual integrity, autonomy, and goals in doing so." In this shift in emphasis from insisting on the separation of church and state to protecting the spiritual mission under public funding arrangements, evangelicals were encouraged by the indirectness of higher education funding streams and the absence of intrusive government control. As Forrester emphasized, government loans carried "no danger of control" since "the government functions as a fiduciary agent only." He also regarded federal funds to higher education as more acceptable to evangelicals because they were available via tuition waivers, rather than via direct grants and contracts.[148] In the wake of the 1963 conference this position gradually emerged as the new consensus on higher education within the NAE. At that year's convention, the NAE refrained from criticizing schools and accepted public funding. While counseling "extreme caution" in order to "maintain the freedom which derives from carefully hewing to the line of church-state separation," the organization nonetheless recognized the reality of government aid and that laws providing this aid were consistent with constitutional clauses.[149] Crucially, the NEA increasingly used worries about federal control, rather than the principle of church-state separation, as the yardstick for measuring public funding proposals.[150]

Despite the recognition that federal support posed little danger to the content of Christian education, evangelicals did not relent in their denunciations of the "syndromes of socialism" and "the penetration of naturalistic humanism" in publicly funded colleges and universities. By the late 1960s, the NAE regularly expressed concern about "encroaching federal controls" and that "both public and private institutions of higher learning are feeling the effect of public influence from the level of the federal government." The 1969 General Convention, for example, cited incidences where campus buildings constructed by churches with federal money were not allowed to be used to hold religious classes, pray, or teach the Bible. While on the surface these sentiments suggested a return to a separationist position, in reality they were a way of demanding federal support without strings attached. When the NAE resolutions during the Convention condemned government for blocking the use of federally funded campus buildings for religious purposes, delegates used this not to reject federal aid but to call for types of funding that allowed private schools to "receive the support they need if they are to survive and provide a truly Christian education."[151]

This paved the way for yet another revision of the evangelical church-state stance. "Our office has written and presented to key people on the hill a suggested plan for direct taxpayer aid to our schools of higher education in the form of a Tax Credit Plan," Taylor reported to the EAC in April 1969. According to this proposal, "taxpayers would be permitted to give a percentage of their Federal tax contributions to the college of their choice."[152] The NAE convention delegates duly concurred. "A possible solution lies in some plan designed to provide tax relief to all citizens supporting education, whether private or public, and without discrimination," the 1969 resolution read.[153] By the early 1970s the NAE had firmed up this embrace of federal aid to higher education along the lines of tax credits.[154] By 1983 any lingering reservations had disappeared almost completely as the organization endorsed tuition tax credits with a 91 percent majority. "This is an historical reversal," NAE director Robert P. Dugan proudly declared, "Ten years ago, probably more than 91% would have opposed tuition tax credits, ascribing it to a Roman Catholic conspiracy to get parochiaid. Even four years ago, a resolution on the subject was considered too controversial to bring to the floor of the convention."[155]

Since then, significant amounts of public funds have gone to evangelical colleges and universities under a variety of direct and indirect aid programs. Indeed, by the 1990s, conservative Protestant colleges and universities were outstripping Catholic and mainline Protestant entities in the receipt of public funds, with 35 percent of conservative Protestant institutions receiving more than 20 percent of their income from public sources. Moreover, the vast majority (78 percent) of conservative Protestant colleges and universities receiving public funds reported no problems with government pressures to limit their sectarian practices.[156] Recalling the impact of federal support ranging from student aid to grants and loans, a professor at Azusa Pacific University, a leading evangelical college in California, concluded in 2005 that "without federal aid, the institution would not have flourished. With federal aid, the university took flight and grew into a significant institution that produces thousands of graduates. This is an example of how the government aided a religious organization without intruding on its autonomy or its faith-based mission."[157] Evangelical colleges and universities thus became an inseparable part of the postwar public-private funding arrangement.

Primary and Secondary Education

In contrast to higher education, where the acceptance of various forms of public aid by evangelical colleges threw doubts on the credibility of the NAE campaign against federal support, evangelicals were much less hampered by embarrassing instances of sectarian primary and secondary schools taking public money. Eager to nip Catholic desires for "parochiaid" in the bud and bolstered in their opposition by Supreme Court rulings that put severe restrictions on federal funding, the NAE and POAU ran a vitriolic campaign against federal aid for religious schools. Resuscitating the anti-Catholicism of the nineteenth-century public school movement, evangelicals also made the fight against school funding a main focus of their postwar political mobilization.

Lobbying against legislation in this field was among the OPA's earliest tasks. In March 1947, Taylor warned Decker about the pending "Taft Bill," which he feared would allow states to provide further public funds to Roman Catholic schools and thus needed to be opposed at the congressional hearings. Noting that the mainline Federal Council of the Churches of Christ in America (FCCCA) had not been called into the debates, Taylor saw this as an opportunity for evangelicals to be present at the hearings and suggested Harold John Ockenga and Bishop Leslie R. Marston of the Free Methodists as possible spokesmen.[158] A year later, Frank Gigliotti, a leading member of the NAE's Committee on Christian Liberty, declared that "the National Catholic Welfare Conference has appropriated approximately $500,000,00 and employed eight priests in Washington to work on Federal Aid to Parochial Schools in the next Congress." In turn, the committee agreed on a plan to urge NAE members to lobby their congressmen to oppose any legislation along these lines and to prepare briefs for congressional hearings.[159] Furthermore, in 1962 Taylor denounced the "G. I. Bill for Junior" introduced by James J. Delaney (D-N.Y.) that proposed subsidies for each child in public and private schools as "simply a gimmick for federal aid to Roman Catholic schools."[160] While the NAE found itself unable to oppose a bill granting aid to church colleges at the abovementioned House Subcommittee on Education hearings that year, it had no such compunction about preventing the passage of similar bills aiding private and parochial schools.[161]

However, even this cause célèbre of evangelical separationism eventually led down the path of accommodation. As explored in Chapter 1, although Supreme Court rulings put severe constitutional limits on federal funding, and no direct government aid legislation was passed, church-state ties in primary and secondary schooling continued to strengthen in the postwar period. Tax money subsidized school transportation, textbooks, teaching inducements, and indirect federal funds to students, particularly in "federally impacted areas."[162] More important than the availability of indirect funding in softening separationist attitudes to school aid, however, was the growing fear of secularism. Already in the mid-1950s, Taylor had raised serious concerns that "we find belligerent groups, either racial or religious, endeavoring to take the Christian witness and all religion out of the public schools and, if possible, to make of our nation a completely materialistic organization."[163]

More than anything, however, the Supreme Court's decision prohibiting Bible reading and compulsory prayer in public schools left evangelicals fearful that secularists "will succeed if God-fearing people abandon government and society to the godless." In turn, the evangelical campaign gradually shifted away from denunciations of Catholic control and toward mobilizing grassroots sentiment around apprehensions over morality and values.[164] After a thorough review of the biblical, historical and judicial context, delegates at the 1964 NAE General Convention agreed that "while Church and State must be separate, the State has an irrevocable obligation . . . to inculcate in rising generations the belief that religion, morality and knowledge are essential to good government and the happiness of its citizens."[165]

Ironically, help in this crusade came from quarters that evangelicals normally regarded as antagonistic to their aspirations. The Great Society's 1965 Elementary and Secondary Education Act laid the foundation for the use of vouchers as a means of providing federal aid to religious schools. Administered by the OEO, the quintessential Great Society agency, this provision of indirect federal funds to students offered evangelicals a way out of getting caught between traditional separationism and fears of secularist control. It ushered in a long-term debate about school vouchers and the large-scale conversion of conservatives to public funding for private schools (see Chapter 5). Southern Baptists in particular could take credit for the adoption of the child-benefit principle in the new law, by which aid went to pupils rather than to schools.[166] Although the NAE did not support the Act, and continued to voice "protest against any federal aid to church related schools whether directly or indirectly given," it adopted a motion in 1966 that declared some contractual arrangements with the government "acceptable and beneficial" as long as they did not incur government control.[167] Moreover, rather than advocating outright opposition, many evangelicals suggested that the courts were the proper place for adjudicating these tricky state-church questions. This, however, contrasted with anxieties that "if our courts continue to permit nothing but an atheistic philosophy to prevail in our schools, we will inevitably end up with the equivalent of a Marxist philosophy of something worse."[168]

In the ensuing decade the NAE first grappled with and then embraced the proposal developed under the auspices of the OEO to provide parents with tuition vouchers to be used in public, private, or parochial schools. Discussions during a 1971 consultation session of the Evangelical Social Action Commission concluded that "the plan can contribute much to the basic reform of American education. It may reinforce parental rights, provide for the special concern of minorities, permit experimentation with various philosophical and pedagogical approaches, and respond to the needs of those whom it serves." Instead of simply rejecting voucher-based public funding of parochial schools, the Commission stated that "when specific issues are raised by an actual operation, the matter will be reviewed."[169]

This stance was largely code for shifting the focus from separationist orthodoxy to efforts to limit regulatory intervention—as became apparent in 1977 when Senator Jesse Helms (R-North Carolina) introduced a bill proposing that any institution that did not receive more than $300,000 or 5 percent of its annual budget from the federal government would not be covered by federal regulations. Designed to curb federal intrusion in the educational field, the proposal covered a significant number of evangelical entities. It "would rejoice the hearts of many people if it were enacted into law," Floyd Robertson, who had succeeded Taylor as secretary of public affairs, summarily declared.[170] These sentiments mirrored a broader shift in evangelical church-state thinking. A 1986 poll among *Christianity Today* readers showed more almost two-thirds (65 percent) in support of "the federal government taking a strong role to improve the quality of public education," with over a fifth (21 percent) regarding this as the most important educational issue. The runner-up was "mandating the teaching of creationism along with evolution in science courses," which, while only regarded as the most important issues by 18 percent, was supported by 74 percent of those surveyed.[171]

Evangelical Health Care and Social Service Agencies

In the health and social services arena, similar patterns prevailed. Throughout the 1950s and 1960s, the condemnation of Catholic efforts to obtain Hill-Burton funding for their hospitals occupied a top spot in evangelical campaigning both within and outside of the NAE. Conservative Protestants accused Catholic institutions of greed, subterfuge, and seeking to undermine the separation of church and state. "Projects by Roman Catholics, who claim 20 per cent of the population, got roughly 80 per cent of Hill-Burton funds awarded to church-related institutions," Carl Henry complained in *Christianity Today*.[172] Taylor charged that across the country the Catholic Church was encouraging communities to secure land and funds for new hospitals only to "hand this all over to one of the Orders of Nuns" who "in turn furnish the additional subsidy in order to get a Federal grant of money." As a result, both the government and the members of Protestant denominations in the respective neighborhoods were contributing to hospitals "that operate under the Catholic Medical Code."[173] And in the early 1960s evangelicals campaigned hard against a 79–acre land grant valued at $1 million to Loyola University for the establishment of a medical center. This was excess land of the Veterans Administration (VA) that eventually created a significant windfall profit for Loyola when the university sold it. Meanwhile, as a chagrined C. Stanley Lowell noted, the VA ended up needing another site and paid taxpayer money for land for its own hospital.[174]

As in the case of higher education, however, anti-Catholic rhetoric often did not match the reality on the ground. Although Catholic denominations received the majority of federal health care funds, hospitals, child services, and nursing homes operated under the auspices of conservative Protestant organizations, particularly those run by Southern Baptists and Seventh-Day Adventists, kept increasing their percentage. As Henry bemoaned, "American Protestants were also entangled, even if on smaller scale."[175] A 1963 survey of aid to Southern Baptist institutions revealed that grants under the Hill-Burton Act amounted to almost $12.8 million. By then, Southern Baptist hospitals received 30 percent of their funds from public sources. Evangelical hospitals were also the prime beneficiaries of surplus government property and equipment donated for welfare and educational uses. In this way they obtained valuable land, buildings, and other property at a heavy discount. According to a 1964 report of the Department of Housing, Education and Welfare, the Assemblies of God, a NAE member denomination, was second in total acreage donation only to the Catholics.[176]

Once again, competition with Catholic providers, the availability of funds, and growing financial pressures largely accounted for the shift in emphasis among conservative Protestants from insisting on separation toward ensuring that evangelical institutions would receive their fair share while retaining operational autonomy. As heavy costs for equipment and operational expenses made it ever more difficult for administrators to stick to church doctrine, Southern Baptists in particular promoted public funding while seeking to make it less visibly a government subsidy. By the late 1950s, they were actively lobbying for less direct funding options such as low-interest loans as an alternative to grants. These options, added in 1958, made it easier for all evangelicals to accept federal support.[177]

The crucial breakthrough in evangelical support for subsidiarity, however, came via the expansion of public aid to sectarian social service providers in the 1960s. In contrast to the other areas of public funding for church-based provision, evangelicals tended to quietly condone the practice in the welfare realm, since funding ties, particularly for foster care, had a long tradition on the state and local levels. When the Great Society dramatically increased the amount of money available to nonprofit welfare organizations, the federalization of aid initially reawakened fears of government control and Catholic dominance. As the War on Poverty loosened long-standing restrictions on federal funding of religious social services, however, it gradually broke down the last vestiges of traditional evangelical separationism. Noting in 1963 that a number of evangelical social service organizations had applied for and received loans under FHA provisions, R. L. Decker acknowledged that "there seems to be little if any disposition on the part of the government . . . to supervise the program in these institutions, after taking precautions to see that the elderly people are physically provided for in the best possible manner."[178]

Although much maligned by conservative Protestants, the extensive growth of welfare programs during the Great Society effectively broke the ground for the institutional and ideological integration of evangelical social service providers into the subsidiarist system. By the 1970s, Southern Baptist and other evangelical hospitals, mental health institutions, and nursing homes were avid participants in funding streams implemented by the Great Society, especially Head Start, Medicaid, and Medicare.[179] A study of a midwestern agency of the Lutheran Church-Missouri Synod revealed that it received 38 percent of its total budget from public funds in 1950, largely on the basis of purchase-of-service contracting; by 1980, the figure had increased to 59 percent, mainly due to Title XX funds. Overall, the study found few differences between evangelical and mainline agencies in the percentage of government funding received. Most striking, however, was the case of the NAE-affiliated Salvation Army. Prior to the availability of OEO funds, public aid had played only a limited role in overall agency income, except for some purchase-of-service contracting. In the 1970s, however, government funding increased rapidly from 4 percent of the overall budget in 1974–1975 to 17 percent by fiscal year 1979–1980. The budgets for social services, including community centers, services for ex-offenders, temporary shelter, counseling agencies, and residences for alcoholics, showed a particularly pronounced reliance on public funds. In these areas 45 percent of income originated in government sources.[180]

In accepting that social welfare subsidiarity had become the norm, evangelicals once again shifted from ubiquitous warnings about opening the floodgates for a church-state combine to discussing the finer differences between types of public funding. By the 1980s, the NAE concentrated its energies in this area on pushing for tax credits, though it continued to oppose service contracts, direct subsidies, block grants, or vouchers. In an indication that fear of secularism and pragmatic considerations had won the day, NAE counsel Forest Montgomery in 1988 rejected "absolutist concepts of the separation of church and state" embedded in legislative proposals through which "child care would be dichotomized," with "secular child care receiving government financial assistance, while private religious child care would have had to compete against government-supported and regulated secularized care." His admission that not allowing religiously affiliated child care centers to participate "will tend to drive those centers out of business," revealed the level of dependence of many conservative Protestant facilities on public funding.[181] Especially in a nation whose motto was "In God We Trust," Montgomery argued in front of the Senate Committee on Finance, it made "little sense, if there is a child care crisis, to fail to help them on the same basis as their secular counterparts." In addition, his stance revealed that the use of religious liberty arguments had won out over separationist dogma. Excluding religiously oriented child care from federal benefits, Montgomery declared, "cannot be squared with our first liberty" and "subordinates religion to irreligion."[182]

Similarly, the Southern Baptists had come around to openly supporting public aid in the aftermath of the divisive conservative takeover of the denomination and its agencies. Particularly Richard D. Land, executive director of the SBC's Christian Life Commission, supported child care block grants whereby federal funds were given but regulation was left to state and local government.[183] Nonetheless, public funding remained controversial within the SBC. In 1988, it urged member churches "to conduct their childcare programs as ministries of the local church or through cooperation among churches, without financing from the federal government" and demanded that "any program of childcare include adequate safeguards to maintain the separation of church and state."[184] Correspondingly, the Baptist Joint Committee on Public Affairs, which included representatives from eight national Baptist bodies with a membership of almost 30 million, noted that "any child care program that provides grants and contracts to churches and other pervasively sectarian institutions is constitutionally suspect." Nonetheless, the Committee also maintained that "unlike child care welfare programs, child care tax proposals generally do not raise significant constitutional problems.[185]

When it became apparent that the tax credit proposal would not be successful, the NAE, rather than reverting to a traditional separationist position, pushed instead for child care vouchers it had previously rejected as a matter of principle. Though dismissing previous concerns that vouchers would mean state regulatory control, Robert Dugan demanded "explicit language permitting these vouchers to be used in facilities providing religious instruction, and inclusion of moral tenets protection."[186] Since vouchers, unlike federal grants and contracts, constituted aid to parents, not to the recipient institution, he insisted that regulations should not limit religious instruction and restrictive hiring.[187] In other words, the child care arena shows that the NAE no longer opposed public funding as such, but only when it imposed constraints on religious providers taking public funds. It rejected regulation when this infringed on the autonomy of religious providers, but demanded it as a means of making sure sectarian practices were protected.[188]

This position made sense in light of the reality of both regulatory leniency and growing public aid dependency. As Stephen Monsma found, although conservative Protestant child service agencies headed the field in exclusive hiring, compulsory religious activities, and religious commitment, the percentage reporting problems with government was only marginally higher (34 percent) than the average for all religiously based agencies (30 percent). While 22 percent felt forced to curtail practices, the highly religious agencies reported the most positive effects of public funding, with 89 percent viewing it as a means of expanding services. By the same token, 39 percent of conservative Protestant child service agencies surveyed in the 1990s reported receiving more than 60 percent their income from public funds, and a further 18 percent reported receiving 20–60 percent.[189] In overall terms, however, evangelical social service agencies received a lower percentage of their total income from public sources than Catholic or mainline agencies. To some extent the lower percentage of public funds for religiously committed child care agencies was due to more resistance on the part of conservative Protestants to government funding. Nonetheless, the disparity can also in part be explained by diverse funding patterns for different institutions. For example, children's institutions, which traditionally have closer financial relationships with government, make up a higher number of agencies in Catholicism than in Judaism and Protestantism.[190]

*   *   *

In summation, starting out in the 1940s on a strict separationist platform, the NAE had by the late 1960s moved toward a much more integrationist stance; it sought to protect the organizational autonomy and spiritual mission of religious providers under public funding arrangements and focused on ensuring equal access to public subsidies. While still adhering to a rhetoric of separation, the organization not only acknowledged that many member churches had benefited from public monies, but also began to embrace the subsidiarist policies it used to eschew. The impetus for this originated both with the social awakening of postwar evangelicalism and with Cold War public policies. In particular the programs of the Great Society were crucial in pushing forward the revision of separationist attitudes and practices among evangelicals. The indirect funding streams and absence of effective restrictions on evangelizing that characterized the War on Poverty encouraged closer links between evangelicals and the state, as the examples of education, health care, and social services indicate. Great Society programs largely privileged nongovernmental over public social provision, reduced the state to a role of paymaster, and sanctioned faith-based practices. This suggests that the significance of Great Society social policies for the political mobilization of conservative Protestants lay not simply in their being an easy target for charges of "immorality" and "permissiveness," but in the role they played in integrating evangelical agencies into the subsidiarist welfare state.

The "subsidiarist turn" of evangelicalism was characterized by a two-pronged approach. On the one hand, evangelicals continued to position themselves as staunch adversaries of the state and sought to uphold a separationist identity. On the other hand, they worked on building funding networks with government agencies and influencing public policy. In short, they combined reacting against the rise of the state with taking advantage of the benefits it offered. Although evangelicals continued to conjure up the specter of secular intrusion in the educational, health care, and social services arenas, they no longer used this to reject public aid, but to limit federal restrictions on their agencies under public funding arrangements. By making the preservation of autonomy within a system of state subsidies the key of the church-state attitude, their main concern was no longer the size of government, but the specifics of the funding arrangement. Evangelicals rejected state subsidies when they threatened to infringe upon religious providers, but demanded them when it came to making sure religious agencies were not excluded from public aid.

Removed from the realm of unquestioned dogma, church-state separationism thus became largely a matter of pragmatic policy that covered up the growing closeness to the structures of the Cold War state in the ensuing decades. As the next chapter shows, this ambivalent position, rather than the outright rejection of the welfare state, formed the basis for the political mobilization of evangelicals under the auspices of its increasingly powerful conservative wing.

CHAPTER 5

CHURCH-STATE RELATIONS AND THE RISE OF THE EVANGELICAL RIGHT

The participation of evangelical agencies in the Cold War national security and welfare state not only brought church and state closer together institutionally and ideologically, it also shaped the dynamics of the political mobilization of evangelicals. The new church-state attitudes emerged only gradually from often heated internal conflicts over political partisanship, civil religion, military power, and government aid. These debates are altogether too easily ignored in analyses of evangelical politics. However, they are vital in understanding postwar evangelicalism's public policy agenda and its relationship to the state. In particular, they proved significant for the rise of the evangelical Right. Conservative forces within the movement used the "statist" and "subsidiarist" turns of postwar evangelicalism to develop a coherent political ideology, foster ties to secular conservatism, and sideline evangelical liberals and the resurgent Left. This helped the Right to emerge triumphant from the intra-evangelical battles in the 1970s and 1980s.

Initially, however, it was a resurgent evangelical Left that politicized the movement. During the Vietnam War era it challenged the evangelical establishment's support for and spiritualization of America's Cold War foreign policy era. Building on evangelical pacifism and antimilitarism the Left denounced the arms race, demanded nuclear disarmament, and deplored the military-industrial complex. Likewise, in the social welfare arena, many left-wing evangelical activists embraced notions of "social sin," criticized capitalism, and called for a new focus on redistribution and social justice.[1] Deeply worried about these developments, conservatives within the movement began to counteract the left-wing drift. In doing so, they formulated an ideology that negotiated between antistatism and the new political realities in church-state relations. On the one hand, the cultural and political upheaval in the aftermath of the 1960s gave new credence to the Right's biblical endorsement of limited government, laissez-faire, and market-based moral reconstruction. On the other hand, however, conservatives did not reject government as such. Instead, the ties to the Cold War state that had developed in the postwar period formed the crucial backdrop for their political assertion within the evangelical fold.

Foreign Policy and the Evangelical Struggle

Despite the apparent political and institutional successes explored in Chapter 3, foreign policy remained a deeply controversial topic within evangelical ranks throughout the Cold War period. Skepticism about America's global role and international entanglements not only found expression in isolationism and unilateralism. Significant elements within evangelical ranks also expressed pacifist sentiments, retained a strong aversion to civil religion, rejected the spiritual sanctification of U.S. foreign policy, denounced the arms race, and demanded nuclear disarmament. As George Marsden put it, "the vision more critical of nation and self-interest is an equally venerable part of a heritage that goes back at least to Roger Williams."[2] Although the demand for "an aggressive spiritual-moral international policy was a recurring plea," a 1956 *Christianity Today* poll of evangelical clergy showed significant support for "world security built on a trusting spiritual level, and less on military spending." Evangelicals not only favored a tough stance against the Soviet Union and opposed recognition of Red China, they also called for decolonization and "less nationalism, more world vision." Likewise, a significant minority called for "less emphasis on bombs and materials for war," more international disarmament negotiations, and even efforts to strengthen international relations through the UN.[3]

Surprisingly, some of the clearest condemnations of the tendency toward civil religion came from the neo-evangelical establishment. In 1967, soon-to-be *Christianity Today* editor Harold Lindsell insisted that the NAE should be brought back to its intellectual roots. Giving voice to traditional premillennialism, he asserted that the church's role was not to "make peace with Caesar's kingdom," but to "witness against the kingdoms of this world," because the solution to the world's moral problems as spelled out in the Bible was "a catastrophic intervention of God." In his view, this included the church not committing itself to either a free market or a managed economy. "The church ought not identify itself with governments, political parties, economic systems, the status quo, revolutionaries or lawbreakers," he declared, warning that if it embraced a particular political agenda, it would become "the voice of those who have managed to seize control of the power structures."[4]

The diversity of evangelical opinion, ranging from strict pacifism to biblical support for militarism, remained a salient feature of the NAE particularly in the post-Vietnam period. In 1977, the NAE reaffirmed its 1952 resolution against "the militarization of the nation in peacetime" and spoke out against universal military training and the proliferation of nuclear weapons. While acknowledging the wide variety of views within its constituency, the resolution stated that "we unite in deploring the mind-set that assumes the way to solve problems is by might and power."[5] In a confidential 1986 *Christianity Today* poll, 23 percent of subscribers listed "continuing arms negotiations with the Soviets" as the most pressing foreign policy issue, and 80 percent expressed support or strong support for further talks with Russia. In regard to defense policies, "pursuing increased nuclear disarmament treaties with the Soviets" and "making substantial cuts in the overall defense budget" were the top priorities (23 and 21 percent respectively), with 72 percent supporting the former and 36 percent the latter; 13 percent even picked unilateral U.S. disarmament as the most important issue. This cause won the support of an impressive 25 percent of those surveyed. In contrast, only 13 percent declared "pursuing the Strategic Defense Initiative" the key issue, backed by 42 percent of respondents.[6]

Similarly, "cutting defense spending to reduce the federal deficit," picked as the third most important economic issue (13 percent), received the support of 50 percent of those polled, while increasing federal spending on defense was favored by only 15 percent. Anticommunism, however, remained high on the agenda: 13 percent each picked the need for the United States to work harder at fighting communism and giving aid to Nicaraguan resistance as the most important issue. However, only 55 percent supported the former—a low figure considering traditional evangelical anticommunism—and 47 percent the latter. Finally, among other issues, "seeing the US initiate a peace process between Israel and the Palestinians" received 71 percent support, imposing economic sanctions on South Africa 39 percent, and maintaining a military presence in the Persian Gulf 71 percent. More support for "the way Israel is handling tensions in the Gaza strip" was supported by only 19 percent.[7]

Conservatives in the movement were increasingly alarmed about this pacifist drift within the evangelical fold, which they feared had the potential to derail their project to build up evangelicals as a coherent religious voting block within the Republican party. In his address on "Christian Responsibility and Government" at the NAE Washington Leadership Briefing in April 1977, Colorado Representative William L. Armstrong, a key figure in engineering links between the NAE and the Republicans, warned about "the evident decline in the willingness of our people to support an adequate national defense." Stoking anticommunist fears and dramatizing the "gap between our expenditure for military research and development and that of the Soviets," he denounced the lack of American resolve and defense funding.[8]

By the early 1980s, however, things still looked bleak as nuclear disarmament continued to attract significant support in the NAE.[9] In turn, OPA director Robert Dugan's invite to President Reagan to speak at the 1983 NAE convention in Orlando explicitly asked for a contribution on military and nuclear defense matters. "An address to NAE could be strategic politically, were the President to articulate his position on national defense," Dugan wrote to Michael K. Deaver, Reagan's deputy chief of staff. While the NCC had already positioned itself on the Left and Catholics were "drifting in the same direction," according to Dugan the NAE stance was still up for grabs. He also assured Deaver that the OPA was "working behind the scenes to counteract some of the drift toward the nuclear freeze position. We are influencing some of our leading evangelical journals and are one of the conveners of the first major national conference for evangelicals on the subject of peacemaking in this nuclear age."[10]

The conference Dugan referred to took place in May 1983 at Fuller Seminary in Pasadena. Designed to explore biblical perspectives on war and peace issues, this seminal gathering on "The Church and Peacemaking in the Nuclear Age" brought together 1,400 registrants who represented a broad cross-section of the North American evangelical constituency.[11] Dugan was actively trying to stack the conference with conservative speakers on defense issues. "We are attempting to assure that strong conservative voices will be heard," he told Deaver.[12] For this purpose, Dugan invited assistant secretary of defense Arthur E. Dewey, Representative Kenneth Kramer, and a number of military officers active in the Officers' Christian Union or teaching at Cal Tech.[13] Although Carl Henry dropped out and Harold O. J. Brown, a prominent evangelical writer and theologian, declined to participate, Dugan was able to rely on Bill Armstrong. He also urged renowned evangelical theologian Francis A. Schaeffer to "bring balance to the program," expressing to "Fran" his concern that evangelicals might end up embracing a nuclear freeze position. "Those on the left in the evangelical community are much more eager to speak out on the subject of national defense and the nuclear arms race," he warned. "We fear that if evangelicals who are conservative on national defense issues are unwilling to enter the dialogue, supporters of the nuclear freeze will win evangelicals' minds by default."[14]

Dugan combined this appeal with his long-term political aspiration to mobilize evangelicals for the Republican party. "I am deeply concerned that the public not perceive evangelicals as irretrievably leaning to the left on the issue of national defense," he declared, concluding that "Frankly, we think that the White House is looking to evangelicals as the one major religious bloc that may support the President's position."[15] He put this even more bluntly in a letter to retired Lieutenant General Daniel O. Graham: "Our concern, quite candidly, is that evangelicals not wind up, in a few years, with the same problem as the mainline Christian denominations—an elite, radical fringe dominating a sullen but coopted majority."[16]

Instead of providing the reassurances he sought, however, the conference dramatically highlighted Dugan's problem. Though listed on the program, several of the well-known evangelical leaders who identified with the aggressive "peace through strength" politics of the Reagan administration did not show up, and it was left to the NAE's Dave Breese to summarize the conservative position. Breese argued that nuclear arms in the hands of the United States had kept the peace and that the country had no intention toward world conquest.[17] However, Breese came across as "a militant patriot with no apparent hesitation about using nuclear weapons to rid the world of communism." Meanwhile, the evangelical Left was represented by a number of articulate spokesmen. In turn, the "enthusiastic response to major addresses by Ronald Sider and Jim Wallis suggested that the doves outnumbered the hawks."[18]

The spin conservatives put on a nuclear arms race poll commissioned by the NAE in the year of the conference illustrated just how controversial their position remained within the movement. It also indicated their continuing worries about the evangelical position on national defense. Although the poll actually revealed little evangelical deviation from general public opinion, the text of the news release suggested that evangelicals were in support of Reagan policies. For example, a lower percentage of evangelicals (41 percent) than of the general public (43 percent) approved of the way Reagan dealt with the nuclear arms situation. By excluding those who expressed no opinion, the news release suggested that 61 percent of evangelicals but only 56 percent of the general public supported Reagan. The significantly higher number of abstentions among evangelicals as compared to the general public, however, was more indicative of the traditional apolitical stance of many conservative Protestants than of their tacit approval of government policies. Nonetheless, the news flash construed the figures to indicate overwhelming evangelical support for Reagan's view that the United States was falling behind the USSR in the nuclear field and needed to match Soviet arms capabilities.

The news release had to resort to even more rhetorical gymnastics in order to put a similar conservative twist on evidence that the movement contained a large liberal or undecided contingent on the nuclear freeze issue. According to the poll, the majority of evangelicals demanded an immediate freeze on the testing, production, and deployment of nuclear weapons (60 percent, or 77 percent with "no opinion" excluded). "The results may initially seem surprising, considering the general peace through strength stance of evangelicals revealed by this poll," the news release admitted. Yet it concluded that "it is apparent that evangelical approval of a nuclear freeze is heavily dependent on any such freeze being verifiable and bilateral." In backing up this statement, the report noted that most evangelicals did not believe that the Soviet Union would allow on-site inspections, 82 percent opposed a unilateral American freeze, and 85 percent felt that possession of nuclear weapons for defensive purposes was not inconsistent with being a Christian. Once again these figures combined the "yes" and the "no opinion" votes. Disaggregated, however, they showed that evangelicals were less likely than the general public to think that the Soviet Union would oppose on-site inspections (76 compared to 78 percent). The figures also indicated that only 67 percent opposed a unilateral nuclear freeze, and that more members of the general public (77 percent) than of the evangelical community (72 percent) thought owning nuclear weapons could be reconciled with being a Christian.[19]

It was clearly time for conservatives to act if they wanted to bring evangelical opinion in line with their partisan political aspirations. Disturbed by the influence of pacifist or near-pacifist voices, the NAE Executive Committee authorized the OPA in Washington to conduct a "feasibility study on how the NAE could best provide leadership in questions of war and peace" in response to "concerns many expressed over the Pasadena Conference on Biblical Peacemaking." The objective was clear: While the NAE had in the past mainly focused on domestic public policy, "Evangelical concern for the moral dimension in all aspects of public life, including international affairs, needed to be transmitted to decision-makers." The result was the launch of the NAE's Peace, Freedom and Security Studies Program (PFSS) in 1984.[20]

Coordinated by OPA intern Brian O'Connell, whom Dugan lauded for knowing both the evangelical leadership and major players in Washington, the ambitious PFSS task included organizing correspondence courses, study kits, a Sunday school curriculum, a speaker's bureau, a college conference series, a media Leadership Network, ministry consultations, and lunches on foreign policy issues.[21] Reporting to the NAE board, Dugan saw PFSS as providing "unique leadership to the evangelical community with a biblically responsive quest for peace, that includes advocacy of international human rights and recognizes the legitimacy of the constitutional duty of government 'to provide for the common defense.'"[22] By 1985 the program was well under way. "Currently a major working group is being developed to prepare the process by which guidelines for the war/peace discussion in the evangelical community can be formulated," Dugan told the NAE board.[23] By 1989 the PFSS leadership network had grown to over five hundred, and plans were afoot to move the thrust "away from consultations across the nation toward the increase of evangelical influence in the foreign and defense policy arenas."[24] Despite some successes in obtaining outside funding, however, financial problems continued to beset the organization.[25]

A key supporter and non-evangelical member of the PFSS advisory board was Robert Pickus, a Jewish peace activist and president of the World Without War Council (WWWC). The organization was formed in the late 1960s after a Vietnam-related split within Turn Toward Peace (TTP), a cooperative venture of some sixty peace and liberal internationalist organizations. Rather than just working with pacifist groups opposed to the war in Indochina, WWWC engaged with a broader spectrum of organizations interested in America's role in world affairs.[26] One of its sister organizations was The James Madison Foundation. Its founding president, George Weigel, was the second non-evangelical on the twenty-member PFSS advisory board. Together with other conservative Catholics, including the American Enterprise Institute's Michael Novak and the Institute on Religion and Public Life's Richard John Neuhaus, Weigel subsequently emerged as a leading "theoconservative," a group of religious intellectuals who regarded the United States as first and foremost a Christian nation. Later based at the conservative Ethics and Public Policy Center (EPPC), he was a charter signatory of the neoconservative Project for the New American Century (PNAC).[27]

An old hand at foreign policy issues, Pickus was seen as both an inspiration and a nuisance by conservative evangelicals. On the one hand, he helped shape an evangelical position on foreign policy by giving voice to an embryonic version of the neoconservative agenda that combined unilateralist intervention with universalist claims. Although Pickus lambasted both pacifists within the evangelical movement for making America the villain and conservatives for thinking that America was always right, Dugan was pleased to note that Pickus found the Right more open than the Left. In particular, Dugan approved of his linking peace to freedom, supporting America's role in the world, and suggesting the use of the church as a center for studying peace issues.[28] Likewise, Dugan endorsed Pickus's poignant criticism of the peace movement as "carriers of [the] Soviet agenda" and his efforts to tie peace to the spread of American-style democracy while rejecting "world government."[29]

On the other hand, O'Connell in particular sought to limit the incursions by WWWC into PFSS seminars. In a memo to Dugan and NAE director Billy Melvin he complained that "the role of Bob Pickus seemed too dominant for an evangelical audience." Although acknowledging that Pickus was "the person to help bring NAE and PFSS from where we were to where we are," O'Connell doubted that he was "the person to lead us where we want to go." PFSS, he suggested, should keep him as a consultant, but "I think we need to make his role a less prominent one in the future."[30]

The PFSS stance, which verged on a civil religious identification of peace with American-style democracy, was not without its critics even within the NAE's upper echelons. Controversies about how to represent the diversity of evangelical sentiments continued throughout the 1980s.[31] "The American Enterprise Institute, American Heritage Foundation, Institute for Religion and Democracy, Hoover Institute, and the N.A.E. Office of Public Affairs all seem to agree on the same positions," NAE Social Action Commission chairman Wilbert Hill complained: "nowhere do I see organizations like Physicians for Social Responsibility, Beyond War, Center for Defense Information, or Union of Concerned Scientists acknowledged as expressing valid viewpoints." He criticized O'Connell for ignoring groups on the evangelical Left, such as Sojourners, and for misrepresenting the positions of Mennonite PFSS advisory board member Myron Augsburger and Messiah College. "Is N.A.E.'s purpose to take opposite stands to Sojourners and Evangelicals for Social Action on its biblical positions? Is Dallas Seminary expressing the only viewpoints that N.A.E. wishes to accept as biblical?," he asked. Charging the NAE with ignoring Augsburger, Evangelical for Social Action's Ron Sider, Sojourner Community's Jim Wallis, and Calvary Ministries' John Perkins, Hill concluded that "I hope that the word liberal will not become a bad word in N.A.E."[32]

Although conservative evangelicals ultimately managed to sideline pacifist sentiments, they nonetheless took on board left-wing evangelical concerns. In effect, they asserted their claim to political leadership within the evangelical fold by forging a distinctive policy profile that combined Cold War intransigence with concerns about human rights and political oppression. As Robert Dugan put it, "unlike other religious agencies, we are committed to linking international peace with both national security and human rights."[33] Though largely a mouthpiece of conservatism, PFSS sought to mediate between Left and Right. It aimed to avoid the most conspicuous error of the Right, namely "unquestioning support of any and all U.S. defense programs," while also sidestepping the most conspicuous error of the Left, that is, "seeing America as the source of evil in the international community."[34] Its funding request to the Pew Trust in the early 1990s declared that in contrast to "highly partisan, crises-centered" programs dominated by church leaders "with already committed military/patriotic or Third World/Liberationist perspectives," PFSS was in the vanguard of building "a consensus on the moral purpose of America's role in world affairs." Its main objective was to remedy "the inadequate response of American Christians to dilemmas of moral purpose and power in the foreign and defense policy arena" and to tie "civic education on freedom and democracy to wider concepts of community values."[35] In short, PFSS connected "peace" and "freedom" in ways that anticipated the neoconservative agenda of the late 1990s.

The Welfare State, the Evangelical Left, and the Right-Wing Resurgence

As in the case of foreign policy, the growing ties between evangelicals and the subsidiarist welfare state proved beneficial for conservatives in the evangelical fold and their ability to calibrate between contradictory positions, build effective political networks, and marginalize internal opponents. In the 1960s, the newly resurgent Left had broadly supported expanding the social responsibilities of the state. "We should not begrudge the extra money that is withheld from our pay check to insure that all of our citizens receive proper medical care," Rufus Jones, who later joined the left-leaning Evangelicals for Social Action, argued in expressing his sympathies with the War on Poverty. Although the poor needed not only "good housing, welfare checks, and a retraining program," but also the Gospel of Christ, he reminded his fellow evangelicals that foreign missionaries had not only built churches but also sought to "minister to the total needs of the people" by erecting schools and hospitals.[36]

Support for the welfare state on the part of progressive evangelicals drew upon an established strain of anticapitalist thought in conservative Protestantism. Encompassing about 20–30 percent of believers in the evangelical spectrum, those in the "prophet of justice/professional caregiver" category (Timothy Clydesdale) saw poverty as rooted in structural and societal evil. They called for enhanced government regulation of economic life, increased social spending, and redistributive politics. Many within this spectrum urged the state to guarantee employment, housing, food, and health care. They viewed the lack of funding, rather than personal iniquity or dubious moral messages, as the main problem of the welfare system.[37] "Too often evangelicals have blindly accepted arguments for limiting government action to combat social evil in the mistaken belief that expanded government intervention is necessarily a greater evil than that to which it is directed," Carl Henry's son Paul declared. Because of this, he warned, "the well-intentioned convictions of evangelicals have been exploited by those who benefit from the government's inability to attack social evil and injustice."[38] Arguing that freedoms were won not only *against* government, but also through it, liberal and left-leaning evangelicals regarded state intervention as a force that could change behavior patterns and transform the moral climate. They noted the ambiguity of sacred texts on social and economic issues, remained critical of capitalism, and rejected the link between conservative religion and right-wing politics. Urging evangelicals to become involved in issues such as social housing, equal opportunity, civil rights, and drug treatment, they deplored the Right's antilabor biases, rabid anticommunism, latent racism, patriotic chauvinism, and tendency toward civil religion.[39]

This, however, was exactly where the Left's problem lay. In effect, its anticapitalist and community-action impulse, and opposition to civil religion and militarism, translated into a renewed rejection of the liberal state in the aftermath of the Vietnam and Watergate debacles. Politicized by the Civil Rights Movement, and disillusioned by the pitfalls of the Great Society, the war in Southeast Asia, and corruption in high places, many left-leaning evangelicals turned their backs on the state. As their social awakening coincided with the crisis of government in general and the welfare state in particular, they were torn between pursuing political involvement and finding spiritual meaning and renewal in separationist social action. Support for state intervention was thus countermanded by antiliberal, countercultural, and anti-establishmentarian sentiments in the post-1960s era. By the late 1960s it was apparent that the commitment to social action and the desire to make their voice heard in government had diverged within the left-leaning evangelical spectrum.

Fragmented, polarized, and weakened, the evangelical Left and mainstream were by the mid-1970s in no position to rein in the newly assertive Right within the movement. Benefiting from the crisis of liberalism and the failure of the NAE to form a strong center, the conservatives emerged victorious from the drawn-out internal political and doctrinal battles. On the surface the message from the Right was blunt and uncompromising in its rejection of left-wing evangelical positions. Outright opposition to the welfare state informed its main social and economic agenda and sat alongside its ferocious anticommunism and flag-waving patriotism. These attacks on the welfare state were grounded in the Right's embrace of the social and economic dogmas of late nineteenth-century liberalism. Discarding traditional misgivings about the "materialistic" theory of free enterprise and laissez faire, conservatives depicted idealized market capitalism as a biblically endorsed system and regarded the welfare state as an expression of secular humanism and materialism.

Despite its biblical grounding, the Right's position was thus largely indistinguishable from secular conservative attacks on the welfare state. Mesmerized by an atomistic view of individuals and a contractual concept of society, conservative evangelicals zealously denounced "collectivism" as automatically leading to a police state. They fervently adopted the secular New Right's "new class theories," which blamed unaccountable bureaucratic elites for creating a welfare system that turned the poor into dependents, undermined their moral stamina, rewarded the indolent, and served to perpetuate a parasitic class of administrators. Depicting America as engaged in a moral and spiritual war between capitalism and socialism, they called for biblically mandated limits on the power of the state. They also regarded redistributive taxation as theft prohibited by the Eighth Commandment, denounced social welfare schemes as ungodly perversions based on the politics of resentment, and declared efforts to even out socioeconomic injustices undesirable.[40]

Superficially, the Right's wholehearted embrace of laissez faire and antiwelfarism thus suggested a return to traditional separationist positions. A closer look, however, shows that a much closer relationship to the state was at the heart of the right-wing position. What characterized the Right was not outright denunciation, but the embrace of state building embedded in an antistatist message. In many ways evangelical conservatives completed the statist and subsidiarist turns of postwar evangelicalism and used them to strengthen their position within the movement. We can trace this process by looking at three aspects of the political assertion of the evangelical Right: its focus on moral issues in social policy in conjunction with its embrace of subsidiarity; its efforts to establish a political presence within the Republican party; and its campaign to disavow left-wing evangelical separationism. The analysis suggests that the way in which conservatives used church-state issues in the context of the internal battles within the evangelical movement was characterized by three main strategies of political mobilization. The Right's moral issues orientation reflected efforts to *calibrate* between retaining an antistatist message and building on the institutional integration into the Cold War state. Its various proposals for public aid for religious agencies became a key agenda in its broader political *networking*. And its rejection of traditional church-state separation turned out to be an effective tool in *marginalizing* internal critics.

Calibrating: Subsidiarity and "Moral Issues"

Viewed in the context of the transformation of evangelical church-state attitudes, the emphasis on "moral issues" in evangelical politics neither indicates the rejection of the welfare state nor suggests a return to traditional pietism. Instead, "morality politics" was indicative of the tension between the ideology of separation and the embrace of public aid for religious agencies that had developed under the aegis of subsidiarity, particularly since the 1960s. The Right's focus on moral issues in social policy reflected an evangelical effort to develop a coherent political agenda that mediated between cultural alienation and institutional integration. Hence, when conservative evangelicals decried abortion, homosexuality, and "permissiveness," they were no longer concerned with public aid to religion but were attempting to ensure the normative content of social policies in an allegedly secularist welfare state threatening to undermine Christian morality. Likewise, when they called for a renewed emphasis on market solutions, suggested the replacement of government programs with charities, and elevated spiritual conversion over social equity, they did not revive separationist mantras but sought to assert church influence in social provision in an era of increasing public subsidies.

The politics of morality so effectively invoked by evangelicals in the 1970s and 1980s as a tool for political mobilization thus needs to be understood as part and parcel of the movement's statist turn. Rather than solely reflecting a post-1960s backlash against the liberal state, it was a particular conservative way of reasserting the trajectory of Cold War state building. This function of morality politics mirrors that of its ideological precursor, namely, anticommunism. As discussed in Chapter 3, anticommunism combined fiery antistatist rhetoric with the embrace of the expanded national security state. Similarly, the moralistic dimension of anticommunism, which the critical literature has identified as the inspiration for the "social issues" focus of the Right in the 1980s, helped reassert the repressive state. In the same vein, morality politics, while broadcasting the moral failures of the liberal state, sanctioned the expansion of the welfare state via punitive, growth-oriented, and subsidiarist policies.

First, evangelicals tended to support means and morals testing and other economistic and punitive social policies. Based on "measurable outcomes," "cost effectiveness," and invidious social distinctions, a vast bureaucratic apparatus was often required to administer these programs that reserved "respectable" entitlements for "worthy" groups and offered meager welfare as a "gratuity" for the "undeserving" poor. While largely perpetuating a segmented system of social provision along race and gender lines, however, this complex set-up at the same time militated against the large-scale dismantling of the welfare state (see Chapter 1). Retrenchment targeted mainly the fiscally insignificant programs benefiting the poor and minorities, such as employment training funds, AFDC, and food stamps. During the Reagan years, for example, the main casualty of retrenchment was welfare, rather than the welfare state. Indeed, devolution and block grants did not lead to a reduction in federal expenditure. As many observers have argued, the Reagan administration's unique contribution to dismantling the U.S. version of the welfare state lay not so much in cutting funding in general as in reducing benefits for specific groups of welfare recipients.[41] By the same token, retrenchment affirmed the police power dimension of social policy. It emphasized behavioral requirements and intrusive regulation, and demanded that the poor exert moral self-control, be responsible, and seek gainful employment. Evangelical activists, for example, reserved their most fiery criticism for AFDC, the assistance program that, in their view, embodied the "moral failures" of the welfare state by encouraging young women to "flout parental authority and indulge in their sexuality."[42] In turn, the Reagan revolution also meant a return to a discretionary welfare system under state control and an increasing reliance on restrictive measures, such as workfare policies, expanding the police force, the use of curfews, and antiloitering laws.[43]

Second, in advocating an antipoverty policy that linked moral conversion to the market participation of autonomous, competitive individuals, conservatives effectively extolled the virtues of the American consumer economy and located the solution to deprivation in growth-oriented economic policies. As David Watt has argued, the explicit embrace of free enterprise, private ownership, and postwar consumer society constituted one of the key changes of fundamentalism in the postwar period. This "consumerist turn" involved basic support for government-induced and bureaucratically administered macroeconomic intervention and constituted another element in the postwar secularization of fundamentalism.[44]

And last, but not least, morality politics, in denouncing "the New Deal-Great Society welfare structure [that] systematized and expanded care for the poor, but in a way that had little room . . . for the religious organizations," sanctioned the expansion of state-funded social provision.[45] In calling for the spiritualization of social service via religious providers, and linking the effectiveness of welfare policy to the individual experience of faith, morality politics demanded public funding for the "mediating structures" that would "constitute vehicles by which personal beliefs and values could be transmitted" between the private worlds of individuals and the large impersonal structures of society.[46] While evangelicals continued to voice a deep distrust in the state and to depict charitable service providers as alternatives to public institutions, they simultaneously affirmed the basic features of Cold War subsidiarity.

In combining moralism with a pro-public funding stance, conservatives both undermined and built upon left-wing social action impulses. On the one hand, they actively sought to assert moral themes over and against socioeconomic and structural concerns. Whereas a vocal evangelical Left attacked the military-industrial complex and economic oppression inherent in the capitalist order, conservative evangelicals reduced social problems to sinful individuals and argued that there was no biblical mandate for state interference in the economy.[47] The advantage of focusing on abortion, homosexuality, and similar themes was that while evangelicals were deeply split on socioeconomic issues they were largely united on moral concerns. Particularly in the post-1960s age when many were searching for moral certainty, the Right's campaign could rely on the broad resonance of normative anxieties within the evangelical spectrum in ways the Left's calls for socioeconomic change could not. The conservatives' renewed emphasis on moral causes and biblical orthodoxy thus amounted to an effective response to the constituency's desire for a unified political and theological voice.

On the other hand, the Right's focus on morality built on the emphasis on social concern and political involvement that 1960s evangelicals had succeeded in placing at the center of the postwar resurgence. The moral campaigns of the Christian Right drew particular strength from the insurgent, countercultural, and anti-establishmentarian dimensions of the renewed emphasis on social action pioneered by the Left. The Right exploited the dilemma of a Left caught between a social concern impulse that saw the state as a necessary instrument of redistribution and social justice, and a growing aversion to large-scale organizations and Vietnam-era frustration with "managerial liberalism." In combining traditional moralism and antiliberalism with a continued commitment to social involvement, the Christian Right perpetuated the specific sentiments and settings that had motivated the Left.[48]

Similarly, the embrace of subsidiarist thinking and practices by the Right enabled conservatives to appropriate and absorb left-wing impulses. More often than not, left-leaning evangelicals in the 1960s had been quite willing to participate in public aid arrangements, particularly in the area of housing and homelessness.[49] However, as disillusionment with Vietnam-era government grew among evangelical grassroots activists, the debate about the attitude toward the liberal state extended into the area of public funding. Despite the explosion of evangelical charitable activism under the auspices of a newly resurgent evangelical Left, many activists in the 1970s turned away from the federal government and toward local and neighborhood organizations. The effect was that by the 1980s the evangelical establishment was largely immobilized and left-wing groups had withdrawn into a small group and communitarian culture.[50]

This withdrawal opened up new opportunities for the resurgent Right. While the Left was calling for church-state separation and was distancing itself from government, many conservative evangelicals renewed their commitment to bringing about a Christian state and nurtured closer funding ties with government. In short, the Left's sense of alienation from government generated by Vietnam and Watergate ran deeper than the Right's sense of alienation nurtured by permissive social policies. While the social concern of the evangelical Left tended to lead *away* from government involvement, the moral reform impulse of the Right tended to lead *toward* government involvement.

As conservative evangelicals discovered the instrumentalities of third-sector funding in the aftermath of the expansion of subsidiarist policies by the Johnson administration, they built on the Left's experience of legislative campaigning, direct lobbying, and renewed social involvement to set up the organizational networks and structures required for effective internal political mobilization. Although the explicit aim of conservative evangelicals was to create a church-centered alternative to the welfare state based on charitable efforts, the reality was a symbiosis of government and nonprofits.[51] It is this combination that developed broad-based appeal in the evangelical movement in the post-1960s era. Indeed, the charitable sector became a meeting ground that facilitated crossovers between both ends of the evangelical spectrum.[52]

One example of this process is Prison Fellowship Ministries (PFM), an evangelical agency founded in 1976 by Charles Colson, the "evil genius" of the Nixon administration who spent seven months in prison after his Watergate-related conviction in the break-in at the office of Daniel Ellsberg's psychiatrist.[53] PFM programs include running special prison wings, state-financed biblical immersion courses, lessons in creationism, substance abuse counseling, and vocational training. They also extend to "biblically based therapy" designed to transform prisoners through an "instantaneous miracle," convert them out of homosexuality, and cure sex offenders.[54] In prisons where PFM has a significant presence, the religious activities of other faith groups are often restricted. Meanwhile, prisoners who turn to God can expect improved conditions and visitation rights, better prison jobs, and enhanced prospects for parole. As an inmate in a Kansas prison that had partially been turned over to PFM stated, "The Christians do lots of stuff the state used to do, like vocational programs, but now they're only for believers."[55]

PFM grew out of the social action impulses of 1970s evangelicalism. It attributed the gap between Christian belief, behavior, and influence within society to the singular focus of the church on evangelism and placed itself in the tradition of the social gospel and the Salvation Army.[56] It also cultivated contacts with left-wing evangelical organizations such as ESA, Sojourners, and Voice of Calvary. At the same time, its efforts to take public funds put it at odds with the evangelical Left. Providing Colson with background information on Sojourners, PFM aide Michael Cromartie, for example, noted that Jim Wallis saw a tension between state permission to work in prisons and a religious approach "that ultimately might put us in conflict with the state by the very essence of the prophetic message we preach."[57]

At the same time Colson enjoyed cordial relations with the NAE and evangelical conservatives. He regarded homosexuality as sinful and evil and warned that to legalize it "would be for society to sanction the deterioration of the family and encourage the destruction of the human race." He expressed strong support for Anita Bryant's campaign in the mid-1970s to prevent gay equality, and denounced sexual liberation, abortion, Islam and the teaching of evolution.[58] Nonetheless, Colson sought to distance PFM from the more lurid dimensions of the resurgent Christian Right. He warned against the "paranoid prattlings of the John Birches in our ranks" and against conforming "the Gospel to a so called conservative political framework." In his view, the danger was that this would "exclude liberals from our ranks" and further exacerbate the differences between mainline churches and evangelicals. "I love Pat Robertson and Jerry Falwell," he declared, "They are both beautiful brothers, but either one could get carried away by his own notion of himself as a Messianic political figure."[59] This caused some irritation among the more outspoken advocates of allying mainstream evangelicalism with the resurgent Right. "I share your tacit concern that many of Chuck Colson's nuanced observations have kept the trumpet from giving a certain sound," the NAE's Robert Dugan confided in a letter to James Dobson, the founder of the conservative Focus on the Family organization.[60]

Michael Cromartie, a former ESA board member who became active in PFM, exemplifies the transition from left- to right-wing evangelicalism. While working for Colson, Cromartie was in the forefront of seeking to prevent the organization from getting sucked into resurgent neofundamentalism. He advised Colson against appearing on Jim Bakker's PTL television show. Offended by the "crass materialism and appearances of hucksterism" of PTL, he noted that Bakker drove around in a Rolls Royce and that Billy Graham's son-in-law Leighton Ford refused to appear on the show.[61] Likewise, Cromartie was shocked by the mixture of fire-and-brimstone preaching and frenzied nationalism that awaited PFM staff on a trip to a Revival Fires Chapel event in Joplin, Missouri. The "Americanized 'Gospel'" of founder Cecil Todd "seemed to be playing upon their worst fears and anxieties by screaming out against smut, filth, pornography, immorality, homosexuality, and rape," a disheartened Cromartie recorded. He admonished Colson not to appear in Revival Fires' national TV specials that promoted "American nationalism alongside Christianity." This "whoop-tee-do about God, Country, and legalistic morality may be impressive to some people, but I don't think the fusion of such doctrines is something you would want to condone," he asserted. Colson agreed. "Mike is correct," he noted on the margin of the memorandum, "it was bad, very bad—I'd rather return the 5,000—maybe we should anyway."[62] Nonetheless, despite these efforts to disassociate evangelicals from the Right, Cromartie had by the 1980s joined the conservative Washington think tank Ethics and Public Policy Center.[63]

PFM was among the evangelical social service agencies most adept at cultivating ties with politicians and like-minded organizations for the purpose of obtaining public funding. Its push for public support for Christian alternatives to incarceration for nonviolent offenders reflected the subsidiarist turn of evangelicalism that privileged expanded state funding over limited government.[64] Fearing that Republicans would "let pass" legislation imposing mandatory minimum sentences, preventive detention and fixed sentences without the possibility of parole, PFM Counsel Daniel Van Ness urged Colson to meet with Sam Nunn (D-Ga.) and others to "convince them that alternatives is the true conservative (fiscally) issue."[65] Moreover, PFM embodied the basic ideological premise of the evangelical embrace of subsidiarity, namely that individual conversion eliminated the need for social programs focused on structural economic issues. As Tanya Erzen has noted, the "testimonial politics" of organizations such as PFM shored up a vision of welfare in which social services were privatized rather than run by the federal government.[66]

By 2003 PFM had grown into the largest prison ministry worldwide as numerous states, aided by the federal government's efforts to increase funding for faith-based organizations, had turned over portions of their prison budgets to this evangelical organization. PFM officials also ran "Dare Mighty Things," which received a $2.2 million grant from the Department of Health and Human Services to function as a clearinghouse for faith-based and community groups applying for federal money. Moreover, policy makers held out the prospect of a complete takeover of prisons by organizations such as PFM. There was also a revolving door between the public and religious sectors in this area, with former PFM staff landing jobs as prison officials.[67] Indeed, although PFM activists stress that their movement is local and grassroots, it is tied to a national campaign of the Christian Right to pursue access to state resources.[68]

Ironically, it was AU, the NAE's former separationist ally, that temporarily put a wrench in the PFM works. In 2003 it filed a successful lawsuit against PFM in an effort to challenge faith-based initiatives on constitutional grounds. The District Court ruling ordered the Iowa program of the PFM's InnerChange Freedom Initiative to be shut and made the organization repay the state the $1.5 million it had been given for services. However, this ruling was largely overturned in 2007 by the Court of Appeals for the Eighth Circuit. In reversing the prior ruling, the court rejected the "pervasively sectarian" standard used by the District Court and affirmed that religious organizations were not barred from cooperating with government simply because they were faith-based.[69]

THE NAE AND "CULTURAL CONSERVATISM"

PFM illustrates the confluence of efforts to create a church-centered alternative to the welfare state with the embrace of the subsidiarist state. It also highlights the links between left-leaning evangelicalism and the conservative resurgence. The NAE's links to Paul Weyrich and the concept of "cultural conservatism," meanwhile, exemplify the emergence of a conservative evangelical agenda that combined statism, subsidiarity, and the embrace of economic growth politics with an antistatist, separationist, and moralistic message. OPA director Robert Dugan in particular was attracted by Weyrich and his Free Congress Research and Education Foundation. "The more I learn about this, the more enthused I become," he wrote to Weyrich, lauding in particular the "shift from a predominant focus on economics to questions of morals and values."[70]

By the early 1990s Dugan had emerged as a key figure in politicizing evangelicals around the culture war theme, particularly via the NAE's Christian Citizenship Campaign. Seeking to "enlist an all-volunteer army to win the culture war in a campaign of prayer and voting," he declared that evangelical churches were "battling against secularism in 'a new civil war.'"[71] His fundraising efforts for the campaign were designed "to arm evangelical churches" with "the spiritual power of prayer" and "the political weapon of the vote, through non-partisan registration in the churches."[72] Writing to Weyrich in order to get himself placed in a working group on the culture war at the Heritage Foundation, he flaunted his impeccable conservative credentials: "I am strongly committed to calling the evangelical community to a warfare status, with a November to November strategy leading to the 1992 elections."[73]

The appeal of cultural conservatism to evangelicals rested on four features that neatly summed up the NAE's revised social policy agenda. First, cultural conservatism maintained that solutions to social problems involved the federal government and not just markets. "Too many conservatives believe one can govern simply by saying, 'Get the government out of such and such,'" Weyrich declared. In contrast, he suggested that "government not only can but must be a positive force, a force for good."[74] Much of this grew out of the disappointment with the Reagan and Bush administrations' failure to push for a moral agenda. As William Lind, director of the Institute for Cultural Conservatism put it: "If it is 'morning in America', it is a morning bleak and gray. The dawn proved false."[75]

Second, Weyrich called for New Deal-like experimentation, the devolution of government functions to the state level and, most importantly, for providing public funds to churches and community organizations via contracting. "Families, churches, service organizations, and community groups can provide the non-material support that people need far better than government can, because they work through people who have made a personal commitment," he asserted. In his view, "Public policy's proper role is to encourage and support mediating institutions. That may mean contracting out to such institutions, including churches and synagogues, the delivery of government-funded services."[76]

Mirroring the transformation of church-state thinking within the evangelical fold, Weyrich drew a clear distinction between church-state issues and the relationship between religion and public policy. Whereas the former involved questions about whether the state should profess a specific religious belief, he argued, the latter looked at the functional value of religious commitment for the delivery of social policy goals. Religious observance and traditional values, he maintained, were socially beneficial on a mass scale. They lowered drug abuse, crime, suicide rates, and teen-age pregnancy, while facilitating higher voter turnout and job retention rates. In his view, policy goals should include the recognition "that a general encouragement of religion does not violate the principle of separation of church and state." In this context he called for returning to government and public schools "a measure of legal flexibility, so that they can experiment with mutually beneficial partnerships with religious institutions," including help with the "financial burden on parents who seek to give their children a religious education." Moreover, he strongly encouraged using religious agencies for delivery of social services, noting that "churches, synagogues and other religious and moral institutions located among the poor should be regarded as major sources of talent and expertise in the distribution of welfare benefits."[77]

Third, Weyrich linked subsidiarity to social policies that explicitly rewarded traditional values, such as delayed gratification, self-improvement, and the rejection of drugs and casual sex. "Subsidies must be structured to uphold and reward traditional values, not undermine them," he declared. He called for a new "social compact" under which the state would support adequate funding for welfare. In exchange, charities should work toward integrating welfare programs with traditional values. Instead of "dollar welfare," which merely provided money, "cultural welfare" included giving payments only to intact families, requiring those under age twenty-one to live with their parents, the adoption of tenant management programs, and "education vouchers to facilitate the establishment of alternative, high-quality inner-city schools, characterized by strong discipline."[78]

Finally, in conjunction with this shift from income maintenance to restoring people to the role of individual producers, cultural conservatism embraced the modern concept of economic growth. "Prosperity is one of the important 'glues' that holds our diverse society together," Weyrich announced, listing a focus on job growth, taxing consumption rather than income, protectionism, and employee ownership as means of uniting labor and management among his key public policy objectives.[79] This entailed basic support for government-induced and bureaucratically administered macroeconomic intervention. By making his case in broad normative and functional terms, Weyrich regarded cultural conservatism as a strategy to build bridges across the partisan divide. "If conservatives intend to seek a mandate to govern, they must be prepared to govern, prepared with a broad array of policy actions" in their effort to uphold and rebuild national culture.[80]

Weyrich's concept neatly encapsulated what the conservative embrace of subsidiarity was all about. Allocative policies were not simply functional policy instruments that structured the relationship between government, business, and nonprofit organizations. They were ideological constructs that asserted the normative basis of Cold War social policy, demarcated the role of government in social and economic affairs, defined the nature of economic well-being, and framed social problems. By defining individuals either as self-interested consumers operating freely in a marketplace, or as morally deficient "sinners" in need of punitive intervention and moral rehabilitation, they helped maintain the tiered structure of social provision. They sanctioned both the expansion of state-funded social provision and affirmed the antistatist ethic of individual self-help and economic self-sufficiency. In so doing, subsidiarist structures transported specific gender, race, and class divides. Depicting the market in terms of "self-regulation" and "free enterprise," and the public sphere in terms of regulatory intervention and punitive control, they guaranteed economic freedom on the basis of a segmented workforce, unequally remunerated work, and the maldistribution of the economic costs of reproduction. In other words, the evangelical embrace of subsidiarity was tied to reasserting white masculine authority in a postsegregationist, postpatriarchal, and postindustrial age.[81]

Dugan shared Weyrich's critique of New Right antistatism as well as his pragmatic conception of religious values, his subsidiarist policy prescriptions, and his desire for a broad-based coalition. He assured Weyrich that he could "count on us at the National Association of Evangelicals to be involved in the intellectual process of developing cultural conservatism and in the political process of bringing it to bear upon the nation."[82] Economic conservatism, Dugan concurred, was insufficient to deal with the nation's problems. The New Right and religious Right agenda "was too narrowly framed" by excluding culture as the basis of society.[83] This applied in particular to social policy where the "free market doesn't solve welfare problems."[84]

Likewise, shedding the last vestiges of evangelical separationism, Dugan embraced a functional concept of religion that saw a "necessary, unbreakable, and causal relationship between traditional Western, Judeo-Christian values . . . and the secular success of Western societies" in which traditional values "give us . . . a society where things work."[85] He also actively employed this argument in his fundraising efforts for the NAE's Christian Citizenship Campaign. "In this time of culture war over the values that have historically made America great," he contended, companies and private charities could surely not stand aside.[86] Finally, Dugan, shared Weyrich's hopes for an inclusive political movement. "In constructing this broader and more profound conservative agenda," he concluded, "all evangelical political leaders should come aboard, including some who may have found themselves at odds with the 'New Right.'"[87] At the same time, however, Dugan clearly placed his bets with the Republican party. He participated in Weyrich's briefings in 1988 on defeating the Democrats and stressed that Republicans needed an issue-oriented campaign to counter the Democratic majority.[88]

Subsidiarity and Networking

Combining the instrumentalities of federal aid with a conservative social agenda, subsidiarity became an important element in the developing nexus between secular and religious conservatism and in infusing an evangelical agenda into the Republican party. In addition to morality politics and economic conservatism, public funding policies formed the third pillar of evangelical social policy lobbying by the 1980s. Various forms of public aid, primarily tax credits and vouchers in education, health care, and social services, were no longer simply grudgingly accepted by evangelicals, but constituted one of their major political demands.

Well into the 1970s, questions of church-state separation had divided the NAE and political conservatives. Ironically, Kennedy's views on separationism in 1960 were closer to evangelical sentiments than those of many Republicans. When tuition voucher programs as a form of government aid to parochial schools emerged as a potent political issue in the 1970s, evangelicals denounced Republican support as a campaign lure to cater to the Catholic vote. *Christianity Today* in 1972 condemned proposals presented to Congress by Nixon for "parochiaid" as another blatant attempt to swing the normally Democratic Catholic vote to the Republicans—as blatant, in fact, as his anti-abortion stance. The magazine also criticized Supreme Court decisions that had declared various "parochiaid" laws constitutional, and lauded voters who had rejected the proposal in state referenda.[89] C. Stanley Lowell of AU was similarly scathing in his critique. "It is the Republicans who have now seized upon this legacy of LBJ," he complained, suggesting that the ensuing shift of the Catholic vote from the Democrats to the Republicans had been "a factor in the election of Richard Nixon over Hubert Humphrey in 1968."[90]

Going even further in his condemnation, Lowell charged that support for state aid was linked to the politically motivated racism that underlay the Republicans' southern strategy. Support for private schools, he maintained, "appeals to conservatives by enabling them to do what they have long wanted to do," namely "to maintain segregated schools serving the skimmed off, better students, and to do it with tax funds." While recognizing that the appeal of the voucher plan lay in its putative "aura of impartiality, fairplay and freedom of choice," he dismissed it as a sinister threat to the institutions of American democracy. Government subsidies on this scale, he warned, would undermine public schools, turn them into "the dumping ground for private school rejects," and threaten to achieve "what our free, democratic concepts have always sought to avoid."[91]

The initial modification to the NAE's oppositional stance happened in the area of higher education funding. As discussed in the previous chapter, by the early 1970s the NAE avidly supported federal aid to religious colleges along the lines of tax credits and no longer had the same qualms about Goldwater's and Rockefeller's softness on church-state issues. By the same token, evangelicals were no longer primarily concerned with the dangers of public aid and instead focused on warding off secular intrusions, such as co-ed physical education classes, sex education, and limits on discriminating on the basis of sexual orientation. In an address given at the Washington Leadership Briefing sponsored by the NAE in April 1977, Representative William Armstrong attacked the "excessive federal involvement" in Christian colleges in the aftermath of increased federal funding. Stressing that evangelical colleges had played a unique and influential role "in the development of America and in producing Christian leadership for the world," he demanded protections from government efforts to impose its "secular moral philosophy." He also depicted federal infringements that limited the ability of colleges to inquire into the marital status of job applicants, fire employees if they had an extramarital pregnancy or an abortion, and discriminate on the basis of gender as a threat to religious liberty.[92]

In the aftermath of the volte-face in higher education the NAE's tone changed markedly even in the significantly more controversial area of public funding for religious primary and secondary education. By the early 1980s the NAE had made federal funding of parochial schools via vouchers a cornerstone of its political platform and lobbying. Next to the anti-abortion campaign, the issues of tuition vouchers and tax credits respectively emerged as central planks in the campaign to infuse an evangelical platform into the Republican party.[93] When Dugan wrote to Reagan's chief of staff James A. Baker shortly after the president's seminal address at the NAE Convention in March 1983 in Orlando, he included tax credits as one of the main issues that would "garner strong support for his administration's positions" among evangelicals. "You can thus count on us for official support on this educational issue," he concluded, noting that the espousal of tuition tax credits represented a major shift in evangelical thinking.[94] Similarly, the NAE campaign in support of the controversial nomination of judge Robert Bork to the Supreme Court in 1987 highlighted the significance of this issue. In addition to Bork's opposition to *Roe v. Wade*, support for capital punishment, and calls to criminalize homosexuality, NAE backing hinged on his view that legislative chaplains did not violate the First Amendment and his support for "state or federal tuition tax credit legislation (or vouchers)." "If Bork is defeated President is mortally wounded for remainder of term," a hastily scribbled memo to NAE director Billy Melvin from the OPA stated bluntly.[95]

The NAE's lobbying for public aid for religious child care in the run-up to the 1990 Child Care and Development Block Grant further highlights the link between changing attitudes to separationism and inroads into the Republican party. Child care legislation emerged as the "number one priority" for the NAE in the late 1980s.[96] By that time the NAE had decided to concentrate its energies on pushing for tax credits, though it still rejected vouchers and block grants. Meanwhile, the alleged secularist implications of a Democratic child care bill provoked vigorous evangelical opposition. Denouncing its "grim details," NAE counsel Forest Montgomery charged that the Act for Better Child Care (ABC) bill was "apparently designed to preserve absolutist concepts of the separation of church and state" and to ensure "that no child care facilities with any religious or spiritual dimensions would be eligible to participate in the federal program."[97]

Once again, the NAE's main concern was no longer breaches in the wall of separation, but a mix of secularist fears and pragmatic considerations. Although changes to the bill made by the Subcommittee on Human Resources meant that "the language blatantly hostile to religion has all been eliminated," Montgomery warned that "the melody lingers on." The new version allowed church-related child care providers to exercise religious preference in hiring staff, but continued to proscribe discrimination among children and to exclude financial assistance for sectarian activities, including worship and instruction. The danger, Montgomery argued, was that this was "broad enough for the courts to construe it as effectively prohibiting any spiritual dimension in church-related child care." As an alternative to the Democratic bill, which was "supported by Dukakis, labor unions, women's groups, the NEA, childcare professionals, and a broad coalition of liberal groups," he promoted the Republican Holloway-Wallop bill, which called for annual tax credits to parents of all preschool children and did not discriminate against religious child care providers.[98]

As competing child care bills were debated in Congress, defeating restrictions on religious agencies in the ABC bill and pushing for tax credits became the main objectives of NAE lobbying. Dugan campaigned hard for these goals, meeting with Vice-President Quayle and urging President Bush to veto the ABC bill.[99] In a letter to Bush he reiterated his testimony before the Republican Convention Platform Committee in 1988, where he had implored Republicans to support tax credits because of fears that "a regulatory and voucher regime" would benefit institutional care, rather than support home care or religious day care.[100] Though his opposition to the Democratic bill was packaged in vigorous opposition to a "huge spending program," his real concern was not expenditure but "subjecting child care to pervasive federal regulation and control."[101]

Conversely, Dugan reacted with great dismay in April 1989 when President Bush apparently rejected tuition tax credits. Calling it a retreat from a campaign commitment, he requested—and was granted—a personal meeting with Bush on this issue. "Your comments have produced a crisis of confidence among those who supported you in 1988," he declared.[102] Yet the NAE soon returned to a more pragmatic stance. As it became apparent that Bush would not stick to the tax credit proposal, the organization, in contrast to its earlier stance, began to push for a voucher system. "If the President's original tax credit approach is to be compromised," Dugan was cited in a NAE press release, there must be "guarantees of a voucher or certificate for parents" that could explicitly be used in religious institutions.[103] The change of heart was made apparent in a letter from Dugan to White House chief of staff John H. Sununu. The OPA director urged Sununu not only to continue supporting a voucher program, but to push for a statute that provided "that vouchers may be used in religious day care, and that this will not compromise the liberty of states to exempt that religious day care from regulation." Neither should the bill force churches and synagogues providing day care "to suppress or sacrifice their religious nature."[104]

In turn, the NAE was visibly pleased when the Bush administration favored the Stenholm-Clay bill (see Chapter 1), which offered to boost federal aid for child care through an increase in the Title XX Social Services Block Grant. The bill was called "child care's version of food stamps" or "kid stamps" by its House sponsor, conservative Christian Representative Charles Stenholm (D-Texas). It required states to aid child care by offering vouchers to parents. It thus ensured that aid could go to sectarian child care programs.[105] It also allowed sectarian organizations to require employees to adhere to their religious tenets and permitted them to give preference to children of church members in slots not funded with public money. While the NAE, together with Pat Robertson and a range of religious broadcasters, supported the bill and pressured Bush to make the vouchers mandatory, opposition came from a range of Jewish, Presbyterian, Episcopal, and Baptist groups.[106]

Throughout the debates about the bill the NAE lobbied forcefully to ensure that religious providers would retain their autonomy regarding staff and content, and that no restrictions were placed on the availability of funds. A letter signed by NAE leaders warned Bush that if the new legislation did not guarantee that vouchers could be used for religious child care or undermined state exemptions from religious day care regulation, "a thoroughly secularized child care system will shape the values of millions of America's children from their earliest years."[107] Likewise, NAE counsel Montgomery complained in a letter to Sununu that the pending White House-Senate compromise "falls short of preserving rights of religiously observant day care centers to operate according to their faith" by limiting preferential hiring, prohibiting religiously based selection, and imposing mandatory health training that undermined state exemptions from federal regulation. Without amendments, he concluded, "we would have to advise our constituency that the conditions of accepting vouchers violate the autonomy of religious day care organizations by subordinating crucial aspects of their operations to government control." [108]

The evangelical clout in pushing through subsidiarist legislation was increasingly recognized inside the Beltway. After a luncheon with the NAE, Jack Kemp, committed evangelical and secretary of the Department of Housing and Urban Development, told Dugan that "your effectiveness in bringing a message of faith and hope to those less fortunate in our society, will help us win the conservative war on poverty."[109] Speaking to the NAE about federal child care policy, Charles Stenholm credited grassroots evangelicals with providing the crucial political momentum. "Folks like you were responsible for flooding the Capitol Hill switchboards. . . . As one of my staffers said, we definitely noticed a lot of 'pent-up energy' from good Christian folks who wanted to get involved in a positive, constructive issue." Regarding the child care bill as an example of coalition building between social conservatives, fiscal conservatives, and the business community, he commended the NAE's involvement as "one of the finest examples of how the great 'moral imperatives' can be applied to the modern exigencies of public policy development."[110]

Similarly, Ralph Reed's analysis of how the 1992 Bush campaign would be able to mobilize both churchgoing evangelical Protestants in the South and pro-family ethnic Roman Catholics in the North as key swing constituencies indicated the political salience of subsidiarity. In addition to involving evangelical leaders in the campaign structure and administration, Reed argued that Bush needed to address the movement's political demands. "'Family friendly' policies," such as "introducing the 'G.I. Bill for Kids'" and "increasing funding for Title XX," he declared, "are all things that evangelicals could get excited about." The former was, of course, essentially the same policy Democratic Representative James Delaney had proposed in 1962 (see Chapter 4). Back then the NAE's Clyde Taylor had denounced it as "a gimmick for federal aid to Roman Catholic schools." Thirty years later, however, Ralph

Reed regarded it as vital to rallying an evangelical electorate that "will no longer be swayed by words and token commitments and a few political crumbs,
but only by sustained political commitment."[111]

After the passage of the 1990 child care legislation, the NAE continued to
monitor the implementation of the new law and to lobby for favorable treatment of religious agencies. OPA staffers attended White House and Capitol
Hill meetings and worked behind the scenes to infuse evangelical demands
into the administration's agenda.[112] Meanwhile, Dugan continued to insist
that indirect funding via vouchers or certificates did not constitute undue
federal financial assistance to the child care provider. Noting that the "child
care statute implicitly recognizes that constraints appropriate to use of federal
grant and contract money need not apply to parental choice with certificates,"
he declared that regulations should not limit religious instruction and restrictive hiring.[113] A new conservative evangelical consensus had come about that
merged expanded public funding with the rhetorical emphasis on limited
government, market forces, and nongovernmental provision.

Marginalizing Separationism

Finally, lobbying for public funding helped split the "separationist" Left from
the "statist" Right within the evangelical movement. Although the NAE as
a whole was on record for its tough separationist stance, conservative Protestantism traditionally contained a wide variety of factions that did not see
eye to eye on issues of church-state relations and public funding. On the one
hand, the strict separation of church and state had been historically espoused
by denominations that traced their legacy to left-wing Puritanism. Baptists
and peace churches in particular resisted any form of church-state linkage.
In the same vein, the NAE throughout the 1950s and 1960s was closely allied with separationist organizations, ran a vitriolic campaign against public
funding, and included a significant pacifist contingent. The POAU's call for
"a new leadership in American Protestantism that is not ashamed to oppose
subsidy grants to any church" during the 1963 church-state conference mirrored the sentiments of the majority of NAE denominations.[114] Likewise,
Clyde Taylor was far from subversive when he not only railed against federal
subsidies for religious educational institutions, but also against funding for
the military chaplaincy where the chaplain thought of himself "not as a member of a specific church but as a military man."[115]

On the other hand, many leading figures in the NAE grudgingly acknowledged that strict separationism was increasingly out of sync with the practices

of many members. A frustrated Harold Lindsell complained that even the NAE, which in theory stood on the side of church-state separation, has "annually made pronouncements, as has the NCC, that dilute if not extinguish its adherence to full state-church separation."[116] "Opposition to our position has grown among Protestants," Glenn L. Archer, AU executive director, noted with dismay about his NAE allies in 1974: "In the early days it was possible to line up nearly all the Jews, Protestants and secular communities behind church-state separation. Now Protestant groups are less unanimous in their support." The biggest change in the church-state situation since the 1940s, he concluded, was that "the issue is no longer a Roman Catholic issue."[117]

By the 1970s the threat of secularization had triumphed over the fear of breaching the wall of separation. As the issue of public funding rose to the top of the conservative evangelical agenda, the NAE disassociated itself from its former allies in the separationist camp. The changing relationship between the NAE and POAU provides a telling illustration of the political repercussions of the transformation of church-state attitudes among evangelicals. Founded in 1948, POAU was among the most radical groups advocating complete separation.[118] Throughout the anticommunist and anti-Catholic campaigns from the mid-1940s to the early 1960s discussed in the previous chapters, the NAE was closely allied with this organization. POAU "is our most important agency responsible for conserving, uniting, motivating, and mobilizing the great grass-roots strength of Separatism which unquestionably still thrives in the major denominations of Protestantism today," *United Evangelical Action* editor Murch noted in 1963.[119] Both organizations officially opposed not only Great Society efforts to involve sectarian organizations in the delivery of social services, but also the more innocuous school voucher proposals put forward by the Nixon administration.[120]

In the ensuing decade, however, NAE and POAU, by then renamed Americans United for the Separation of Church and State (AU), increasingly found themselves on opposite sides of church-state issues. Whereas the NAE embraced subsidiarist policies and mobilized in open opposition to separationist Supreme Court decisions, AU steadfastly resisted any softening of church-state separation. The two issues that had by then become the cornerstones of the NAE's new church-state stance—tuition tax credits for religious education and the campaign against the Supreme Court's "secularist" school prayer decision—continued to be rejected by AU on separationist grounds.[121] Reiterating his opposition, Glenn Archer identified "fiscal and administrative entanglements between religion and political institutions; the role of religion in public education; and attempts to revise the First Amendment to accommodate parochiaiders and school prayer extremists" as the big church-state issues of the future.[122] Similarly, the NAE supported tax exemptions for churches while AU continued to oppose them. Meanwhile, in a shot across the bow of its erstwhile ally, Clyde Taylor exclaimed in 1974 that "the viewpoint of Americans United, that carries separation of Church and State to an extreme, is typical of the viewpoint that has provoked the idea of getting a constitutional amendment to permit prayer in public institutions."[123]

Hence, by the mid-1970s, the evangelical Left was calling for continued church-state separation and was distancing itself from government, while the evangelical Right renewed its social involvement and extended its ties to government. In the subsequent decades, the NAE leadership used subsidiarist policies to build coalitions with other religious conservatives and the Republican party. Meanwhile, AU both rejected public funding legislation and disassociated itself from the Christian Right.[124] Instead of sharing the political journey of its evangelical wayfarers, it found itself in the same camp as an array of liberal religious and secular groups that had taken up the mantle of separationism, declaring that "in child care, as in education, the federal government must not finance religious or discriminatory practices."[125] The odd man out in the Cold War state was thus no longer evangelicalism, but "that assortment of strict separationists, leftist critics, and theological liberationists who from their various perspectives find government funding of religiously grounded activities abhorrent to the best interests of American democracy."[126] Indeed, faith-based policies have remained controversial in progressive evangelicalism well into the twenty-first century. While Ron Sider and Jim Wallis, for example, eventually supported school vouchers and Charitable Choice, Richard Pierard continued to defend the separation of church and state.[127]

*   *   *

In summation, this chapter challenges the widespread assumption that the right-wing political mobilization of evangelicals was primarily a reaction against the growth of the secular state. Instead, it suggests that in this story the integration of evangelicals into the structures of postwar state building takes center stage. Conservatives within the evangelical movement combined an insurgent message with the affirmation of the Cold War military-industrial complex; the entrepreneurial market subject with moral traditionalism; and church-centered social provision with state funding. Calibrating their position in this way gave them a competitive edge in the post-1960s climate of opinion. In organizing around the politics of patriotism, morality, and subsidiarity, they emerged triumphant from the often agonizing debates of the 1970s and developed new links between religious and secular conservatives in the 1980s.

In the foreign policy arena, they forged new ties with policy elites and the institutions of the Cold War state, while at the same time projecting an anti-establishmentarian image. This enabled them to negotiate the movement's internal ambiguities and marginalize its separationist left-wing groups during a period of internal fragmentation. The NAE's Peace, Freedom and Security Studies Program, for example, mobilized these links to engineer the dominance of a "peace through strength" platform. Likewise, in the social policy field the Right used antistatist rhetoric to capitalize on the widespread alienation from the liberal state while at the same time embracing the established patterns of subsidiarity. Many conservative evangelical agencies, such as Prison Fellowship Ministries, kept alive the countercultural rejection of managerial liberalism while thriving on public funds, and combined left-wing evangelical social impulses with right-wing political connections.

The tension between a separationist ideology and an integrationist reality that had developed as a result of the evangelicals' growing involvement in the national security and welfare state in the 1950s and 1960s thus benefited the Right in the movement more than liberal and left-leaning groups. Moreover, it also played a central role in cementing ties between conservative evangelicals and the Republican party. Whereas in the early 1960s evangelicals had found themselves more in tune with John F. Kennedy's opposition to public aid to religion, their "subsidiarist turn" brought them in line with mainstream Republicanism. In the 1980s and 1990s, the NAE infused evangelical demands for public funding with limited regulatory control into the Republican party. Supportive of Paul Weyrich's "cultural conservatism," the organization maintained that solutions to poverty involved the federal government, not just markets. It called for government contracting with churches and community groups, and embraced the concept of economic growth and consumer capitalism.

As the Conclusion shows, conservative evangelicalism thus mirrored the broader transformation of postwar conservatism. Its foreign policy engagement fed into conservative policies that employed the rhetoric of limited government but supported a hawkish foreign policy and large-scale military spending. Likewise, the evangelical embrace of subsidiarity echoed resurgent conservatism's combination of attacking the welfare state while becoming increasingly adept at using the instrumentalities of public funding for nonprofits.

RESURGENT CONSERVATISM AND THE
PUBLIC FUNDING OF RELIGIOUS AGENCIES

The partisan realignment of evangelicals constitutes the most striking case of belief-based change in party identities since World War
II. Having been one of the most loyal components of the Democratic
party in the South and West well into the 1970s, conservative Protestants became steadily more Republican in the 1980s and 1990s. Today, as Geoffrey
Layman notes, they form "the most strongly Republican group in the religious spectrum."[1] What is more, the Republican mobilization of evangelicals
strengthened significantly the electoral fortunes of conservatism by providing
the party with a socioeconomic base beyond its affluent upper-middle-class
and business clientele. By achieving the elusive goal of mobilizing lower- and
middle-class voters who had traditionally viewed Republicans as unfriendly
to their economic interests, the party was finally able to overcome one of its
fundamental obstacles to electoral success in the postwar period. Mobilizing
evangelicals was thus part of the emergence of a new populist conservatism
that constituted a "momentous break with an elitist conservatism unable to
shed its association with the smug and wealthy."[2]

Most scholarship on the New Right attributes the political resurgence and
partisan realignment of evangelicalism to the so-called "backlash" against the
political and cultural upheaval of the 1960s.[3] It depicts the rise of the Christian Right *sui generis* as a spontaneous moral outburst against the growing
radicalization of the insurgent movements, the post-Vietnam upheaval, the
rise of the counterculture, and the iniquities of the welfare state. As 1950s
grassroots conservative organizing and 1960s cultural alienation met with the
economic crisis of the 1970s, advocates of the backlash argument contend,
the traditional link between the Democratic party and white, lower-middle-
and working-class voters—including evangelicals—was severely strained.

While the Democratic party was torn apart, the Republicans gradually embraced right-wing populism and built a power base among the disaffected. The New Christian Right played a key role in this political realignment. By emphasizing "social issues" such as abortion, homosexuality, and the Equal Rights Amendment, it adroitly exploited the "moral rift" within the Democratic party and effectively replaced the shared economic interests that had held the Democratic coalition together with a political allegiance based on moral and cultural issues.[4] This provided the resurgent Right with both a populist agenda and a new electorate that embraced strict morality, the traditional family, the work ethic, and American patriotism. Naturally drawn to resurgent secular conservatism, which was fostered intellectually by neoconservative intellectuals and institutionally by big business, the Christian Right became part of a new conservative alliance. By the 1980s, disaffected Democrats, conservative Republicans, Christian Fundamentalists, and the right-wing fringe had combined in a movement which centered ideologically on an amalgam of moral intolerance, religious orthodoxy, and the cult of the free market, and institutionally on Republican party grassroots campaigning, church organizing and fundraising, think tanks, and big business funding.[5]

In contrast, the analysis of church-state relations presented in this study contributes to a growing body of literature that has been revising the backlash thesis over the past few decades. By exploring the evangelical repositioning in Cold War foreign and social policy, it suggests that the religious Right's cultivation of an insurgent image coalesced with evangelicalism's gradual integration into the Cold War state. As the national security and welfare state made evangelical agencies part of its administrative structure, conservative Protestants combined an "outsider" message of free enterprise and moral awakening with the sanctification of state building. This combination, rather than simply the fight against the secularist elites and bureaucracies of Cold War liberalism, underpinned the political mobilization of evangelicalism.

This raises the question of what role the transformation of evangelical church-state relations played in the larger story of the resurgence of conservatism in the United States since the late 1970s. As Chapter 5 has argued, the convergence between religious and secular conservatives centered on an ideology that combined aversion to the state with embracing the instrumentalities of government. Seen from this perspective, the evangelical reorientation in church-state matters can be understood as part of the emergence of the broader "antistatist statism" of populist conservatism. The push for subsidiarist policies, particularly tuition vouchers and child care grants, both carried forward the basic structures of the Cold War state and projected an antistatist identity. It simultaneously appropriated liberal policies and presented them as alternatives to liberal state building. This helped bridge the ideological gap between postwar conservatives, who had largely accepted the structures of the liberal state, and neoconservatives, who adulated the market.

Evangelicals, therefore, were not just moralistic fellow travelers in the Republican party who had nowhere else to go when faced with the rise of liberal secular culture. Instead, they were a valuable ingredient in conservatism's electoral and ideological amalgam that, rather than spearheading a fundamental challenge to postwar state building, constituted a particular way of shoring up the Cold War state in a post-1960s climate of opinion. This stance had tremendous political resonance during the polarized and disillusioned atmosphere of the 1970s, particularly in the South and West, where visceral opposition to big government, managerial liberalism, Washington bureaucrats, and welfare chiselers merged with underlying support for the defense and welfare state. As William Hixson has noted, the "fundamentalist-evangelical role in the right wing . . . better accounts both for its ideology . . . and for its relatively diverse base than do alternative explanations."[6]

The "Statist Turn" of Postwar Conservatism

The institutional and ideological construction of Cold War public policies not only formed the bedrock of postwar liberalism, it also induced the broader retreat from antistatism among conservatives. Although postwar Republicans initially demanded welfare state retrenchment and a balanced budget under the leadership of Robert Taft, the Right gradually abandoned fiscal conservatism and embraced the commercial Keynesianism and deficit spending that had become the trademark of postwar Democratic economic policies. Granted, hard-line *rhetorical* opposition to New Deal "collectivism" remained a key mantra of the Right. Yet postwar conservatives and their big business allies, while continuing to denounce the interventionist state, largely joined in the liberal consensus by supporting macroeconomic management and limited social welfare expansion by the federal government.[7] Hence, when the Republicans gained control of Congress in 1946 for the first time in sixteen years, they did not repeal New Deal reforms nor push for the withdrawal of the United States from the international scene. For the first time in the nation's history, domestic welfare programs and foreign assistance had broad bipartisan support. By the late 1950s, the welfare agendas of Republicans and Democrats had largely merged.[8]

The defeat of Barry Goldwater in the 1964 presidential elections "marked the end of the conservative battle against the ghost of Roosevelt and the New Deal," as Kurt Schuparra has noted. Moreover, "the creation of new bureaucracies during the Johnson years prompted conservatives to finally abandon their attempt to roll back the welfare state and instead focus on thwarting its burgeoning new growth."[9] In turn, Richard Nixon's domestic policies did not constitute a substantial break with Cold War social policies. During his administration government services expanded, both because of pressure from a Democratic Congress and because Nixon himself desired it. He proposed the Family Assistance Plan, new health and safety legislation, and new housing allowances. As a result, the Nixon administration built more subsidized housing units than any administration before, signed the Environmental Protection Act, expanded the food stamp program, and allocated more federal money to local government.[10]

This "statist turn" of postwar conservatism was most apparent in the foreign policy arena. For conservatives, as for evangelicals (see Chapter 3), anticommunism was a central means of embracing big government. By arguing that they were fighting totalitarianism, conservatives abandoned rigid antiinterventionism and foreign policy isolationism in favor of expanded military spending and support for America's new global role in the struggle against the Soviet Union. In what effectively amounted to a type of right-wing statism, they relinquished the mantra of budget balancing. As Cold War realities superseded their fears of the growing state, they justified the massive buildup of the Cold War military-industrial complex and the national security state. William F. Buckley's *National Review*, for example, denounced the noninterventionist arguments of the libertarian journal *The Freeman*, particularly its criticism of imperialism and the military-related expansion of state power.[11]

A similar conservative turn toward the state took place in regard to the subsidiarist dimension of liberal social policy. Subsidiarity was part and parcel of the normative basis of postwar liberal state building, which combined reliance on public funds with faith in the efficacy of nongovernmental providers and market solutions. On the one hand, subsidiarity allowed the state to mobilize the organizational capacities and ideological resources of third-sector agencies in order to meet the political exigencies of Cold War social and foreign policy. On the other hand, funding nongovernmental bodies was a means of rendering the postwar expansion of government compatible with the ideology of limited government. The devolutionary emphasis in federal policies meant that government purposes were carried out by nonprofit providers and private players via elaborate funding arrangements that frequently did not appear in the federal budget.[12]

Government-by-proxy had the clear benefit of removing a wide range of public programs and services from the scrutiny of a highly skeptical public that suspected waste, inefficiency, and bloated bureaucracies whenever the government was directly involved in the running of public services. It helped mobilize political support for social welfare initiatives by making big government palatable to an electorate that associated support for nongovernmental agencies with cost reduction, self-help, and the responsiveness of local services.[13] As Smith and Lipsky noted, "Politicians are regularly criticized if the number of public employees has increased while they have been in office. They are virtually never criticized if the number of employees working for agencies under contract to the state has increased dramatically."[14] Contracting for services thus greatly increased government expenditures without engendering public opposition. It helped to "resolve the dilemma created by a continuing desire for social services provided by the welfare state and opposition to taxation and spending by government bureaucracies" because the public "more readily accepts government funding and standard setting if nongovernmental organizations deliver the public goods and services."[15]

At the same time, devolving functions to nongovernmental providers depicted them as intrinsically superior to public institutions and provided them with significant administrative leeway and procedural autonomy. While bolstering the fiscal and macroeconomic role of the state, subsidiarity set up significant roadblocks to government infringements on the organizational and substantive independence of publicly funded charities. Since government support often reached nonprofits indirectly through vouchers, reimbursement schemes, and block grants, in many instances business or nonprofit organizations succeeded in gaining control over the provision of services at the expense of the state.[16] Agency policies, rather than a state-mandated approach, came to determine policy content. Confining the state largely to a funding body effectively sanctioned the social welfare ideologies of a wide range of private and nonprofit providers.[17]

Subsidiarist policies thus transformed nongovernmental agencies into quasi-public agencies while at the same time nurturing their image as alternatives to the bureaucratic welfare state. As the rhetoric of a "third sector" substitute for the welfare state increasingly hid the reality of the dependence on expanding government aid, the ability of nongovernmental organizations to navigate carefully between an alternative and an auxiliary to the state became a key component in their political identity and in the functioning of state-private networks. Ironically, maintaining a sense of the failure of public action and conveying the image of keeping the growth of the state in check was instrumental in legitimizing "third-party government" funding structures.

Indeed, the most significant effort to expand the welfare state during the Cold War best illustrates this dichotomy. The Great Society massively expanded public funding for private and nonprofit social services. At the same time its allocative policies "reflected, either explicitly or implicitly, a vote of no confidence in governmental services as then being delivered."[18] The funding of nonprofit agencies, which formed "the intellectual centerpiece of the War on Poverty," was designed to circumvent traditional mediating levels of state and local bureaucracies and to create alternatives to existing public delivery.[19] Saturated in antigovernment rhetoric that denounced the failure of government to address social needs, its lack of responsiveness, and its demeaning service, Great Society planners relied on direct federal-to-nonprofit allocation. The nonprofit Community Action agencies created under the 1964 EOA exemplified this shift from government programs to the public funding of private, community-based organizations that promoted small-scale personalized efforts, emphasized rehabilitation over maintenance, and sought to foster self-reliance. The Great Society thus set in motion an unprecedented expansion of the nonprofit sector and the American welfare state while paradoxically nurturing a sense of disenchantment with public action.[20]

It was on the basis of this duality that postwar conservatives actively embraced the instrumentalities of the subsidiarist state. Though a stalwart defender of traditional Republican values of limited government, Robert Taft once again hinted at the new direction. Instrumental in defeating federal aid to education during the war, he became nonetheless convinced that the measure was necessary.[21] Taft's change of heart was indicative of a larger trend as conservative think tanks and foundations discovered that Cold War public policy, rather than weakening conservative nonprofit organizations, underwrote their postwar expansion and safeguarded their organizational and ideological autonomy. In turn, conservatives were increasingly savvy in making use particularly of the changes in the tax treatment of charitable giving and the tax status of philanthropies. This fueled a wave of New Right giving and foundation formation, particularly on the state and local levels in the South and West. Fed by the postwar economic boom and the growth of new defense-related industries, wealthy southern and western non-WASP conservatives, such as financier William E. Simon, economist Alan Greenspan, and defense contractor and corporate lawyer Caspar Weinberger, created a conservative counterestablishment and policy elite via a new attitude to philanthropy. Their efforts combined deeply conservative convictions with extraordinary sophistication about governmental and corporate institutions. By the 1980s, large conservative foundations, such as Lilly, Pew, Olin, and Smith-Richardson, "were demanding a voice in shaping the national philanthropic agenda." At the same time, conservative think tanks, including the Heritage Foundation, the Hoover Institution, the American Enterprise Institute, and the Cato Institute, "began to serve as policy counterparts to such venerable liberal centers as the Brookings Institute and the Twentieth Century Fund."[22]

As Lisa McGirr concluded in her study of conservative grassroots mobilization, "the world of the New Deal state thus first marginalized, then reshuffled, and eventually invigorated American conservatism."[23] In putting the accent on ever-increasing economic output, state-private networks, and moral categorizing, postwar liberal policies inadvertently shored up the Right's social welfare discourse centered on "wealth creators," "privatization," and the "undeserving poor." The very framework put in place to safeguard the liberal welfare state nurtured the institutions and ideologies that were in the forefront of its undoing. They simultaneously generated an attachment to the underlying policy trajectories of postwar state building and enabled conservatives to solidify their ideological and institutional power base. In turn, an ideology altogether different from the limited-government conservatism that had traditionally dominated the Republican party emerged triumphant and nudged the Right into embracing the tools of the state.

The Crisis of Consensus Liberalism

As long as the postwar economic boom more or less addressed socioeconomic deprivation, these contradictions did not become a palpable problem for liberal policy making. The economic downturn and the cultural crises of the late 1960s and 1970s, however, revealed the political pitfalls of the paradoxical construction of public policies that simultaneously constituted the strength of the Cold War state and the structural weakness of Cold War liberalism. They rocked the foundations of a consensus liberalism based on a fragile alliance between disparate groups reliant upon patronage politics and the largesse of the New Deal state.[24]

The growing fragmentation of the volatile constituency of the Democratic party—which included urban working-class voters, African Americans, Southern Democrats, liberal intellectuals, Catholics, Jews, evangelical Protestants, and western progressives—had a variety of causes. Desegregation and the Civil Rights movement alienated white southerners from the Democrats; the Vietnam War split the party as protests ran afoul of the patriotic instincts of middle America; and deindustrialization, the decline of unions, and the demise of traditional party machines effectively disenfranchised significant segments of the working-class electorate. Social policies, however, also played an important role in this unfolding drama. Growth-inducing welfare and defense spending, state-private networks, and the behavioralist approach to problems of poverty had helped build up the American welfare state, yet inadvertently hindered an extended public sphere of control, embedded the rhetoric of retrenchment, sanctified market solutions, and perpetuated a fragmented and segmented structure. Although by the mid-1970s social welfare expenditures in the United States approached those of European welfare states, liberal public policies had failed to sustain an electoral coalition on the basis of inclusive social provision, redistributive justice, and a civic conception of the public sphere.[25]

Three problems were at the core of this malaise. First, as discussed in Chapter 2, liberal state building perpetuated gendered and racialized hierarchies in the welfare state that weakened the sense of social solidarity. While noncontributory assistance programs for the poor offered insufficient support with many restrictions for a largely female and minority population, Social Security provided substantial benefits to a largely male working- and middle-class clientele. In this segmented arrangement, entitlements were administered by the federal government, whereas means and morals-tested welfare was devolved to state and local levels. Doubtlessly, liberal planners in the 1960s had made a fervent effort to part with this politically divisive tradition of morally charged categorizing. Indeed, the Great Society was in part an attempt to integrate public assistance into the established regulatory and social insurance models of the welfare state. The Kennedy, Johnson, and even Nixon administrations extended policies adopted during the New Deal to cover large parts of the low-wage working population previously excluded under social insurance and not covered by private benefit plans.[26]

However, while the War on Poverty helped undermine race and gender

as grounds for exclusion from government support, it was at no point accompanied by a cultural redefinition of poverty. In actuality, liberal campaigns
to remove discriminations from the statutes continued to locate the origins
of poverty in the behavioral characteristics of the poor, not in the maldistribution of wealth. As explored in Chapter 2, the liberal "culture of poverty"
argument, which underlay much of Great Society thinking and was virtually
institutionalized in research by the 1960s, depicted the poor as intrinsically
hedonistic, improvident, unable to defer gratification, trapped in cycles of
dependency, and in need of punitive measures. Welfare experts largely substi-
tuted the language of deviance and deprivation for the language of class and
inequality in poverty analysis. Daniel Patrick Moynihan's influential 1965
book *The Negro Family: The Case for National Action*, for example, traced
the origins of deprivation once again to black deviance from the moral and
behavioral norms of white middle-class families. Blaming the socioeconomic
malaise of African Americans on the disintegration of families as a result of
historical and cultural factors, Moynihan revived traditional stereotypes of
African Americans as immoral, childlike, and victimized.[27]

In turn, liberal policies expanded welfare expenditures, but left the established tiered structure and moral underpinnings of the welfare state in
place to deal with poverty. The Great Society's expansion of targeted, noncontributory, and means-tested income maintenance programs, such as AFDC,
Medicaid, and food stamps, retained conceptions of a moral difference between welfare recipients and social insurance beneficiaries. While invoking
the rhetoric of rights, and attempting to bridge the gap between insurance
and assistance programs, it extended benefits based on a rehabilitative welfare concept.[28] Although Lyndon Johnson had hoped that the Great Society's
weakening of the boundary between contributory and assistance programs
would unite the social program clientele, his policies actually heightened animosities between the poor and the middle classes.[29]

Likewise, Great Society subsidiarity militated against the formation of an
effective welfare state coalition. Allocative social policy meant that federal
income support programs, nonwage benefits due to unionized welfare capitalism, a range of federal and local in-kind transfer programs, and publicly
funded nongovernmental agencies continued to serve different social groups
based on separate administrative mechanisms. While Medicaid and Medicare
established a rudimentary public health insurance system, and food stamps
and AFDC laid the foundation for welfare entitlements, the involvement of
state, local, and nongovernmental providers left discretionary leeway to em-

ploy traditional exclusionary policies.[30] The urge to preserve a prominent role for publicly funded for-profit and nonprofit agencies thus undermined the effort to expand inclusive, coordinated, centralized provision. As Great Society planners happily entered the quagmire of public-private partnerships in their desire to bypass the swamp of the established federal-state grant-in-aid system, they cemented the tiered structure of welfare provision, uneven coverage, and the stratification along racial, class, and gender lines. Ironically, the Great Society programs, vilified by the Right as promoting moral decline and big government, thus pioneered the transfer of public business to private organizations that has been associated with resurgent conservatism.[31]

Second, the use of regressive taxation as a means of financing the extension of welfare programs to cover large parts of the low-wage working population exacerbated the strains in the Democratic political coalition. The Kennedy, Johnson, and Nixon administrations frequently relied on highly regressive payroll and state-based sales taxes—traditionally a volatile tax, and one that people were painfully aware of—to pay for the large-scale increase in means-tested cash and in-kind transfers to those previously excluded under social insurance and not covered by private benefit plans. Rather than helping to overcome the glaring discrepancies of the American welfare state, however, these efforts in fact heightened the awareness of social divisions, since they reinforced "a sharp separation between the distribution of benefits and the responsibility of paying for them." The middle and working classes did not benefit much from welfare state expansion in the 1960s and the 1970s, but ended up paying for its programs.[32] As Ira Katznelson has concluded, the Great Society, with its reliance on economic growth, regressive taxation, rejection of redistributive policies, and faith in market mechanisms, embedded the public policy trajectory of the 1940s and left Democrats vulnerable to assaults from the Right.[33]

Finally, as Barbara Ehrenreich has noted, by adhering to a belief in abundance and the distribution of ever-increasing economic output as a social cure-all, postwar liberalism failed to develop a convincing radical critique of capitalism that addressed the meaning of "more" in a consumer culture.[34] The postwar dominance of visions of consumer-oriented social policies settled the conflict between participatory and distributive conceptions of the democratic welfare state in progressive thought in favor of the latter. While proponents of the participatory view focused on industrial democracy and social ethics, advocates of the distributive view made access to consumer goods and wealth distribution their overriding goal. Rather than promoting civic consciousness, public control, and workplace codetermination, they encouraged primarily the development of consumption habits.[35] This constituted a qualitative shift in liberal social and economic thought. In the mid to late 1940s, as Steve Fraser and Gary Gerstle remind us, "business Keynesianism" with its emphasis on fiscal incentives, deficit spending and subsidies to private businesses and nonprofit organizations gained dominance in the Democratic party and over the state's administrative structures.[36] "Vital center" liberals, such as Oscar Ewing and Leon Keyserling, conceptualized the welfare state as part of a vision of sustaining economic expansion.[37] In the words of Daniel Bell, the politics of growth emerged as a new ideology of consensus, implying that the basic contradictions and tensions in capitalist society had been resolved.[38] As critics such as C. Wright Mills and Herbert Marcuse have pointed out, Cold War liberalism thus shifted the focus away from questions of social justice and industrial democracy, disavowed the idea of an alternative model to capitalism, and denied the need for an expanded sphere of public control. In short, "there was little room on ship for liberal politicians who kept alive an aggressive and articulate concern with income redistribution, economic planning, or international idealism."[39]

When the hopeful beginnings of the Great Society gave way to gloomier realities, and tax increases due to the Vietnam War began to eat up the real income of the lower and middle classes in the 1970s, a fateful divide developed within a Democratic party bereft of the power to forge an electoral coalition on the basis of race and gender equality, redistributive justice, and civic participation. Blue-collar workers, hit hard by inflation, social unrest, and deindustrialization, resented rising welfare costs. Self-confidently defining themselves as "workers" and as "middle class," they were increasingly hostile to the nonworking, able-bodied poor on welfare. Rather than seeing welfare benefits as a way of helping those who would otherwise lose their social bearings, many traditional Democratic voters, including evangelicals, maligned public assistance programs for promoting laziness, licentiousness, and moral iniquity. They regarded welfare recipients, primarily African Americans and single mothers, as promiscuous and irresponsible, and blamed them for spreading the socially destructive and morally reprehensible lifestyles of the 1960s to the poor. Significant segments of the Democratic constituency thus came to regard persistent social problems as due to a moral breakdown, rather than to socioeconomic inequalities. To them, the War on Poverty appeared to condone immoral behavior and create welfare dependency; the growth of a "secular humanist" state relegated traditional religion to the sidelines; and

1960s "permissiveness" clashed with their culture organized around family, church, and neighborhood.[40]

The Rise of Neoconservative Statism

In turn, a new generation of conservatives stepped into the breach. Initially nurtured in the 1950s and 1960s by a small coterie of neoconservatives, including William F. Buckley and Norman Podhoretz, and a few publications, such as *Human Events, The Freeman, Modern Age, Conservative Digest*, and *American Spectator*, the movement reshaped the political landscape in the aftermath of the upheavals of the 1970s. On the surface, neoconservatives gave voice to the groundswell of populist antiwelfarism and antistatism. Leading conservative thinkers, such as Leo Strauss, Eric Voegelin, Robert Nisbet, Russell Kirk, Richard Weaver, and Friedrich von Hayek, invoked stark images that pitted their moral agenda of personal responsibility, voluntarism, and retrenchment against oppressive federal control, stifling bureaucratism, rampant secularization, and moral permissiveness allegedly nurtured by liberal social policies. Disregarding the antitraditionalist and amoral implications of market commodification, they developed a new moral justification for capitalism. They located the emergence of social discipline required for the functioning of society purely in the operations of the free market, rather than in traditional social ties, moral legislation, or regulatory intervention.[41]

In presenting themselves as uncompromising antistatists, however, the neoconservatives faced a political dilemma: Cold War policies, while failing to forge an effective electoral coalition in support of the liberal welfare state, continued to generate general popular support for government spending. Many polls in the mid-1970s recorded entrenched support for macroeconomic intervention and the expansion of the human services infrastructure. They showed that many Americans supported both redistribution of income and a tough stance on social issues. In the same vein, Christopher Lasch maintained that the tax revolt of the 1970s was not a mandate for supply side economics since it was directed against regressive property taxes, not the more progressive federal income tax.[42] Indeed, many political scientists attribute the backlash of the 1970s and 1980s to a crisis of the Democratic party and its postwar social agenda, rather than to a serious shift to the Right in the ideological outlook of the electorate. As Mickey Kaus surmised in the

New York Times, Republicans discovered that "the voters never really hated government, they just hated welfare."[43]

The evangelicals were no exception. While Republicans managed to mobilize the evangelical electorate on the basis of moral issues, a significant percentage of evangelicals, despite severing their links with the Democratic party, remained comfortable with Democratic economic policies and the New Deal/Great Society state. As George Gallup put it, the future of the Democratic party lay in crafting a platform that defended traditional democratic economic policies and promoted a moderate image on social issues, especially on crime.[44] Similar to the Republican party in the early 1950s, evangelicals embraced the expansion of the military-industrial complex, macroeconomic planning, and the basic social security state. They combined an antistatist and separationist attitude with support for the basic axioms of the Cold War state. Although in their political self-identification evangelicals increasingly shunned the term "liberal"—associating it with attacks on "family values" and softness on crime rather than with New Deal or Great Society social programs—their broader centrist political outlook largely survived the partisan realignments since the 1970s.[45]

Therefore, the upheavals of the 1970s, while exposing the contradictions of Cold War liberalism, did not question the institutional or ideological construction of the Cold War state as such. Instead, they increasingly separated culturally liberal supporters of the welfare state from culturally conservative supporters. Indeed, the key to mobilizing new voter groups lay in conservatism's ability to reconcile antistatist sentiments with the embrace of the welfare and national-security state, rather than solely in its pervasive rhetoric of retrenchment and limited government. The Right needed to develop an ideology compatible with a climate of opinion that, as voter surveys have consistently shown, was dominated by a mistrust of government but also demanded a social safety net and macroeconomic stability.

Hence, although vociferous antistatism resurfaced with a vengeance in the 1970s, the New Right did not revolt against government as such. Instead, it offered primarily an "antistatist" ideology of state building that appropriated a range of liberal policies. The Right engaged in a rhetorical assault on big government without abandoning growth-oriented policies and deficit spending. It posited devolution and voluntarism as substantive alternatives to the welfare state without questioning the role of government in funding and structuring the field of nonprofit social provision.[46] Indeed, the Republican administrations in the 1980s and again after 2000 largely accepted or expanded on the existing level of government activity and involvement. Reagan, for example, combined fiery right-wing rhetoric with a legacy of moderate policies based on the New Deal consensus in what Alonzo Hamby has called "reactionary Keynesianism." As explored in Chapters 1 and 5, Reagan administration social policies attacked the welfare state, yet oversaw no wholesale dismantling of New Deal social provision or net reduction in social or educational spending.[47] Efforts to dismantle the Department of Education and reduce federal funding for elementary and secondary education, for example, failed in the face of opposition from conservatives who embraced an active federal role in this field.[48] As Rebecca Klatch has concluded, the Reagan legacy lay in the diminution of governmental authority to remedy social inequality, not in the reduction of government expenditure and power.[49]

Similarly, in fiscal policy the Reagan administration was only at the very beginning serious about balancing the budget when it raised business taxes in response to the 1982 recession. Later on its concern with running up the budget deficit waned rapidly. The Federal Reserve continued to lower interest rates, encouraging a ballooning deficit and making borrowing a way of life. Driven by a sense that deficits did not really matter, Reagan engaged in the classic policies of big government conservatism, namely the expansion of the military-industrial complex. Resurgent conservatism thus remained wedded to growth-oriented public policies by propounding consumerist stimulants and regarding tax cuts as more important than budget cuts. As a result, the United States saw the biggest deficit ever, with cumulative debt surging to $3 trillion and interest consuming more than 20 percent of the budget. For the first time in its history the country was transformed into a debtor nation.[50]

What is more, the New Right's emphasis on market solutions and devolved delivery ironically engineered a new identification with the subsidiarist dimension of American public policy among conservatives. On the one hand, the New Right invoked traditional ideas about the intrinsic opposition of government and private action. It demanded welfare state retrenchment and called for the empowerment of mediating structures. On the other hand, however, "those who advocate a larger role for charity (or simply a smaller welfare state) are unprepared to present a blueprint for reduced entitlements."[51] Even after the cutbacks during the Reagan administration, there was only minor retrenchment in overall levels of nonprofit funding, since real reductions would have threatened to close off revenue flows to conservative nonprofits that had become dependent on government grants and contracts. "A Republican leadership that owed its power to a significant degree to its adroit use of nonprofit vehicles in policy making (American Enterprise Institute, Heritage Foundation), propagandizing (Christian Coalition), and campaign financing (Newt Gingrich's GOPAC)," Peter Dobkin Hall aptly remarked, "seemed hardly likely to kill the goose that laid its golden egg."[52]

The evangelical reconceptualization of church-state relations further tempered the antigovernmentalism of the neoconservatives. As Christopher Lasch has noted, "the architects of the new right were by no means unanimously committed to free-market economics." Supported by the NAE, Paul Weyrich, one of key religious figures of the New Right, called for a "morally based conservatism," not free-market economics, and combined the critique of government with that of big corporations. As explored in Chapter 5, Weyrich's "cultural conservatism" showed that the right-wing political mobilization was not rooted solely in the rejection of government. Indeed, in Lasch's view, Weyrich felt intellectually much closer to William Jennings Bryan than to Friedrich von Hayek.[53]

In the same vein, other neo- and theoconservative advocates of the devolution of social provision to charities, such as Nathan Glazer, Peter L. Berger, and Richard John Neuhaus, simultaneously called for state subsidies for religious social service providers and packaged this in the rhetoric of a third sector as an alternative to government-run services. They voiced concerns about the erosion of the religious character of church agencies by being turned into quasi-governmental agencies, yet also demanded increased public funding for churches to turn them into "implementing agents of policy goals." As Berger and Neuhaus put it, "the mediating structure proposal is not antigovernment. We are favorably disposed toward government. We strongly support the form of government which has marked the American experiment at its best, namely, self-government."[54]

The conservatism that emerged triumphant from the crisis of Cold War liberalism was thus broadly characterized by combining the ideology of limited government with support for the national security and welfare state, and the belief in voluntary self-help with public funding for nongovernmental providers. Of course, this virtual adoption of liberal policies eventually did incite the ire of true-blue conservatives who turned against Reagan and renewed their call for spending cuts and a balanced budget in the "Contract with America." As neoconservative Ben Wattenberg lamented, "The numbers may not work, but economics is symbolic. Forget the numbers. It's growth economics. That's New Deal economics. That's Democratic economics. That ain't Republican economics."[55] Despite these concerns, however, Republican administrations, while liberally employing the rhetoric of limited government, continued to run up unprecedented deficits and engage in massive military spending. In 1968, the federal share of GNP had reached 20.6 percent. In 2006, after almost four decades of heated controversies about cutting government spending, it was 20.8 percent.[56]

Calibrating in this fashion between support for federal funding and the preservation of cognitive lines of defense formed the "paradoxical combination" political scientist Jerome Himmelstein has identified as the main strength of the conservative movement. In his view, it brought together "insider resources— support from business and the upper middle class as well as solid roots within the Republican party—and a capacity to use antiestablishment rhetoric to talk to the growing range of discontents that grew out of the 1960s." As he aptly concluded, "the contradictions were time-honored, and conservatives had considerable experience managing them."[57] This "antistatist statism" generated by conservatism's integration into consensus politics in the postwar period helped engineer the political realignments in the South and the West that became the basis for a new Republican majority. On the one hand, it resonated with the libertarianism, entrepreneurial individualism, and social conservatism that permeated the region's culture and formed the right-wing ideological bedrock of a mobile and anxious suburban middle class.[58] On the other hand, it appealed to a populace whose Sunbelt affluence was largely due to government-generated growth and social benefits. By the 1990s, Cold War liberalism as an effective means of ensuring the loyalty of lower-middle-class southern and western voters to the Democratic party had been replaced by "big government" conservatism as an instrument of Republican mobilization of the same voter groups.[59]

Although liberalism's electoral basis collapsed, the Cold War state itself thus emerged largely unscathed from both the large-scale cultural upheaval of the 1960s and 1970s and the conservative politics of retrenchment in the 1980s and 1990s. The growth-oriented, subsidiarist, and normative underpinnings of Cold War public policy formed the basis of a broad political consensus that cut across partisan positions. They were staple features of both Democratic and Republican administrations and became the basis upon which they embraced the expansion of the state. As Gareth Davies has shown, the distancing of American conservatism from its antistatist traditions paved the way for today's big government conservatism, and the coalescence of liberals and conservatives preserved significant parts of the Great Society legacy.[60] In Lawrence Mead's words, "The two sides now differ more sharply on questions of social authority than they do about the scale of government."[61]

From Conservative State Building to the Faith-Based Initiative

This analysis also suggests a different reading of the two key pieces of legislation that have opened up further opportunities for religious agencies to participate in federal funding streams since the end of the Cold War: the Clinton administration's little noticed Charitable Choice provision of the landmark 1996 Personal Responsibility and Work Opportunity Reconciliation Act (PRWORA) and the more recent efforts by the George W. Bush administration to funnel public funds into religious groups via the White House Office of Faith-Based and Community Initiatives. They neither ushered in unprecedented financial ties between church and state, as opponents alleged, nor constituted a radical challenge to the welfare state, as proponents promised. Instead, the two measures showcase the three main processes discussed in this study.

First, Charitable Choice and the Faith-Based Initiative highlight that subsidiarist policies are part of a well-established policy pattern sustained by a long-term political consensus that connects postwar federal programs, the Great Society of the 1960s, and 1980s-style devolution.[62] They show that partisan conflicts no longer revolved around whether public funds should support nongovernmental social service delivery, but around the level of government support for which type of private or nonprofit agency. In spite of the clamoring of conservative despisers of big government and liberal jeremiads against devolution and privatization, both 1960s Democrats and 1990s Republicans looked to nongovernmental organizations in general, and religious agencies in particular, to play major roles in the American system of social provision. Although the rhetoric of "retrenchment," "privatization," and "empowerment of mediating structures" emanated from the political Right, it described the same kind of devolution of social services that liberals had pioneered during the War on Poverty.[63] "To conservatives, government contracting is part of the broad appeal of privatization that promises smaller government and more reliance on private initiative. To liberals, government contracting with nonprofit agencies can be a way to expand the boundaries of the welfare state."[64]

Subsidiarist policies thus resulted from the confluence of "strands of thought and action" that had been "entertained by influential groups across the political spectrum." By the mid-1990s these groups, despite deep-seated historical animosities, could form a consensus on such issues as expanding the rights of religious institutions, government funding of faith-based services, and turning key government roles over to nonprofit groups, whether secular or religious.[65] That the reforms of 1996 and the Faith-Based Initiative are frequently depicted by proponents as radical challenges to the welfare state, and by its opponents as fundamental breaches in the wall of separation, is more indicative of the power of antistatist rhetoric in the post-1960s era than of the policies constituting a real departure from established patterns of American social provision.

Second, the two measures marked the final step in the process of making evangelicals an explicit part of the nation's subsidiarist welfare system. Charitable Choice, sponsored by Missouri Senator John Ashcroft, a conservative Christian who later became Attorney General in the George W. Bush administration, not only prohibited discrimination against religious nonprofits in the contracting process. It "specifically required state and local governments to open the door to faith-based organizations when buying services from nongovernmental sources."[66] In so doing, the provision allowed states to use federal funds to enter into service contracts with charitable and faith-based organizations while removing elements of federal oversight. It permitted restrictive hiring of employees by religious agencies contracting with government, and abandoned requirements for religious social service agencies to be separately incorporated and tax exempt under IRS codes as a prerequisite for receiving public funds. It also allowed the display of religious icons and other symbols where government services were provided.[67] Similarly, the Faith-Based Initiative allowed for federal funds to be given directly to churches, rather than just denominational charities, and further limited the ability of the state to interfere with religious content.[68]

The two programs thus addressed the remaining concerns evangelicals had in regard to public funding. First, they broadened the definition of eligible recipients of aid and loosened restrictions on religious agencies, while at the same time limiting the potential for government intrusion. Second, they strengthened the legislative basis for the overt embrace of religious content in social welfare, which had previously been tolerated via a policy of benign neglect, but had not been written into the statutes. Under the new laws, religious providers retained autonomy from all levels of government and control over the definition, development, practice, and expression of religious beliefs. They were able to assert their spiritual dimension, which strengthened the influence of religious imagery and narratives in the welfare debates.[69]

Finally, the faith-based policies since the 1990s put the finishing touches on the long-term ideological process of turning a religious group that had traditionally adhered to a strict separation of church and state into a champion of state funding. By 1999, prior to the Faith-Based Initiative, 28 percent of white evangelical denominations were willing to apply for federal funding. This continued to trail expressions of interest on the part of Catholics (40 percent) and liberal Protestants (41 percent), and lagged far behind predominantly African American congregations (64 percent). Nonetheless, it was a startling percentage for a grouping that had traditionally been adamantly opposed to any government aid.[70] Meanwhile, the availability of funds continued to exert its own subtle pressure. According to a nine-state study, 20 of the 84 contracts engaged conservative and evangelical faith-based organizations in Charitable Choice contracting.[71] Likewise, a 2007 survey concluded that evangelical Protestants shared the basic ideas behind Charitable Choice. According to its findings, only one quarter to one-third of congregations felt that government should have little or no role in the care for the needy and that the religious community should not work directly with government in providing these services. In contrast, more than eight out of ten (82 percent) agreed with the statement that "meeting the needs of the poor demands collaboration between government, the religious community, and the secular community." These views were held almost uniformly across the congregational divides, with evangelical Protestants and theological conservatives only modestly less likely to subscribe to them.[72]

That evangelicals have since moved to the forefront of what the *Wall Street Journal* has called the "Blaine game" further highlights the magnitude of this change in church-state attitudes. As mentioned in Chapter 1, in the late nineteenth century, James G. Blaine's campaign against direct government aid to religious educational institutions had succeeded in putting in place restrictive provisions in 37 state constitutions. While widely hailed by evangelicals at the time, these laws became the object of evangelical ire in the twentieth century when opponents of public aid used them to challenge religious school funding. Encouraged by the Supreme Court's approval of a school voucher program in *Zelman v. Simmons-Harris* (2002), however, a remarkably ecumenical coalition of evangelicals, libertarians, conservatives, African Americans, Catholics, and Orthodox Jews mobilized to bury Blaine once and for all.[73]

The new evangelical church-state ideology amalgamated both separationist and statist elements. On the one hand, evangelicals continued to voice concerns about government intrusion, were fiercely protective of their organizational autonomy, denounced the moral failures of the liberal state, and depicted religious agencies and the state as inhabiting separate spheres. They viewed faith-based social service delivery as more effective than government, demanded that welfare provision shift from income maintenance to a focus on the behavioral roots of poverty, and asserted that religious belief exerted an "empowering" effect on the poor.[74] On the other hand, the growing experience of evangelical agencies with public funding had convinced them that subsidiarity protected religious providers and tacitly condoned the transformative power of faith as an effective antipoverty policy. In turn, in interacting with the subsidiarist state, evangelicals shifted their emphasis from the anti-establishment clause to the free exercise clause of the First Amendment in ways that enabled them to legitimize their transformation from advocates of strict separationism to beneficiaries of government funding.

* * *

In summation, the analysis of white evangelicalism during the Cold War presented in this book shows that, in their desire to regain cultural legitimacy and political influence within the political climate of the liberal consensus, conservative Protestants underwent a "statist" and "subsidiarist" turn. They came to embrace a level of government activity they had previously objected to as a matter of doctrine. In particular, identification with Cold War anticommunism, fears of the rise of Catholic influence, growing concern that secularists were forcing religion out of the public sphere, and purely pragmatic considerations prompted evangelicals to part with their traditional separationism. Despite their fledgling ties to the Cold War order, however, evangelicals continued to project a traditional separationist image and to hone their antistatist credentials. The NAE remained closely allied with separationist organizations, included a significant pacifist contingent, denounced Catholic efforts to obtain public aid, pilloried the secular state, and worried about intrusive federal oversight. Hence, as the Cold War national security and welfare state made evangelical agencies part of its administrative structure, conservative Protestants had to struggle with the dilemma of rejecting public funds in principle while accepting them in practice. What distinguished the experience of conservative Protestants from that of other religious groups, however, was not that they were being marginalized, but that they had to make a larger ideological leap in order to reconcile their established church-state stance with participation in the Cold War order.

This assimilation of evangelical entities into the structures of the state was eased by "liberal" Cold War policies that enabled conservatives to assert concrete political and cultural power. Growth-oriented policies embedded a conservative ideology of limited government; the public funding of nongovernmental organizations facilitated the build-up of conservative nonprofits and their antistatist ethos; and the moralistic framework of welfare policies preserved gender discrimination, racialized welfare provision, and a segmented workforce. Particularly in evangelicalism's strongholds of the South and the West, growth-oriented policies had engendered underlying support for the defense and welfare state; subsidiarity was crucial in building up the religious nonprofit infrastructure; and the moral construction of poverty militated against overcoming the race and class divisions within the Democratic coalition.

Together these findings suggest that the evangelical involvement with the Cold War state and its inherent contradictions, rather than simply the rejection of liberal public policies, was at the center of the political mobilization of conservative Protestantism. Indeed, the liberal state emerged as both an enabler and a nemesis for the evangelical resurgence. As the New Deal coalition fragmented in the context of the economic and cultural crises of the late 1960s and 1970s, evangelicals blended an insurgent message with the institutional embrace of the Cold War state. Their growing support for subsidiarity in particular helped them marginalize internal critics, forge ties with resurgent secular conservatism, and formulate a moral and cultural narrative of "antistatist state building" for the post-1960s age.

In this way the evangelical resurgence became part and parcel of a larger "big government conservatism" that, while vilifying the liberal state, did not question the institutional or ideological construction of Cold War public policy. Viewed from this vantage point, the main story since the 1960s is not the replacement of New Deal/Great Society welfare state building with the politics of conservative retrenchment and culture warring. Indeed, the differences between the "liberal consensus" and "resurgent conservatism" have been overestimated, and the much-touted "culture war" is more rhetorical than real. The "stealth state building" of conservatism suggests that the answer to the "what's the matter with Kansas" enigma is not that morality politics is a deflection from socioeconomic concerns based on the false consciousness of a disillusioned electorate.[75] Instead, it indicates that morality politics transported the foundations of the Cold War state into a post-1960s age after liberalism had succeeded in generating popular support for state social provision, but had failed to forge an effective electoral coalition in support of an inclusive, redistributive welfare state.

NOTES

Introduction: How Evangelicals Learned to Stop Worrying and Love the State

1. On the role of state-private networks during the Cold War see Hogan, "Corporatism," 363–67; McCormick, "Drift or Mastery," 318–29; Laville and Wilford, *U.S. Government, Citizen Groups and Cold War.*

2. Wuthnow, "Improving Our Understanding of Religion." Wuthnow regards "the ways in which government, media, and the for-profit sector impinge on the activities of religious organizations" as areas in need of further research (218). N. J. Demerath and Rhys Williams note the gap between cultural conceptions of separation and structural realities of the church-state relationship. See Demerath and Williams, "Mythical Past," 77–83.

3. Monsma, *Sacred and Secular*, 1.

4. This is in contrast to the copious literature on the relationship between religion and state formation in the nineteenth century, which highlights the key role of religion in fashioning the nation-state. See, for example, Ahlstrom, *Religious History*; Thomas, *Revivalism and Cultural Change.*

5. See Hall and Burke, "Historical Statistics," 9, 27–28.

6. Salamon, *Partners in Public Service*, 21. See also Hall and Burke, "Historical Statistics," 12.

7. Nichols, *Uneasy Alliance*, 206.

8. Hall and Burke, "Historical Statistics," 16–17, 28. This lack of statistical data is part and parcel of the larger scholarly neglect of state-nonprofit relations. According to Peter Dobkin Hall, the "inability of legislators, policy makers, journalists, and academics to discern the character of the welfare state being created after the war" has resulted in a lack of reliable information on government support for voluntary sector and its impact on nonprofits. Hall, "Welfare State and Careers," 366. Likewise, Lester Salamon complains that no government-wide overview of federal support to nonprofit institutions is available, and few state or local government collected relevant data. Salamon, *Partners in Public Service*, 86. And Stephen Monsma notes the "surprising disinterest both in the government-nonprofit relationship in general and religiously based organizations within the nonprofit sector in particular." Monsma, *Sacred and Secular*, 12. On the problems of obtaining reliable information see also Wuthnow, "Improving Our Understanding of Religion," 271–83.

9. Butler, "Jack-in-the-Box Faith."

10. Heclo and McClay, *Religion Returns to the Public Sphere*, 11; Fogel, *Fourth Great Awakening*, 179–80, 217; Skocpol, "Religion, Civil Society," 45. See also Noll, *Religion and American Politics*.

11. Carlson-Thiess, "Charitable Choice," 109.

12. Hall, "Philanthropy," 1.

13. Monsma, *Sacred and Secular*, 9.

14. In 2011 the Supreme Court in *Arizona Christian School Tuition Organization v. Winn* upheld tuition tax credits as a constitutional way of indirectly channeling tax funds to aid religion.

15. Forrester, "Federal Aid to Higher Education," 6–8 March 1963.

16. Cnaan et al., *Newer Deal*, 280. See also Hall, "Philanthropy," 36.

17. Lasch, *True and Only Heaven*, 532.

18. Ehrenreich, "New Right Attack," 181.

Chapter 1. The Cold War State and Religious Agencies

1. Berkowitz, *America's Welfare State*, 52. On the political and administrative impact of wartime mobilization on state building and postwar public policy, see Sherry, *Shadow of War*, 71–86; Skocpol, *Social Policy in the United States*, 167–208; Berkowitz and McQuaid, *Creating the Welfare State*, 149–54; Fraser and Gerstle, *Rise and Fall*, xv; Yergin and Stanislaw, "Democrats and Republicans," 477–78; Himmelstein, *To the Right*, 17ff.; Neustadt, "Congress and the Fair Deal." See also Collins, *More*; Wolfe, *America's Impasse*; Brinkley, *Liberalism and Its Discontents*; Friedberg, *Shadow of the Garrison State*; Bell, *Liberal State on Trial*; Polenberg, *War and Society*; Conkin, *The New Deal*; Freidel, *Franklin D. Roosevelt*; Sparrow, *From the Outside In*. For a recent assessment of the impact of 1940s public policy on the Cold War order, see "Round Table: A Critical Moment." For a good summary of the postwar European embrace of economic planning and state intervention, see Judt, *Postwar*, 67–77.

2. Sherry, *Shadow of War*, 78. On liberal state building that combines the expansion of national administrative capacities with antistatist rhetoric, see Hawley, "New Deal State"; Karl, *Uneasy State*; Morone, *Democratic Wish*. Historically, federal expenditure levels never returned to prewar levels, and this rule applied even more to World War II than to any previous war. Between 1940 and 1960, federal spending as a percentage of GNP roughly doubled from 9.8 percent in 1940 to 18 percent in 1960. For details on federal government receipts and expenditures, see U.S. Bureau of the Census, *Historical Statistics*; and U.S. Office of Management and Budget, *Budget of the United States Government, Fiscal Year 2000, Historical Tables*. See also Berkowitz and McQuaid, *Creating the Welfare State*, 147, 149; and Campbell, *Growth of American Government*.

3. On the associative state and corporatism of the 1920s see Hawley, *Great War*; Hogan, *Informal Entente*; Hogan, "Corporatism"; Schwarz, *Interregnum of Despair*. On the history of public-private relations prior to World War II, see Katz and Sachsse, *Mixed*

Economy; Salamon, *Partners in Public Service*, 85; Finkenbine, "Law, Reconstruction"; Skocpol, "Religion, Civil Society," 26. On New Deal separation between public and private agencies, see Schottland, "Introduction," viii; McKeown, "Claiming the Poor," 156. On efforts to fuse the resources of the public and private sectors in an associational arrangement and on the role of this pattern of state building in war mobilization, national security, and social welfare prior to and during World War II, see Koistinen, *Planning War, Pursuing Peace*; Hamilton, *From New Day to New Deal*; Karl and Katz, "American Private Philanthropic Foundation."

4. On postwar public funding of nongovernmental organizations and on subsidiarity becoming the norm, see Salamon, *Partners in Public Service*, 18–28, 45–50, 83, 90; Smith and Lipsky, *Nonprofits for Hire*, 5, 15–16, 46, 70–71, 179–80; Hall, "Welfare State and Careers," 363–83; Hall and Burke, "Historical Statistics," 9–10, 12, 18, 23; Kramer, *Voluntary Agencies*, 67–69; Monsma, *Sacred and Secular*, 4; Garr, *Reinvesting in America*, 5–6; Critchlow, "Family Planning"; Schäfer, "Religious Nonprofit Organizations."

5. Hall, "Welfare State and Careers," 380.

6. See Salamon, *Partners in Public Service*, 19; Hall, "Philanthropy," 17; Critchlow, "Family Planning," 212.

7. Nichols, *Uneasy Alliance*, 206.

8. Critchlow, "Family Planning," 211–12; Greenberg, "Doing Whose Work?" 179. For figures, see also Salamon, *Nonprofit Sector*, 45–46; and Salamon, *Partners in Public Service*, 86–88, 90.

9. Salamon, *Partners in Public Service*, 93; see also 86–93, 99.

10. Hall, "Welfare State and Careers," 381–82, 380. For details on government becoming the main source of nonprofit income, see Salamon, *Nonprofit Sector*, 25–26, 45–46; Hall, "Welfare State and Careers," 363–65, 375, 381–82; Hall and Burke, "Historical Statistics," 8–9, 29–30, and tables; Thiemann, Herring, and Perabo, "Responsibility and Risks," 54; Critchlow, "Family Planning," 213; Kramer, *Voluntary Agencies*, 152; Smith and Lipsky, *Nonprofits for Hire*, 4, 66–70; O'Neill, *Third America*, 98; Smith and Stone, "Unexpected Consequences."

11. Hall and Burke, "Historical Statistics," 29–30. On postwar public funding for religious nonprofits see Skocpol, "Religion, Civil Society," 21–50; Glenn, *Ambiguous Embrace*; Monsma, *Sacred and Secular*; Wineburg, *Limited Partnership*; Epstein, *Dilemma of American Social Welfare*, 63; Netting, "Secular and Religious Funding"; Weber and Gilbert, *Private Churches and Public Money*; Coughlin, *Church and State*. For a thoughtful recent exploration of public funding of religious social services by an academic-turned-minister, see Daly, *God and the Welfare State*. On religious providers as part of the nonprofit sector, see Wuthnow, *Saving America?*; Wuthnow, Hodgkinson, and Associates, *Faith and Philanthropy*; O'Neill, *Third America*.

12. Carpenter, "Revive Us Again," 118, see also 114. On the role of war in renewing the commitment to mission work and on military imagery in the missions movement, see also Carpenter, *Revive Us Again*, 178–79. On the war shoring up religion, see Wuthnow, *Restructuring of Religion*, 59–60; Carpenter, "Youth for Christ," 361, 370;

Sittser, *Cautious Patriotism*. On the role of religion in early Cold War foreign policy, see Inboden, *Religion and American Foreign Policy*.

13. Quoted in "A Nation Under God," 38.

14. Elson, "Worship in the Life of the Nation," 10–11, 19.

15. Hoover, "Communist Propaganda and the Christian Pulpit," 5.

16. Quoted in Pierard and Lindner, *Civil Religion*, 189, 197–98.

17. Miller, *Piety Along the Potomac*, 41.

18. Pierard and Lindner, *Civil Religion*, 184, 201–4.

19. On this famous quote and its various uses see Henry, "'And I Don't Care What It Is'" (the correct quote is on 41).

20. On the Cold War and religion generally, see Ellwood, *Fifties Spiritual Marketplace*, 18, 38, 48–51; Wuthnow, *Restructuring of American Religion*, 39–43, 47, 50–51; Preston, "Death of a Peculiar Special Relationship."

21. Flipse, "Save 'Free Vietnam,'" 209.

22. Hall and Burke, "Historical Statistics," 9; Monsma, *Sacred and Secular*, 8–9, 67.

23. O'Neill, *Third America*, 20–21. For examples of religious institution building in the late nineteenth and early twentieth centuries see 30ff.

24. Hammack, "Failure and Resilience," 280; Salamon, *Partners in Public Service*, 50.

25. Skocpol, "Religion, Civil Society," 25.

26. On public funding during the eighteenth and nineteenth centuries, see Salamon, *Partners in Public Service*, 84–86; Smith and Lipsky, *Nonprofits for Hire*, 47–50. Monsma, *Sacred and Secular*, 5–6; O'Neill, *Third America*, 24–30. On the role of religion and public funding of religious primary and secondary education in the nineteenth century, see Viteritti, *Last Freedom*, 74–86. On public funding ties with the Catholic church, see Adloff, "Civil Society, Civic Engagement"; Adloff, "Religion and Social-Political Action"; Adloff, "Catholic Charities und der amerikanische Wohlfahrtsstaat." On religious narratives shaping the public discussion on social policies, see also Reich, *Tales of a New America*; O'Connor, *Poverty Knowledge*; Bane and Mead, *Lifting Up the Poor*; Heimert, *Religion and the American Mind*; Smith, *Revivalism and Social Reform*; Loveland, *Southern Evangelicals*.

27. Having witnessed the failure of charitable institutions during the Great Depression, the federal administrators who pioneered the massive antipoverty programs of the New Deal were skeptical of charitable and religious organizations and relied largely on public agencies as the core of the delivery system. For example, the very first regulation by the Federal Emergency Relief Administration (FERA), established in 1933 to funnel federal relief through state and local agencies, blocked the formal participation of private welfare organizations. It ruled that all public monies had to be distributed by public agencies. This preempted attempts by Catholic charities to establish themselves on local and state levels as administrators of federal and state welfare funds for FERA. Although church organizations, such as Jewish Vocational Services, the National Conference of Catholic Charities, and the Salvation Army eventually ended up becoming part of the public welfare delivery system, their influence and involvement in the New Deal welfare

state remained limited. See McKeown, "Claiming the Poor," 155–56; Carlson-Thiess, "Charitable Choice," 111; Lowell, *Church-State Fraud*, 173–74; Brown and McKeown, *The Poor Belong to Us*, chap. 5; Rosenthal, "Public or Private," 10–11. On successes of the charitable sector in securing federal funding during the New Deal, see Hammack, "Failure and Resilience"; Salamon, *Partners in Public Service*, 50.

28. Murch, "The Protestant Position Today," 6–8 March 1963, 5.

29. Netting, "Secular and Religious Funding," 587, 601; Bogle, "Survey of Congregation-Based Child Care," 227–28; Salamon, *Partners in Public Service*, 86; Monsma, *Sacred and Secular*, 12–13.

30. Hall and Burke, "Historical Statistics," 9, 16–17, 27. See also Coughlin, *Church and State*, 66.

31. Hall and Burke, "Historical Statistics," 28.

32. Monsma, *Sacred and Secular*, 8–9, 67.

33. Nichols, *Uneasy Alliance*, 210. On foreign aid policy during the Cold War and the development of close ties between state and philanthropies, see Hess, "Waging the Cold War"; Parmar, "Conceptualising."

34. Flipse, "Save 'Free Vietnam,'" 208–9.

35. [Henry], "Peace Drive in the Churches," 20.

36. Fowler Hamilton to Clinton P. Anderson, 9 November 1962; U.S. Congress, House, Subcommittee of the Committee on Foreign Affairs, *Final Report on Foreign Aid*, Report 1845, 80th Cong., 2nd sess., 1948; Section 202 of amended Agricultural Trade and Development Assistance Act; Section 635(c) of the Act for International Development (PL 87-195).

37. Nichols, *Uneasy Alliance*, 208–10.

38. Lowell, *Church-State Fraud*, 12, 168.

39. Hostetter, "Government Overseas Programs and the Churches," 6–8 March 1963, 1.

40. Nichols, *Uneasy Alliance*, 207–8.

41. Fowler Hamilton to Clinton P. Anderson, 9 November 1962; USAID, "Involvement of Religious Affiliated Institutions," 1–2. See also Lowell, *Church-State Fraud*, 164.

42. Fowler Hamilton to Clinton P. Anderson, 9 November 1962.

43. Nichols, *Uneasy Alliance*, 93, 209

44. Lowell, *Church-State Fraud*, 165–67, quote 166. Lowell notes that R. Sargent Shriver, then head of the Peace Corps, acknowledged that the provision of government funds for the maintenance of missionary operations and personnel abroad was a frequent practice (167).

45. Bachmann, *The Emerging Perspective*, 161.

46. Nichols, *Uneasy Alliance*, 93.

47. Bachmann, *The Emerging Perspective*, 160–61.

48. "Peace Drive in the Churches," 20.

49. Nichols, *Uneasy Alliance*, 100–131, 210; Monsma, *Sacred and Secular*, 79; Flipse, "Save 'Free Vietnam,'" 206–22.

50. Loveland, *Evangelicals and the Military*, 139–64.

51. Nichols, *Uneasy Alliance*, 200, 211.

52. Monsma, *Sacred and Secular*, 9–10, 65, 67–68, 72–73, 78.

53. On the G.I. Bill, see Skocpol, "G.I. Bill and U.S. Social Policy," 96–101; Ravitch, *Troubled Crusade*, 12, 14; Berkowitz and McQuaid, *Creating the Welfare State*, 157.

54. On the history of public funding of higher education in general, see Hall and Burke, "Historical Statistics," 12, 16–17, 29–30; Hall, "Welfare State and Careers," 364, 378–80; Skocpol, "Religion, Civil Society," 26. See also Murch, "The Protestant Position Today," 6–8 March 1963, 3–4.

55. Lowell, *Church-State Fraud*, 54, 154–61. The anti-Catholic campaign this subsidy engendered among evangelicals is discussed in Chapter 4.

56. Eighmy, *Churches in Cultural Captivity*, 160; Lowell, *Church-State Fraud*, 11; Ravitch, *Troubled Crusade*, 41–42. Ravitch identifies race and religion as the key issues that militated against the passage of a federal aid to education bill prior to 1965. On the debates about public funding of sectarian primary and secondary education, see also 27–42. On impacted areas, see also Taylor, "Report of the Office of Public Affairs," 14 September 1961, 2.

57. Viteritti, *Last Freedom*, 82.

58. On Hill-Burton and subsequent expansions of public funding for nongovernmental health care, see Coughlin, *Church and State*, 47; U.S. Department of Health and Human Resources, "Hill-Burton"; Hall, "Welfare State and Careers," 365; Lowell, *Church-State Fraud*, 11–12, 148–49.

59. Eighmy, *Churches in Cultural Captivity*, 160; Coughlin, *Church and State*, 47, 69–73, 159–62. Among Protestant hospitals, the institutions that benefited the most from Hill-Burton funding were in the Northwest (30.1 percent) and the Northeast (18.2 percent) of the country. These were closely followed by the Rocky Mountain states (16.1 percent) and the Southwest (11.4 percent), figs. 162. See also Decker, "Government Grants and Loans to Charitable Institutions." 6–8 March 1963.

60. Lowell, *Church-State Fraud*, 12, 152–54, 163.

61. Wuthnow, *Restructuring of Religion*, 42; Carpenter, "Youth for Christ," 363.

62. Henry, "Soul Searching in Social Welfare," 31–32.

63. Salamon, *Partners in Public Service*, 85–86; Smith and Lipsky, *Nonprofits for Hire*, 50–51, 53, 71; Thiemann, Herring, and Perabo, "Responsibility and Risks," 53; Smith and Stone, "Unexpected Consequences," 235; Rosenthal, "Public or Private," 10–11, 12. See also Wedel, Katz, and Weick, *Social Services*, 2.

64. Eighmy, *Churches in Cultural Captivity*, 160.

65. Coughlin, *Church and State*, 2, 60, 64, 67–68, 130.

66. Smith and Lipsky, *Nonprofits for Hire*, 54, 71; O'Neill, *Third America*, 96–97. On the Community Mental Health Centers Act (1963), see Smith and Stone, "Unexpected Consequences," 236; Hall and Burke, "Historical Statistics," 12, 19. On the community action component of the 1964 Economic Opportunity Act, see Smith and Stone, "Unexpected Consequences," 235. On subsidies to private nursing homes and other agencies provided via the 1965 Medical Care Act (Medicare and Medicaid), see Smith and Lipsky, *Nonprofits for Hire*, 65–66, 68; Wedel, Katz, and Weick, *Social Services*, vi.

67. Eighmy, *Churches in Cultural Captivity,* 164–65.

68. Taylor, "Report of the Office of Public Affairs," 7 October 1963, 2.

69. Hall, "Welfare State and Careers," 364, 378; Hall and Burke, "Historical Statistics," 14; Salamon, *Partners in Public Service,* 89, 90–91.

70. Eighmy, *Churches in Cultural Captivity,* 164–65; Lowell, *Church-State Fraud,* 188.

71. For an insightful analysis of the conservative embrace of federal aid to education and the way Republican administrations since the 1980s built on the legacy of Lyndon Johnson's Great Society by expanding funding for public education, see Davies, *See Government Grow.*

72. Monsma, *Sacred and Secular,* 9–10, 68–70, 72–73, quote 47.

73. Ibid., 10.

74. Lowell, *Church-State Fraud,* 168–69, 170.

75. Salamon, *Partners in Public Service,* 88–91.

76. Eighmy, *Churches in Cultural Captivity,* 160, 164–66.

77. Bogle, "Survey of Congregation-Based Child Care," 226; Smith and Lipsky, *Nonprofits for Hire,* 60–61, 71; Garr, *Reinvesting in America,* 7; Lowell, *Church-State Fraud,* 147, 173–74, 176–82. Lowell regarded the churches as "prime beneficiaries" of the EOA. In particular, he attributes this to two provisions. Section 213 authorized antipoverty grants to "private, nonpublic organizations to pay all or part of the costs of development of community action programs." Section 113 provides that both federal funds and federal employees can be used for "local projects sponsored by private, nonprofit organizations" (176–77).

78. *Catholic Standard,* 17 February 1966, quoted in Lowell, *Church-State Fraud,* 178.

79. On the 1967 changes, see Smith and Lipsky, *Nonprofits for Hire,* 55–56; Smith and Stone, "Unexpected Consequences," 236; Rosenthal, "Public or Private," 34–36.

80. Lowell, *Church-State Fraud,* 184, 13, 173–74, 178.

81. Smith and Stone, "Unexpected Consequences," 237. Figures in Derthick, *Uncontrollable Spending,* 8; and Smith and Lipsky, *Nonprofits for Hire,* 54. See also Wedel, Katz, and Weick, *Social Services,* vi–vii.

82. Smith and Lipsky, *Nonprofits for Hire,* 55–56. See also Thiemann, Herring, and Perabo, "Responsibility and Risks," 54.

83. Smith and Stone, "Unexpected Consequences," 239, details on Title XX, 238–39; Wedel, Katz, and Weick, *Social Services,* 3. On lobbying by nongovernmental groups for Title XX, see O'Neill, *Third America,* 96–97.

84. Salamon, *Partners in Public Service,* 94. See also Oates, "Faith and Good Works," 291. On legislation since the 1970s, see also Greenberg, "Doing Whose Work?" 180–82, 193; Smith and Lipsky, *Nonprofits for Hire,* 54–57, 62–63, 67; Bogle, "Survey of Congregation-Based Child Care," 226–27; Gottschalk and Gottschalk, "Reagan Retrenchment," 61–71; Smith and Stone, "Unexpected Consequences," 381–82.

85. Smith and Lipsky, *Nonprofits for Hire,* 71, figures on 54; O'Neill, *Third America,* 96–97. See also Gottschalk and Gottschalk, "Reagan Retrenchment," 66; Thiemann, Herring, and Perabo, "Responsibility and Risks," 54.

86. Smith and Lipsky, *Nonprofits for Hire*, 62–63; O'Neill, *Third America*, 97; Gott-schalk and Gottschalk, "Reagan Retrenchment," 62–63.

87. Netting, "Secular and Religious Funding," 592–93.

88. Smith and Lipsky, *Nonprofits for Hire*, 63, 10; Smith and Stone, "Unexpected Consequences," 239–40; Piven and Cloward, "Popular Power," 75–76. However, Michael Givel points out that in the case of the 1981 Community Service Block Grant Act, the states "generated little or no budgetary resources to compensate for the federal budget cuts," Givel, *War on Poverty Revisited*, 213–14. On Reagan cuts and their impact on nonprofit funding, see also Schiff, *Charitable Giving*, 4, 141–43. On churches making up for the shortfall of federal funding, see Rabinowitz, *Social Change Philanthropy*, 123.

89. Hall, "Philanthropy," 36. See also Smith and Stone, "Unexpected Consequences," 234; Piven and Cloward, "Popular Power," 75–76, 88, 92; Gottschalk and Gottschalk, "Reagan Retrenchment," 71.

90. Stenholm, "A Christian's Response to Federal Child Care Policy," 27 April 1990, 5–6.

91. Bogle, "Survey of Congregation-Based Child Care," 226–27.

92. Monsma, *Sacred and Secular*, 1; Greenberg, "Doing Whose Work?," 180. According to Hall and Burke, the Catholic Church is "probably the most active provider of the widest range of educational, health, and human services," and Catholic Charities USA, "perhaps the largest faith-based charity, is a secular corporation that is substantially supported by government subsidies." See "Historical Statistics," 27.

93. Monsma, *Sacred and Secular*, 10, 68–69, 72–73.

94. Demerath and Williams, "Mythical Past," 77–90; Monsma, *Sacred and Secular*, 30–31; Hammond, "Church/State Jurisprudence." Hammond points out that since the 1940s, Supreme Court decisions have exhibited a clear tendency to expand the range of religious behaviors entitled to constitutional protection and at the same time to restrict government involvement in, or sponsorship of, religious activity (456). The most detailed source of information is Miller and Flowers, *Toward Benevolent Neutrality*. For a review of the 13 cases on aid to parochial schools between 1947 and 1997 and their inconsistencies, see Viteritti, *Last Freedom*, 121–38. Diane Ravitch points out that "it became an accepted axiom of the American political scene in the years between 1950 and 1965 that it was impossible to pass general federal aid to education." See Ravitch, *Troubled Crusade*, 41. See also Long, "Drawing the Line."

95. Monsma, *Sacred and Secular*, 30–31; Carlson-Thiess, "Charitable Choice," 114.

96. Coughlin, *Church and State*, 129. For details on the legal sanctioning of the partnership between government and sectarian welfare institutions, see 44–48; Monsma, *Sacred and Secular*, 13; Hall and Burke, "Historical Statistics," 17. In the 1899 *Bradfield v. Roberts* decision, the Supreme Court upheld state aid to a religious hospital. The ruling argued that the state entered into a contract with a religious institution as a civil entity, not a religious body.

97. Greenberg, "Doing Whose Work?" 180; Monsma, *Sacred and Secular*, 31–41, 45–46. The long-standing practice of limiting state support for religious institutions by

defining them as "pervasively sectarian" has recently come under attack. The U.S. Court of Appeals for the 10th Circuit ruled in July 2008 that Colorado may not distinguish between sectarian and "pervasively sectarian" colleges to deny state funds to students in the latter category, because this amounted to illegal state preferences for some religious groups over others. "U.S. Court Rejects 'Pervasively Sectarian' Test," *Inside Higher Ed*, http://www.insidehighered.com/news/2008/07/24/ccu.

98. Lowell, *Church-State Fraud*, 189. See also Coughlin, *Church and State*, 44–48, 129.

99. Lowell, *Church-State Fraud*, 192, 206.

100. On the special treatment of religious bodies under tax and regulatory regimes, see Hall and Burke, "Historical Statistics," 16. These exemptions were rooted both in common law tradition, which accorded exemption to religious groups that discharged certain governmental burdens, and in equity law, which accorded exemptions to all churches that dispensed certain social benefits. On tax exemptions, see also Demerath and Williams, "Mythical Past," 83–89; Lowell, *Church-State Fraud*, 12, 204–5. On efforts to limit them, see Hall, "Welfare State and Careers," 373; Witte, "Piety or Charity," 160–61; Demerath and Williams, "Mythical Past," 89.

101. Pfeffer, "Religion Exemptions," 104, 106–7; Witte, "Piety or Charity," 136. On the impact of tax policies in the 1980s on charitable giving, see Schiff, *Charitable Giving*, 135–36.

102. Hall and Burke, "Historical Statistics," 17.

103. Monsma, *Sacred and Secular*, 13, 40–41; Viteritti, *Last Freedom,* 136–37.

104. Although the Vermont Supreme Court found tuition vouchers in violation of the Constitution, and the Supreme Court at the time refused to review the case. Lowell, *Church-State Fraud*, 186.

105. Monsma, *Sacred and Secular*, 31–33; Viteritti, *Last Freedom*, 134–35. In tracking the record of the Supreme Court, Viteritti finds little that is redeeming about its inconsistencies. The Court upheld religious tax exemptions, but outlawed school prayer and bible reading. It struck down benefits for students at parochial schools, but approved tax deduction for tuition, textbook, and transportation expenses.

106. Viteritti, *Last Freedom*, 138–40. In *PEARL v. Nyquist* (1973), the Court ruled that tuition tax credits were not distinguishable from grants for tuition reimbursement. It struck down a tuition grant program for the state of New York that provided partial reimbursement to low-income parents whose children attended private schools, arguing that grants offered as an incentive to parents to send their offspring to religious schools violated the Establishment Clause.

107. For examples of church-state conflicts and warnings about the corrupting influence of public funding, see Carlson-Thiess, "Charitable Choice," 112; Greenberg, "Doing Whose Work?," 189–90; Monsma, *Sacred and Secular*, 11–12; Rosenthal, "Public or Private," 3; Netting, "Secular and Religious Funding," 588–89; Lowell, *Church-State Fraud*, 147–50, 177, 184–86; Berger and Neuhaus, *To Empower People*, 150–52, 185–93; Olasky, "Corruption of Religious Charities," 95–96, 99.

108. Coughlin, *Church and State*, 87–88; Netting, "Secular and Religious Funding," 591–92; Bachmann, *The Emerging Perspective*, 156; Smith and Stone, "Unexpected Consequences," 235, 240; Smith and Lipsky, *Nonprofits for Hire*, 10, 17–18, 204; Hall and Burke, "Historical Statistics," 24

109. Bachmann, *The Emerging Perspective*, 156.

110. Netting, "Secular and Religious Funding," 592.

111. Carlson-Thiess, "Charitable Choice," 114–15.

112. Salamon, *Partners in Public Service*, 19–21, 28, 93–96, 99; Monsma, *Sacred and Secular*, 5, 64–66.

113. Smith and Lipsky, *Nonprofits for* Hire, 10; Smith and Stone, "Unexpected Consequences," 239; Kramer, *Voluntary Agencies*, 72.

114. Coughlin, *Church and State*, 57; Lowell, *Church-State Fraud*, 212; Hall and Burke, "Historical Statistics," 24, see also 10; Smith and Lipsky, *Nonprofits for Hire*, 10–11, 203; Salamon, *Partners in Public Service*, 22, 27.

115. Salamon, *Partners in Public Service*, 21.

116. Monsma, *Sacred and Secular*, 82–85, 90–91.

117. Rosenthal, "Public or Private," 13, 18, 26; Bachmann, *The Emerging Perspective*, 161–62; Monsma, *Sacred and Secular*, 85–86, 90–91.

118. Monsma, *Sacred and Secular*, 85–86, 95–96, 96–98, quote 95.

119. Hall, "Welfare State and Careers," 375

120. Piven and Cloward, "Popular Power," 90. In 1939, 12,500 charitable nonprofits were registered with the Internal Revenue Service. By 1967 there were 300,000; by 1992, there were approximately 1.4 million, with a total income of $316 billion. Hall, "Welfare State and Careers," 363–64. See also Weisbrod, *Nonprofit Economy*. For a contrasting view, see Kramer, *Voluntary Agencies*, 67–69.

121. Wuthnow, "Religion and Voluntary Spirit," 15–16; Hall and Burke, "Historical Statistics."

122. Bogle, "Survey of Congregation-Based Child Care," 218, 223–24; Rosenthal, "Public or Private," 16; Bachmann, *The Emerging Perspective*, 157. See also Lindner, Mattis, and Rogers, *When Churches Mind the Children*.

123. Smith and Lipsky, *Nonprofits for Hire*, 40, 62.

124. Wald, *Religion and Politics*, 27; Garr, *Reinvesting in America*, xii.

125. Hunter, *Evangelicalism: Coming Generation*, 257 n35. According to a survey from the late 1980s, congregations used 46 percent of donated funds for activities other than religious ministry and education. Roughly 87 percent of congregations reported being involved in a human service or welfare program, 80 percent reported participation in family counseling, 71 percent sent relief and aid abroad, 56 percent supported hospitals, nursing homes, or hospices, 46 percent were involved in community development programs, 38 percent reported support for schools and colleges, and 31 percent provided day care centers. Hodgkinson, Weitzman, and Kirsch, "From Commitment to Action," 96; Wuthnow, "Religion and Voluntary Spirit," 16.

126. Coughlin, *Church and State*, 104.

127. Ibid., 102–3, 105; Rosenthal, "Public or Private," 13. Jewish organizations in particular played a leading role in federal lawsuits on issues of church-state cooperation. See Ivers, *To Build a Wall.*

128. Oates, "Faith and Good Works," 288.

129. Coughlin, *Church and State*, 105.

130. Ibid., 47.

131. Hunter, *American Evangelicalism*, 8; Stone, *Boundaries of Evangelicalism*, 27.

132. Coughlin, *Church and State*, 63, 87–88, 105, 116–21. On attitudes to taking federal funds among administrators in mainline Protestant denominations, see 82ff.

133. Ibid., 55, 64, 84, 104, 108, 130–31. See also Netting, "Secular and Religious Funding," 603.

134. Nichols, *Uneasy Alliance*, 206, quotes 201, 202.

135. Coughlin, *Church and State*, 121–23.

136. Bachmann, *The Emerging Perspective*, 155, 159, see also 160–61.

137. Ibid., 159.

138. Coughlin, *Church and State*, 123. See also Bachmann, *The Emerging Perspective*, 157–58.

139. Monsma, *Sacred and Secular*, 106.

Chapter 2. The Evangelical Rediscovery of the State

1. Carpenter, *Revive Us Again*, 233. On the rise of postwar neo-evangelicalism, see also Noll, *History of Christianity*, 463–69; Marsden, *Understanding Fundamentalism*, 1–6, 62–82; Hatch and Hamilton, "Taking the Measure"; Hankins, *Uneasy in Babylon*; Hunter, *American Evangelicalism*; Warner, *New Wine*, 1–30; Stone, *Boundaries of Evangelicalism*.

2. Taylor, "Church and State-1963," 13 November 1963, 1.

3. See Lasch, *True and Only Heaven*, 52.

4. Carpenter, *Revive Us Again*, 233; Dayton, "Social and Political Conservatism," 74.

5. On neo-evangelicalism and its efforts to carve out a position distinct from both prewar fundamentalism and modernist liberalism, see Marsden, "Fundamentalism and Evangelicalism," 29–30; Marsden, *Understanding Fundamentalism*, 63–70; Carpenter, "Revive Us Again," 109–16; Carpenter, *Revive Us Again*, 153, 173–75, 188–89, 233; Carpenter, "Youth for Christ," 368, 374; Hunter, *American Evangelicalism*, 41–45; Stone, *Boundaries of Evangelicalism*, 10, 113; Wuthnow, *Restructuring of Religion*, 133–43; Watt, *Transforming Faith*, 49–71; Noll, *Old Religion*, 155.

6. "Evangelicals and Fundamentals," 21. On Henry, see also Weeks, "Carl F. H. Henry's Moral Arguments for Evangelical Political Activism"; Weeks, "Carl F. H. Henry on Civic Life."

7. The best example of the neo-evangelical critique of the dogmatic separatism and cultural isolationism of prewar fundamentalism can be found in Henry, *Uneasy Con-*

science. See also Carpenter, *Two Reformers*; Marsden, *Reforming Fundamentalism*; Matthews, *Standing Up, Standing Together*; Nelson, *Making and Unmaking*.

8. Henry, "Dare We Revive the Modernist-Fundamentalist Conflict?" 6. On attempts to demarcate evangelicalism theologically from both fundamentalism and liberalism, see also Henry, "Dare We Renew the Controversy? III. The Contemporary Restoration"; Henry, "Dare We Renew the Controversy? The Evangelical Responsibility"; Bromiley, "Fundamentalism-Modernism"; "Resurgent Evangelism."

9. Henry, *Remaking the Modern Mind*, 22, 265, 267.

10. Taylor, "NAE Celebrates 30 Years."

11. Hunter, *American Evangelicalism*, 45; Hunter, *Evangelicalism: Coming Generation*, 46. On the tension between evangelicalism's integration into mainstream culture and its preservation of a militant and subcultural identity, as well as on this mixture of alienation and engagement as key to the cultural strength of conservative Protestantism, see Carpenter, *Revive Us Again*, 242–43; Smith, *American Evangelicalism*, 153; Ellwood, *Fifties Spiritual Marketplace*, 8, 48; Watt, "Private Hopes"; Wuthnow, *Restructuring of Religion*, 142–43; Stone, *Boundaries of Evangelicalism*, 7–15, 28–29, 43–48, 83–84, 183. See also Hammond, "Evangelical Politics," 190; Himmelstein, *To the Right*, 78; Williams, "Culture Wars, Social Movements," 286–93; Layman, *Great Divide*, 53–54. I have discussed this in detail in Schäfer, *Countercultural Conservatives*.

12. Sweet, "Crisis of Liberal Christianity," 45.

13. Reid, "Age of Anxiety," 3–4. On Reid's contribution to the intellectual profile of neo-evangelicalism, see MacLeod, *W. Stanford Reid*.

14. Taylor, "Citizens of Heaven and Earth," 8 August 1954, 4, 7–8.

15. Ibid., 7–9. Taylor's April 1960 report to the NAE Board of Administration exemplifies the tension between pietistic separatism and participation. See Taylor, "Report to NAE Board of Administration, Office of Public Affairs," 25 April 1960, 1.

16. "Christian Responsibility in Political Affairs," 24.

17. On the NAE, see Carpenter, *Revive Us Again*, 150–54, 188–89; Marsden, "Fundamentalism and Evangelicalism," 29–30; Marsden, *Understanding Fundamentalism*, 71–72; Stone, *Boundaries of Evangelicalism*, 76–77, 127, 132; Matthews, *Standing Up, Standing Together*. Ostling, "Religious Landscape," 12. See also National Association of Evangelicals, "History of the NAE."

18. Carpenter, *Revive Us Again*, 144, 157–58.

19. "Temporary Committee for United Action," [1941].

20. "Thirty Short Months," 19–20 September 1945, 14b-14c; Taylor, "NAE Celebrates 30 Years," 12. I have also discussed the range of NAE commissions and affiliates in Schäfer, *Countercultural Conservatives*.

21. Evangelical Action Committee, "Minutes," [Clyde W. Taylor], 5 June 1957, 1–2.

22. Taylor, "NAE Celebrates 30 Years," 11–12. See also "Thirty Short Months," 19–20 September 1945, 14b-14c.

23. Taylor, "Citizens of Heaven and Earth," 8 August 1954, 5; Taylor, "Watchman in Washington," [1955], 1.

24. Taylor, "NAE Celebrates 30 Years," 9; "The Washington Office," 53. On problems with the FCC regarding renewal of licenses for religious broadcasters, see also Taylor, "Supplementary Report on Legislation," 9 October 1961, 2.

25. Taylor, "Mid-Year Report, Secretary of Affairs," 1 October 1952.

26. Taylor, "NAE Celebrates 30 Years," 12.

27. In its clarification of the OPA's task, the NAE declared that the director of public affairs was employed by the Board of Administration upon nomination by the Executive Committee and was responsible for representing the NAE in Washington, rendering service to evangelicals relating to government agencies, watching legislation and government activities pertaining to religious issues, representing evangelical interests to government agencies, and informing evangelicals on relevant issues. See Board of Administration, "Minutes, Third Session," 23 April 1963, 11.

28. Taylor, "Mid-Year Report of the Secretary of Affairs," 1 October 1949, 1. See also Taylor, "Citizens of Heaven and Earth," 8 August 1954, 5.

29. Pfeffer, "Religion Exemptions," 105.

30. Taylor, "N.A.E. Washington Watchmen," February 1956, 1.

31. Henry, "Evangelicals in the Social Struggle," 7, 11.

32. Taylor, "Report of the Secretary of Public Affairs," 1 April 1957, 1; "Seminar on Federal Service," *Spiritual Unity in Action: The Program of the N.A.E. for 1963*, 4.

33. Cairns, "Church-State Relations in the United States," 6–7 February 1961, 10.

34. Discussion of Rutherford L. Decker's message "How Others Look at Us," 6–7 February 1961, 4.

35. Taylor, "Citizens of Heaven and Earth," 8 August 1954, 5.

36. Taylor, "Report of the Office of Public Affairs," 10–14 April 1961, 2.

37. Taylor, "Report of the Office of Public Affairs," 14 September 1961, 1.

38. Taylor, "Report of the Office of Public Affairs," 3 December 1962, 2; [Taylor], "Christian Responsibility in Public Affairs," 3 December 1962,

39. Taylor, "Report of the Secretary of Public Affairs," 6–7 October 1959, 4.

40. Taylor, "Report of the Secretary of Public Affairs," 1 April 1957, 1,

41. Taylor, "Dynamic Performance," 4 April 1957, 4–5. For a study of the relatively widespread success of evangelicals in becoming leaders in business, government, and even entertainment, see Lindsay, *Faith in the Halls of Power*.

42. Robertson, "Semi-Annual Report to the Board of Administration," 4 October 1977," 1.

43. Macy, "Report of the Field Director, Upper Midwest Region," 4–6 April 1967.

44. Discussion of Rutherford L. Decker's message, "How Others Look at Us," 6–7 February 1961, 4.

45. "Resolutions," 25 April 1963, 7.

46. Quoted in Taylor, "The Church in the World—#4: Involvement," 19 March 1974, 33.

47. Coughlin, *Church and State*, 124.

48. Lowell, *Church-State Fraud*, 14.

49. "The Washington Office," 53.

50. Horn to Christian Leaders, "Confidential Memorandum," February 1987.

51. Dugan to John R. Dellenback, 30 August 1982.

52. Fairbanks, "Politics and the Evangelical Press," 245, 251–55. See also Toulouse, "*Christianity Today* and American Public Life."

53. Murch, "The Protestant Position Today," 6–8 March 1963, 3.

54. On conservative movement organizing prior to the 1970s see, for example, Diamond, *Roads to Dominion*; Wilcox, *Onward Christian Soldiers?*; Bruce, *Conservative Protestant Politics*; Liebman and Wuthnow, eds. *New Christian Right*; Ribuffo, *Old Christian Right*, 263; Lienesch, *Redeeming America*, 8; Jelen, "Culture Wars and the Party System," 150; Himmelstein, *To the Right*, 136, 138–39; Wuthnow, *Restructuring of Religion*, 195. For excellent recent books on the evangelical resurgence, see Dochuk, *From Bible Belt to Sun Belt*; Williams, *God's Own Party*; Miller, *Graham and the Republican South*; Turner, *Bill Bright and Campus Crusade*; Eskridge and Noll, *More Money, More Ministry*.

55. Fogel, *Fourth Great Awakening*, 179. See also Harding and Bright, eds., *Statemaking and Social Movements*.

56. On solidifying the role of wartime military expenditure in social policy and economic planning, see Hall, "Welfare State and Careers," 369; Hall and Burke, "Historical Statistics," 13; and Polenberg, *War and Society*, 94. In contrast, Michael Sherry sees the concern with national security and economic recovery as mainly running separately and parallel to each other; Sherry, *Shadow of War*, 78. On combining social service provision and the "garrison state" in the form of a "security state," see also Miller, *Private Government and the Constitution*. For contemporary critiques, see Laswell, "Garrison State"; Mills, *Power Elite*.

57. "NSC 68."

58. Hall, "Welfare State and Careers," 369.

59. U.S. Office of Management and Budget, *Budget of the United States Government, Fiscal Year 2007, Historical Tables*, Table 6.1: Composition of Outlays, 1940–2011, 118–25.

60. Clayton, "Defense Spending," 280; Clayton, "Impact of the Cold War," 449.

61. Ward, "From backwater to outer space."

62. Salamon, *Partners in Public Service*, 96–98. The author challenges the conventional image of government and the nonprofit sector as competitors. Where nonprofits were a major presence, as in the West, government turned to them for help in delivering services. Where there was less of a nonprofit infrastructure, as in the South, government tended to carry more of the delivery burden, but also supplied more nonprofit funds.

63. Jackson, *Crabgrass Frontier*, 215–16. On the growth of the wartime and postwar South and West, see McGirr, *Suburban Warriors*, 25–51, 215. A concise overview of the impact of the New Deal, World War II, and the Cold War on the West can be found in White, *It's Your Misfortune*, 472–612. See also McMillan with Cobb and Sosna, *Remaking Dixie*; Badger, *Prosperity Road*.

64. Himmelstein, *To the Right*, 75; Ravitch, *Troubled Crusade*, 41; Gallup and Castelli, *People's Religion*, 94; Kellstedt and Noll, "Religion, Voting for President," 370–76; Hunter, *American Evangelicalism*, 46–47, 53–56, 117; Rothenberg and Newport, *Evangelical Voter*, 27, 31–35; Conn, *American City*, 145; Warner, *New Wine*, 61; Ellwood, *Fifties Spiritual Marketplace*, 9–10; Wuthnow, *Restructuring of Religion*, 36; Lienesch, *Redeeming America*, 10–11. Many observers have pointed out that the growth of evangelical churches and the decline of mainlines has less to do with liberalism or involvement in social issues than with demographics. See, for example, Wood, "Liberal Protestant Action," 180–81. According to Gallup and Castelli (*People's Religion*, 94), 46 percent of evangelicals live in the South, 25 percent in the Midwest, 15 percent in the West, and 13 percent in the East.

65. Harrison, "Is America's Spiritual Vigor Waning?" Harrison had by then become executive director of the Evangelical (Child) Welfare Agency in Chicago.

66. White, "Philanthropic Giving," 69.

67. Carpenter, "Youth for Christ," 358–63; Wuthnow, *Restructuring of Religion*, 42.

68. Wuthnow, *Restructuring of Religion*, 27–28, 31–35; McGirr, *Suburban Warriors*, 241–42, 254–56.

69. O'Neill, *Third America*, 34; see also 32.

70. Sherry, *Shadow of War*, 73.

71. On the corporate takeover of the war effort see Berkowitz and McQuaid, *Creating the Welfare State*, 149–51. See also Sparrow, *From the Outside In*.

72. On the New Deal as part of the emergence of modern corporate capitalism and on the growing influence of conservatism due to wartime business ties, see Polenberg, *War and Society*; Conkin, *The New Deal*; and Freidel, *Franklin D. Roosevelt*.

73. Sherry, *Shadow of War*, 75. On sidelining New Deal "service intellectuals," such as Rexford Tugwell, Henry Wallace, and Adolph Berle during the war years and the failure to create a comprehensive welfare state, see Berkowitz and McQuaid, *Creating the Welfare State*, 154; Himmelstein, *To the Right*, 17ff.; Neustadt, "Congress and the Fair Deal."

74. Sherry, *Shadow of War*, 75. On the retreat of government and the emphasis on fiscal stimulants as a social policy tool during and after World War II, see Collins, *More*; Wolfe, *America's Impasse*; Brinkley, *Liberalism and Its Discontents*.

75. Brinkley, "World War II and American Liberalism," 446; Berkowitz and McQuaid, *Creating the Welfare State*, 157–58. A good analysis of the link between Fair Deal and New Deal is found in Hamby, *Truman and the Fair Deal*. On the 1946 Employment Act and the Council of Economic Advisors, see Hall, "Welfare State and Careers," 369; and Neustadt, "Congress and the Fair Deal." On the Housing Acts of 1949 and 1954, see Jackson, *Crabgrass Frontier*, 203–18; and Gotham, "City Without Slums."

76. Quoted in Woods, *Quest for Identity*, 80.

77. Patterson, "Poverty and Welfare," 194, 206.

78. Galbraith and Williams, *Essential Galbraith*, 52–53. On growth-oriented policies

and public-private networks primarily benefiting a middle-class clientele, see Skocpol, "G.I. Bill and U.S. Social Policy," 96–101; Brown, "Segmented Welfare System," 191. On Social Security, unemployment insurance, and welfare programs, see Berkowitz, *America's Welfare State*, 50–51, 54, 62–63. On welfare capitalism and union-based benefits, see Berkowitz and McQuaid, *Creating the Welfare State*, 149–51.

79. McGirr, *Suburban Warriors,* 27, 29–30, 40, 51–52, 161, 271; Hall, "Welfare State and Careers," 379; Himmelstein, *To the Right,* 129, 143; Hixson, *American Right Wing*, xxi.

80. McGirr, *Suburban Warriors,* 25–29, quote 29. On the impact of World War II on the West, see also Nash, *World War II and the West*; Nash, *American West Transformed*; and Markusen, Hall, Campbell, and Deitrick, *Rise of the Gunbelt.*

81. See, for example, White, *It's Your Misfortune.*

82. O'Connor, *Poverty Knowledge,* 15–16.

83. Ibid. See also Brown, "Segmented Welfare System," 188.

84. O'Connor, *Poverty Knowledge,* 14, 18–19. O'Connor regards the cultural lag and social ecology approach pioneered by Chicago School sociologists Robert Park and Ernest Burgess in the 1920s as key to diverting attention from economic interpretations of poverty.

85. Katz, *Undeserving Poor,* 122–23. See also Handler and Hasenfeld, *Moral Construction*; Reich, *Tales of a New America.*

86. Sklansky, *Soul's Economy.* See also Cohen, *Reconstruction of American Liberalism.* On historicist understandings of market society and relativistic conceptions of social norms in progressive social thought, particularly as they developed in a transatlantic reform context, see Kloppenberg, *Uncertain Victory*; Rodgers, *Atlantic Crossings*; Schäfer, *American Progressives.*

87. Reich, *Tales of a New America,* 6–7. Robert Reich identifies four basic "myth-based morality tales that determine when we declare a fact a problem, how policy choices are characterized, how the debate is framed."

88. Epstein, *Dilemma of American Social Welfare,* 204, see also 8. In a similar vein Herbert Marcuse criticized the therapeutic mind-set as a way of delegitimizing an effective critique of socioeconomic structures. Citing investigations of worker complaints, he noted that focusing on their concreteness, and judging the success of interventions on the basis of effectiveness in adjusting the individual to society, meant forestalling their larger socioeconomic implications. Hence, complaints such as "wages are too low" were seen as a reflection not of general malaise, but of personal discontent. Marcuse, *One-Dimensional Man*, 108–13.

89. On moral categorizing and the shift in the policy discourse from "class" to "conduct," see also Handler and Hasenfeld, *Moral Construction*, 202–5; Mead, *New Politics of Poverty,* 2–4, 16–23; and Patterson, "Poverty and Welfare," 202–4, 213–14.

90. Freeden, "Democracy and Paternalism."

91. O'Connor, *Poverty Knowledge,* 17.

92. Katz, *Undeserving Poor,* 122–23. For links between liberal and conservative con-

ceptualizations of poverty, see Handler and Hasenfeld, *Moral Construction*, 201; Ehrenreich, "New Right Attack," 175. On the sanctification of traditional core social norms
combined with the rejection of civic conceptions of a common good in social policy,
see Rawls, *Theory of Justice*; Walzer, *Spheres of Justice*; and Sandel, *Limits of Justice*. For a
contrasting perspective, see Carlson-Thies, "Charitable Choice," 112.

93. Jacobson, *Whiteness of a Different Color*.

94. On gender-related discrimination in social policy, see Sarvasy, "Reagan and
Low-Income Mothers"; Handler and Hasenfeld, *Moral Construction*, especially 22–25
and 37; and Patterson, "Poverty and Welfare," 201. See also Gordon, *Women, the State,
and Welfare*; Gordon, *Pitied But Not Entitled*; Abramowitz, *Regulating the Lives of
Women*; Wikander et al., eds., *Protecting Women*. For an alternative reading of social
policy see SenGupta, *From Slavery to Poverty*. The author shows that subaltern groups
devised imaginative ways of using public resources like alms houses, orphanages, prisons, and juvenile reformatories as material resources for disciplining or educating
truant children, obtaining medical assistance, and settling family disputes. Moreover,
a significant body of research has shown that, whereas traditional moral categorizing
reasserts gender hierarchies, the politics of economic growth potentially undermines
them. Considering that "consumption" is traditionally associated with female traits, the
rise of consumer society has, to an extent, strengthened the role of women in American
society and challenged established gender hierarchies. See, for example, Cohen, *Consumers' Republic*.

95. On racial divisions inscribed into the system of social provision, see Lieberman,
Shifting the Color Line, 1–22. On social security exclusions, see Handler and Hasenfeld,
Moral Construction, 34. On the G.I. Bill and housing policies, see Jackson, *Crabgrass
Frontier*, esp. 203–18; Davies, *Housing Reform*. On race and social policy, see also Davies
and Derthick, "Race and Social Welfare Policy"; Hamilton and Hamilton, *Dual Agenda*;
Jencks, *Rethinking Social Policy*; Lasch-Quinn, *Black Neighbors*; Quadagno, *Color of Wel-
fare*; Gutman, "Mirrors"; Wilson, *Truly Disadvantaged*.

96. Handler and Hasenfeld, *Moral Construction*, 2, 15, 29.

97. O'Connor, *Poverty Knowledge*, 15.

98. Handler and Hasenfeld, *Moral Construction*, 40.

99. Bell, "Interpretations," 61, 63–64.

100. Heclo, *Christianity and American Democracy*, 94.

101. Ehrenreich, "New Right Attack," 179, 181–82, 192; Lasch, *True and Only
Heaven*, 516, 518, 521–23; Himmelstein, *To the Right*, 89.

102. May, *Homeward Bound*; Westbrook, "Fighting for the Family," 409–11, 414.
On the role of Cold War moral and family discourses in U.S. foreign policy see Briggs,
Reproducing Empire; Klein, *Cold War Orientalism*. For an alternative assessment empha-
sizing the transformation in race and gender relations caused by the war see Ravitch,
Troubled Crusade, 19–22.

103. Miller and Nowak, *The Fifties*, 122.

104. Lieberman, *Shifting the Color Line,* 5; Handler and Hasenfeld, *Moral Construc-*

tion, 27. The lower life expectancy of African Americans, however, means that they still receive proportionally fewer benefits from Social Security than whites.

105. On this issue see especially Moreton, *To Serve God and Wal-Mart*. On the false dichotomy between "moral" and "economic" issues, particularly from a gender perspective, see also *Duggan, Twilight of Equality?*; MacLean, *Freedom Is Not Enough*; Harding, *The Book of Jerry Falwell*; Luker, *Abortion and the Politics of Motherhood*; Kintz, *Between Jesus and the Market*. For a good example of the application of gender analysis for understanding conservative populism, see also MacLean, *Behind the Mask of Chivalry*.

Chapter 3. Evangelicals, Foreign Policy, and the National Security State

1. This apolitical and separationist stance was grounded in premillennialist dispensationalism. It saw Christian political efforts as largely futile, the current "church age" as marked by corruption, and considered only a remnant of true believers to be able to remain pure. See Marsden, *Understanding Fundamentalism*, 100–101.

2. Carpenter, *Revive Us Again*, 171. Carpenter identifies the advocates of a Puritan-Reformed notion of cultural responsibility and their desire for a "Christian America" as the most active members of the NAE (157–58). For evangelical attitudes toward patriotism, see Fowler, *New Engagement*, 90. On evangelicals and the Cold War, see Lahr, *Millennial Dreams and Apocalyptic Nightmares*; Cromartie, *Evangelicals and Foreign Policy*; Carpenter, "Youth for Christ," 361, 370–71; Carpenter, "Revive Us Again," 114, 118; Ellwood, *Fifties Spiritual Marketplace*, 38, 51.

3. Henry, *Uneasy Conscience*, 23, 29, 76.

4. Henry, "Why Christianity Today," 20. See also Reid, "Age of Anxiety."

5. Kamm, "Is America Losing Her Cultural Distinctives?" 4.

6. "Eisenhower, Khrushchev and History's Inevitable Course," 26.

7. Quoted in Loveland, *Evangelicals and the Military*, 37. See also Ockenga, "Communist Issue Today," 12.

8. See, for example, Kuhn, "Christian Surrender to Communism." 9; Taylor, "Why Communism Is Godless," 13. See also Lienesch, *Redeeming America*, 199.

9. Boyer, *When Time Shall Be No More*, xii; Carpenter, *Revive Us Again*, 149.

10. Ockenga, "Communist Issue Today," 12.

11. Harrison, "Is America's Spiritual Vigor Waning?" 24.

12. On the role of anticommunist statism in conservative mobilization, see Himmelstein, *To the Right*, 42; and McGirr, *Suburban Warriors*, 166.

13. Quoted in Murch, "The Protestant Position Today," 6–8 March 1963.

14. Carpenter, "Youth for Christ," 371. George Marsden sees a continuous tension in fundamentalism between "positive revivalism and polemics." While fundamentalists cultivate an outsider identity and see themselves as separate from the power centers of worldly life, this does not preclude their economic participation or patriotic engagement. See Marsden, *Understanding Fundamentalism*, 110–11. See also Ellwood, *Fifties Spiritual Marketplace*, 48; Wacker, "Uneasy in Zion," 384–86.

15. Henry, "Why Christianity Today," 20. See also "Declaration of Principles," 20.

16. Harrison, "Christianity and Peace in Our Day," 16.

17. Marsden, *Understanding Fundamentalism*, 110–11.

18. See, for example, Harrison, "Reminiscences and a Prophecy," 14. See also Lienesch, *Redeeming America*, 228–33; Boyer, *When Time Shall Be No More*, 185–87.

19. Discussion of Rutherford L. Decker's message, "How Others Look at Us," 6–7 February 1961.

20. Lienesch, *Redeeming America*, 231–32; Boyer, *When Time Shall Be No More*, 208–24; Watt, *Transforming Faith*, 58. Conversion also remained the goal as far as Catholics were concerned. In outlining the evangelical strategy "for the Roman Catholic problem," Clyde Taylor suggested at a staff retreat "to evangelize the Catholics as an answer to the problem." See NAE, "Minutes of the NAE Staff Retreat in Glen Eyrie," 10–12 January 1961, 8.

21. Harrison, "Reminiscences and a Prophecy," 15. See also Boyer, *When Time Shall Be No More*, 174–76; Carpenter, *Revive Us Again*, 149; Fowler, *New Engagement*, 31.

22. See, for example, Judd, "World Issues and the Christian"; Elson, "Worship in the Life of the Nation."; "Joint Moscow-Peking Threat"; [Henry], "Low Tide in the West"; Manning, "The Integrity of Nations." See also Boyer, *When Time Shall Be No More*, 248; Lienesch, *Redeeming America*, 195, 198, 201; Pierard and Lindner, *Civil Religion*, 189, 194–99.

23. "UN: Town Meeting? Or Tragedy?" 20. See also "Spiritual-Moral Unity Wanes in United Nations," 22; Lippincott, "World Government and Christianity." Lippincott, a former ambassador, argued that a UN not controlled by the United States would pose a serious threat to Christians.

24. Taylor, "Dynamic Performance," 4 April 1957.

25. Henry, "Evangelicals in the Social Struggle," 9.

26. [Taylor], "Watchman in Washington," [1955]. On evangelical attitudes to supranationalism and international organizations, see also Preston, "Universal Nationalism."

27. See, for example, Mearsheimer and Walt, *Israel Lobby*; Marsden, "US-Israel Relations."

28. "Graham Describes Three Great American Crises." On evangelical views of communism and the Soviet Union, see also Harrison, "Reminiscences and a Prophesy," 13–15; Boyer, *When Time Shall Be No More*, 156, 170–71; Lienesch, *Redeeming America*, 211–27.

29. Ockenga, "Communist Issue Today," 12; Martin, *With God on Our Side*, 29; Lienesch, *Redeeming America*, 214–15; Wuthnow, *Restructuring of Religion*, 51–52.

30. Hoover, "Communism: The Bitter Enemy of Religion," 4.

31. "Joint Moscow-Peking Threat," 23. See also Lienesch, *Redeeming America*, 220–22.

32. Bell, "A Layman and his Faith: Christianity and Communism," 19.

33. Hoover, "The Communist Menace," 3.

34. Schwarz, "Can We Meet the Red Challenge," 13; Martin, *With God on Our Side*, 39. Schwarz was the leader of the Christian Anti-Communist Crusade.

35. See, for example, Knowland, "Admit Red China?"; "Red China and World Morality"; "Left Wing Attacks on FBI and House Un-American Activities Group"; Martin, *With God on Our Side*, 34.

36. Taylor, "Citizens of Heaven and Earth," 8 August 1954.

37. Taylor, "Report of the Office of Public Affairs," 10–12 April 1962.

38. Ockenga, "Communist Issue Today," 11. In the same vein, Billy Graham maintained that about 1,100 "social sounding institutions" were infiltrated by communists. See Martin, *With God on Our Side*, 34. On conspiracy theories and the sense of betrayal, see also Lienesch, *Redeeming America*, 204; Gay, *Liberty and Justice*, 94.

39. Hoover, "The Communist Menace," 3. See also Hoover's "Soviet Rule or Christian Renewal," and "Communist Propaganda and the Christian Pulpit," 5.

40. Arnold, "Communism Report," 10–12 January 1961.

41. Ockenga, "Communist Issue Today," 12. See also Lienesch, *Redeeming America*, 213.

42. Ellwood, *Fifties Spiritual Marketplace*, 38, 51. See also "Joint Moscow-Peking Threat," 24.

43. Peachey, "Beyond Christian-Communist Strife," 16.

44. Henry, "Fragility of Freedom in the West," 8–9; Henry, "Christian-Pagan West," 3–5; Henry, *Remaking the Modern Mind*, 25–26, 267.

45. See, for example, "What Is the Target?" See also Martin, *With God on Our Side*, 35–39; Hunter, *American Evangelicalism*, 43–45; Ribuffo, *Old Christian Right*.

46. Arnold, "Communism Report," 10–12 January 1961.

47. Taylor, "Report of the Secretary of Affairs," 9 April 1962. See also Taylor, "Report of the Secretary of Public Affairs," 5 December 1961.

48. See, for example, "Red China and World Morality"; Knowland, "Admit Red China?" 11; Taylor, "Report to NAE Board of Administration, Office of Public Affairs," 25 April 1960; Taylor, "Report of the Secretary of Public Affairs," 5 December 1961.

49. Taylor, "Report of the Secretary of Public Affairs," 5 December 1961. On the renewed anticommunist drive, see also Murch, "Report of the Commission on Evangelical Action," April 1961; Murch, "Report of the Commission on Evangelical Action," 10–12 April 1962.

50. NAE, "Minutes of the NAE Staff Conference," 10–13 January 1962.

51. Marsden, *Understanding Fundamentalism*, 109; Himmelstein, *To the Right*, 212–22; McGirr, *Suburban Warriors*, 168, 176, 186, 260.

52. McGirr, *Suburban Warriors*, 16, 186, 213–14; Lasch, *True and Only Heaven*, 505, 509; Ehrenreich, "New Right Attack," 165–66; Bell, "Interpretations," 62; Himmelstein, *To the Right*, 71.

53. See, for example, "Billy Graham and the Pope's Legions"; "Bigotry or Smear?" In a 1957 news item, *Christianity Today* criticized that an immigration bill proposed by Senator John F. Kennedy to redistribute unused quotas under the McCarran-Walter Act of 1952 threatened to allow more Catholics to enter the country. It depicted the bill as linked to communist attempts to destroy the Act. See "Immigration Bill."

54. Taylor, "Mid-Year Report, Secretary of Affairs," 1 October 1952.

55. See, for example, Taylor, "Citizens of Heaven and Earth," 8 August 1954.

56. Henry, "Christian-Pagan West," 4, 5. On Catholicism being perceived as a perverted form of Christianity, see Watt, *Transforming Faith*, 57.

57. See, for example, "NAE Reaffirms Strong Anti-Communist Stand."

58. On the rapid expansion of foreign missionary activities after World War II and its effects in generating interest in foreign policy, see Carpenter, *Revive Us Again*, 177–80; Lienesch, *Redeeming America*, 222; Wuthnow, *Restructuring of Religion*, 41.

59. Taylor, "Citizens of Heaven and Earth," 8 August 1954.

60. Taylor, "Mid-Year Report of the Secretary of Affairs," 1 October 1949; [Taylor], "Watchman in Washington," [1955].

61. Taylor, "Dynamic Performance," 4 April 1957.

62. Taylor, "Mid-Year Report of the Secretary of Affairs," 1 October 1949.

63. See, for example, [Taylor], "Watchman in Washington," [1955].

64. Taylor, "Citizens of Heaven and Earth," 8 August 1954.

65. [Taylor], "Watchman in Washington," [1955].

66. Ibid.; Taylor, "Dynamic Performance," 4 April 1957. For similar examples of successful cooperation with the state department, see Taylor, "15th Annual Report, N.A.E. Office of Affairs," 6 April 1959; Taylor, "Report to NAE Board of Administration, Office of Public Affairs," 25 April 1960.

67. Taylor, "Mid-Year Report of the Secretary of Affairs," 1 October 1949.

68. Taylor, "Citizens of Heaven and Earth," 8 August 1954.

69. Taylor, "Religious Liberty in America," 6–8 March 1963.

70. Taylor, "Dynamic Performance," 4 April 1957.

71. [Taylor], "Watchman in Washington," [1955].

72. Taylor, "Religious Liberty in America," 6–8 March 1963.

73. [Henry], "Human Rights in an Age of Tyranny."

74. Robertson, "Office of Public Affairs, NAE, Semi-Annual Report," 4 October 1977.

75. Dugan, "NAE Office of Public Affairs Report," 8–9 October 1985. For further indications of the significance of the religious freedom campaign see, for example, Dugan, "NAE Office of Public Affairs Semi-Annual Report," 3–4 October 1989.

76. A 1966 NAE circular of policy statements by NAE staff showed how much attitudes had started to change with a new spirit of tolerance in the wake of the Second Vatican Council. See "Confrontation: a sharp look at the issues facing Evangelicals in 1966." See also Watt, *Transforming Faith*, 65–67.

77. Wuthnow, *Restructuring of Religion*, 142–43.

78. See, for example, Taylor, "Report of the Evangelical Action Commission and the NAE Office of Public Affairs," 14 April 1969.

79. Dugan, "NAE Office of Public Affairs Annual Report," 5 March 1984.

80. Pierard, "Billy Graham and the U.S. Presidency," 116. For a good discussion of the relationship between Graham and Eisenhower, see Pierard and Lindner, *Civil Religion*, 184–205; Graham, *Just As I Am*, 188–206.

81. Quoted in Pierard and Lindner, *Civil Religion*, 199; Pollock, *Billy Graham*, 166.

82. Pierard, "Billy Graham and the U.S. Presidency," 118. On ties between religious and secular conservatives, see also Lienesch, *Redeeming America*, 195, 211.

83. Miller, *Piety Along the Potomac*, 42.

84. Taylor, "Citizens of Heaven and Earth," 8 August 1954.

85. Taylor, "Dynamic Performance," 4 April 1957.

86. Taylor, "15th Annual Report, N.A.E. Office of Affairs," 6 April 1959.

87. Judd, "World Issues and the Christian."

88. On ties between ICL and NAE, see Taylor, "Report of the Office of Public Affairs," 10–12 April 1962.

89. Loveland, *Evangelicals and the Military*, 38; Martin, *With God on Our Side*, 30–31.

90. Taylor, "Citizens of Heaven and Earth," 8 August 1954.

91. [Henry], "The Sprit of Foreign Policy," 22. See also [Henry], "The Peace Drive in the Churches," 20.

92. "Resolutions," 1–4 April 1957. Clyde Taylor commended the "presentation of American religious viewpoints to peoples of other parts of the world," and urged the NAE "to give every possible support and assistance to the USIA program." Taylor, "Report of the Secretary of Public Affairs," 1 April 1957.

93. [Henry], "Christ and the Atom Bomb," 20.

94. Taylor, "15th Annual Report, N.A.E. Office of Affairs," 6 April 1959.

95. [Henry], "The Spirit of Foreign Policy," 22.

96. "Ministers Favor Eisenhower 8 to 1."

97. [Henry], "Where Do We Go From Here?" 16.

98. Miller, *Piety Along the Potomac*, 34, 42.

99. [Henry], "Where Do We Go from Here?" 17; Miller, *Piety Along the Potomac*, 19, 34, 43; Pierard and Lindner, *Civil Religion*, 199, 184; Pollock, *Billy Graham*, 165–66. On Eisenhower and foreign policy, see Bowie and Immerman, *Waging Peace*; Craig, *Destroying the Village*; Greenstein, *Hidden-Hand Presidency*.

100. Loveland, *Evangelicals and the Military*, xi–xii, quote 164.

101. Carpenter, *Revive Us Again*, 180, see also 177–78.

102. Pierard, "Billy Graham and the U.S. Presidency," 110. See also Carpenter, *Revive Us Again*, 178, 180.

103. Loveland, *Evangelicals and the Military*, 42.

104. Ibid., 10, see also 11–13.

105. Ibid., 1, 9; Wuthnow, *Restructuring of Religion*, 42; Carpenter, "Youth for Christ," 363. See also "The Pentagon's Responsibility," 22, which records an increase in cases of misconduct and crimes by U.S. military personnel abroad and urges the need to do more to indoctrinate them in the reasons for being overseas.

106. Martin, *With God on Our Side*, 28; Taylor, "NAE Celebrates 30 Years."

107. Loveland, *Evangelicals and the Military*, 56–58.

108. Ibid., 10–13, 56–64. Broger was AFIE deputy director beginning in 1956 and became agency director in 1961. On his involvement with the NAE see, for example,

Taylor, "Report of the Office of Public Affairs," 12 June 1962; Taylor, "Report of the Office of Public Affairs," 7 October 1963.

109. Loveland, *Evangelicals and the Military*, 42, 44, 76; Pierard, "Billy Graham and the U.S. Presidency," 110.

110. Harrison, "Reminiscences and a Prophecy," 14; Loveland, *Evangelicals and the Military*, 51–53, 55.

111. Loveland, *Evangelicals and the Military*, 10–13.

112. Coughlin, *Church and State*, 108. During the same time period, the publicly funded prison chaplaincy moved into the field of vision of the NAE's Chaplains Commission. According to a 1959 report, there were numerous openings, but the consensus was that "we simply did not have the personnel nor resources to enter this field at the present time." However, the report noted that the National Council of Churches was unable "to meet the demand and this alone opens the door to qualified men from our ranks." It urged evangelicals to fill these openings. See Taylor, "Report of the Secretary of Public Affairs," 6–7 October 1959.

113. Robertson, "The Military Chaplaincy," 10–12 January 1961; Loveland, *Evangelicals and the Military*, 84–93.

114. Taylor, "Religious Liberty in America," 6–8 March 1963.

115. Loveland, *Evangelicals and the Military*, 83, 95.

116. See, for example, [Taylor], "Watchman in Washington," [1955].

117. Taylor, "Dynamic Performance," 4 April 1957.

118. Taylor, "Report to NAE Board of Administration, Office of Public Affairs," 25 April 1960; Loveland, *Evangelicals and the Military*, 95–96.

119. Taylor, "NAE Celebrates 30 Years," 12.

120. Loveland, *Evangelicals and the Military*, xii; see also 51–52 on Harrison and Vietnam and 96–99 for linking the rise of the New Christian Right to this expanded influence within the military.

121. Nichols, *Uneasy Alliance*, 92. For a concise summary of the evangelical approach to foreign aid and missions, see 168–69.

122. "Pressures Rise for Federal Handouts," 22. The text quotes the POAU's monthly magazine *Church & State*.

123. Lowell, *Church-State Fraud*, 202.

124. "Pressures Rise for Federal Handouts."

125. [Henry], "Where Do We Go From Here?" 17–18.

126. [Henry], "The Spirit of Foreign Policy," 20–22.

127. Nichols, *Uneasy Alliance*, 92–93, 200–206.

128. [Henry], "The Spirit of Foreign Policy," 20.

129. Ibid., 21.

130. "Eisenhower, Khrushchev and History's Inevitable Course," 26.

131. Hostetter, "Government Overseas Programs and the Churches," 6–8 March 1963.

132. Taylor, "Citizens of Heaven and Earth," 8 August 1954.

133. See, for example, Taylor, "Report of the Secretary of Affairs," 9 April 1962.

134. See, for example, [Henry], "The Spirit of Foreign Policy," 20; "Pressures Rise for Federal Handouts," 22.

135. Judd, "World Issues and the Christian," 8.

136. Nichols, *Uneasy Alliance*, 92.

137. Hostetter, "Government Overseas Programs and the Churches," 6–8 March 1963.

138. Nichols, *Uneasy Alliance*, 200.

139. Executive Committee, NAE, "Minutes," 6 April 1964.

140. Henry, "Evangelicals: Out of the Closet but Going Nowhere?" 20. On World Vision, see also Carpenter, *Revive Us Again*, 182; Nichols, *Uneasy Alliance*, 92–93; Fowler, *New Engagement*, 182.

141. Executive Committee, NAE, "Minutes," 19 November 1948, 9.

142. Gertrude D. Clark to Board Members, 1 November 1948; R.L. Decker to Fellow Workers, 10 November 1948. The discrepancy between the Executive Committee minutes and the way Clark and Decker describe the incidence is indicative of the NAE's desire for legitimacy. In contrast to the minutes, the letters state that Taylor "was called into a committee meeting of the State Department, where he was told that they recognized N.A.E. as a responsible group with a real desire to help in the Displaced Persons situation." See also Nichols, *Uneasy Alliance*, 208.

143. Executive Committee, NAE, "Minutes," 19 November 1948, 10.

144. Taylor, "Report of the Secretary of Affairs to the Executive Committee," 7 March 1949.

145. Taylor, "Mid-Year Report of the Secretary of Affairs," 1 October 1949

146. Ibid.

147. Taylor, "Report of the Secretary of Public Affairs," 1 April 1957. The NAE's Evangelical Action Committee also discussed this issue and asked the Social Education Committee "to determine the attitude of Evangelicals toward foreign aid, especially with regard to governments limiting the freedom of the individual in matters of religious freedom and worship." See Evangelical Action Committee, "Minutes," [Clyde W. Taylor], 5 June 1957.

148. Taylor, "Report to NAE Board of Administration, Office of Public Affairs," 25 April 1960. See also Taylor, "Report of the Office of Public Affairs," 12 June 1962.

149. Henry, "Soul-Searching in Social Welfare," 32; Nichols, *Uneasy Alliance*, 93.

150. Rockey, "Report of the Executive Director World Relief Commission," 10 October 1960.

151. Rockey, "Report of the Executive Director N.A.E. World Relief Commission," 4 April 1967.

152. In a project planned jointly with the WRC, for example, USAID approved over 5,000 tons of Food for Freedom provisions to support land reclamation in Korea. Both the food valued at almost $400,000 and the ocean freight costs of roughly $200,000 were paid for by the U.S. government. See USAID, "Self-Help Land Reclamation in Korea Assisted with Food for Freedom," 6–12 December 1966.

153. Rockey, "Report of the Executive Director World Relief Commission, N.A.E.,"

13 April 1961. See also NAE, "Minutes of the NAE Staff Retreat in Glen Eyrie," 10–12 January 1961. Wendell Rockey also reported in October that the Department of Agriculture had made available additional foodstuffs for the South Korean disaster area, which necessitated a special appeal for ocean freight funds amounting to approximately $14,000. See Rockey, "Report of the Executive Director World Relief Commission, N.A.E.," 9 October 1961.

154. Rockey, "Report of the Executive Director World Relief Commission, N.A.E.," 7 October 1963.

155. "Miscellaneous," Executive Committee of the World Relief Commission, 13–14 November 1973.

156. Taylor, "Report of the Office of Public Affairs," 13 March 1961. See also Taylor, "Report of the Office of Public Affairs," 10–14 April 1961; Taylor, "Report of the Office of Public Affairs," 3 December 1962; Taylor, "Religious Liberty in America," 6–8 March 1963; Lowell, *Church-State Fraud*, 167.

157. Taylor, "Report of the Secretary of Public Affairs," 5 December 1961. In September 1961, the NAE Executive Committee already reported on plans to establish relationships between the NAE and the Peace Corps.

158. Taylor, "Report of the Office of Public Affairs," 10–12 April 1962. On fears of being outstripped by Catholics and mainline Protestants, see also Nichols, *Uneasy Alliance*, 203.

159. Taylor, "Report of the Office of Public Affairs," 12 June 1962.

160. Taylor, "15th Annual Report, N.A.E. Office of Affairs," 6 April 1959.

161. Taylor, "Religious Liberty in America," 6–8 March 1963; Taylor, "Report of the Office of Public Affairs," 10–12 April 1962.

162. See, for example, "Confrontation: a sharp look at the issues facing Evangelicals in 1966."

163. Taylor, "Report of the Office of Public Affairs," 10–12 April 1962. See also Taylor, "Report of the Office of Public Affairs," 12 June 1962; Taylor, "Report of the Secretary of Affairs," 9 April 1962.

164. Taylor, "Religious Liberty in America," 6–8 March 1963.

165. Rockey, "Report of the Executive Director World Relief Commission, N.A.E.," 7 October 1963.

166. "Additional Findings not included in above," March 1964.

167. Taylor, "Report of the Office of Public Affairs," 8–9 October 1962. See also USAID Policy Determination #10, "Religious Organizations and the United States Aid Program"; Taylor, "Report of the Office of Public Affairs," 22–25 April 1963.

168. Fowler Hamilton to Clinton P. Anderson, 9 November 1962.

169. Taylor, "Report of the Office of Public Affairs," 3 December 1962; Taylor, "Report of the Office of Public Affairs," 8–9 October 1962.

170. See, for example, World Relief Commission, "Minutes of the Executive Committee," 14–15 September 1972; Rockey, "Report of the Executive Director N.A.E. World Relief Commission," 4 April 1967; Nichols, *Uneasy Alliance*, 203.

171. Monsma, *Sacred and Secular*, 79. See also Nichols, *Uneasy Alliance*, 100–31; Flipse, "Save 'Free Vietnam,'" 208–9.

172. Nichols, *Uneasy Alliance*, 170–71, 201; World Relief Commission, "Minutes of the Executive Committee," 14–15 September 1972.

173. "Miscellaneous," Executive Committee of the Word Relief Commission, 13–14 November 1973. On reorganization plans, see "Plans Proposed for the Re-Organization of WRC," 7 February 1974.

174. See, for example, "Sectional Reports-Section IV: World Relief Corporation," 7 October 1980, 5.

175. Nichols, *Uneasy Alliance,* 211.

176. Monsma, *Sacred and Secular*, 10, 72–73.

177. Ibid., 95; see also 78, 93–99; Nichols, *Uneasy Alliance*, 93, 200.

Chapter 4. Evangelicals, Social Policy, and the Welfare State

1. See Kellstedt, "Neglected Variable," 289; Gallup and Castelli, *People's Religion*, 218; Fowler, *New Engagement*, 153–54; Gay, *Liberty and Justice*, 11, 81, 93–94. On fears of government control over church agencies, see Coughlin, *Church and State*, 87–88, 105; Netting, "Secular and Religious Funding," 591–92; Bachmann, *The Emerging Perspective*, 156.

2. Quoted in Ford, "Memorandum Containing a Collection of Statements," [1956], 6. See also Clyde W. Taylor to J. D. Murch, 16 November 1956.

3. Bundy, *Collectivism in the Churches*, 73.

4. Watt, *Transforming Faith*, 56; McGirr, *Suburban Warriors*, 156–60.

5. Fowler, *New Engagement*, 88, 153–54.

6. On the lack of a clear link between religious and political conservatism, see Wuthnow, "Religious Commitment and Conservatism," 126, also 117–32; Hood and Morris, "Boundary Maintenance," 143; Davis and Robinson, "A War for America's Soul?"56–57; Jelen, "Culture Wars and the Party System," 149; Himmelstein, *To the Right*, 78–79, 121; Layman, *Great Divide*, 171–72, 176, 198, 299; Gallup and Castelli, *People's Religion*, 102, 220.

7. [Henry], "Where Do We Go From Here?" 17–18.

8. Fowler, *New Engagement*, 47, 49.

9. Bailey, *Southern White Protestantism*, 134.

10. Himmelstein, *To the Right*, 89–90.

11. Quoted in Lasch, *True and Only Heaven*, 505.

12. Coughlin, *Church and State*, 109. On the role of the NAE in extending social security coverage to ministers and church workers, see also Taylor, "Dynamic Performance," 4 April 1957, 5.

13. Fowler, *New Engagement*, 26–27.

14. Monsma, *Sacred and Secular*, 56.

15. According to John H. Simpson, 54.7 percent of "sectarians" voted for Carter,

41.5 percent for Reagan, and 3.8 percent for Anderson. This group included fundamentalist, Pentecostal, Wesleyan holiness, Mormon, and Adventist churches, and thus reflected a good cross section of smaller evangelical groups. This contrasts with well over 50 percent support for Reagan among northern Baptists, Lutherans, Methodists, and Presbyterians, and over 80 percent among Episcopalians. Simpson, "Socio-Moral Issues," 119. On Carter and the evangelical vote, see also Marsden, *Understanding Fundamentalism*, 105; Kellstedt and Noll, "Religion, Voting for President," 375; Jelen, "Culture Wars and the Party System," 150.

16. Gallup and Castelli, *People's Religion*, 16. On the continuing link between evangelicals and the Democratic party, see also Rothenberg and Newport, *Evangelical Voter*, 77–78; Lipset and Raab, "The Election and the Evangelicals"; Smith et al., "Myth of Culture Wars," 182; Himmelstein, *To the Right*, 78–79; Layman, *Great Divide*, 172.

17. "*Christianity Today* Confidential Survey," 29 April 1986, 1–3.

18. Gallup and Castelli, *People's Religion*, 19, 94, 98, 167, 215, 217.

19. Ibid., 202, 217, 239–40, 249.

20. Davis and Robinson, "War for America's Soul?" 51.

21. Gallup and Castelli, *People's Religion*, 249.

22. Davis and Robinson, "War for America's Soul?" 52–54; Layman, *Great Divide*, 34; Hammond, "Evangelical Politics," 189.

23. Gallup and Castelli, *People's Religion*, 225–26.

24. Layman, *Great Divide*, 34; Davis and Robinson, "War for America's Soul?" 44, 52–54.

25. Henry, *Uneasy Conscience*, 32.

26. Taylor, "Report to NAE Board of Administration, Office of Public Affairs," 25 April 1960, 3.

27. Ribuffo, *Old Christian Right*, 122; Lienesch, *Redeeming America*, 126–27.

28. Fowler, *New Engagement*, 80.

29. Taylor, "Citizens of Heaven and Earth," 8 August 1954, 8.

30. Henry, *Uneasy Conscience*, 23, 29, 76.

31. Watt, *Transforming Faith*, 62; Lienesch, *Redeeming America*, 47, 50, 125, 128–29, 132–34; Hunter, *American Evangelicalism*, 47; Cerillo, "Survey of Recent Evangelical Social Thought," 273–74; Fowler, *New Engagement*, 54, 145.

32. Lienesch, *Redeeming America*, 47, 128–33; Watt, *Transforming Faith*, 55.

33. Quoted in Miller, "American Religion and American Political Attitudes," 108. See also Hofstadter, *Age of Reform*.

34. A good example of this bifurcation is the attitude among evangelicals toward AIDS. A 1986 poll among *Christianity Today* subscribers showed that while punitive measures, such as mandatory AIDS testing for marriage licensing (77 percent), restricting homosexual rights (51 percent), and even quarantining AIDS patients (28 percent) received significant support, the most important issue for half of those polled was "focusing more on abstinence and fidelity to combat AIDS" (98 percent), followed by "finding new ways to compassionately deal with AIDS patients" (92 percent) and "allocating

more federal money for AIDS research" (72 percent). "*Christianity Today* Confidential Survey," 29 April 1986.

35. On the historical variety of evangelical social thought, ranging from a private and individuated view of poverty to a public and societal conceptualization, see also Clydesdale, "Soul-Winning and Social Work," 188–92, 197.

36. Hall, "History of Religious Philanthropy," 56, 58; Lienesch, *Redeeming America*, 125–27, 133–34; Greenstone, "Decline and Revival," 172; Warner, *New Wine*, 8. See also Henry, "Evangelicals in the Social Struggle."

37. Henry, "Evangelicals in the Social Struggle," 7–8.

38. "Confrontation: a sharp look at the issues facing Evangelicals in 1966," 4.

39. Henry, "Soul Searching in Social Welfare"; "Protestant Muddle in Social Welfare."

40. Taylor, "Report to NAE Board of Administration, Office of Public Affairs," 25 April 1960, 2.

41. Lienesch, *Redeeming America*, 121.

42. Henry, "Evangelicals in the Social Struggle," 8.

43. [Henry], "Foundations: Tilt to the Left," 20–24.

44. See, for example, Murch, "Report of the Commission on Evangelical Action," 10–12 April 1962, 1; Taylor, "Report of the Secretary of Affairs," 9 April 1962, 1.

45. Henry, "Evangelicals in the Social Struggle," 5.

46. Henry, "Church-State Issues Facing N.A.E. Leaders," 6–7 February 1961, 1.

47. Executive Committee, "Minutes," 22 November 1960; Taylor, "Report of the Secretary of Public Affairs," 22 November 1960, 2.

48. Conference on Church-State Relations, "Minutes," 6–7 February 1961, 1; Murch, "Report of the Commission on Evangelical Action," April 1961, 1.

49. Henry, "Soul Searching in Social Welfare," 33.

50. Conference on Church-State Relations, "Minutes," 6–7 February 1961, 1–7; Taylor, "Report of the Office of Public Affairs," 14 September 1961, 5.

51. Murch, "Report of the Commission on Evangelical Action," April 1961, 1.

52. Cairns, "Church-State Relations in the United States," 6–7 February 1961, 11–12.

53. Henry, "Church-State Issues Facing N.A.E. Leaders," 6–7 February 1961, 1.

54. Conference on Church-State Relations, "Minutes," 6–7 February 1961, 7.

55. Murch, "Report of the Evangelical Action Commission," 8–9 October 1962, 1–2.

56. Murch, "Report of the Evangelical Action Commission," 22–25 April 1963.

57. Nichols, *Uneasy Alliance*, 201; Berg, "Anti-Catholicism and Modern Church-State Relations." For details on Catholic social teachings and success in obtaining public funding, see Rosenthal, "Public or Private," 13.

58. Taylor, "Church and State-1963," 13 November 1963, 4.

59. [Taylor], "Watchman in Washington," [1955], 1, 8. See also Taylor, "Dynamic Performance," 4 April 1957, 1–6; Taylor, "Report of the Office of Public Affairs," 10–14 April, 1961, 1; Murch, "The Protestant Position Today," 6–8 March 1963, 1–7.

60. Taylor, "Citizens of Heaven and Earth," 8 August 1954, 2–3.

61. Taylor, "Dynamic Performance," 4 April 1957, 4.

62. Lowell, *Church-State Fraud*, 14–15, 148, 202–3, 211, 217.

63. Ibid., 170, 213–14.

64. Murch, "Report of the Commission on Evangelical Action," 10–12 April 1962, 1; Taylor, "Report of the Secretary of Affairs," 20 July 1960, 2.

65. [Taylor], "Watchman in Washington," [1955], 3.

66. Taylor, "Report to NAE Board of Administration, Office of Public Affairs," 25 April 1960, 4.

67. Taylor, "Religious Liberty in America," 6–8 March 1963, 5–6.

68. "Bigotry or Smear?" 20. See also "NAE Resolutions"; Eighmy, *Churches in Cultural Captivity*, 169–71.

69. Taylor, "Report of the Secretary of Affairs," 20 July 1960, 4–5. See also Murch, "Report of the Commission on Evangelical Action," April 1961, 1. On the anti-Kennedy campaign, see also Taylor, "Report of the Secretary of Affairs," 11 October 1960, 1–2; Taylor, "Report of the Secretary of Public Affairs," 22 November 1960, 1.

70. Conference on Church-State Relations, "Minutes," 6–7 February 1961, 1.

71. Taylor, "Report of the Office of Public Affairs," 10–14 April 1961, 2.

72. "Confrontation: A Sharp Look at the Issues Facing Evangelicals in 1966," 2.

73. Murch, "Report of the Commission on Evangelical Action," April 1961, 1. See also Murch, "Report of the Commission on Evangelical Action," 10–12 April 1962, 2.

74. Taylor, "Report of the Office of Public Affairs," 10–14 April 1961, 1.

75. "Confrontation: A Sharp Look at the Issues Facing Evangelicals in 1966," 2.

76. Lowell, "Federal Aid to Education," 6–8 March 1963, 6.

77. Ibid. See also Lowell, *Church-State Fraud*, 216

78. Quoted in Murch, "The Protestant Position Today," 6–8 March 1963, 4.

79. Ibid., 4, 6.

80. Taylor, "Church and State-1963," 13 November 1963, 4.

81. Taylor, "Citizens of Heaven and Earth," 8 August 1954, 7. See also Taylor, "Report of the Secretary of Public Affairs," 6–7 October 1959, 6; "Billy Graham and the Pope's Legions."

82. Dawson, "The Christian View of the State," 5. See also Stone, *Boundaries of Evangelicalism*, 27.

83. Demerath and Williams, "Mythical Past," 77. On the rise of Catholicism in the nineteenth century, see also O'Neill, *Third America*, 30–32.

84. Marsden, *Understanding Fundamentalism*, 64, 108.

85. Hatch and Hamilton, "Taking the Measure," 404. See also Watt, *Transforming Faith*, 69.

86. Taylor, "Report to NAE Board of Administration, Office of Public Affairs," 25 April 1960, 4.

87. Taylor, "Citizens of Heaven and Earth," 8 August 1954, 2.

88. Taylor, "Report of the Office of Public Affairs," 10–12 April 1962.

89. Conference on Church-State Relations, "Minutes," 6–7 February 1961, 6.

90. Taylor, "Report of the Office of Public Affairs," 10–12 April 1962. See also Watt, *Transforming Faith*, 70.

91. Ford, "Religion and the Public Schools," 6–8 March 1963, 1, 3.

92. Decker, "Government Grants and Loans to Charitable Institutions," 6–8 March 1963, 5. See also Harmon, "Church and State—A Relation in Equity."

93. "Religion in National Life Resolution," 10 December 1963, 8. On EAC discussions, see Taylor, "Report of the Office of Public Affairs," 7 October 1963, 1.

94. See, for example, Elliott, "The Christian Amendment to the Constitution," 6–8 March 1963, 1.

95. Robertson, "Semi-Annual Report to the Board of Administration," 4 October 1977, 2. See also Watt, *Transforming Faith*, 70.

96. See Dugan, "NAE Office of Public Affairs Semi-Annual Report," 2–3 October 1990; Dugan, "NAE Office of Public Affairs Semi-Annual Report," 9 October 1991.

97. Harmon, "Church and State—A Relation in Equity," 5–6.

98. Taylor, "The Church in the World: 2. Evangelicals, Church and State," 20 March 1974, 12.

99. [Taylor], "Watchman in Washington," [1955], 3.

100. "Religious Subsidy by Tax Exemption," 13 April 1961.

101. Taylor, "Report of the Secretary of Public Affairs," 22 November 1960, 1.

102. Taylor, "Report of the Office of Public Affairs," 8–9 October 1962, 2–3.

103. Pfeffer, "Religion Exemptions," 105.

104. Coughlin, *Church and State*, 81–82, 108–10, 160; Eighmy, *Churches in Cultural Captivity*, 160, 165.

105. "Protestant Muddle in Social Welfare." See also Henry, "Soul Searching in Social Welfare."

106. Henry, "Church-State Issues Facing N.A.E. Leaders," 6–7 February 1961, 1–2.

107. "Confrontation: a sharp look at the issues facing Evangelicals in 1966," 8. See also Lowell, *Church-State Fraud*, 148, 170–71, 216.

108. Conference on Church-State Relations, "Minutes," 6–7 February 1961, 2, 5.

109. Coughlin, *Church and State*, 81–82, 108, 110.

110. Lowell, *Church-State Fraud*, 215.

111. Coughlin, *Church and State*, 63, 110, 130–31. See also Lindsell, "An Evangelical Evaluation of the Relationship between Churches and the State in the United States," 11–13 October 1967.

112. Thiemann, Herring, and Perabo, "Responsibility and Risks," 54, 59; Bailey, *Southern White Protestantism*, 135–36; Hunter, *Evangelicalism: Coming Generation*, 42; Nichols, *Uneasy Alliance*, 92.

113. Coughlin, *Church and State*, 102–3.

114. Murch, "Report of the Commission on Evangelical Action," April 1961, 2. See also Taylor, "Report of the Secretary of Affairs," 20 July 1960, 3; Murch, "Report of the Commission on Evangelical Action," 10–12 April 1962, 2; Murch, "Report of the Evangelical Action Commission," 8–9 October 1962, 2.

115. Carpenter, *Revive Us Again*, 158–60.

116. Hall and Burke, "Historical Statistics," 17.

117. Lowell, *Church-State Fraud*, 147, 177; see also 184–86.

118. Ibid., 212.

119. Taylor, "Religious Liberty in America," 6–8 March 1963, 5.

120. "Church-State Separation Policy Statements," 8 April 1964, 9.

121. Taylor, "Shriver and the Mission Budget," 25 October 1966, 1–2.

122. Monsma, *Sacred and Secular*, 67, 69, 73–77, 98, 104–5.

123. Hall and Burke, "Historical Statistics," 17; see also 9, 27–28; Salamon, *Partners in Public Service*, 86; Netting, "Secular and Religious Funding," 587, 601.

124. Executive Committee, "Minutes," 31 January 1958. On NAE debates about public funding for higher education, see also [Taylor], "Watchman in Washington," [1955], 5; Taylor, "Report of the Office of Public Affairs," 10–14 April 1961, 2; Taylor, "Report of the Secretary of Affairs," 9 April 1962, 1.

125. Taylor, "Report to NAE Board of Administration, Office of Public Affairs," 25 April 1960, 2.

126. Lowell, *Church-State Fraud*, 213–14.

127. Ann Smith to Glenn Archer, 22 November 1956. On the Lincoln Square campaign, see also Gill, "Sectarian Subsidy via Slum Clearance," [1956]; "Fact Sheet Lincoln Square Project, New York City," [1956]; "Lincoln Square Project—Add to Fact Sheet," [1956]; Albert M. Cole to John J. Allen Jr., 26 February 1957; Taylor, "Dynamic Performance," 4 April 1957, 3–4.

128. Taylor, "Supplementary Report on Legislation," 9 October 1961, 3.

129. Murch, "Report of the Evangelical Action Commission," 22–25 April 1963.

130. Taylor, "Report of the Secretary of Affairs," 20 July 1960, 1.

131. Taylor, "Supplementary Report on Legislation," 9 October 1961, 2.

132. Conference on Church-State Relations, "Minutes," 6–7 February 1961, 2–3. See also Eighmy, *Churches in Cultural Captivity*, 171.

133. Taylor, "Report of the Office of Public Affairs," 10–14 April 1961, 2. It is worth noting that this passage was cut out of the Annual Report in the official minutes of the Annual Convention. See Taylor, "Report of the Office of Public Affairs," 10–14 April 1961.

134. Taylor, "Report of the Secretary of Affairs," 9 April 1962, 1.

135. Forrester, "Federal Aid to Higher Education," 6–8 March 1963, 1, 6. The NAE Executive Committee requested in 1962 that the EAC and the Education Commission invite representatives of evangelical colleges to discuss principles and practices in response to federal aid, loans, and gifts. See Executive Committee, "Minutes," 8 October 1962.

136. Clydesdale, "Soul-Winning and Social Work," 196; Carpenter, *Revive Us Again*, 181. See also Monsma, *Sacred and Secular*, 9, 47, 71.

137. Forrester, "Federal Aid to Higher Education," 6–8 March 1963, 1, 6.

138. Eighmy, *Churches in Cultural Captivity*, 164–66.

139. Lowell, *Church-State Fraud*, 163.

140. Eighmy, *Churches in Cultural Captivity*, 164–65; Lowell, *Church-State Fraud*, 188; Coughlin, *Church and State*, 110.

141. Taylor, "Report of the Office of Public Affairs," 10–12 April 1962. For examples of Taylor monitoring federal aid legislation and the gradual softening of the NAE stance, see Taylor, "Report of the Office of Public Affairs," 14 September 1961, 2; Taylor, "Report of the Office of Public Affairs," 12 June 1962, 2; Taylor, "Report of the Office of Public Affairs," 8–9 October 1962, 2–3; Murch, "Report of the Evangelical Action Commission," 8–9 October 1962, 2; Taylor, "Report of the Office of Public Affairs," 22–25 April 1963; Taylor, "Report of the Office of Public Affairs," 7 October 1963, 1; and Taylor, "Church and State-1963," 13 November 1963.

142. Murch, "Report of the Evangelical Action Commission," 8–9 October 1962, 1.

143. Murch, "Report of the Commission on Evangelical Action," 10–12 April 1962, 1.

144. Taylor, "Report of the Secretary of Affairs," 9 April 1962, 1.

145. Forrester, "Federal Aid to Higher Education," 6–8 March 1963, 1–2, 6.

146. Ibid., 5–6. On the funding crisis of evangelical colleges, see also Pruyne, "The Church and Higher Education," 17 November 1987.

147. Henry, "Dare We Renew the Controversy?" 24.

148. Forrester, "Federal Aid to Higher Education," 6–8 March 1963, 6. See also Forrester, "New Paths in Christian Higher Education."

149. "Resolutions, Church and State, Aid to Church-Related Schools," 25 April 1963, 8.

150. See, for example, "Resolutions Committee Report, Federal Aid to Education," 20 April 1966, 5.

151. National General Convention, "Minutes," 17 April 1969, 10.

152. Taylor, "Report of the Evangelical Action Commission and the NAE Office of Public Affairs," 14 April 1969, 2.

153. National General Convention, "Minutes," 17 April 1969, 10.

154. "Resolution on Higher Education," 20 April 1972.

155. Robert P. Dugan, Jr., to Morton C. Blackwell, 22 March 1983. See also Robert P. Dugan, Jr., to James A Baker III, 22 March 1983.

156. Monsma, *Sacred and Secular,* 9–10, 68–70, 72–74, 77, 84.

157. David Weeks, personal communication with the author, 23 July 2005.

158. Taylor, "Memo to show Dr. Decker," 28 March 1947.

159. Committee on Christian Liberty, "Minutes," 19 October 1948, 5.

160. Taylor, "Report of the Office of Public Affairs," 12 June 1962, 2.

161. Murch, "Report of the Commission on Evangelical Action," 10–12 April 1962, 1.

162. Ravitch, *Troubled Crusade,* 27–42; Viteritti, *Last Freedom,* 134–35; Eighmy, *Churches in Cultural Captivity,* 160, 164. On the NAE monitoring "impacted areas" aid and related legislation, see Taylor, "Report of the Office of Public Affairs," 14 September 1961, 2; Taylor, "Report of the Office of Public Affairs," 7 October 1963, 2.

163. Taylor, "Dynamic Performance," 4 April 1957, 1.

164. Taylor, "Church and State-1963," 13 November 1963, 2. On education emerging as a critical arena of right-wing grassroots activism due to fears of "losing control" over children and growing "permissiveness," see also McGirr, *Suburban Warriors,* 179–81.

165. National General Convention, "General Convention Business Session Minutes," 8 April 1964, 6–7.

166. Eighmy, *Churches in Cultural Captivity*, 160, 164; Lowell, *Church-State Fraud*, 11, 188.

167. "Resolutions Committee Report, Federal Aid to Education," 20 April 1966, 5.

168. "Confrontation: a sharp look at the issues facing Evangelicals in 1966," 2, 4–5.

169. "Educational Voucher System," 15–16 January 1971.

170. Robertson, "Semi-Annual Report to the Board of Administration," 4 October 1977, 2.

171. "*Christianity Today* Confidential Survey," 29 April 1986, 1.

172. Henry, "Soul Searching in Social Welfare," 31. On evangelical opposition to Hill-Burton, see also Coughlin, *Church and State*, 109–10; Lowell, *Church-State Fraud*, 215.

173. Taylor, "Report to NAE Board of Administration, Office of Public Affairs," 25 April 1960, 2.

174. Lowell, *Church-State Fraud*, 152–54; Taylor, "Supplementary Report on Legislation," 9 October 1961, 2.

175. Henry, "Soul Searching in Social Welfare," 31. See also Henry, "Church-State Issues Facing N.A.E. Leaders," 6–7 February 1961, 1; Lowell, *Church-State Fraud*, 215.

176. Eighmy, *Churches in Cultural Captivity*, 160, 165; Coughlin, *Church and State*, 69–73, 109–10; Lowell, *Church-State Fraud*, 149, 161, 163.

177. Coughlin, *Church and State*, 81–82; Lowell, *Church-State Fraud*, 148; Eighmy, *Churches in Cultural Captivity*, 160.

178. Decker, "Government Grants and Loans to Charitable Institutions," 6–8 March 1963, 4.

179. Lowell, *Church-State Fraud*, 170–71, 179–80.

180. Netting, "Secular and Religious Funding," 589–91, 602. See also Salamon, *Partners in Public Service*, 94; Greenberg, "Doing Whose Work?" 180.

181. Forest D. Montgomery to Robert P. Dugan, Jr., "Memorandum Re: Child Care," [1988], 2, 5.

182. Montgomery, "Statement . . . on the Federal Role in Child Care," 22 September 1988.

183. Land, "Child Care Legislation," 12 April 1989. See also Ammermann, *Baptist Battles*; Hankins, *Uneasy in Babylon*.

184. "Resolution on Institutional Childcare," Southern Baptist Convention, 14–16 June 1988.

185. Thomas, "Statement of the Baptist Joint Committee on Public Affairs," 17 April 1989, 2–3.

186. Robert P. Dugan, Jr., to George Bush, 8 July 1988; "Will President Bush Sell out Evangelicals?" 29 January 1990.

187. Robert P. Dugan, Jr., to John H. Sununu, 1 May 1991. See also Dugan, "NAE Office of Public Affairs Semi-Annual Report," 9 October 1991. As Mary M. Bogle has

noted, whereas grants or contracts prohibit religious instruction, employment and/or admission discrimination on the basis of belief, the key appeal of vouchers was that they prohibited none of these and allowed for faith-based provision in child care. Bogle, "Survey of Congregation-Based Child Care," 226–27.

188. See, for example, Dugan, "Statement . . . on Child Care Welfare Programs and Tax Credit Proposals," 19 April 1989, 1–7.

189. Monsma, *Sacred and Secular*, 68–69, 72–78, 84–86, 90–91, 93; Bogle, "Survey of Congregation-Based Child Care," 228. The NAE Records contain numerous letters from ministers in member churches requesting information on voucher money available to pastors and local NAE chapters, especially after California had made $104 million available for child care vouchers in 1993.

190. Coughlin, *Church and State*, 60, 68.

Chapter 5. Church-State Relations and the Rise of the Evangelical Right

1. For an excellent study of left-wing evangelicalism, see Swartz, "Left Behind." For an insightful analysis that traces the right-wing political mobilization of evangelicals to developments in the 1940s and 1950s while acknowledging the significance of an indigenous evangelical Left, see Watt, *Transforming Faith*, 49–71. On the evangelical Left, see also Flowers, *Religion in Strange Times*, 55–56; Cerillo, "Survey of Recent Evangelical Social Thought," 276–80; Marsden, *Understanding Fundamentalism*, 74–76; Erickson, *Evangelical Left*; Gay, *Liberty and Justice*; Fowler, *New Engagement*, 185; Ammermann, *Baptist Battles*; Dayton and Johnston, *The Variety of American Evangelicalism*; Schäfer, *Countercultural Conservatives*; Quebedeaux, *Young Evangelicals*, 38; Quebedeaux, *Worldly Evangelicals*, xi, 147–62. In a recent conversation with the author, Richard Pierard argued that Quebedeaux's focus on the "young evangelicals" underestimated the role older evangelicals played in the emergence of the evangelical Left in the 1970s.

2. Marsden, *Understanding Fundamentalism*, 97. See also Fowler, *New Engagement*, 30–31; Cerillo, "Survey of Recent Evangelical Social Thought," 277.

3. [Henry], "Where Do We Go From Here?" 17.

4. Lindsell, "An Evangelical Evaluation of the Relationship between Churches and the State in the United States," 11–13 October 1967.

5. "Resolutions—The Use of Force," 24 February 1977.

6. "*Christianity Today* Confidential Survey," 29 April 1986.

7. Ibid.

8. Armstrong, "Christian Responsibility and Government," 18–22 April 1977.

9. See, for example, Executive Committee, "Minutes," 7 June 1982.

10. Robert P. Dugan, Jr., to Michael K. Deaver, 3 December 1982. In turn, Reagan's Orlando speech asked for evangelical support for the administration's defense policy.

11. For details on the Pasadena conference and on debate between peace churches and the NAE, see Burkholder, "Mennonites in ecumenical dialogue on peace and justice," Part III. See also Swartz, "Left Behind," 580.

12. Robert P. Dugan, Jr. to Michael K. Deaver, 3 December 1982.

13. Robert P. Dugan, Jr. to Arthur E. Dewey, 10 November 1982; Dugan to Kenneth Kramer, 1 December 1982; Dugan to Col. Don Martin, 1 December 1982; Dugan to Gen. Lew Allen, 1 December 1982; Dugan to Lt. Gen. Daniel O. Graham, 1 December 1982.

14. Robert P. Dugan, Jr. to Francis A. Schaeffer, 23 November 1982.

15. Ibid.

16. Robert P. Dugan, Jr. to Lt. Gen. Daniel O. Graham, 1 December 1982.

17. Dave Breese to Robert P. Dugan, Jr., 4 August 1983. Other "hawks" included Catholic scholar George Weigel. On NAE participation in this and other foreign policy conferences, see also Dugan, "NAE Office of Public Affairs Semi-Annual Report," 4–5 October 1983; [Dugan], "PFSS: 'First Steps of NAE Leadership,'" [1989].

18. Burkholder, "Mennonites in ecumenical dialogue on peace and justice," Part III.

19. "NAE Commissioned Gallup Poll," 5 July 1983; "Views of Evangelicals on the Nuclear Arms Race," June 1983.

20. "NAE's Peace, Freedom and Security Studies Program," [c. 1985]; Burkholder, "Mennonites in ecumenical dialogue on peace and justice," Part III; Dugan, "NAE Office of Public Affairs Semi-Annual Report," 2–3 October 1984.

21. Dugan, "NAE Office of Public Affairs Semi-Annual Report," 2–3 October 1984; Dugan, "Semi-Annual Report to the Board of Administration," 6–7 October 1987.

22. Dugan, "NAE Office of Public Affairs Report," 8–9 October 1985.

23. Dugan, "NAE Office of Public Affairs Annual Report," 4 March 1985.

24. Dugan, "NAE Office of Public Affairs Annual Report," 6 March 1989.

25. See, for example, Dugan, "Semi-Annual Report to the Board of Administration," 6–7 October 1987; Dugan, "NAE Office of Public Affairs Semi-Annual Report," 9 October 1991.

26. For a succinct history of the WWWC, see "World Without War Council—Midwest, Brief History."

27. On the theocons and their relationship to neoconservatism, see Heilbrunn, "Neocon v. Theocon."

28. [Dugan] to "Pick" [Bob Pickus], [c. 1988].

29. [Dugan], "27th Consultation, Columbus, Ohio," [1989].

30. Brian F. O'Connell to Billy A. Melvin and Robert P. Dugan, Jr., Memorandum, 12 September 1988.

31. "Sharing Groups, II. Peace, Freedom and Security Studies Program," [c. 1985].

32. Wilbert Hill to Social Action Commission, 28 September 1988.

33. Robert P. Dugan, Jr., to Carol Hayes, 25 February 1987.

34. "NAE's Peace, Freedom and Security Studies Program," [c. 1985]. See also [Dugan], "PFSS: 'First Steps of NAE Leadership,'" [1989].

35. "Peace, Freedom and Security Studies Program: Encouraging Evangelical Leadership in International Affairs," [c. 1991]. See also Davis, "Evangelical program takes on war and peace," 5D.

36. Jones, "What Program and Activities Should Evangelicals Be Promoting," May 1965, 4–5. On evangelical support for the War on Poverty, see also Fowler, *New Engagement*, 56–58.

37. Clydesdale, "Soul-Winning and Social Work," 192, 202; Fowler, *New Engagement*, 89, 155, 186; Watt, *Transforming Faith*, 53; Cerillo, "Survey of Recent Evangelical Social Thought," 276; Gay, *Liberty and Justice*, 32–33, 45–46.

38. Henry, *Politics for Evangelicals*, 40; see also 115.

39. Cerillo," Survey of Recent Evangelical Social Thought," 275–77; Davis and Robinson, "A War for America's Soul?" 44; Pierard, *Unequal Yoke*, 185–86.

40. Gay, *Liberty and Justice*, 3, 17–18, 73, 78–79, 84, 86–87, 92–93, 97; Fowler, *New Engagement*, 26–27, 154; Cerillo, "Survey of Recent Evangelical Social Thought," 273–74; Dayton, "Social and Political Conservatism"; Hamby, *Liberalism and Its Challengers*, 356–57. See also "Inflation and the Breakdown of Trust"; Howard, "Christian Approach to Economics"; Elzinga, "Demise of Capitalism."

41. Although cutbacks during the Reagan administration hit some nonprofit human service providers hard, the federal government increased expenditures in established entitlement programs, such as Social Security, Medicaid, and Medicare, which involved extensive financial support for nonprofit organizations. While means-tested programs such as AFDC continued to decline, human resource programs grew from 32.6 percent of federal outlays in 1967 to 48.7 percent in 1986, mainly as a result of Social Security funding. See Gottschalk and Gottschalk, "Reagan Retrenchment," 62–63, 65–66, 71; Smith and Stone, "Unexpected Consequences," 240; Smith and Lipsky, *Nonprofits for Hire*, 67, 69, n 101.

42. Ehrenreich, "New Right Attack," 179; see also 164, 166, 173.

43. On both the affirmation of state police power and the preservation of the welfare state despite retrenchment, see Hall, "Philanthropy," 36; Gottschalk and Gottschalk, "Reagan Retrenchment," 65, 67–69; Piven and Cloward, "Popular Power," 75–76; Cnaan et al., *Newer Deal*, 279.

44. Watt, *Transforming Faith*, 65–67; Lienesch, *Redeeming America*, 114–15, 124; Gay, *Liberty and Justice*, 91.

45. Carlson-Thiess, "Charitable Choice," 113.

46. Berger and Neuhaus, *To Empower People*, 145, 148.

47. Fowler, *New Engagement*, 35–39; Watt, *Transforming Faith*, 67.

48. Carroll, "New Populists," 532–33, 539.

49. For a good example of a left-wing evangelical organization securing governmental support for its activities and struggling with the implications, see the Records of Voice of Calvary Ministries, Collection 362, Billy Graham Center Archives, Wheaton College, Illinois. Voice of Calvary Ministries in Jackson, Mississippi, was created by John Perkins, an African American minister who was a member of ESA and the NAE's Social Action Commission. On increasing efforts to secure government support for low-income housing, see also Social Concerns Commission, "Minutes," 1–3 May 1973, 2–3; Conn, *American City*, 158.

50. Carroll, "New Populists," 528, 532; Hall, "Welfare State and Careers," 381; Marsden, *Understanding Fundamentalism*, 79.

51. Lienesch, *Redeeming America*, 137; O'Neill, *Third America*, 105.

52. One example was the litigation campaign that led to deinstitutionalization of the mentally ill and creation of alternative settings for the disabled in the 1970s and 1980s. Spearheaded by the ACLU, it was supported by a loose alliance of critics, including religious conservatives, who advocated the formation of a system of nonprofits as a substitute for government-run group homes. This led to the establishment of a program that steered billions of dollars into acquiring, renovating, and operating facilities and funneled funds into agencies that in many instances linked left-wing countercultural origins with reliance on right-wing political connections. See Hall and Burke, "Historical Statistics," 19; Hall, "Philanthropy," 31–32; Hall, "Welfare State and Careers," 380–81; Smith and Stone, "Unexpected Consequences," 236.

53. Colson showed little contrition, either. Listing the flaws and failures of those who pushed the Watergate case, he noted with *Schadenfreude* that "those who conquered in the Watergate came away so flushed with victory that their lives all ended up messed up." Chuck [Colson] to David [Bovenizer], Memorandum, 9 October 1979.

54. Shapiro, "Jails for Jesus," 55–56, 59.

55. Ibid., 57.

56. David [Bovenizer?] to Gordon [Loux], Draft of "The 'Sept. 4' Letter," 20 August 1980; Mike [Cromartie] to Chuck [Colson], handwritten note. Cromartie recommended chapter 8 ("Prison Philanthropy") of Norris Magnuson's *Salvation in the Slums* to Colson, noting that "I see exciting parallels with what Maud Booth was doing and what we are doing."

57. Mike [Cromartie] to Chuck [Colson], Memorandum "Re: Sojourner's Interview," [1977]. On contacts with left-wing evangelical organizations, see also David [Bovenizer?] to Gordon [Loux], Memorandum, 11 February 1980. On the origins of PFM, see also Oliver, "Attica, Watergate."

58. Charles Colson to Margaret Shannon, 9 August 1977; Shapiro, "Jails for Jesus," 58.

59. Chuck [Colson] to David [Bovenizer], Memorandum, 3 October 1979.

60. Robert P. Dugan, Jr., to James Dobson, 10 March 1994.

61. Mike [Cromartie] to Chuck [Colson], Memorandum, 29 August 1977. See also see DWV [Daniel W. Van Ness] to RDV [Ralph D. Veerman] and GDL [Gordon Loux], Memorandum "Re: Meeting with Bob Dugan," 24 September 1981.

62. Mike [Cromartie] to Chuck [Colson], Memorandum "RE: On our trip to Joplin, Missouri with Revival Fires," 4 October 1977.

63. Swartz, "Left Behind," 580.

64. See, for example, PLK [Paul Kramer?] to File, Memorandum "Re: Recommendations to follow-through with New Mexico Proposal," 26 July 1978; David [Bovenizer?] to Gordon [Loux], "Friday Report," 5 September 1980; Dan [Van Ness] to Chuck [Colson], Memorandum, "Re: South Carolina Prison Reform Legislation," 23 March 1981; DWV [Daniel W. Van Ness], "Special Project Status Report, Project: Federal Legislation," 22

September 1981. See also PFM Records, Box 10, Folder 12 for Colson's drafts of the goals of the organization and strategy to create networks with individuals and organizations. PFM also created a 501(c)(4) Political Action Organization to conduct legislative activity while being funded by the 501(c)(3) Charitable Organization. See, for example, DWV [Daniel W. Van Ness] to RDV [Ralph D. Veerman], CWC [Charles W. Colson], GDL [Gordon Loux], Memorandum "Re; Tax Status of PF," 26 June 1981.

65. DWV [Daniel W. Van Ness] to CWC [Charles W. Colson], Memorandum "Re: Federal Legislation on Alternatives," 9 July 1981. See also Milton G. Rector to Daniel W. Van Ness, 30 June 1981.

66. Erzen, "Testimonial Politics."

67. Shapiro, "Jails for Jesus," 56–58, 98.

68. Erzen, "Testimonial Politics."

69. On the AU lawsuit, see Roundtable on Religion and Social Welfare Policy, "Americans United for Separation of Church and State et al. v. Warden Terry Mapes, Prison Fellowship Ministries, InnerChange Freedom Initiative, et al."; Americans United for the Separation of Church and State, "Faith-Based Initiatives"; InnerChange Freedom Initiative, "IFI Ruling Information: Eighth Circuit Issues Ruling." For a detailed analysis of the case, see Sullivan, *Prison Religion.*

70. Robert P. Dugan, Jr., to Paul M. Weyrich, 30 June 1987.

71. Dugan, "NAE Office of Public Affairs Semi-Annual Report," 9 October 1991.

72. Robert P. Dugan, Jr., to Mrs. Arthur S. DeMoss, 4 March 1994. See also Robert P. Dugan, Jr., to Rick DeVoss, 4 March 1994. Dugan contacted both companies, such as Amway, and private charities, such as the Arthur S. DeMoss Foundation. A $25,000 grant from the latter was among the contributions received. Nancy S. DeMoss to Robert P. Dugan, Jr., 10 July 1992; Robert P. Dugan, Jr., to Mrs. Arthur S. DeMoss, 17 July 1992.

73. Robert P. Dugan, Jr., to Paul Weyrich, 12 August 1991.

74. Weyrich, "Cultural Conservatism: Toward a New National Agenda," 1 December 1987. See also Ehrenreich, "New Right Attack," 183.

75. Lind, "Cultural Conservatism: Toward a New National Agenda," 1 December 1987. On Reagan adopting little more than fundamentalist rhetoric while doing almost nothing to push fundamentalist issues, see also Marsden, *Understanding Fundamentalism*, 77; Lienesch, *Redeeming America*, 2; Rothenberg and Newport, *Evangelical Voter*, 5.

76. Institute for Cultural Conservatism, "Summary of Chapters," 1 December 1987.

77. Ibid.

78. Ibid.

79. Ibid.

80. Weyrich, "Cultural Conservatism: Toward a New National Agenda," 1 December 1987.

81. On the gender politics involved in demarcating public and private, see Moreton, "Why Is There So Much Sex in Christian Conservatism"; Duggan, *Twilight of Equality?*

82. Robert P. Dugan, Jr., to Paul M. Weyrich, 30 June 1987.

83. [Dugan], Marginalia in statement of William S. Lind, "Cultural Conservatism: Toward a New National Agenda," 1 December 1987.

84. [Dugan], Marginalia in William S. Lind and William H. Marshner, "Fact Sheet: Cultural Conservatism: Toward a New National Agenda," [1 December 1987].

85. Lind, "Cultural Conservatism: Toward a New National Agenda," 1 December 1987.

86. Robert P. Dugan, Jr., to Mrs. Arthur S. DeMoss, 4 March 1994.

87. Robert P. Dugan, Jr., to Paul M. Weyrich, 30 June 1987.

88. [Dugan], "Weyrich Briefing, 1988."

89. "Parochaid: Looking for a Loophole," 39–40; Eighmy, *Churches in Cultural Captivity,* 171.

90. Lowell, *Church-State Fraud,* 193; see also 186–87, 194.

91. Ibid., 187, 195–97.

92. Armstrong, "Christian Responsibility and Government," 18–22 April 1977, 4–6.

93. See, for example, Dugan, "Testimony before the Republican National Convention Platform Committee," 31 May 1988; Spring, "Bob Dugan: Representing Evangelicals in Washington," April 1984, 6–7. See also McGirr, *Suburban Warriors,* 179–81. On federal educational policy in this period, see Kosar, *Failing Grades.*

94. Robert P. Dugan, Jr., to James A Baker III, 22 March 1983. See also Dugan to Morton C. Blackwell, 22 March 1983.

95. [Dugan?] "Bork-To BAM [Billy A. Melvin]," [1987].

96. Robert P. Dugan, Jr., to Barry Lindsey, Memorandum "Re: Child Care legislation," 15 June 1989.

97. Forest D. Montgomery to Robert P. Dugan, Jr., Memorandum "Re: Child Care," [1988], 2.

98. Ibid., 3–5. See also Montgomery, "Statement . . . on the Federal Role in Child Care," 22 September 1988.

99. Robert P. Dugan, Jr., to Barry Lindsey, Memorandum "Re. Child Care legislation," 15 June 1989. See also Dugan, "NAE Office of Public Affairs Semi-Annual Report," 3–4 October, 1989; [Dugan], "Bush Hdqter, 3:00," [Fall 1988].

100. Robert P. Dugan, Jr., to George Bush, 8 July 1988.

101. Dugan, "Statement . . . on Child Care Welfare Programs and Tax Credit Proposals," 19 April 1989, 3. See also Robert P. Dugan, Jr., to George Bush, 5 January 1990.

102. Robert P. Dugan, Jr., to The President [George H. W. Bush], 7 April 1989; Dugan, "NAE Office of Public Affairs Semi-Annual Report," 3–4 October 1989.

103. "Will President Bush Sell out Evangelicals?" 29 January 1990.

104. Robert P. Dugan, Jr., to John H. Sununu, 24 February 1990.

105. Stenholm, "A Christian's Response to Federal Child Care Policy," 27 April 1990, 6.

106. "Church-State Squabble Stalls Child-Care Bill in House."

107. John H. White, Billy A. Melvin, B. Edgar Johnson, Robert P. Dugan, Jr., to The President [George H. W. Bush], 7 March 1990. See also Dugan, "NAE Office of Public Affairs Semi-Annual Report," 2–3 October 1990.

108. Forest Montgomery to John H. Sununu, 22 October 1990.

109. Jack Kemp to Robert P. Dugan, Jr., 10 October 1990.

110. Stenholm, "A Christian's Response to Federal Child Care Policy," 27 April 1990, 1, 10.

111. Ralph Reed to Mimi Dawson, Memorandum "Bush and the Evangelical Vote—Executive Summary," 19 June 1992; Taylor, "Report of the Office of Public Affairs," 12 June 1962, 2.

112. This applied in particular to Richard Cizik and Curran Tiffany. See, for example, Dugan, "NAE Office of Public Affairs Semi-Annual Report," 9 October 1991.

113. Robert P. Dugan, Jr., to John H. Sununu, 1 May 1991.

114. Murch, "The Protestant Position Today," 6–8 March 1963, 7.

115. Taylor, "Religious Liberty in America," 6–8 March 1963, 2–3.

116. Lindsell, "An Evangelical Evaluation of the Relationship Between Churches and the State," 11–13 October 1967, 10–11.

117. "The Church-State Wall: Glenn L. Archer," 6.

118. Coughlin, *Church and State*, 107–8.

119. Murch, "The Protestant Position Today," 6–8 March 1963, 7. See also Murch, "Report of the Commission on Evangelical Action," 10–12 April 1962, 1.

120. Lowell, *Church-State Fraud*, 175–76, 186–87, 198, 201–2.

121. "United for Separation." By the 1970s, AU campaigned against issues where evangelicals had changed their separationist position, namely tuition tax credits for religious education and prayer in public schools. For example, AU filed a lawsuit against the OEO over funding for Lutheran Resources Mobilization and "dangers of religious liberty implicit in parochiaid and voucher plans." See Kucharsky, "War on Church Establishment," 44. See also Gogdell, "Statement . . . to Study Public Financial Aid to Nonpublic Primary and Secondary Schools," 1 December 1970, 1–6; "Educational Voucher System," 15–16 January 1971.

122. "The Church-State Wall: Glenn L. Archer," 9–10.

123. Taylor, "The Church in the World: 2. Evangelicals, Church and State," 20 March 1974, 13.

124. See, for example, Americans United Press Release, 25 November 1986. On conservatism linked to the embrace of the religious nature of the state, see also McMaster, "Church/State: Separate or Not?" 26–27, 66–67. On AU attitudes toward Charitable Choice, see Greenberg, "Doing Whose Work?" 191. On the debates about public funding in the broader evangelical fold, see also Minow, "Choice or Commonality," 165.

125. "Church-State Squabble Stalls Child-Care Bill in House." However, AU remained loyal to an earlier position that distinguished between areas of funding. "The organized groups that raise the barricades against virtually any form of public money going to religious elementary and secondary schools are largely silent when it comes to aid to religious colleges and universities," Steven Monsma observed. "One such organization is Americans United for the Separation of Church and State. An analysis of its monthly periodical, *Church and State*, published between January 1989 and December

1993, reveals there were 24 editorials related to the issue of aid to elementary and secondary schools and only four editorials related to the issue of aid to religious colleges and universities." Monsma, *Sacred and Secular*, 47.

126. Nichols, *Uneasy Alliance*, 206. The 1977 *Wolman v. Walters* Supreme Court decision threw into sharp relief the remarkable changes that had taken place. In its ruling, the Court largely upheld various forms of aid to mostly sectarian nonpublic schools in Ohio. William Brennan, the only Catholic judge, voted to strike down all types of aid provisions and thus expressed the sentiments of AU, which had been fervently anti-Catholic well into the early part of the decade. Meanwhile, three justices, including conservative William Rehnquist, voted for upholding the majority of the provisions, while the remainder supported the whole package. See Robertson, "Semi-Annual Report to the Board of Administration," 4 October 1977, 1.

127. Tseng and Furness, "Reawakening of Social Consciousness," 125.

Conclusion: Resurgent Conservatism and the Public Funding of Religious Agencies

1. Layman, *Great Divide*, 199; Green, Guth, and Hill, "Faith and Election," 80–91.

2. Kazin, "Grass-Roots Right," 148. See also Himmelstein, *To the Right*, 28; Hixson, *American Right Wing*, 297.

3. For good summaries of the backlash argument, see Layman, *Great Divide*, 175–76; McGirr, *Suburban Warriors*, 238–40; Lasch, *True and Only Heaven*, 476–77, 479–80, 484–88, 492–93; Hunter, *Culture Wars*.

4. Himmelstein, *To the Right*, 104; Simpson, "Socio-Moral Issues," 115–23; McGirr, *Suburban Warriors*, 186, 198–99; Layman, *Great Divide*, 68. Davis and Robinson, "A War for America's Soul?" 42, 49–52. On the "moral rift" and the extent to which social issues define the chasm within the Democratic party coalition, see Lasch, *True and Only Heaven*, 486–91, 495, 504–9, 512, 516, 518, 529–30.

5. On the electoral, ideological, and organizational origins of the new populist conservatism, see Himmelstein, *To the Right*, 69–71, 73, 78–79, 129, 136, 138–39, 143; McGirr, *Suburban Warriors*, 45, 186; Layman, *Great Divide*, 199; Wuthnow, *Restructuring of Religion*, 195; Green, Guth, and Hill, "Faith and Election." For good discussions of the link between social policy and the New Christian Right, see Brown et al., *Remaking the Welfare State*; Liebman and Wuthnow, eds., *New Christian Right*.

6. Hixson, *American Right Wing*, xxvi.

7. Himmelstein, *To the Right*, 6–7, 134, 164; Fraser and Gerstle, *Rise and Fall*, xv. On conservative thought in the postwar era, especially the rise of neoliberalism and its new acceptance of big government, see also *WZB Mitteilungen*, 25–27. On conservatives and Social Security, see Berkowitz, *America's Welfare State*, 64–65.

8. Krock, *In the Nation*, 255–57.

9. Schuparra, *Triumph of the Right*, 149.

10. Ravitch, *Troubled Crusade*, 8.

11. Himmelstein, *To the Right*, 30–32, 38–40; McGirr, *Suburban Warriors*, 172–75, 261.

12. Despite the marked increase in the range of federal responsibilities between the mid-1950s and the late 1970s, the federal budget as part of the Gross National Product remained comparatively stable at around 20 percent before leaping to close to 24 percent by 1983. At the same time, combined local, state, and federal government expenditure increased from around 25 percent to close to 30 percent, reaching over 33 percent by 1983. See Salamon, *Partners in Public Service*, 19; Smith and Lipsky, *Nonprofits for Hire*, 203. Federal budget figures are in U.S. Office of Management and Budget, *Budget of the United States Government, Fiscal Year 2007, Historical Tables*, Table 1.2: Summary of Receipts, Outlays, and Surpluses or Deficits (-) as Percentages of GDP: 1930–2011, 23–24; Gottschalk and Gottschalk, "Reagan Retrenchment," 61, 63, 66; Salamon, *Nonprofit Sector*, 45–46. See also Critchlow, "Family Planning," 211.

13. Bendick, "Privatizing the Delivery," 101.

14. Smith and Lipsky, *Nonprofits for Hire*, 203–4.

15. Kramer, *Voluntary Agencies*, 72. See also Smith and Lipsky, *Nonprofits for Hire*, 203; Salamon, *Partners in Public Service*, 28–30; Rosenthal, "Public or Private," 2.

16. Salamon, *Partners in Public Service*, 21, see also 19–20; Berkowitz and McQuaid, *Creating the Welfare State*, 149; Smith and Lipsky, *Nonprofits for Hire*, 13–14; Smith and Stone, "Unexpected Consequences," 233.

17. Smith and Lipsky, *Nonprofits for Hire*, 11.

18. Gurin, "Responsibility and Privatization," 182.

19. Smith and Stone, "Unexpected Consequences," 235.

20. Gurin, "Responsibility and Privatization," 181, 183; Kramer, *Voluntary Agencies*, 75; Smith and Lipsky, *Nonprofits for Hire*, 16–17, 53, 60; Garr, *Reinvesting in America*, vii.

21. Ravitch, *Troubled Crusade*, 26.

22. Hall, "Welfare State and Careers," 380; Hall, "Philanthropy," 25, 28, 37.

23. McGirr, *Suburban Warriors*, 17; see also 12–14, 45, 152–56. See also Piper, *Ideologies and Institutions*.

24. Piven and Cloward, "Popular Power," 79–83, 85, 89–90; Brown, "Segmented Welfare System," 204; see also 185–86.

25. Brown, "Segmented Welfare System," 187–88, 203; McGirr, *Suburban Warriors*, 238. On deindustrialization, the decline of unions and traditional parties, and their role in the realignment and disfranchisement of lower classes, see Blumenthal and Edsall, *Reagan Legacy*.

26. Brown, "Segmented Welfare System," 188; Davies, *From Opportunity to Entitlement*.

27. O'Connor, "Neither Charity nor Relief"; Ehrenreich, "New Right Attack," 175–77, 188; Carlson-Thies, "Charitable Choice," 115; Gurin, "Governmental Responsibility and Privatization," 182; Gottschalk and Gottschalk, "Reagan Retrenchment," 61–62; Givel, *War on Poverty Revisited*, 211–12. On Daniel Patrick Moynihan's study of African American families, see Moynihan, *The Negro Family*; Gutman, "Mirrors." For an in-depth study of Great Society social policy, see Matusow, *Unraveling*.

28. See Lockhart, *Gaining Ground*, 19.

29. Davies, *From Opportunity to Entitlement*. The author highlights the clash between a liberal push for entitlement-based income support and Johnson's own adherence to a more traditional conception of social provision as a major cause for the division of the New Deal coalition.

30. Brown, "Segmented Welfare System," 187–91.

31. See Smith and Stone, "Unexpected Consequences," 234. On subsidiarity replicating the segmentation of the welfare state, see Salamon, *Partners in Public Service*, 30.

32. Brown, "Segmented Welfare System," 188, 196–97, quote 188. On income redistribution, see also Gottschalk and Gottschalk, "Reagan Retrenchment," 62; Piven and Cloward, "Popular Power," 87.

33. Katznelson, "Great Society," 185–211, esp. 186.

34. Ehrenreich, "New Right Attack," 190. See also Michael Sandel's critique that American government had become a "procedural republic" defined in purely functional terms. Sandel, *Democracy's Discontent*.

35. In his incisive critique of progressivism, Christopher Lasch maintained that liberal social thought in the United States was torn between the two positions. On the one hand, advocates of the participatory view, including John Dewey, Herbert Croly, Thorstein Veblen, Louis Mumford, and Van Wyck Books, developed a social-relational theory of democracy beyond laissez faire and limited government. Instead of locating liberty and the formation of values in economic independence, natural rights, and proprietary individualism, they contended that opportunities for meaningful public participation via an extended sphere of public control were the basis for the development of ideas of the social good. In their pursuit of the cooperative commonwealth of public ownership and industrial democracy, these progressives displayed strong affinities with French syndicalism, British guild socialism, and German revisionist social democracy. In contrast, the distributive approach, promoted by economist Simon N. Patten and journalist Walter Weyl, among others, associated democracy with the creation of prosperity and universal abundance. Its advocates adopted the concept of a surplus economy and linked progress to the democratization of consumption and leisure. In turn, they primarily concerned themselves with developing administrative techniques to distribute the fruits of an ever-expanding industrial economy via tax policies and growth-oriented economic planning. See Lasch, *True and Only Heaven*, 68–71, 340–48, 531.

36. Fraser and Gerstle, *Rise and Fall*, xv.

37. Hamby, "Vital Center." On Cold War liberalism, see Brinkley, "War and Liberalism," 448.

38. Bell, *End of Ideology*, 403.

39. Wolfe, *America's Impasse*, 23. See also Mills, *Power Elite*; Marcuse, *One-Dimensional Man*; Bell, *End of Ideology*, 401–2, 404–5; Schäfer, "Liberal State and Conservative Social Policy." In his insightful analysis of Bell's "postcapitalist vision," historian Howard Brick challenges the view that American thought and culture succumbed in the 1940s to a conservative Cold War consensus that put aside reform ideology and social theory. Rather, expectations of a shift to a new social economy persisted and contributed to the

revival of dissenting thought and practice in the 1960s. See Brick, *Transcending Capitalism*. For an excellent study of C. Wright Mills, see Geary, *Radical Ambition*.

40. Lasch, *True and Only Heaven*, 486–88, 493–96, 531; Ehrenreich, "New Right Attack," 175. For an incisive analysis of the role of social policies in the fragmenting of the New Deal coalition, see Davies, *From Opportunity to Entitlement*. In contrast to Davies, however, I see the conservative construction of Cold War liberalism, rather than the liberal push for entitlement-based polices, as the key factor in undermining the Democratic party and American liberalism.

41. Himmelstein, *To the Right*, 13, 31, 28, 45; Hixson, *American Right Wing*, xxvi–xxvii, 297. See also Lasch, *True and Only Heaven*, 528. On the neoconservative revival of traditional antistatist rhetoric, see Carroll, "New Populists," 534; Skocpol, "Religion, Civil Society," 46.

42. Lasch, *True and Only Heaven*, 506; Ehrenreich, "New Right Attack," 174.

43. Kaus, "Revival of Liberalism"; Brown, "Segmented Welfare System," 198; Kelley, "Democracy and the New Deal Party System," 185, 191, 194–96.

44. Gallup and Castelli, *People's Religion*, 217, 249. See also Layman, *Great Divide*, 299.

45. Gallup and Castelli, *People's Religion*, 246.

46. Rebecca Klatch's examination of the Young Americans for Freedom (YAF) provides a good illustration of this process. YAF entered the public arena in 1960 as a movement opposing Eisenhower Republicanism. Finding intellectual expression in the 1960 Sharon Statement, YAF identified with Goldwater and the American Conservative Union in the 1964 presidential campaign. As libertarians they regarded the U.S. government, rather than communism, as the main threat. By the 1970s, however, after a series of purges in which traditionalists used strong-arm tactics to push out libertarians, YAF rejected the antistatist agenda. In the end, most traditionalist members of YAF became integrated into mainstream politics and seated in institutional positions of political power, while libertarians ended up in universities and colleges. Klatch, *Generation Divided*, 213, 222, 236, 270, 285; Andrews, *Other Side of the Sixties*, 8–10.

47. Hamby, *Liberalism and Its Challengers*, 340, 363–67, 371, 385.

48. Davies, *See Government Grow*.

49. Klatch, *Generation Divided*, 146, 148.

50. Yergin and Stanislaw, "Democrats and Republicans," 482–483; Himmelstein, *To the Right*, 89–90. See also Morgan, *Age of Deficits*.

51. Smith and Lipsky, *Nonprofits for Hire*, 17. See also Salamon, *Partners in Public Service*, 96–98.

52. Hall, "Philanthropy," 33; see also 25; Hall, "Welfare State and Careers," 378–88.

53. Lasch, *True and Only Heaven*, 505. See also Ehrenreich, "New Right Attack," 181.

54. Berger and Neuhaus, *To Empower People*, 152, 187, 193.

55. Ben Wattenberg quoted in Blumenthal, *Rise of the Counter-Establishment*, 130.

56. U.S. Office of Management and Budget, *Budget of the United States Government, Fiscal Year 2007, Historical Tables*, Table 1.2: Summary of Receipts, Outlays, and Surpluses or Deficits (-) as Percentages of GDP: 1930–2011, 23–24.

57. Himmelstein, *To the Right*, 78, 90.

58. McGirr, *Suburban Warriors*, 45.

59. Hixson, *American Right Wing*, xxv; Layman, *Great Divide*, 302.

60. Davies, *See Government Grow*.

61. Mead, *New Politics of Poverty*, 2.

62. Greenberg, "Doing Whose Work?" 180. Charitable Choice and the Faith-Based Initiative embody two contradictory characteristics of subsidiarity. On the one hand, they continued the tendency towards fragmented provision by devolving implementation to the state and local levels. On the other hand, however, they reflected "an extension of the earlier efforts through which government effectively took over the domain of donative voluntary associations and transformed them into quasi-governmental entities." On this dichotomy, see Greenberg, "Doing Whose Work?" 183–86; Carlson-Thiess, "Charitable Choice," 117; Hall, "Philanthropy," 36. In addition, several new welfare laws have since the mid-1990s opened up further opportunities for religious agencies to participate in federal funding streams. Under these arrangements, faith-based organizations can either accept vouchers from welfare recipients or enter into contracts with state government to deliver welfare services, including Temporary Aid to Needy Families (TANF), food stamps, Medicaid and Supplemental Security Income (SSI). Likewise, many federal agencies have developed programs and expanded grant eligibility for faith-based groups. One example is the Center for Community and Interfaith Partnerships. Created by Housing Secretary Andrew Cuomo in 1997, and headed by a Catholic priest, it is designed to increase participation of religious groups in HUD initiatives by allowing them to bid for $20 million of grants and assistance to build affordable housing and promote economic development. See Greenberg, "Doing Whose Work?" 181–83, 194 n24.

63. Smith and Lipsky, *Nonprofits for Hire*, 16–17, 53; Salamon, *Partners in Public Service*, 23; Hall, "Welfare State and Careers," 380–81.

64. Smith and Lipsky, *Nonprofits for Hire*, 17. On subsidiarity as a factor in the statist turn of postwar conservatism, see also Monsma, *Sacred and Secular*, 7; Smith and Stone, "Unexpected Consequences," 234, 240; Salamon, *Partners in Public Service*, 23; Hall, "Welfare State and Careers," 380–81.

65. Hall, "Philanthropy," 32.

66. Carlson-Thiess, "Charitable Choice," 118.

67. On changes in statutes and procedures relating to church-state funding relations, see Hall, "Philanthropy," 35–36; Carlson-Thiess, "Charitable Choice," 117–18; Greenberg, "Doing Whose Work?" 183. On exemptions from the Civil Rights Act and the Americans with Disabilities Act under Charitable Choice, see also Cnaan et al., *Newer Deal*, 280–83.

68. On the most recent legislation, see Kennedy and Bielefeld, *Charitable Choice at Work*; Pipes and Ebaugh, "Faith-Based Coalitions"; Carlson-Thiess, "Charitable Choice," 114–15; Greenberg, "Doing Whose Work?"; Davis and Hankins, *Welfare Reform and Faith-Based Organizations*.

69. Greenberg, "Doing Whose Work?" 180–81, 183; Carlson-Thiess, "Charitable Choice," 116–18; Cnaan with Wineburg and Boddie, *Newer Deal*, 281–83. See also Sherman, "Testimony."

70. Green, "Congregations and Social Service," 51; Greenberg, "Doing Whose Work?" 181–83, 187–90; Chaves, "Religious Congregations and Welfare Reform." Chaves analyzes data from the National Congregations Study (NCS). On black evangelicals and subsidiarity, see also Carson, "Patterns of Giving in Black Churches," 240. For a succinct review of the literature, see Montiel et al., "The Use of Public Funds For Delivery of Faith-Based Human Services.

71. Sherman, "Testimony," 27. Approximately $2.15 billion was channeled to faith-based charities in 2005, constituting close to 11 percent of competitive federal grants. See Goldenberg, "US religious charities win $2.15bn in state grants."

72. Green, "Congregations and Social Service," 47–49, quote 49.

73. Viteritti, *Last Freedom*, 135; "The Blaine Game."

74. Greenberg, "Doing Whose Work?" 180–81, 183; Carlson-Thiess, "Charitable Choice," 116–18; Cnaan et al., *Newer Deal*, 281–83.

75. Frank, *What's the Matter with Kansas?*

BIBLIOGRAPHY

Archival Materials

ABBREVIATIONS

CTI Records. Christianity Today International Records, Collection 8, Billy Graham Center Archives, Wheaton, Illinois.

ESA Records. Evangelicals for Social Action Records, Collection 37, Billy Graham Center Archives, Wheaton, Illinois.

NAE Records. National Association of Evangelicals Records, Wheaton College Archives and Special Collections, Buswell Memorial Library, Wheaton College, Illinois. At the time of writing the records were in the process of being moved to the Billy Graham Center Archives in Wheaton, Illinois.

PFM Records. Prison Fellowship Ministries Records, Collection 274, Billy Graham Center Archives, Wheaton, Illinois.

REPORTS, NEWS RELEASES, STATEMENTS, MEMORANDA, ETC. (WITHOUT NAMED AUTHORS)

"Additional Findings not included in above." Draft for Church-State Findings. National Association of Evangelicals, March 1964. NAE Records.

Americans United Press Release. 25 November 1986. NAE Records.

"*Christianity Today* Confidential Survey of Subscribers: A Political Opinion Poll," 29 April 1986. NAE Records.

"Church-State Separation Policy Statements." In "General Convention Business Session Minutes," National General Convention, NAE, 8 April 1964. NAE Records.

"Confrontation: A Sharp Look at the Issues Facing Evangelicals in 1966." Circular. National Association of Evangelicals, [1966]. NAE Records.

Discussion of Rutherford L. Decker's message "How Others Look at Us in Church-State Relations." Conference on Church-State Relations. National Association of Evangelicals, 6–7 February 1961. NAE Records.

"Educational Voucher System." Findings of the Evangelical Action Consultation. National Association of Evangelicals, 15–16 January 1971. NAE Records.

"Fact Sheet Lincoln Square Project, New York City." National Association of Evangelicals, [1956]. NAE Records.

The Institute for Cultural Conservatism of the Free Congress Research and Education Foundation. "Summary of Chapters, *Cultural Conservatism: Toward a New National Agenda*," 1 December 1987. NAE Records.

"Lincoln Square Project—Add to Fact Sheet." National Association of Evangelicals, [1956]. NAE Records.

"Miscellaneous." Agenda. Executive Committee of the Word Relief Commission, November 1973. NAE Records.

"NAE Commissioned Gallup Poll Released on Evangelical Views about the Nuclear Arms Race." News Release. National Association of Evangelicals, 5 July 1983. NAE Records.

"NAE's Peace, Freedom and Security Studies Program." National Association of Evangelicals, [c. 1985]. NAE Records.

"Peace, Freedom and Security Studies Program: Encouraging Evangelical Leadership in International Affairs." "Draft of Proposal sent to Pew." National Association of Evangelicals, [c. 1991]. NAE Records.

"Plans Proposed for the Re-Organization of WRC." Agenda. Executive Committee of the World Relief Commission, 7 February 1974. NAE Records.

"Religion in National Life Resolution." In "Executive Committee Minutes," Executive Committee, NAE, 10 December 1963. NAE Records.

"Religious Subsidy by Tax Exemption." In "Minutes of General Convention Business Sessions," National General Convention, NAE, 13 April 1961. NAE Records.

"Resolution on Higher Education." In "General Convention Minutes. Third Session," National General Convention, NAE, 20 April 1972. NAE Records.

"Resolution on Institutional Childcare." Southern Baptist Convention, 14–16 June 1988. NAE Records.

"Resolutions." In "Minutes of the Fifteenth Annual Conference of NAE." National General Convention, NAE, 1–4 April 1957. NAE Records.

"Resolutions." In "General Convention Business Session Minutes," National General Convention, NAE, 25 April 1963. NAE Records.

"Resolutions Committee Report, Federal Aid to Education." In "General Convention Minutes. Second Session," National General Convention, NAE, 20 April 1966. NAE Records.

"Resolutions, Church and State, Aid to Church-Related Schools." In "General Convention Business Session Minutes." National General Convention, NAE, 25 April 1963. NAE Records.

"Resolutions—The Use of Force." In "General Session Minutes. Second Session." National General Convention, NAE, 24 February 1977. NAE Records.

"Sectional Reports-Section IV: World Relief Corporation." NAE Board of Administration. National Association of Evangelicals, 7 October 1980. NAE Records.

"Seminar on Federal Service." In *Spiritual Unity in Action: The Program of the N.A.E. for 1963*. National Association of Evangelicals, 1963. NAE Records.

"Sharing Groups, II. Peace, Freedom and Security Studies Program." National Association of Evangelicals, [c. 1985]. NAE Records.

"Temporary Committee for United Action Among Evangelicals." Circular. National Association of Evangelicals, [1941]. NAE Records.

"Thirty Short Months: A partial record of the achievements of the National Association of Evangelicals since its organization was completed in May 1943." In "Minutes of the Meeting of the Board of Administration," Board of Administration, NAE, 19–20 September 1945 [dated "Release October 1, 1945"]. NAE Records.

U.S. Agency for International Development. Policy Determination 10, "Religious Organizations and the United States Aid Program." Marginalia "approved 16 July 1962, withdrawn 21 August 1962." NAE Records.

———. "Involvement of Religious Affiliated Institutions in the U.S. Foreign Aid Program." Typescript enclosed in Fowler Hamilton to Clinton P. Anderson, November 9, 1962. NAE Records.

———. "Self-Help Land Reclamation in Korea Assisted with Food for Freedom." Press Releases, 6–12 December 1966. NAE Records.

"Views of Evangelicals on the Nuclear Arms Race: A Survey conducted for the National Association of Evangelicals by the Gallup Organization, Inc." National Association of Evangelicals, June 1983. NAE Records.

"Will President Bush Sell Out Evangelicals?" NAE press release. National Association of Evangelicals, 29 January 1990. NAE Records.

LETTERS, MEMORANDA, REPORTS, ETC. (WITH NAMED AUTHORS)

Armstrong, William L. "Christian Responsibility and Government." Address at Washington Leadership Briefing sponsored by NAE. National Association of Evangelicals, 18–22 April 1977. NAE Records.

Arnold, Ron. "Communism Report." In "Minutes of NAE Staff Retreat in Glen Eyrie," National Association of Evangelicals, 10–12 January 1961. NAE Records.

[Bovenizer?], David, to Gordon [Loux]. Memorandum, 11 February 1980. PFM Records, Box 16, Folder 6.

———, David, to Gordon [Loux]. "Friday Report," 5 September 1980. PFM Records, Box 16, Folder 7.

[———], David, to Gordon [Loux]. Draft of "The 'Sept. 4' Letter," 20 August 1980. PFM Records. Box 16, Folder 7.

Breese, Dave, to Robert P. Dugan, Jr., 4 August 1983. NAE Records.

Cairns, Earle. "Church-State Relations in the United States," Conference on Church-State Relations. Appendix B. National Association of Evangelicals, 6–7 February 1961. NAE Records.

Clark, Gertrude D., to Board Members, 1 November 1948. NAE Records.

Cole, Albert M. [Housing and Home Finance Agency Administrator] to John J. Allen Jr., 26 February 1957. NAE Records.

Colson, Charles, to Margaret Shannon, 9 August 1977. PFM Records, Box 10, Folder 12.

[———], to David [Bovenizer]. Memorandum, 3 October 1979. PFM Records, Box 14, Folder 2.

———, to David [Bovenizer]. Memorandum, 9 October 1979. PFM Records. Box 14, Folder 2.

[Cromartie], Mike, to Chuck [Colson]. Handwritten note with copy of Chapter 8 "Prison Philanthropy" of Norris Magnuson's *Salvation in the Slums*. PFM Records. Box 11, Folder 1.

———, to Chuck [Colson]. Memorandum "Re: Sojourner's Interview," [1977]. PFM Records, Box 10, Folder 12.

———, to Chuck [Colson]. Memorandum, 29 August 1977. PFM Records, Box 10, Folder 12.

———, to Chuck [Colson]. Memorandum "RE: On our trip to Joplin, Missouri with Revival Fires," 4 October 1977. PFM Records, Box 10, Folder 12.

Decker, R. L., to Fellow Workers, 10 November 1948. NAE Records.

———."Government Grants and Loans to Charitable Institutions." National Conference on Church-State Relations, NAE, Winona Lake, Indiana, 6–8 March 1963. NAE Records.

DeMoss, Nancy S., to Robert P. Dugan, Jr., 10 July 1992. NAE Records.

Dugan, Robert P., Jr., to John R. Dellenback, 30 August 1982. NAE Records.

———, to Arthur E. Dewey, 10 November 1982. NAE Records.

———, to Francis A. Schaeffer, 23 November 1982. NAE Records.

———, to Gen. Lew Allen, 1 December 1982. NAE Records.

———, to Lt. Gen. Daniel O. Graham, 1 December 1982. NAE Records.

———, to Kenneth Kramer, 1 December 1982. NAE Records.

———, to Col. Don Martin, 1 December 1982. NAE Records.

———, to Michael K. Deaver, 3 December 1982. NAE Records.

———, to James A. Baker III [Chief of Staff and Assistant to the President], 22 March 1983. NAE Records.

———, to Morton C. Blackwell [Special Assistant to the President for Public Liaison], 22 March 1983. NAE Records.

———. "NAE Office of Public Affairs Semi-Annual Report to the Board of Administration." National Association of Evangelicals, 4–5 October 1983. NAE Records.

———. "NAE Office of Public Affairs Annual Report to the Board of Administration." National Association of Evangelicals, 5 March 1984. NAE Records.

———. "NAE Office of Public Affairs Semi-Annual Report to the Board of Administration." National Association of Evangelicals, 2–3 October 1984. NAE Records.

———. "NAE Office of Public Affairs Annual Report to the Board of Administration." National Association of Evangelicals, 4 March 1985. NAE Records.

———. "NAE Office of Public Affairs Report to the Board of Administration." National Association of Evangelicals, 8–9 October 1985. NAE Records.

[———?]. "Bork—To BAM [Billy A. Melvin]." National Association of Evangelicals, [1987]. NAE Records.

———, to Carol Hayes, 25 February 1987. NAE Records.

———, to Paul M. Weyrich, 30 June 1987. NAE Records.

———. "Semi-Annual Report to the Board of Administration." [With marginalia]. National Association of Evangelicals, 6–7 October 1987. NAE Records.

[———]. Marginalia in Statement of William S. Lind, "Cultural Conservatism: Toward a New National Agenda." Free Congress Research and Education Foundation News Conference, National Press Club, Washington, D.C., 1 December 1987. NAE Records.

[———]. Marginalia in William S. Lind and William H. Marshner, "Fact Sheet: Cultural Conservatism: Toward a New National Agenda." Free Congress Research and Education Foundation, [1 December 1987]. NAE Records.

[———]. "Bush Hdqter, 3:00." Handwritten notes. National Association of Evangelicals, [1988]. NAE Records.

[———], to "Pick" [Bob Pickus]. National Association of Evangelicals, [c. 1988]. NAE Records.

[———]. "Weyrich Briefing, 1988." Handwritten notes. National Association of Evangelicals, 1988. NAE Records.

———. "Testimony before the Republican National Convention Platform Committee." Kansas City, Missouri, 31 May 1988. NAE Records.

———, to George Bush, 8 July 1988. NAE Records.

[———]. "27th Consultation, Columbus, Ohio." Handwritten notes. National Association of Evangelicals, [1989]. NAE Records.

[———]. "PFSS: 'First Steps of NAE Leadership.'" Handwritten notes. National Association of Evangelicals, [1989]. NAE Records.

———. "NAE Office of Public Affairs Annual Report to the Board of Administration." [With marginalia]. National Association of Evangelicals, 6 March 1989. NAE Records.

———, to The President [George H. W. Bush], 7 April 1989. NAE Records.

———. "Statement of Robert P. Dugan Jr., Director, Office of Public Affairs, National Association of Evangelicals on Child Care Welfare Programs and Tax Credit Proposals Before the Committee on Finance, United States Senate." National Association of Evangelicals, 19 April 1989. NAE Records.

———, to Barry Lindsey. Memorandum "Re: Child Care legislation," 15 June 1989. NAE Records.

———. "NAE Office of Public Affairs Semi-Annual Report to the Board of Administration." [With marginalia]. National Association of Evangelicals, 3–4 October 1989. NAE Records.

———, to George Bush, 5 January 1990. NAE Records.

———, to John H. Sununu [White House Chief of Staff], 24 February 1990. NAE Records.

———. "NAE Office of Public Affairs Semi-Annual Report to the Board of Administration." [With marginalia]. National Association of Evangelicals, 2–3 October 1990. NAE Records.

———, to John H. Sununu [White House Chief of Staff], 1 May 1991. NAE Records.

———, to Paul Weyrich, 12 August 1991. NAE Records.

———. "NAE Office of Public Affairs Semi-Annual Report to the Board of Administration." National Association of Evangelicals, 9 October 1991. NAE Records.

———, to Mrs. Arthur S. DeMoss, 17 July 1992. NAE Records.

———, to Mrs. Arthur S. DeMoss, 4 March 1994. NAE Records.

———, to Rick DeVoss, 4 March 1994. NAE Records.

———, to James Dobson, 10 March 1994. NAE Records.

Elliott, D. Howard. "The Christian Amendment to the Constitution of the United States," National Conference on Church-State Relations, NAE, Winona Lake, Indiana, 6–8 March 1963. NAE Records.

Ford, George L. [Executive Director, NAE]. "Memorandum Containing a Collection of Statements from Individual NAE Leaders in Answer to Questions by Mr. George Cornell of Associated Press." National Association of Evangelicals, [1956]. NAE Records.

———. "Religion and the Public Schools." National Conference on Church-State Relations, NAE, Winona Lake, Indiana, 6–8 March 1963. NAE Records.

Forrester, James. "Federal Aid to Higher Education and the Church Related College." National Conference on Church-State Relations, NAE, Winona Lake, Indiana, 6–8 March 1963. NAE Records.

Gill, Donald H. "Sectarian Subsidy via Slum Clearance." National Association of Evangelicals, [1956]. NAE Records.

Gogdell, Gaston D. "Statement of Gaston D. Gogdell, on Behalf of the Massachusetts State Organization of Americans United for Separation of Church and State to the Special Commission to Study Public Financial Aid to Nonpublic Primary and Secondary Schools." Boston. National Association of Evangelicals, 1 December 1970. NAE Records.

Hamilton, Fowler [USAID Director] to Clinton P. Anderson [US Senator], 9 November 1962. NAE Records.

Henry, Carl F. H. "Church-State Issues Facing N.A.E. Leaders." Conference on Church-State Relations. Appendix A. National Association of Evangelicals, 6–7 February 1961. NAE Records.

Hill, Wilbert, to Social Action Commission, 28 September 1988. NAE Records.

Horn, Carl, to Christian Leaders. "Confidential Memorandum." February 1987. NAE Records.

Hostetter, C. N., Jr. "Government Overseas Programs and the Churches." National Conference on Church-State Relations, NAE, Winona Lake, Indiana, 6–8 March 1963. NAE Records.

Jones, Rufus. "What Program and Activities Should Evangelicals Be Promoting and Implementing." Consultation on Christian Unity, Evangelicals for Social Action, May 1965. ESA Records, Box 1, Folder 1.

Kemp, Jack, to Robert P. Dugan, Jr., 10 October 1990. NAE Records.

[Kramer, Paul?] to File. Memorandum "Re: Recommendations to follow-through with New Mexico Proposal," 26 July 1978. PFM Records, Box 13, Folder 8.

Land, Richard D. "Child Care Legislation." House Republican Study Committee, 12 April 1989. NAE Records.

Lind, William S. "Cultural Conservatism: Toward a New National Agenda." Free Congress Research and Education Foundation News Conference. National Press Club, Washington, D.C., 1 December 1987. NAE Records.

Lindsell, Harold. "An Evangelical Evaluation of the Relationship between Churches and the State in the United States." Consultation on the Church in a Secular World. National Association of Evangelicals, 11–13 October 1967. NAE Records.

Lowell, C. Stanley. "Federal Aid to Education: Private and Parochial Elementary and Secondary Schools." National Conference on Church-State Relations, NAE, Winona Lake, Indiana, 6–8 March 1963. NAE Records.

Macy, Mahlon L. "Report of the Field Director, Upper Midwest Region, to the NAE Board of Administration." National Association of Evangelicals, 4–6 April 1967. NAE Records.

Montgomery, Forest D., to Robert P. Dugan, Jr. "Memorandum Re: Child Care," [1988]. NAE Records.

———. "Statement of Forest D. Montgomery, Counsel, Office of Public Affairs, National Association of Evangelicals on the Federal Role in Child Care before the Committee on Finance, United States Senate." National Association of Evangelicals, 22 September 1988. NAE Records.

———, to John H. Sununu [White House Chief of Staff], 22 October 1990. NAE Records.

Murch, James De Forest. "Annual Report of the Commission on Evangelical Action to the NAE Board of Administration." National Association of Evangelicals, April 1961. NAE Records.

———. "Report of the Commission on Evangelical Action to the Board of Administration." National Association of Evangelicals, 10–12 April 1962. NAE Records.

———. "Report of the Evangelical Action Commission to the Board of Administration." National Association of Evangelicals, 8–9 October 1962. NAE Records.

———. "The Protestant Position Today." National Conference on Church-State Relations, NAE, Winona Lake, Indiana, 6–8 March 1963. NAE Records.

———. "Report of the Evangelical Action Commission to the Board of Administration, NAE." National Association of Evangelicals, 22–25 April 1963. NAE Records.

O'Connell, Brian F., to Billy A. Melvin and Robert P. Dugan, Jr. Memorandum, 12 September 1988. NAE Records.

Pruyne, James W. "The Church and Higher Education." Typescript for Great Rivers Presbytery, 17 November 1987. CTI Records, Box 17, Folder 94.

Rector, Milton G. [President, National Council on Crime and Delinquency] to Daniel W. Van Ness, 30 June 1981. PFM Records, Box 18, Folder 7.

Reed, Ralph, to Mimi Dawson. Memorandum "Bush and the Evangelical Vote-Executive Summary," 19 June 1992. NAE Records.

Robertson, Floyd. "The Military Chaplaincy." In "Minutes of the NAE Staff Retreat in Glen Eyrie," National Association of Evangelicals, 10–12 January 1961. NAE Records.

———. "Office of Public Affairs, National Association of Evangelicals, Semi-Annual Report to the Board of Administration." National Association of Evangelicals, 4 October 1977. NAE Records.

Rockey, Wendell L. "Report of the Executive Director World Relief Commission, N.A.E. to the Executive Committee and the Board of Administration of N.A.E." National Association of Evangelicals, 10 October 1960. NAE Records.

———. "Report of the Executive Director World Relief Commission, N.A.E., to the Executive, 13 April 1961. NAE Records.

———. "Report of the Executive Director World Relief Commission, N.A.E., to the Executive Committee and the Board of Administration of N.A.E." National Association of Evangelicals, 9 October 1961. NAE Records.

———. "Report of the Executive Director World Relief Commission, N.A.E., to the Executive Committee and the Board of Administration of N.A.E." National Association of Evangelicals, 7 October 1963. NAE Records.

———. "Report of the Executive Director N.A.E. World Relief Commission, Inc. to the Executive Committee and the Board of Administration of N.A.E." National Association of Evangelicals, 4 April 1967. NAE Records.

Smith, Ann, to Glenn Archer, 22 November 1956. NAE Records.

Spring, Beth. "Bob Dugan: Representing Evangelicals in Washington." *Focus on the Family*, April 1984, 6–7. NAE Records.

Stenholm, Charles. "A Christian's Response to Federal Child Care Policy by Congressman." National Association of Evangelicals, 27 April 1990. NAE Records.

Taylor, Clyde W. "Memo to show Dr. Decker," 28 March 1947. NAE Records.

———. "Report of the Secretary of Affairs to the Executive Committee, NAE." In "Minutes of the Meeting of the Executive Committee," Executive Committee, NAE, 7 March 1949. NAE Records.

———. "Mid-Year Report of the Secretary of Affairs to N.A.E. Board of Administration." National Association of Evangelicals, 1 October 1949. NAE Records.

———. "Mid-Year Report, Secretary of Affairs, Washington, D.C. Office to N.A.E. Board of Administration." National Association of Evangelicals, 1 October 1952. NAE Records.

———. "Citizens of Heaven and Earth." Typescript "condensed from address given at Winona Lake, Indiana." "Broadcast over WBMI-Chicago." National Association of Evangelicals, 8 August 1954. NAE Records.

[———]. "Watchman in Washington." National Association of Evangelicals, [c. 1955]. NAE Records.

———. "N.A.E. Washington Watchmen." Typescript dated "Feb. 1956, for UEA [*United*

Evangelical Action]." National Association of Evangelicals, February 1956. NAE Records.

————, to J. D. Murch, 16 November 1956. NAE Records.

————. "Report of the Secretary of Public Affairs to the NAE Board of Administration." National Association of Evangelicals, 1 April 1957. NAE Records.

————. "The Dynamic Performance of An Alert Minority." Address given at the fifteenth Annual Convention of the National Association of Evangelicals, Buffalo, New York, 4 April 1957. NAE Records.

————. "15th Annual Report, N.A.E. Office of Affairs, Washington, D.C., to the N.A.E. Board of Administration." National Association of Evangelicals, 6 April 1959. NAE Records.

————. "Report of the Secretary of Public Affairs to the Board of Administration." National Association of Evangelicals, 6–7 October 1959. NAE Records.

————. "Report to NAE Board of Administration, Office of Public Affairs." National Association of Evangelicals, 25 April 1960. NAE Records.

————. "Report of the Secretary of Affairs to the NAE Board of Administration." National Association of Evangelicals, 20 July 1960. NAE Records.

————. "Report of the Secretary of Affairs to the Board of Administration." National Association of Evangelicals, 11 October 1960. NAE Records.

————. "Report of the Secretary of Public Affairs to the NAE Executive Committee." National Association of Evangelicals, 22 November 1960. NAE Records.

————. "Report of the Office of Public Affairs to the N.A.E. Executive Committee." National Association of Evangelicals, 13 March 1961. NAE Records.

————. "Report of the Office of Public Affairs to the Board of Administration." National Association of Evangelicals, 10–14 April, 1961. NAE Records.

————. "Report of the Office of Public Affairs to the NAE Executive Committee." National Association of Evangelicals, 14 September 1961. NAE Records.

————. "Supplementary Report on Legislation." In "Report to the Mid-Year Meeting, NAE Board of Administration." National Association of Evangelicals, 9 October 1961. NAE Records.

————. "Report of the Secretary of Public Affairs to the Executive Committee, N.A.E." National Association of Evangelicals, 5 December 1961. NAE Records.

————. "Report of the Secretary of Affairs to the NAE Board of Administration." National Association of Evangelicals, 9 April 1962. NAE Records.

————. "Report of the Office of Public Affairs to the 20th Annual Convention, NAE," National Association of Evangelicals, 10–12 April 1962. NAE Records.

————. "Report of the Office of Public Affairs to the Executive Committee, N.A.E." National Association of Evangelicals, 12 June 1962. NAE Records.

————. "Report of the Office of Public Affairs to the Board of Administration, N.A.E." National Association of Evangelicals, 8–9 October 1962. NAE Records.

————. "Report of the Office of Public Affairs to the NAE Executive Committee Meeting." National Association of Evangelicals, 3 December 1962. NAE Records.

[———]. "Christian Responsibility in Public Affairs, A Seminar for Pastors and Laymen sponsored by the Office of Public Affairs," 3 December 1962. In Clyde W. Taylor, "Report of the Office of Public Affairs to the NAE Executive Committee Meeting." National Association of Evangelicals, 3 December 1962. NAE Records.

———. "Religious Liberty in America." National Conference on Church-State Relations, NAE, Winona Lake, Indiana, 6–8 March 1963. NAE Records.

———. "Report of the Office of Public Affairs to the Board of Administration, N.A.E." National Association of Evangelicals, 22–25 April 1963. NAE Records.

———. "Report of the Office of Public Affairs to the NAE Board of Administration." National Association of Evangelicals, 7 October 1963. NAE Records.

———. "Church and State-1963, A Year of Re-examination." Typescript for article in *Eternity Magazine,* 13 November 1963. NAE Records.

———. "Shriver and the Mission Budget." Typescript for *Clyde W. Taylor Report*, 25 October 1966. NAE Records.

———. "Report of the Evangelical Action Commission and the NAE Office of Public Affairs to the Board of Administration." National Association of Evangelicals, 14 April 1969. NAE Records.

———. "The Church in the World, Lecture Series by Clyde W. Taylor at Belhaven College, dated 3/19/74, # 4, Involvement." NAE Records.

———. "The Church in the World, Lecture Series by Clyde W. Taylor at Belhaven College, dated 3/20/74, # 2, Evangelicals, Church and State." NAE Records.

Thomas, Oliver S. "Statement of the Baptist Joint Committee on Public Affairs on Child Care Welfare Programs and Tax Credit Proposals to the Committee on Finance, United States Senate," 17 April 1989. NAE Records.

[Van Ness], Dan, to Chuck [Colson]. Memorandum "Re: South Carolina Prison Reform Legislation," 23 March 1981. PFM Records, Box 18, Folder 7.

[———], to RDV [Ralph D. Veerman], CWC [Charles W. Colson], GDL [Gordon Loux]. Memorandum "Re: Tax Status of PF," 26 June 1981. PFM Records, Box 18, Folder 7.

[———], to CWC [Charles W. Colson]. Memorandum "Re: Federal Legislation on Alternatives," 9 July 1981. PFM Records, Box 18, Folder 7.

[———], "Special Project Status Report, Project: Federal Legislation," 22 September 1981. PFM Records, Box 20, Folder 2.

[———], to RDV [Ralph D. Veerman] and GDL [Gordon Loux]. Memorandum "Re: Meeting with Bob Dugan," 24 September 1981. PFM Records, Box 18, Folder 7.

Weeks, David J. Personal communication with the author, 23 July 2005.

Weyrich, Paul M. "Cultural Conservatism: Toward a New National Agenda." Free Congress Research and Education Foundation News Conference. National Press Club, Washington, D.C., 1 December 1987. NAE Records.

White, John H., Billy A. Melvin, B. Edgar Johnson, Robert P. Dugan, Jr. to The President [George H. W. Bush], 7 March 1990. NAE Records.

MINUTES

Board of Administration. National Association of Evangelicals. "Minutes of the Meeting of the Board of Administration," 19–20 September 1945 [dated "Release October 1, 1945"]. NAE Records.

———. "Minutes. Third Session," 23 April 1963. NAE Records.

Committee on Christian Liberty. National Association of Evangelicals. "Minutes," 19 October 1948. In "Minutes of the Meeting of the Executive Committee," Executive Committee, NAE, 19 November 1948. NAE Records.

Conference on Church-State Relations. National Association of Evangelicals. "Minutes," 6–7 February 1961. NAE Records.

Evangelical Action Committee. National Association of Evangelicals. "Minutes of the Evangelical Action Committee," [Clyde W. Taylor], 5 June 1957. NAE Records.

Executive Committee. National Association of Evangelicals. "Minutes of the Meeting of the Executive Committee," 19 November 1948. NAE Records.

———. "Minutes of the Meeting of the Executive Committee," 7 March 1949. NAE Records.

———. "Executive Committee Minutes," 31 January 1958. NAE Records.

———. "Minutes of the Executive Committee of the NAE," 22 November 1960. NAE Records.

———. "Minutes," 8 October 1962. NAE Records.

———. "Executive Committee Minutes," 10 December 1963. NAE Records.

———. "Executive Committee Minutes," 6 April 1964. NAE Records.

———. "Minutes of the Executive Committee of the NAE," 7 June 1982. NAE Records.

National Association of Evangelicals. "Minutes of the NAE Staff Retreat in Glen Eyrie," 10–12 January 1961. NAE Records.

———. "Minutes of the NAE Staff Conference." Colorado Springs, 10–13 January 1962. NAE Records.

National General Convention. National Association of Evangelicals. "Minutes of the Fifteenth Annual Conference of NAE," 1–4 April 1957. NAE Records.

———. "Minutes of General Convention Business Sessions," 13 April 1961. NAE Records.

———. "General Convention Business Session Minutes," 25 April 1963. NAE Records.

———. "General Convention Business Session Minutes," 8 April 1964. NAE Records.

———. "General Convention Minutes. Second Session," 20 April 1966. NAE Records.

———. "Minutes," 17 April 1969. NAE Records.

———. "General Convention Minutes. Third Session," 20 April 1972. NAE Records.

———. "General Session Minutes. Second Session," 24 February 1977. NAE Records.

Social Concerns Commission, National Association of Evangelicals, "Minutes of the Social Concerns Commission," 1–3 May 1973. NAE Records.

World Relief Commission. National Association of Evangelicals. "Minutes of the Executive Committee, WRC," 14–15 September 1972. NAE Records.

Published Materials

Abramowitz, Mimi. *Regulating the Lives of Women: Social Welfare Policy from Colonial Times to the Present*. Boston: South End Press, 1988.

Adloff, Frank. "Catholic Charities und der amerikanische Wohlfahrtsstaat. Organisatorische und konzeptionelle Transformationen." In *Katholiken in den USA und Deutschland: Kirche, Gesellschaft und Politik*, ed. Wilhelm Damberg and Antonius Liedhegener, 146–67. Münster: Aschendorff, 2006.

———. "Civil Society, Civic Engagement, and Religion: Findings and Research Problems in Germany and the U.S." In *Civil Society, Civic Engagement and Catholicism in the U.S.*, ed. Antonius Liedhegener and Werner Kremp, 63–92. Trier: Wissenschaftlicher Verlag, 2007.

———. "Religion and Social-Political Action: The Catholic Church, Catholic Charities, and the American Welfare State." *International Review of Sociology—Revue Internationale de Sociologie* 16, 2 (2006): 1–30.

Ahlstrom, Sydney E. *A Religious History of the American People*, 2nd ed. New Haven, Conn.: Yale University Press, 2004.

Americans United for the Separation of Church and State. "Faith-Based Initiatives," http://www.au.org/site/PageServer?pagename=issues_faithbased. 19 August 2008.

Ammermann, Nancy. *Baptist Battles: Social Change and Religious Conflict in the Southern Baptist Convention*. New Brunswick, N.J.: Rutgers University Press, 1990.

Andrews, John A., III. *The Other Side of the Sixties: Young Americans for Freedom and the Rise of Conservative Politics*. New Brunswick, N.J.: Rutgers University Press, 1997.

Bachmann, E. Theodore, ed. *The Emerging Perspective*. Vol. 3 of *Churches and Social Welfare*. New York: National Council of Churches of Christ, 1956.

Badger, Anthony J. *Prosperity Road: The New Deal, Tobacco, and North Carolina*. Chapel Hill: University of North Carolina Press, 1980.

Bailey, Kenneth K. *Southern White Protestantism in the Twentieth Century*. New York: Harper and Row, 1964.

Bane, Mary Jo, and Lawrence M. Mead. *Lifting Up the Poor: A Dialogue on Religion, Poverty and Welfare Reform*. Washington, D.C.: Brookings Institution Press, 2003.

Bell, Daniel. *The End of Ideology: On the Exhaustion of Political Ideas in the Fifties*. Glencoe, Ill.: Free Press, 1960.

———. "Interpretations of American Politics." In *The Radical Right: The New American Right*, ed. Daniel Bell. Expanded and updated ed. Garden City, N.Y.: Doubleday, 1963.

Bell, Jonathan. *The Liberal State on Trial: The Cold War and American Politics in the Truman Years*. New York: Columbia University Press, 2004.

Bell, L. Nelson. "A Layman and his Faith: Christianity and Communism." *Christianity Today*, 19 January 1959, 19.

Bendick, Marc, Jr. "Privatizing the Delivery of Social Welfare Services: An Idea to Be

Taken Seriously." In *Privatization and the Welfare State*, ed. Sheila B. Kamerman and Alfred J. Kahn, 99–120. Princeton, N.J.: Princeton University Press, 1989.

Berg, Thomas Charles. "Anti-Catholicism and Modern Church-State Relations." *Loyola University Chicago Law Journal* 33 (Fall 2001): 121–72.

Berger, Peter L., and Richard John Neuhaus. *To Empower People: From State to Civil Society*, ed. Michael Novak. 2nd ed. Washington, D.C.: American Enterprise Institute for Public Policy Research, 1996.

Berkowitz, Edward D. *America's Welfare State: From Roosevelt to Reagan*. Baltimore: Johns Hopkins University Press, 1991.

Berkowitz, Edward D., and Kim McQuaid. *Creating the Welfare State: The Political Economy of Twentieth-Century Reform*. 2nd ed. New York: Praeger, 1988.

"Bigotry or Smear." *Christianity Today*, 1 February 1960, 20–21.

"Billy Graham and the Pope's Legions." *Christianity Today*, 22 July 1957, 20–21.

"The Blaine Game: The ACLU and Its Allies Pick up the Banner of the Know Nothings," *Wall Street Journal*, 7 December 2003.

Bloesch, Donald G. *The Future of Evangelical Christianity: A Call for Unity amid Diversity*. Garden City, N.Y.: Doubleday, 1983.

Blumenthal, Sidney. *The Rise of the Counter-Establishment: From Conservative Ideology to Political Power*. New York: Times Books, 1986.

Blumenthal, Sidney, and Thomas Byrne Edsall. *The Reagan Legacy*. New York: Pantheon, 1988.

Bogle, Mary M. "A Survey of Congregation-Based Child Care in the United States." In *Sacred Places, Civic Purposes: Should Government Help Faith-Based Charity*, ed. E. J. Dionne, Jr., and Ming Hsu Chen, 216–34. Washington, D.C.: Brookings Institution Press, 2001.

Bowie, Robert R., and Richard H. Immerman. *Waging Peace: How Eisenhower Shaped an Enduring Cold War*. New York: Oxford University Press, 1998.

Boyer, Paul S. *When Time Shall Be No More: Prophecy Belief in Modern American Culture*. Cambridge, Mass.: Belknap Press of Harvard University Press, 1992.

Brick, Howard. *Transcending Capitalism: Visions of a New Society in Modern American Thought*. Ithaca, N.Y.: Cornell University Press, 2006.

Briggs, Laura. *Reproducing Empire: Race, Sex, Science, and U.S. Imperialism in Puerto Rico*. Berkeley: University of California Press, 2003.

Brinkley, Alan. *Liberalism and Its Discontents*. Cambridge, Mass.: Harvard University Press, 1998.

———. "World War II and American Liberalism." In *Major Problems in American History, 1920–1945*, ed. Colin Gordon, 443–50. Boston: Houghton Mifflin, 1999.

Bromiley, Geoffrey W. "Fundamentalism—Modernism: A First Step in the Controversy." *Christianity Today*, 11 November 1957, 3–5.

Brown, Dorothy M., and Elizabeth McKeown, *The Poor Belong to Us: Charities and American Welfare*. Cambridge, Mass.: Harvard University Press, 1997.

Brown, Michael K. "The Segmented Welfare System: Distributive Conflict and Retrenchment in the United States, 1968–1984." In *Remaking the Welfare State: Retrenchment and Social Policy in America and Europe*, ed. Michael K. Brown, 182–210. Philadelphia: Temple University Press, 1988.

———, ed. *Remaking the Welfare State: Retrenchment and Social Policy in America and Europe*. Philadelphia: Temple University Press, 1988.

Bruce, Steve. *Conservative Protestant Politics*. Oxford: Oxford University Press, 1999.

Bundy, Edgar C. *Collectivism in the Churches: A Documented Account of the Political Activities of the Federal, National and World Council of Churches*. Wheaton, Ill.: Church League of America, 1958.

Burkholder, John Richard. "Mennonites in ecumenical dialogue on peace and justice, Part III: Back home among the evangelicals." Mennonite Central Committee Occasional Paper 7, August 1988. http://www.mcc.org/respub/occasional/73.html. 11 August 2008.

Butler, Jon. "Jack-in-the-Box Faith: The Religion Problem in Modern American History." *Journal of American History* 90 (March 2004): 1357–78.

Campbell, Ballard C. *The Growth of American Government: Governance from the Cleveland Era to the Present*. Bloomington: Indiana University Press, 1995.

Carlson-Thiess, Stanley. "Charitable Choice: Bringing Religion Back into American Welfare." *Journal of Policy History* 13 (2001): 109–32.

Carpenter, Joel A. "Revive Us Again: Alienation, Hope, and the Resurgence of Fundamentalism, 1930–1950." In *Transforming Faith: The Sacred and Secular in Modern American History*, ed. Malcolm L. Bradbury and James B. Gilbert, 105–25. New York: Greenwood Press, 1989.

———. *Revive Us Again: The Reawakening of American Fundamentalism*. New York: Oxford University Press, 1997.

———. *Two Reformers of Fundamentalism: Harold John Ockenga and Carl F. H. Henry*. New York: Garland, 1988.

———. "Youth for Christ and the New Evangelicals." In *Reckoning with the Past: Historical Essays on American Evangelicalism from the Institute for the Study of American Evangelicals*, ed. D. G. Hart, 354–75. Grand Rapids, Mich.: Baker Books, 1995.

Carroll, Peter N. "The New Populists, the New Right, and the Search for the Lost America." In *Conflict and Consensus in Modern American History*, ed. Allen F. Davis and Harold D. Woodman, 527–40. 7th ed. Lexington, Mass.: Heath, 1988.

Carson, Emmett D. "Patterns of Giving in Black Churches." In *Faith and Philanthropy in America: Exploring the Role of Religion in America's Voluntary Sector*, ed. Robert A. Wuthnow, Virginia Hodgkinson, and Associates, 232–52. San Francisco: Jossey-Bass, 1990.

Cerillo, Augustus, Jr. "A Survey of Recent Evangelical Social Thought." *Christian Scholar's Review* 5 (March 1976): 272–80.

Chaves, Mark. "Religious Congregations and Welfare Reform: Who Will Take Advantage of 'Charitable Choice'?" *American Sociological Review* 64, 6 (1999): 836–46.

"Christian Responsibility in Political Affairs." *Christianity Today*, 1 August 1960, 24.

"Church-State Squabble Stalls Child-Care Bill in House," *Congressional Quarterly*, 24 March 1990, 902–21.

"The Church-State Wall: Glenn L. Archer." *Christianity Today*, 10 May 1974, 6–12.

Clayton, James L. "Defense Spending: Key to California's Growth." *Western Political Quarterly* 15 (June 1962): 280–93.

———. "The Impact of the Cold War on the Economies of California and Utah, 1946–1965." *Pacific Northwest Quarterly* 36 (November 1967): 449–73.

Clydesdale, Timothy T. "Soul-Winning and Social Work: Giving and Caring in the Evangelical Tradition." In *Faith and Philanthropy in America: Exploring the Role of Religion in America's Voluntary Sector*, ed. Robert A. Wuthnow, Virginia Hodgkinson, and Associates, 187–210. San Francisco: Jossey-Bass, 1990.

Cnaan, Ram A., with Robert J. Wineburg and Stephanie C. Boddie. *The Newer Deal: Social Work and Religion in Partnership*. New York: Columbia University Press, 1999.

Cohen, Lizabeth. *A Consumers' Republic: The Politics of Mass Consumption in Postwar America*. New York: Knopf, 2003.

Cohen, Nancy. *The Reconstruction of American Liberalism, 1865–1914*. Chapel Hill: University of North Carolina Press, 2002.

Collins, Robert M. *More: The Politics of Economic Growth in Postwar America*. New York: Oxford University Press, 2000.

Conkin, Paul K. *The New Deal*. 3rd ed. Wheeling, Ill.: Harlan Davidson, 1992.

Conn, Harvie. *The American City and the Evangelical Church: A Historical Overview*. Grand Rapids, Mich.: Baker Books, 1994.

Coughlin, Bernard. *Church and State in Social Welfare*. New York: Columbia University Press, 1965.

Craig, Campbell. *Destroying the Village: Eisenhower and Thermonuclear War*. New York: Columbia University Press, 1998.

Critchlow, Donald T. "Implementing Family Planning Policy: Philanthropic Foundations and the Modern Welfare State." In *With Us Always: A History of Private Charity and Public Welfare*, ed. Donald T. Critchlow and Charles H. Parker, 211–41. Lanham, Md.: Rowman and Littlefield, 1998.

Cromartie, Michael, ed. *Evangelicals and Foreign Policy: Four Perspectives*. Lanham, Md.: University Press of America, 1989.

Daly, Lew. *God and the Welfare State*. Cambridge, Mass.: MIT Press, 2006.

Davies, Gareth. *From Opportunity to Entitlement: The Transformation and Decline of Great Society Liberalism*. Lawrence: University Press of Kansas, 1996.

———. *See Government Grow: Education Politics from Johnson to Reagan*. Lawrence: University Press of Kansas, 2007

Davies, Gareth, and Martha Derthick. "Race and Social Welfare Policy: The Social Security Act of 1935." *Political Science Quarterly* 112 (Summer 1997): 217–35.

Davies, Richard O. *Housing Reform During the Truman Administration*. Columbia: University of Missouri Press, 1966.

Davis, Derek, and Barry Hankins, eds. *Welfare Reform and Faith-Based Organizations.* Waco, Tex.: J. M. Dawson Institute of Church-State Studies, 1999.

Davis, James D. "Evangelical Program Takes on War and Peace." *Fort Lauderdale Sun-Sentinel,* 5 November 1988, 5D.

Davis, Nancy J., and Robert V. Robinson. "A War for America's Soul? The American Religious Landscape." In *Cultural Wars in American Politics: Critical Reviews of a Popular Myth,* ed. Rhys H. Williams, 39–61. New York: de Gruyter, 1997.

Dawson, Joseph M. "The Christian View of the State." *Christianity Today,* 24 June 1957, 3–5.

Dayton, Donald. "The Social and Political Conservatism of Modern American Evangelicalism: A Preliminary Search for the Reasons." *Union Seminary Quarterly Review* 22 (Winter 1977): 71–80.

Dayton, Donald W., and Robert K. Johnston, eds. *The Variety of American Evangelicalism.* Knoxville: University of Tennessee Press, 1991.

"Declaration of Principles." *Christianity Today,* 14 October 1957, 20–21.

Demerath, N. J., III, and Rhys H. Williams. "A Mythical Past and Uncertain Future." In *Church-State Relations: Tensions and Transitions,* ed. Thomas Robbins and Roland Robertson, 77–90. New Brunswick, N.J.: Transaction, 1987.

Derthick, Martha. *Uncontrollable Spending for Social Services.* Washington, D.C.: Brookings Institution, 1975.

Diamond, Sara. *Roads to Dominion: Right-Wing Movements and Political Power in the United States.* New York: Guilford Press, 1995.

Dochuk, Darren T. *From Bible Belt to Sun Belt: Plain Folk Religion, Grassroots Politics, and the Rise of Evangelical Conservatism.* New York: Norton, 2011.

Duggan, Lisa. *The Twilight of Equality? Neoliberalism, Cultural Politics, and the Attack on Democracy.* Boston: Beacon Press, 2003.

Ehrenreich, Barbara. "The New Right Attack on Social Welfare." In *The Mean Season: The Attack on the Welfare State,* ed. Fred Block et al., 161–95. New York: Pantheon, 1987.

Eighmy, John Lee. *Churches in Cultural Captivity: A History of the Social Attitudes of Southern Baptists.* Knoxville: University of Tennessee Press, 1972.

"Eisenhower, Khrushchev and History's Inevitable Course." *Christianity Today,* 12 October 1959, 25–26.

Ellwood, Robert S. *The Fifties Spiritual Marketplace: American Religion in a Decade of Conflict.* New Brunswick, N.J.: Rutgers University Press, 1997.

Elson, E. L. R. "Worship in the Life of the Nation." *Christianity Today,* 12 November 1956, 10–11, 19.

Elzinga, Kenneth G. "The Demise of Capitalism and the Christian's Response." *Christianity Today,* 7 July 1972, 12–16.

Epstein, William M. *The Dilemma of American Social Welfare.* New Brunswick, N.J.: Transaction, 1993.

Erickson, Millard J. *The Evangelical Left: Encountering Postconservative Evangelical Theology.* Grand Rapids, Mich.: Baker Books, 1997.

Erzen, Tanya. "Testimonial Politics: The Christian Right's Faith-Based Approach to Marriage and Imprisonment." *American Quarterly* 59 (September 2007): 991–1015.

Eskridge, Larry, and Mark A. Noll, eds. *More Money, More Ministry: Money and Evangelicals in Recent North American History.* Grand Rapids, Mich.: Eerdmans, 2000.

Fairbanks, James D. "Politics and the Evangelical Press." In *Religion and Political Behavior in the United States,* ed. Ted G. Jelen, 243–57. New York: Praeger, 1989.

Finkenbine, Roy E. "Law, Reconstruction, and African American Education in the Post-Emancipation South." In *Charity, Philanthropy and Civility in American History,* ed. Lawrence J. Friedman and Mark D. McGarvie, 161–78. Cambridge: Cambridge University Press, 2003.

Flipse, Scott. "To Save 'Free Vietnam' and Lose Our Souls." In *The Foreign Mission Enterprise at Home: Explorations in American Cultural History,* ed. Daniel H. Bays and Grant Wacker, 206–22. Tuscaloosa: University of Alabama Press, 2003.

Flowers, Ronald B. *Religion in Strange Times: The 1960s and 1970s.* Macon, Ga.: Mercer University Press, 1984.

Fogel, Robert William. *The Fourth Great Awakening and the Future of Egalitarianism.* Chicago: University of Chicago Press, 2000.

Forrester, James. "New Paths in Christian Higher Education." *Christianity Today,* 28 August 1964, 8-10.

Fowler, Robert Booth. *A New Engagement: Evangelical Political Thought, 1966–1976.* Grand Rapids, Mich.: Eerdmans, 1987.

Frank, Thomas. *What's the Matter with Kansas? How Conservatives Won the Heart of America.* New York: Holt, 2004.

Fraser, Steve, and Gary Gerstle, eds. *The Rise and Fall of the New Deal Order, 1930–1980.* Princeton, N.J.: Princeton University Press, 1989.

Freeden, Michael. "Democracy and Paternalism: The Struggle over Shaping British Liberal Welfare Thinking." In *Democracy and Social Rights in the Two Wests,* ed. Alice Kessler-Harris and Maurizio Vaudagna, 259–77. Turin: Otto Editore, 2009.

Freidel, Frank. *Franklin D. Roosevelt: A Rendezvous with Destiny.* Boston: Little, Brown, 1990.

Friedberg, Aaron L. *In the Shadow of the Garrison State: America's Anti-Statism and Its Cold War Grand Strategy.* Princeton, N.J.: Princeton University Press, 2000.

Friedman, Lawrence J., and Mark D. McGarvie, eds. *Charity, Philanthropy and Civility in American History.* Cambridge: Cambridge University Press, 2003.

Galbraith, John Kenneth, and Andrea D. Williams. *The Essential Galbraith.* Boston: Houghton Mifflin, 2001.

Gallup, George, Jr., and Jim Castelli. *The People's Religion: American Faith in the 90's.* New York: Macmillan, 1989.

Garr, Robin. *Reinvesting in America: The Grassroots Movements That Are Feeding the Hungry, Housing the Homeless, and Putting Americans Back to Work.* Reading, Mass.: Addison-Wesley, 1995.

Gay, Craig. *With Liberty and Justice for Whom? The Recent Evangelical Debate over Capitalism.* Grand Rapids, Mich.: Eerdmans, 1991.

Geary, Daniel. *Radical Ambition: C. Wright Mills, the Left, and American Social Thought.* Berkeley: University of California Press, 2009.

Givel, Michael. *The War on Poverty Revisited: The Community Services Block Grants in the Reagan Years.* Lanham, Md.: University Press of America, 1991.

Glenn, Charles L. *The Ambiguous Embrace: Government and Faith-Based Schools and Social Agencies.* Princeton, N.J.: Princeton University Press, 2000.

Goldenberg, Suzanne. "US Religious Charities Win $2.15bn in State Grants." *The Guardian*, 11 March 2006, 17.

Gordon, Linda. *Pitied But Not Entitled: Single Mothers and the History of Welfare.* Cambridge, Mass.: Harvard University Press, 1995.

———, ed. *Women, the State, and Welfare.* Madison: University of Wisconsin Press, 1991.

Gotham, Kevin Fox. "A City Without Slums: Urban Renewal; Public Housing and Downtown Revitalization in Kansas City, Missouri." *American Journal of Economics and Sociology* 60 (January 2001): 285–316.

Gottschalk, Barbara, and Peter Gottschalk. "The Reagan Retrenchment in Historical Context." In *Remaking the Welfare State: Retrenchment and Social Policy in America and Europe*, ed. Michael K. Brown, 59–72. Philadelphia: Temple University Press, 1988.

Graham, Billy. *Just as I Am: The Autobiography of Billy Graham.* San Francisco: HarperSanFrancisco, 1997.

"Graham Describes Three Great American Crises." *Christianity Today*, 8 July 1957, 28.

Green, John C. "American Congregations and Social Service Programs: Results of a Survey." Roundtable on Religion & Social Welfare Policy, 2007, http://www.religion andsocialpolicy.org/docs/public_resources/AmericanCongregationsReport.pdf. 30 August 2011.

Green, John C., James L. Guth, and Kevin Hill. "Faith and Election: The Christian Right in Congressional Campaigns 1978–1988." *Journal of Politics* 55 (February 1993): 80–91.

Greenberg, Anna. "Doing Whose Work? Faith-Based Organizations and Government Partnerships." In *Who Will Provide? The Changing Role of Religion in American Social Welfare*, ed. Mary Jo Bane, Brent Coffin, and Ronald Thiemann, 178–97. Boulder, Colo.: Westview Press, 2000.

Greenstein, Fred J. *The Hidden-Hand Presidency: Eisenhower as Leader.* New York: Basic Books, 1982.

Greenstone, J. David. "The Decline and Revival of the American Welfare State: Moral Criteria and Instrumental Reasoning in Critical Elections." In *Remaking the Welfare State: Retrenchment and Social Policy in America and Europe*, ed. Michael K. Brown, 165–81. Philadelphia: Temple University Press, 1988.

Gurin, Arnold. "Governmental Responsibility and Privatization: Examples from Four Social Services." In *Privatization and the Welfare State*, ed. Sheila B. Kamerman and Alfred J. Kahn, 181–205. Princeton, N.J.: Princeton University Press, 1989.

Gutman, Herbert G. "Mirrors of Hard, Distorted Glass: An Examination of Some Influential Historical Assumptions About the Afro-American Family and the Shaping of

Public Policy, 1861–1965." In *Social Policy and Social History*, ed. David J. Rothman and Stanton Wheeler, 239–73. New York: Academic Press, 1981.

Hall, Peter Dobkin. "The History of Religious Philanthropy in America." In *Faith and Philanthropy in America: Exploring the Role of Religion in America's Voluntary Sector*, ed. Robert A. Wuthnow, Virginia Hodgkinson, and Associates, 38–62. San Francisco: Jossey-Bass, 1990.

———. "Philanthropy, the Welfare State, and the Transformation of American Public and Private Institutions, 1945–2000." Working Paper 5. Cambridge, Mass.: Hauser Center for Nonprofit Organizations, Harvard University, 2000. http://www.hks.harvard.edu/hauser/PDF_XLS/workingpapers/workingpaper_5.pdf. 7 December 2008.

———. "The Welfare State and the Careers of Public and Private Institutions Since 1945." In *Charity, Philanthropy and Civility in American History*, ed. Lawrence J. Friedman and Mark D. McGarvie, 363–83. Cambridge: Cambridge University Press, 2003.

Hall, Peter Dobkin, and Colin B. Burke. "Historical Statistics of the United States Chapter on Voluntary, Nonprofit, and Religious Entities and Activities: Underlying Concepts, Concerns, and Opportunities." Working Paper 14. Cambridge, Mass.: Hauser Center for Nonprofit Organizations, Harvard University, 2002. http://www.hks.harvard.edu/hauser/PDF_XLS/workingpapers/workingpaper_14.pdf. 9 September 2010.

Hamby, Alonzo, ed. *Harry S. Truman and the Fair Deal*. Lexington, Mass.: Heath, 1974.

———. *Liberalism and Its Challengers: F.D.R. to Reagan*. New York: Oxford University Press, 1985.

———. *Liberalism and Its Challengers: From F.D.R. to Bush*. New York: Oxford University Press, 1992.

———. "The Vital Center, the Fair Deal, and the Quest for a Liberal Political Economy." *American Historical Review* 77 (June 1972): 653–78.

Hamilton, Charles V., and Dona C. Hamilton. *The Dual Agenda: Race and Social Welfare Policies of Civil Rights Organizations*. New York: Columbia University Press, 1997.

Hamilton, David E. *From New Day to New Deal: American Farm Policy from Hoover to Roosevelt, 1928–1933*. Chapel Hill: University of North Carolina Press, 1991.

Hammack, David C. "Failure and Resilience: Pushing the Limits in Depression and Wartime." In *Charity, Philanthropy and Civility in American History*, ed. Lawrence J. Friedman and Mark D. McGarvie, 263–80. Cambridge: Cambridge University Press, 2003.

Hammond, Phillip E. "American Church/State Jurisprudence from the Warren Court to the Rehnquist Court." *Journal for the Scientific Study of Religion* 40, 3 (2001): 455–64.

———. "Evangelical Politics: Generalizations and Implications." *Review of Religious Research* 27 (December 1985): 189–92.

Handler, Joel, and Yeheskel Hasenfeld. *The Moral Construction of Poverty: Welfare Reform in America*. Newbury Park, Calif.: Sage, 1991.

Hankins, Barry. *Uneasy in Babylon: Southern Baptist Conservatives and American Culture*. Tuscaloosa: University of Alabama Press, 2002.

Harding, Susan F. *The Book of Jerry Falwell: Fundamentalist Language and Politics.* Princeton, N.J.: Princeton University Press, 2000.

Harding, Susan F., and Charles C. Bright, eds. *Statemaking and Social Movements: Essays in History and Theory.* Ann Arbor: University of Michigan Press, 1984.

Harmon, Nolan B. "Church and State—A Relation in Equity." *Christianity Today,* 4 February 1972, 4–7.

Harrison, William K. "Christianity and Peace in Our Day." *Christianity Today,* 29 October 1956, 13–16.

———. "Is America's Spiritual Vigor Waning?" *Christianity Today,* 20 January 1958, 24–25.

———. "Reminiscences and a Prophecy." *Christianity Today,* 4 March 1957, 13–15.

Hatch, Nathan O., and Michael S. Hamilton. "Taking the Measure of the Evangelical Resurgence, 1942–1992." In *Reckoning with the Past: Historical Essays on American Evangelicalism from the Institute for the Study of American Evangelicals,* ed. D. G. Hart, 395–412. Grand Rapids, Mich.: Baker Books, 1995.

Hawley, Ellis W. *The Great War and the Search for a Modern Order: A History of the American People and Their Institutions, 1917–1933.* New York: St. Martin's Press, 1992.

———. "The New Deal State and the Anti-Bureaucratic Tradition." In *The New Deal and Its Legacy: Critique and Reappraisal,* ed. Robert Eden, 77–92. New York: Greenwood Press, 1989.

Heclo, Hugh. *Christianity and American Democracy.* Cambridge, Mass.: Harvard University Press, 2007.

Heclo, Hugh, and Wilfred M. McClay, eds. *Religion Returns to the Public Sphere: Faith and Policy in America.* Washington, D.C.: Woodrow Wilson Center Press, 2003.

Heilbrunn, Jacob. "The New Fault Line on the Right: Neocon v. Theocon." *New Republic,* 12 December 1996.

Heimert, Alan. *Religion and the American Mind from the Great Awakening to the Revolution.* Cambridge, Mass.: Harvard University Press, 1966.

[Henry, Carl F. H.], "Christ and the Atom Bomb." *Christianity Today,* 2 September 1957, 20–22.

———. "The Christian-Pagan West." *Christianity Today,* 24 December 1956, 3–5, 34.

———. "Dare We Renew the Controversy? III. The Contemporary Restoration." *Christianity Today,* 8 July 1957, 15–18.

———. "Dare We Renew the Controversy? The Evangelical Responsibility." *Christianity Today,* 22 July 1957, 23–26, 38.

———. "Dare We Revive the Modernist-Fundamentalist Conflict?" *Christianity Today,* 10 June 1957, 3–6.

———. "Evangelicals in the Social Struggle." *Christianity Today,* 8 October 1965, 4–11.

———. "Evangelicals: Out of the Closet but Going Nowhere?" *Christianity Today,* 4 January 1980, 16–22.

———. "The Fragility of Freedom in the West." *Christianity Today,* 15 October 1956, 8–11, 17.

[———]. "Foundations: Tilt to the Left." *Christianity Today*, 28 April 1958, 20–24.

[———]. "Human Rights in an Age of Tyranny." *Christianity Today*, 4 February 1957, 20–22.

[———]. "Low Tide in the West." *Christianity Today*, 24 December 1956, 20–24.

[———]. "The Peace Drive in the Churches." *Christianity Today*, 13 April 1959, 20–21.

———. *Remaking the Modern Mind*. Grand Rapids, Mich.: Eerdmans, 1946.

———. "Soul-Searching in Social Welfare." *Christianity Today*, 2 February 1959, 31–33.

[———]. "The Spirit of Foreign Policy." *Christianity Today*, 29 April 1957, 20–23.

———. *The Uneasy Conscience of Modern Fundamentalism*. Grand Rapids, Mich.: Eerdmans, 1947.

[———]. "Where Do We Go From Here?" *Christianity Today*, 12 November 1956, 16–18.

———. "Why Christianity Today," *Christianity Today*, 15 October 1956, 21.

Henry, Patrick. "'And I Don't Care What It Is': The Tradition-History of a Civil Religion Proof Text." *Journal of the American Academy of Religion* 49 (March 1981): 35–49.

Henry, Paul B. *Politics for Evangelicals*. Valley Forge, Pa.: Judson Press, 1974.

Hess, Gary R. "Waging the Cold War in the Third World: The Foundations and the Challenges of Development." In *Charity, Philanthropy, and Civility in American History*, ed. Lawrence J. Friedman and Mark D. McGarvie, 319–39. Cambridge, Mass.: Cambridge University Press, 2003.

Himmelstein, Jerome L. *To the Right: The Transformation of American Conservatism*. Berkeley: University of California Press, 1990.

Hixson, William B., Jr. *Search for the American Right Wing: An Analysis of the Social Science Record, 1955–1987*. Princeton, N.J.: Princeton University Press, 1992.

Hodgkinson, Virginia A., Murray S. Weitzman, and Arthur D. Kirsch. "From Commitment to Action: How Religious Involvement Affects Giving and Volunteering." In *Faith and Philanthropy in America: Exploring the Role of Religion in America's Voluntary Sector*, ed. Robert A. Wuthnow, Virginia Hodgkinson, and Associates, 93–114. San Francisco: Jossey-Bass, 1990.

Hofstadter, Richard. *The Age of Reform. From Bryan to F.D.R*. New York: Vintage, 1955.

Hogan, Michael J. "Corporatism." *Journal of American History* 77 (June 1990): 153–60.

———. "Corporatism: A Positive Appraisal." *Diplomatic History* 10 (1986): 363–67.

———. *Informal Entente: The Private Structure of Cooperation in Anglo-American Economic Diplomacy, 1918–1928*. Chicago: Imprint Publications, 1991.

Hood, Ralph W., and Ronald J. Morris. "Boundary Maintenance, Social-Political Views, and the Presidential Preference among High and Low Fundamentalists." *Review of Religious Research* 27 (December 1985): 134–45.

Hoover, J. Edgar. "Communism: The Bitter Enemy of Religion." *Christianity Today*, 22 June 1959, 3–5.

———. "The Communist Menace: Red Goals and Christian Ideals." *Christianity Today*, 10 October 1960, 3–5.

———. "Communist Propaganda and the Christian Pulpit." *Christianity Today*, 24 October 1960, 5–7.

——. "Soviet Rule or Christian Renewal." *Christianity Today*, 7 November 1960, 8, 10–11.

Howard, Irving E. "Christian Approach to Economics." *Christianity Today*, 18 August 1958, 7–9.

Hunter, James Davison. *American Evangelicalism: Conservative Religion and the Quandary of Modernity*. New Brunswick, N.J.: Rutgers University Press, 1983.

——. *Culture Wars: The Struggle To Define America*. New York: Basic Books, 1992.

——. *Evangelicalism: The Coming Generation*. Chicago: University of Chicago Press, 1987.

"Immigration Bill." *Christianity Today*, 22 July 1957, 29.

Inboden, William. *Religion and American Foreign Policy, 1945–1960: The Soul of Containment*. Cambridge: Cambridge University Press, 2008.

"Inflation and the Breakdown of Trust." *Christianity Today*, 6 January 1958, 21–23.

InnerChange Freedom Initiative. "IFI Ruling Information: Eighth Circuit Issues Ruling," http://www.ifiprison.org/generic.asp?ID=7277. 19 August 2008.

Ivers, Gregg. *To Build a Wall: American Jews and the Separation of Church and State*. Charlottesville: University of Virginia Press, 1995

Jackson, Kenneth T. *Crabgrass Frontier: The Suburbanization of the United States*. New York: Oxford University Press, 1985.

Jacobson, Matthew Frye. *Whiteness of a Different Color: European Immigrants and the Alchemy of Race*. Cambridge, Mass.: Harvard University Press, 1998.

Jelen, Ted. "Culture Wars and the Party System: Religion and Realignment, 1972–1993." In *Cultural Wars in American Politics: Critical Reviews of a Popular Myth*, ed. Rhys H. Williams, 145–57. New York: de Gruyter, 1997.

Jencks, Christopher. *Rethinking Social Policy: Race, Poverty, and the Underclass*. Cambridge, Mass.: Harvard University Press, 1992.

"Joint Moscow-Peking Threat Calls for Christian Realism." *Christianity Today*, 4 March 1957, 23–24.

Judd, Walter H. "World Issues and the Christian." *Christianity Today*, 23 June 1958, 6–8.

Judt, Tony. *Postwar: A History of Europe Since 1945*. London: Pimlico, 2007.

Kamm, S. Richey. "Is America Losing Her Cultural Distinctives?" *Christianity Today*, 8 July 1957, 3–5.

Karl, Barry. *The Uneasy State: The United States from 1915 to 1945*. Chicago: University of Chicago Press, 1983.

Karl, Barry D., and Stanley N. Katz. "The American Private Philanthropic Foundation and the Public Sphere, 1890–1930." *Minerva* 19 (1981): 236–70.

Katz, Michael. *The Undeserving Poor: From the War on Poverty to the War on Welfare*. New York: Pantheon, 1989.

Katz, Michael, and Christoph Sachsse, eds. *The Mixed Economy in Social Welfare: Public/Private Relations in England, Germany, and the United States, the 1870s to the 1930s*. Baden-Baden: Nomos, 1996.

Katznelson, Ira. "Was the Great Society a Lost Opportunity." In *The Rise and Fall of the*

New Deal Order, 1930–1980, ed. Steve Fraser and Gary Gerstle, 185–211. Princeton, N.J.: Princeton University Press, 1989.

Kaus, Mickey. "The Revival of Liberalism." *New York Times*, 9 August 1996, A 26–27.

Kazin, Michael. "The Grass-Roots Right: New Histories of U.S. Conservatism in the Twentieth Century." *American Historical Review* 97 (February 1992): 136–55.

Kelley, Stanley. "Democracy and the New Deal Party System." In *Democracy and the Welfare State*, ed. Amy Gutman, 185–206. Princeton, N.J.: Princeton University Press, 1988.

Kellstedt, Lyman A. "Religion, the Neglected Variable: An Agenda for Future Research on Religion and Political Behavior." In *Rediscovering the Religious Factor in American Politics*, ed. David C. Leege and Lyman A. Kellstedt, 273–303. Armonk, N.Y.: M. E. Sharpe, 1993.

Kellstedt, Lyman A., and Mark A. Noll. "Religion, Voting for President, and Party Identification, 1948–1984." In *Religion and American Politics*, ed. Mark A. Noll, 355–79. New York: Oxford University Press, 1990.

Kennedy, Sheila Suess, and Wolfgang Bielefeld. *Charitable Choice at Work: Evaluating Faith-Based Job Programs in the States.* Washington, D.C.: Georgetown University Press, 2006.

Kintz, Linda. *Between Jesus and the Market: The Emotions that Matter in Right-Wing America.* Durham, N.C.: Duke University Press, 1997.

Klatch, Rebecca E. *A Generation Divided: The New Left, the New Right, and the 1960s.* Berkeley: University of California Press, 1999.

Klein, Christina. *Cold War Orientalism: Asia in the Middlebrow Imagination, 1945–1961.* Berkeley: University of California Press, 2003

Kloppenberg, James T. *Uncertain Victory: Social Democracy and Progressivism in European and American Thought, 1870–1920.* New York: Oxford University Press, 1986.

Knowland, William F. "Admit Red China?" *Christianity Today*, 29 October 1956, 10–11.

Koistinen, Paul A. C. *Planning War, Pursuing Peace: The Political Economy of American Warfare, 1920–1939.* Lawrence: University Press of Kansas, 1998.

Kosar, Kevin R. *Failing Grades: The Federal Politics of Educational Standards.* Boulder, Colo.: Lynne Rienner, 2005.

Kramer, Ralph M. *Voluntary Agencies in the Welfare State.* Berkeley: University of California Press, 1981.

Krock, Arthur. *In the Nation: 1932–1966.* New York: McGraw-Hill, 1966.

Kucharsky, David. "The War on Church Establishment." *Christianity Today*, 3 March 1972, 44.

Kuhn, Harold B. "Christian Surrender to Communism." *Christianity Today*, 2 March 1959, 9–11.

Lahr, Angela M. *Millennial Dreams and Apocalyptic Nightmares: The Cold War Origins of Political Evangelicalism.* New York: Oxford University Press, 2007.

Lasch, Christopher. *The True and Only Heaven: Progress and Its Critics.* New York: Norton, 1991.

Lasch-Quinn, Elizabeth. *Black Neighbors: Race and the Limits of Reform in the American*

Settlement House Movement, 1890–1945. Chapel Hill: University of North Carolina Press, 1993.

Laswell, Harold B. "The Garrison State." *American Journal of Sociology* 46 (1941): 455–68.

Laville, Helen, and Hugh Wilford, eds. *The US Government, Citizen Groups and the Cold War: The State-Private Network*. London: Routledge, 2006.

Layman, Geoffrey. *The Great Divide: Religious and Cultural Conflict in American Party Politics*. New York: Columbia University Press, 2001.

"Left Wing Attacks on FBI and House Un-American Activities Group." *Christianity Today*, 30 March 1959, 21.

Lieberman, Robert. *Shifting the Color Line: Race and the American Welfare State*. Cambridge, Mass.: Harvard University Press, 1998.

Liebman, Robert, and Robert Wuthnow, eds. *The New Christian Right: Mobilization and Legitimation*. New York: Aldine, 1983.

Lienesch, Michael. *Redeeming America: Piety and Politics in the New Christian Right*. Chapel Hill: University of North Carolina Press, 1993.

Lindner, Eileen W., Mary C. Mattis, and June R. Rogers. *When Churches Mind the Children: A Study of Day Care in Local Parishes*. New York: National Council of Churches of Christ in the U.S.A., 1983.

Lindsay, D. Michael. *Faith in the Halls of Power: How Evangelicals Joined the American Elite*. New York: Oxford University Press, 2007.

Lippincott, H. H. "World Government and Christianity." *Christianity Today*, 3 February 1958, 3–5.

Lipset, Seymour Martin, and Earl Raab, "The Election and the Evangelicals," *Commentary* 71 (March 1981): 25–31.

Lockhart, Charles. *Gaining Ground: Tailoring Social Programs to American Values*. Berkeley: University of California Press, 1989.

Long, Emma J. " 'Drawing the Line': Religion, Education, and the Establishment Clause, 1947–1997." Ph.D. dissertation, University of Kent, 2008.

Loveland, Anne C. *American Evangelicals and the U.S. Military, 1942–1993*. Baton Rouge: Louisiana State University Press, 1996.

———. *Southern Evangelicals and the Social Order, 1800–1860*. Baton Rouge: Louisiana State University Press, 1980.

Lowell, C. Stanley. *The Great Church-State Fraud*. Washington, D.C.: Robert Luce, 1973.

Luker, Kristin. *Abortion and the Politics of Motherhood*. Berkeley: University of California Press, 1984.

MacLean, Nancy. *Behind the Mask of Chivalry: The Making of the Second Ku Klux Klan*. New York: Oxford University Press, 1994.

———. *Freedom Is Not Enough: The Opening of the American Workplace*. Cambridge, Mass.: Harvard University Press, 2006.

MacLeod, A. Donald. *W. Stanford Reid: An Evangelical Calvinist in the Academy*. Montreal: McGill University Press, 2004.

Manning, Ernest C. "The Integrity of Nations." *Christianity Today*, 29 October 1956, 8–10, 18–19.

Marcuse, Herbert. *One-Dimensional Man: Studies in the Ideology of Advanced Industrial Society.* Boston: Beacon Press, 1964.

Markusen, Ann, Peter Hall, Scott Campbell, and Sabina Deitrick. *The Rise of the Gunbelt: The Military Remapping of Industrial America.* New York: Oxford University Press, 1991.

Marsden, George M. "Fundamentalism and American Evangelicalism." In *The Variety of Evangelicalism*, ed. Donald W. Dayton and Robert K. Johnston, 22–35. Knoxville: University of Tennessee Press, 1991.

———. *Reforming Fundamentalism: Fuller Seminary and the New Evangelicalism.* Grand Rapids, Mich.: Eerdmans, 1987.

———. *Understanding Fundamentalism and Evangelicalism.* Grand Rapids, Mich.: Eerdmans, 1991.

Marsden, Lee. "US-Israel Relations: A Special Friendship." In *America's 'Special Relationships': Foreign and Domestic Aspects of the Politics of Alliance*, ed. John Dumbrell and Axel R. Schäfer, 191–207. London: Routledge, 2009.

Martin, William. *With God on Our Side: The Rise of the Religious Right in America.* New York: Broadway Books, 1996.

Matthews, Arthur H. *Standing Up, Standing Together: The Emergence of the National Association of Evangelicals.* Carol Stream, Ill.: National Association of Evangelicals, 1992.

Matusow, Allen J. *The Unraveling of America: A History of Liberalism in the 1960s.* New York: Harper and Row, 1984.

May, Elaine Tyler. *Homeward Bound: American Families in the Cold War.* New York: Basic Books, 1988.

McCormick, Thomas J. "Drift or Mastery: A Corporatist Synthesis for American Diplomatic History." *Reviews in American History* 10 (1982): 318–29.

McGirr, Lisa. *Suburban Warriors: The Origins of the New American Right.* Princeton, N.J.: Princeton University Press, 2001.

McKeown, Elizabeth. "Claiming the Poor." In *With Us Always: A History of Private Charity and Public Welfare*, ed. Donald T. Critchlow and Charles H. Parker, 145–59. Lanham, Md.: Rowman and Littlefield, 1998.

McMaster, R. E., Jr. "Church/State: Separate or Not?" *Christian Life*, June 1981, 26–27, 66–67.

McMillan, Neil R., ed., with James C. Cobb and Morton Sosna. *Remaking Dixie: The Impact of World War II on the American South.* Jackson: University Press of Mississippi, 1997.

Mead, Lawrence M. *The New Politics of Poverty: The Nonworking Poor in America.* New York: Basic Books, 1992.

Mearsheimer, John J., and Stephen M. Walt. *The Israel Lobby and U.S. Foreign Policy.* New York: Farrar, Straus and Giroux, 2007.

Miller, Arthur S. *Private Government and the Constitution*. Santa Barbara, Calif.: Center for the Study of Democratic Institutions, 1959.

Miller, Douglas T., and Marion Nowak. *The Fifties: The Way We Really Were*. Garden City, N.Y.: Doubleday, 1977.

Miller, Robert T., and Ronald B. Flowers. *Toward Benevolent Neutrality: Church, State, and the Supreme Court*. Waco, Tex.: Baylor University Press, 1998.

Miller, Steven P. *Billy Graham and the Rise of the Republican South*. Philadelphia: University of Pennsylvania Press, 2009.

Miller, William Lee. "American Religion and American Political Attitudes," in *Religious Perspectives in American Culture*, ed. James Ward Smith and A. Leland Jamison, 81–118. Princeton, N.J.: Princeton University Press, 1961.

———. *Piety Along the Potomac: Notes on Politics and Morals in the Fifties*. Boston: Houghton Mifflin, 1964.

Mills, C. Wright. *The Power Elite*. New York: Oxford University Press, 1956.

"Ministers Favor Eisenhower 8 to 1." *Christianity Today*, 29 October 1956, 28.

Minow, Martha. "Choice or Commonality: Welfare and Schooling After the Welfare State." In *Who Will Provide? The Changing Role of Religion in American Social Welfare*, ed. Mary Jo Bane, Brent Coffin, and Ronald Thiemann, 147–78. Boulder, Colo.: Westview Press, 2000.

Monsma, Stephen V. *When Sacred and Secular Mix: Religious Nonprofit Organizations and Public Money*. Lanham, Md.: Rowman and Littlefield, 1996.

Montiel, Lisa M., with Jason D. Scott, Joyce Keyes-Williams, and Jun Seop Han. "The Use of Public Funds For Delivery of Faith-Based Human Services: A review of the research literature focusing on the public funding of faith-based organizations in the delivery of social services." 2nd ed. The Roundtable on Religion and Social Welfare Policy, 2003, http://www.religionandsocialpolicy.org/docs/bibliographies/9–24–2002_use_of_public_funds.pdf. 16 July 2008.

Moreton, Bethany. *To Serve God and Wal-Mart: The Making of Christian Free Enterprise*. Cambridge, Mass.: Harvard University Press, 2009.

———. "Why Is There So Much Sex in Christian Conservatism and Why Do So Few Historians Care Anything about It?" *Journal of Southern History* 75 (2009): 717–38.

Morgan, Iwan. *The Age of Deficits: Presidents and Unbalanced Budgets from Jimmy Carter to George W. Bush*. Lawrence: University of Kansas Press, 2009.

Morone, James A. *The Democratic Wish: Popular Participation and the Limits of American Government*. New York: Basic Books, 1990.

Moynihan, Daniel P. *The Negro Family: The Case for National Action*. Washington, D.C.: U.S. Department of Labor, 1965

"NAE Reaffirms Strong Anti-Communist Stand," *Christianity Today*, 9 May 1960, 30.

"NAE Resolutions." *Christianity Today*, 9 May 1960, 30.

Nash, Gerald D. *The American West Transformed: The Impact of the Second World War*. Bloomington: Indiana University Press, 1985.

——. *World War II and the West: Reshaping the Economy.* Lincoln: University of Nebraska Press, 1990.

"A Nation Under God," *Christianity Today,* 4 February 1957, 28, 38.

National Association of Evangelicals. "History of the NAE," http://www.nae.net/index .cfm?FUSEACTION=nae.history. 24 July 2008.

Nelson, Rudolph. *The Making and Unmaking of an Evangelical Mind: The Case of Edward Carnell.* Cambridge: Cambridge University Press, 1987.

Netting, Ellen F. "Secular and Religious Funding of Church-Related Agencies." *Social Service Review* 56 (1982): 586–604.

Neustadt, Richard E. "Congress and the Fair Deal: A Legislative Balance Sheet." In *Harry S. Truman and the Fair Deal,* ed. Alonzo Hamby, 15–41. Lexington, Mass.: Heath, 1974.

Nichols, Bruce. *The Uneasy Alliance: Religion, Refugee Work, and U.S. Foreign Policy.* New York: Oxford University Press, 1988.

Noll, Mark A. *A History of Christianity in the United States and Canada.* Grand Rapids, Mich.: Eerdmans, 1992.

——. *The Old Religion in a New World: The History of North American Christianity.* Grand Rapids, Mich.: William B. Eerdmans, 2002.

——, ed. *Religion and American Politics: From the Colonial Period to the 1980s.* New York: Oxford University Press, 1989.

"NSC 68: United States Objectives and Programs for National Security." Section IX. D, 14 April 1950, http://www.fas.org/irp/offdocs/nsc-hst/nsc-68.htm. 6 July 2008.

Oates, Mary J. "Faith and Good Works: Catholic Giving and Taking." In *Charity, Philanthropy and Civility in American History,* ed. Lawrence J. Friedman and Mark D. McGarvie, 281–99. Cambridge: Cambridge University Press, 2003.

Ockenga, Harold John. "The Communist Issue Today." *Christianity Today,* 22 May 1961, 9–12.

O'Connor, Alice. *Poverty Knowledge: Social Science, Social Policy, and the Poor in Twentieth-Century U.S. History.* Princeton, N.J.: Princeton University Press, 2001.

——. "Neither Charity nor Relief: The War on Poverty and the Efforts to Redefine the Basis of Social Provision." In *With Us Always: A History of Private Charity and Public Welfare,* ed. Donald T. Critchlow and Charles H. Parker, 191–210. Lanham, Md: Rowman and Littlefield, 1998.

Olasky, Marvin. "The Corruption of Religious Charities," In Peter L. Berger and Richard John Neuhaus. *To Empower People: From State to Civil Society,* ed. Michael Novak. 2nd ed., 94–104. Washington, D.C.: American Enterprise Institute, 1996.

Oliver, Kendrick. "Attica, Watergate and the Origin of Evangelical Prison Ministry, 1969–1975." Paper presented at David Bruce Centre for American Studies Colloquium "New Perspectives on American Evangelicalism and the 1960s," Keele University, 16–19 April 2011.

O'Neill, Michael. *The Third America: The Emergence of the Nonprofit Sector in the United States.* San Francisco: Jossey-Bass, 1989.

Ostling, Richard N. "America's Ever-Changing Religious Landscape." *Brookings Review* 17 (Spring 1999): 10–13.

Parmar, Inderjeet. "Conceptualising the American State-Private Network during the Cold War." In *The US Government, Citizen Groups and the Cold War: The State-Private Network*, ed. Helen Laville and Hugh Wilford, 13–27. London: Routledge, 2006.

"Parochaid: Looking for a Loophole." *Christianity Today*, 8 December 1972, 39–40.

Patterson, James T. "Poverty and Welfare in America, 1945–1960." In *Reshaping America: Society and Institutions, 1945–1960*, ed. Robert H. Bremner and Gary W. Richard, 193–221. Columbus: Ohio State University Press, 1982.

Peachey, Paul. "Beyond Christian-Communist Strife." *Christianity Today*, 27 October 1958, 15–17, 24.

"The Pentagon's Responsibility for Servicemen Abroad." *Christianity Today*, 22 July 1957, 21–22.

Pfeffer, Leo. "Religion Exemptions." In *Church-State Relations: Tensions and Transitions*, ed. Thomas Robbins and Roland Robertson, 103–14. New Brunswick, N.J.: Transition, 1987.

Pierard, Richard V. "Billy Graham and the U.S. Presidency." *Journal of Church and State* 22 (Winter 1980): 107–27.

———. *The Unequal Yoke: Evangelical Christianity and Political Conservatism*. Philadelphia: Lippincott, 1970.

Pierard, Richard V., and Robert D. Lindner, *Civil Religion and the Presidency*. Grand Rapids, Mich.: Academie Books, 1988.

Piper, J. Richard. *Ideologies and Institutions: American Conservative and Liberal Governance Prescriptions Since 1933*. Lanham, Md.: Rowman and Littlefield, 1997.

Pipes, Paula F., and Helen Rose Ebaugh. "Faith-Based Coalitions, Social Services, and Government Funding." *Sociology of Religion* 63 (2002): 49–68.

Piven, Frances Fox, and Richard A. Cloward, "Popular Power and the Welfare State." In *Remaking the Welfare State: Retrenchment and Social Policy in America and Europe*, ed. Michael K. Brown, 73–95. Philadelphia: Temple University Press, 1988.

Polenberg, Richard. *War and Society: The United States, 1941–1945*. Westport, Conn.: Greenwood Press, 1980.

Pollock, John. *Billy Graham, Evangelist to the World: An Authorized Biography of the Decisive Years*. San Francisco: Harper and Row, 1979.

"Pressures Rise for Federal Handouts." *Christianity Today*, 12 May 1958, 22.

Preston, Andrew. "The Death of a Peculiar Special Relationship: Myron Taylor and the Religious Roots of America's Cold War." In *America's 'Special Relationships': Foreign and Domestic Aspects of the Politics of Alliance*, ed. John Dumbrell and Axel R. Schäfer, 208–22. London: Routledge, 2009.

———. "Universal Nationalism," in *The Shock of the Global: The 1970s in Perspective*, ed. Niall Ferguson, Charles S. Maier, Erez Manela, and Daniel J. Sargent, 306–18. Cambridge, Mass.: Belknap Press of Harvard University Press, 2010.

"Protestant Muddle in Social Welfare." *Christianity Today*, 2 February 1959, 23.

Quadagno, Jill. *The Color of Welfare: How Racism Undermined the War on Poverty.* New York: Oxford University Press, 1994.

Quebedeaux, Richard. *The Worldly Evangelicals.* San Francisco: Harper and Row, 1978.

———. *The Young Evangelicals: Revolution in Orthodoxy.* New York, Harper and Row, 1974.

Rabinowitz, Alan. *Social Change Philanthropy in America.* New York: Quorum Books, 1990.

Ravitch, Diane. *The Troubled Crusade: American Education, 1945–1980.* New York: Basic Books, 1983.

Rawls, John. *A Theory of Justice.* Cambridge, Mass.: Belknap Press of Harvard University Press, 1971.

"Red China and World Morality." *Christianity Today,* 10 December 1956, 20–22.

Reich, Robert B. *Tales of a New America.* New York: Times Books, 1987.

Reid, W. Stanford. "The Age of Anxiety: A Call to Christian Action." *Christianity Today,* 18 August 1958, 3–4.

"Resurgent Evangelism." *Christianity Today,* 9 June 1958, 20–22.

Ribuffo, Leo. *The Old Christian Right: The Protestant Far Right from the Great Depression to the Cold War.* Philadelphia: Temple University Press, 1983.

Rodgers, Daniel T. *Atlantic Crossings: Social Politics in a Progressive Age.* Cambridge, Mass.: Harvard University Press, 1998.

Rosenthal, Marguerite G. "Public or Private Children's Services? Privatization in Retrospect," http://archive.epinet.org/real_media/010111/materials/rosenthal.pdf. 9 July 2008.

Rothenberg, Stuart, and Frank Newport. *The Evangelical Voter: Religion and Politics in America.* Washington, D.C.: Institute for Government and Politics, 1984.

"Round Table: A Critical Moment: World War II and Its Aftermath at Home." *Journal of American History* 92 (March 2006): 1212–99.

The Roundtable on Religion and Social Welfare Policy. "Americans United for Separation of Church and State et al. v. Warden Terry Mapes, Prison Fellowship Ministries, InnerChange Freedom Initiative, et al. (U.S. District Court, Southern District of Iowa, suit filed 2/12/03)," 14 March 2003, http://www.religionandsocialpolicy.org/legal/legal_update_display-38371.html. 30 August 2011.

Salamon, Lester H. *America's Nonprofit Sector: A Primer.* Baltimore: Johns Hopkins University Press, 1992.

———. *Partners in Public Service: Government-Nonprofit Relations in the Modern Welfare State.* Baltimore: Johns Hopkins University Press, 1995.

Sandel, Michael J. *Democracy's Discontent: America in Search of a Public Philosophy.* Cambridge, Mass.: Harvard University Press, 1981.

———. *Liberalism and the Limits of Justice.* Cambridge: Cambridge University Press, 1982.

Sarvasy, Wendy. "Reagan and Low-Income Mothers: A Feminist Recasting of the Debate." In *Remaking the Welfare State: Retrenchment and Social Policy in America and Europe,* ed. Michael K. Brown, 253–76. Philadelphia: Temple University Press, 1988.

Schäfer, Axel R. *American Progressives and German Social Reform, 1875–1920: Social Ethics, Moral Control, and the Regulatory State in a Transatlantic Context.* Stuttgart: Franz Steiner Verlag, 2000.

———. "The Cold War State and the Resurgence of Evangelicalism: A Study of the Public Funding of Religion Since 1945." *Radical History Review* 99 (Fall 2007): 19–50.

———. *Countercultural Conservatives: American Evangelicalism from the Postwar Revival to the New Christian Right.* Madison: University of Wisconsin Press, 2011.

———. "The Liberal State and Conservative Social Policy: The Politics of Growth, Subsidiarity, and Moral Categorizing in the U.S. After 1945." In *Democracy and Social Rights in the Two Wests*, ed. Alice Kessler-Harris and Maurizio Vaudagna, 259–77. Turin: Otto Editore, 2009.

———. "Religion, the Cold War State, and the Resurgence of Evangelicalism in the U.S., 1942–1990." ZENAF Arbeits- und Forschungsbericht (ZAF), 1/2006, Center for North American Studies, Johann Wolfgang Goethe-Universität Frankfurt, http://web.uni-frankfurt.de/zenaf/zenaf/schaefer_zaf.pdf. 6 December 2008.

———. "Religious Nonprofit Organizations, the Cold War, the State and Resurgent Evangelicalism, 1945–1990." In *The US Government, Citizen Groups and the Cold War: The State-Private Network*, ed. Helen Laville and Hugh Wilford, 175–93. London: Routledge, 2006.

Schiff, Gerald. *Charitable Giving and Government Policy: An Economic Analysis.* New York: Greenwood, 1990.

Schottland, Charles I. "Introduction." In Bernard Coughlin. *Church and State in Social Welfare.* New York: Columbia University Press, 1965.

Schuparra, Kurt. *Triumph of the Right: The Rise of the California Conservative Movement, 1945–1966.* Armonk, N.Y.: M.E. Sharpe, 1998.

Schwarz, Frederick G. "Can We Meet the Red Challenge." *Christianity Today*, 13 April 1959, 13–15.

Schwarz, Jordan A. *The Interregnum of Despair: Hoover, Congress, and the Depression.* Urbana: University of Illinois Press, 1970.

SenGupta, Gunja. *From Slavery to Poverty: The Racial Origins of Welfare in New York, 1840–1918.* New York: New York University Press, 2009.

Shapiro, Samantha M. "Jails for Jesus." *Mother Jones*, December 2003, 55–59.

Sherman, Amy L. Testimony, U.S. Congress. House. Committee on the Judiciary, Subcommittee on the Constitution, "State and Local Implementation of Existing Charitable Choice Programs," 107th Cong., 1st sess., 24 April 2001. http://commdocs.house.gov/committees/judiciary/hju72145.000/hju72145_0.HTM. 17 August 2008.

Sherry, Michael. *In the Shadow of War: The United States Since the 1930s.* New Haven, Conn.: Yale University Press, 1995.

Simpson, John H. "Socio-Moral Issues and Recent Presidential Elections." *Review of Religious Research* 27 (December 1985): 115–23.

Sittser, Gerald L. *A Cautious Patriotism: The American Churches and the Second World War.* Chapel Hill: University of North Carolina Press, 1997.

Sklansky, Jeffrey. *The Soul's Economy: Market Society and Selfhood in American Thought, 1820–1920*. Chapel Hill: University of North Carolina Press, 2002.

Skocpol, Theda. "The G.I. Bill and U.S. Social Policy," *Social Philosophy and Policy* 14 (1997): 95–115.

———. "Religion, Civil Society, and Social Provision in the U.S." In *Who Will Provide? The Changing Role of Religion in American Social Welfare*, ed. Mary Jo Bane, Brent Coffin and Ronald Thiemann, 21–50. Boulder, Colo.: Westview Press, 2000.

———. *Social Policy in the United States: Future Possibilities in Historical Perspective*. Princeton, N.J.: Princeton University Press, 1995.

Smith, Christian. *American Evangelicalism: Embattled and Thriving*. Chicago: University of Chicago Press, 1998.

Smith, Christian, with Michael Emerson, Sally Gallagher et al. "The Myth of Culture Wars: The Case of American Protestantism." In *Cultural Wars in American Politics: Critical Reviews of a Popular Myth*, ed. Rhys H. Williams, 175–95. New York: de Gruyter, 1997.

Smith, Stephen Rathgeb, and Deborah A. Stone. "The Unexpected Consequences of Privatization." In *Remaking the Welfare State: Retrenchment and Social Policy in America and Europe*, ed. Michael K. Brown, 232–52. Philadelphia: Temple University Press, 1988.

Smith, Steven Rathgeb, and Michael Lipsky. *Nonprofits for Hire: The Welfare State in the Age of Contracting*. Cambridge, Mass.: Harvard University Press, 1993.

Smith, Timothy. *Revivalism and Social Reform: American Protestantism on the Eve of the Civil War*. Rev. ed. Baltimore: Johns Hopkins University Press, 1980.

Sparrow, Bartholomew H. *From the Outside In: World War II and the American State*. Princeton, N.J.: Princeton University Press, 1996.

"Spiritual-Moral Unity Wanes in United Nations." *Christianity Today*, 4 March 1957, 21–22.

Stone, Jon R. *On the Boundaries of American Evangelicalism: The Postwar Evangelical Coalition*. New York: St. Martin's Press, 1997.

Sullivan, Winnifred Fallers. *Prison Religion: Faith-Based Reform and the Constitution*. Princeton, N.J.: Princeton University Press, 2009

Supreme Court of the United States. *Arizona Christian School Tuition Organization v. Winn et al.* http://www.supremecourt.gov/opinions/10pdf/09-987.pdf. 24 May 2011.

Swartz, David R. "Left Behind: The Evangelical Left and the Limits of Evangelical Politics, 1965–1988." Ph.D. dissertation, University of Notre Dame, 2008.

Sweet, Leonard. "The 1960s: The Crisis of Liberal Christianity and the Public Emergence of Evangelicalism." In *Evangelicalism and Modern America*, ed. George M. Marsden, 29–45. Grand Rapids, Mich.: Eerdmans, 1984.

Taylor, Clyde W. "NAE Celebrates 30 Years of Service." *Action*, Spring 1972, 8–12.

Taylor, G. Aiken. "Why Communism Is Godless." *Christianity Today*, 22 December 1958, 13–15.

Thiemann, Ronald, Samuel Herring, and Betsy Perabo, "Responsibility and Risks for Faith-Based Organizations." In *Who Will Provide? The Changing Role of Religion in American Social Welfare*, ed. Mary Jo Bane, Brent Coffin, and Ronald Thiemann, 51–70. Boulder, Colo.: Westview Press, 2000.

Thomas, George M. *Revivalism and Cultural Change: Christianity, Nation Building, and the Market in the Nineteenth-Century United States*. Chicago: University of Chicago Press, 1989.

Toulouse, Mark G. "*Christianity Today* and American Public Life: A Case Study." *Journal of Church and State* 35 (Spring 1993): 241–84.

Tseng, Timothy, and Janet Furness, "The Reawakening of the Evangelical Social Consciousness." In *The Social Gospel Today*, ed. Christopher Evans, 114–25. Louisville, Ky.: Westminster/John Knox, 2001.

Turner, John G. *Bill Bright and Campus Crusade for Christ: The Renewal of Evangelicalism in Postwar America*. Chapel Hill: University of North Carolina Press, 2008.

"UN: Town Meeting? Or Tragedy?" *Christianity Today*, 1 April 1957, 20–22.

"United for Separation." *Christianity Today*, 2 March 1973, 51.

U.S. Bureau of the Census. Department of Commerce. *Historical Statistics of the United States: Colonial Times to 1970*. Washington, D.C.: Government Printing Office, 1975, http://www.census.gov/prod/www/abs/statab.html. 6 July 2008.

U.S. Congress. House. Subcommittee of the Committee on Foreign Affairs. *Final Report on Foreign Aid*, Report #1845, 80th Cong., 2nd sess., 1948; Section 202, amended Agricultural Trade and Development Assistance Act; Section 635(c), Act for International Development (PL 87–195).

"U.S. Court Rejects 'Pervasively Sectarian' Test." *Inside Higher Education*. http://www.insidehighered.com/news/2008/07/24/ccu. 15 September 2008.

U.S. Department of Health and Human Resources. "Hill-Burton Facilities Compliance and Recovery," http://www.hrsa.gov/hillburton/compliance-recovery.htm. 9 July 2008.

U.S. Office of Management and Budget. *Budget of the United States Government, Fiscal Year 2000, Historical Tables*, http://www.fas.org/man/docs/fy00/historical/index.html#h10. 4 December 2008.

———. *Budget of the United States Government, Fiscal Year 2007, Historical Tables*, Washington, D.C.: Government Printing Office, 2007, http://www.whitehouse.gov/omb/budget/fy2007/pdf/hist.pdf. 4 December 2008.

Viteritti, Joseph P. *The Last Freedom: Religion from the Public School to the Public Square*. Princeton, N.J.: Princeton University Press, 2007.

Wacker, Grant. "Uneasy in Zion: Evangelicals in Postmodern Society." In *Reckoning with the Past: Historical Essays on American Evangelicalism from the Institute for the Study of American Evangelicals*, ed. D. G. Hart, 376–93. Grand Rapids, Mich.: Baker Books, 1995.

Wald, Kenneth. *Religion and Politics in the United States*. 2nd ed. Washington, D.C.: Congressional Quarterly, 1992.

Walzer, Michael. *Spheres of Justice: A Defense of Pluralism and Equality.* New York: Basic Books, 1983.

Ward, Andrew. "From backwater to outer space." *Financial Times,* 17 February 2006. http://www.ft.com/cms/s/0/2a38db9a-9f5b-11da-ba48-0000779e2340.html?nclick_check=1. 6 July 2008.

Warner, R. Stephen. *New Wine in Old Wineskins: Evangelicals and Liberals in a Small-Town Church.* Berkeley: University of California Press, 1988.

"The Washington Office: A Voice Above the Clamor." *Christianity Today,* 8 October 1982, 53.

Watt, David Harrington. "The Private Hopes of American Fundamentalists and Evangelicals, 1925–1975." *Religion and American Culture* 1, 2 (1991): 155–75.

———. *A Transforming Faith: Explorations of Twentieth-Century American Evangelicalism.* New Brunswick, N.J.: Rutgers University Press, 1991.

Weber Paul J., and Dennis A. Gilbert. *Private Churches and Public Money: Church-Government Fiscal Relations.* Westport, Conn.: Greenwood Press, 1981.

Wedel, Kenneth A., Arthur J. Katz, and Ann Weick, eds. *Social Services by Government Contract: A Policy Analysis.* New York: Praeger, 1979.

Weeks, David L. "Carl F. H. Henry on Civic Life." In *Evangelicals in the Public Square: Four Formative Voices on Political Thought and Action,* ed. J. Budziszewski, 123–40. Grand Rapids, Mich: Baker Group, 2006.

Weeks, David L. "Carl F. H. Henry's Moral Arguments for Evangelical Political Activism." *Journal of Church and State* 40 (Winter 1998): 83–106.

Weisbrod, Burton A. *The Nonprofit Economy.* Cambridge, Mass.: Harvard University Press, 1988.

Westbrook, Robert B. "Fighting for the Family." In *Major Problems in American History, 1920–1945,* ed. Colin Gordon, 408–17. Boston: Houghton Mifflin, 1999.

"What Is the Target: Communism or Anti-Communists." *Christianity Today,* 22 May 1961, 22–23.

White, Arthur H. "Philanthropic Giving." In *Philanthropic Giving: Studies in Varieties and Goals,* ed. Robert Magat, 65–71. New York: Oxford University Press, 1989.

White, Richard. *"It's Your Misfortune and None of My Own": A New History of the American West.* Norman: University of Oklahoma Press, 1991.

Wikander, Ulla, Alice Kessler-Harris, and Jane Lewis, eds., with the assistance of Jan Lambertz. *Protecting Women: Labor Legislation in Europe, the United States, and Australia, 1880–1920.* Urbana: University of Illinois Press, 1995.

Wilcox, Clyde. *Onward Christian Soldiers? The Religious Right in American Politics.* Boulder, Colo.: Westview Press, 1996.

Williams, Daniel K. *God's Own Party: The Making of the Christian Right.* New York: Oxford University Press, 2010.

Williams, Rhys H. "Culture Wars, Social Movements, and Institutional Politics." In *Cultural Wars in American Politics: Critical Reviews of a Popular Myth,* ed. Rhys H. Williams, 283–95. New York: de Gruyter, 1997.

Wilson, William Julius. *The Truly Disadvantaged: The Inner City, the Underclass, and Public Policy.* Chicago: University of Chicago Press, 1987.

Wineburg, Robert J. *A Limited Partnership: The Politics of Religion, Welfare, and Social Service.* New York: Columbia University Press, 2000.

Witte, John, Jr. "Whether Piety or Charity: Classification Issues in the Exemption of Churches and Charities from Property Taxation." In *Religion, Independent Sector and American Culture,* ed. Conrad Cherry and Rowland A. Sherrill, 135–61. Atlanta: Scholars Press, 1992.

Wolfe, Alan. *America's Impasse: The Rise and Fall of the Politics of Growth.* New York: Random House, 1980.

Wood, James R. "Liberal Protestant Action in a Period of Decline." In *Faith and Philanthropy in America: Exploring the Role of Religion in America's Voluntary Sector,* ed. Robert A. Wuthnow, Virginia Hodgkinson, and Associates, 165–86. San Francisco: Jossey-Bass, 1990.

Woods, Russell Bennett. *Quest for Identity: America Since 1945.* New York: Cambridge University Press, 2005.

"World Without War Council—Midwest, Brief History." http://www.worldwithoutwar .org/about_us.php?member_www=b1fe25c80aee6b7ec4eda0c2496cc7b0. 11 August 2008.

Wuthnow, Robert. "Improving Our Understanding of Religion and Giving: Key Issues for Research." In *Faith and Philanthropy in America: Exploring the Role of Religion in America's Voluntary Sector,* ed. Robert A. Wuthnow, Virginia Hodgkinson, and Associates, 271–83. San Francisco: Jossey-Bass, 1990.

———. "Religion and the Voluntary Spirit in the United States: Mapping the Terrain." In *Faith and Philanthropy in America: Exploring the Role of Religion in America's Voluntary Sector,* ed. Robert A. Wuthnow, Virginia Hodgkinson, and Associates, 3–21. San Francisco: Jossey-Bass, 1990.

———. *The Restructuring of American Religion: Society and Faith Since World War II.* Princeton, N.J.: Princeton University Press, 1988.

———. *Saving America? Faith-Based Services and the Future of Civil Society.* Princeton, N.J.: Princeton University Press, 2004.

———. "Religious Commitment and Conservatism: In Search of an Elusive Relationship." In *Religion in Sociological Perspective,* ed. Charles Y. Glock, 117–32. Belmont, Calif.: Wadsworth, 1973.

Wuthnow, Robert, Virginia Hodgkinson, and Associates, eds. *Faith and Philanthropy in America: Exploring the Role of Religion in America's Voluntary Sector.* San Francisco: Jossey-Bass, 1990.

WZB Mitteilungen 110 (December 2005): 25–27.

Yergin, Daniel, and Joseph Stanislaw, "Democrats and Republicans Forge a New Political Economy." In *Major Problems in American History Since 1945,* ed. Robert Griffith and Paula Baker. 2nd ed., 477–96. Boston: Houghton Mifflin, 2001.

INDEX

Faith-Based Initiative, 14, 18, 21, 44, 145, 210–12, 259n62, 260n71

FCC (Federal Communications Commission), 66

FCCCA (Federal Council of the Churches of Christ in America), 154

Federal Communications Commission. *See* FCC

Federal Council of the Churches of Christ in America. *See* FCCCA

First Amendment, 21, 46, 47, 49, 137, 186, 213. *See also* Supreme Court

Flipse, Scott, 27

Fogel, Robert William, 5, 72

Ford, George, 97, 132, 139–40

foreign aid relief: overview, 9, 12–13, 113, 122; Catholicism and, 12, 32–34, 112–13, 115; church-state relations and, 12, 146; Cold War state and, 30–31; communism and, 111, 113; conservative Protestantism and, 12, 13, 112–13, 120; education and, 32; evangelicals and, 6, 12–13, 110, 113; freedom of religion and, 113, 118–19, 121; mainline Protestantism and, 32–34, 56–57, 112; missionary activism and, 13, 32, 53; NAE relief programs and, 66, 111–12, 114–19, 238nn142, 147; nonprofits and, 8, 23; POAU and, 110–11, 114; state, civil, and religious group ties discussion and, 6, 9, 86; statistics, 4; subsidiarity and, 13, 23–24, 27–34, 38, 53, 112–13; Supreme Court decisions and, 46

foreign policy: overview, 1–4, 6, 11–13, 86, 121–22; Catholicism and, 169; conservatism and, 197; conservative Protestantism and, 12, 13, 86, 119, 165–66; conversionism and, 90–91; education and, 13; evangelicals' relation with, 6, 12, 87–89, 103–5, 164, 165; health care and, 13; Israel and, 12, 89, 91–93, 108, 165; Jews and, 169–70; the Left and, 170; left-leaning evangelicals and, 169; millennialism and, 93; missionary activism and, 103–4, 105–6, 236n92; NAE and, 103–4, 119, 164–67, 249n17; national security state and, 104–5; New Christian Right and, 93; nonprofits and, 119; religious groups and, 3, 14–15, 50, 55, 95; right-wing evangelicals and, 164–71; separationism and, 90–91; spiritual renewal and, 87–90; subsidiarity and, 8–9; UN and, 12, 66, 67,

91–93, 92–93, 108, 121, 233n23. *See also* anti-Catholicism; anticommunism; Cold War state; national security state

Forrester, James, 151–52

Freeden, Michael, 80

freedom of religion: overview, 70, 89, 161–62; armed forces and, 107–8, 111; Catholicism and, 67; child care services and, 160, 192, 248n189; church-state relations and, 99; communism versus, 94, 96–97, 107–8, 121; foreign aid relief and, 113, 118–19, 121; missionary activism and, 100–101, 111; national security state and, 121; peace association with, 170–72; peacemaking and, 170–72; state building and, 140; subsidiarity and, 113, 118–19, 120–21; tuition tax credits and, 254n121; voucher system and, 44, 188–90, 247n187, 254n121. *See also* NAE

Fuller Theological Seminary, 63, 149. *See also* neo-evangelicals

fundamentalism: anti-Catholicism and, 97–98, 111; consumer capitalist secularization of, 176; NAE relation with, 65; neo-evangelicals' rejection of, 2, 10, 62–63, 71; separationism and, 111; welfare state and, 127–28. *See also* conservative Protestantism; evangelicals; New Christian Right

Gallup, George, Jr., 126–27, 206

gender discrimination: anticommunism and, 83; Cold War state and, 7; consumer capitalism and, 80–81, 231n94; evangelicals and, 11, 84; New Christian Right and, 7; poverty as moral issue, 78, 80–81, 84, 201–2, 204, 231n94; state building and, 7; subsidiarity and, 19; welfare state and, 7, 78, 80–82, 84, 201, 231n94

G.I. Bill of Rights (1944), 23, 34–35, 39, 52, 81, 141, 149–50

Goldwater, Barry, 149, 197, 258n46

Graham, Billy, 62, 75, 88, 93, 102–4, 125, 234n68

Great Society: education and, 39–40, 150, 155; evangelicals' support for, 206; health care and, 38–39, 40, 158–59; moral issues and, 6; poverty as moral issue, 202, 257n29; social services and, 40–45, 161; subsidiarity and, 6, 24, 38–42, 145, 146, 202–3. *See also* Cold War state; War on Poverty; welfare state; *specific government departments, programs*

and, 83–84, 207; evangelicals and, 10–11,
61–62, 73–75, 228n62; moral issues discussions and, 97; New Deal and, 196; partisan
politics and, 17, 194–95; political activism
and, 97; school voucher system and, 15;
subsidiarity and, 15, 199, 206–7, 258n46;
suburban Sunbelt communities and, 17,
209; welfare state critique by, 173. *See also*
New Christian Right
Nichols, Bruce, 4, 24, 30, 113, 133
Nixon, Richard, and administration: anticommunism and, 26, 97; church-state
relations and, 149; education and, 185, 191;
evangelicals' relation with, 103; regressive
taxation and, 203; welfare state and, 197,
201
nonprofits: foreign aid relief and, 8, 23;
foreign policy and, 119; religious agencies and, 9; socioeconomics and, 75–76,
228n56; statistics, 4, 53, 224n120; subsidiarity and, 42–43, 119–20; War on Poverty,
38–40. *See also* religious agencies

Ockenga, Harold John, 62, 89, 95, 154.
See also NAE (National Association of
Evangelicals)
O'Connor, Alice, 78, 80, 230n84
OEO (Office of Economic Opportunity), 39,
41–42, 146, 155–56, 158, 254n121
OPA (Office of Public Affairs): overview and
role of, 10, 66–67, 227n27; anti-Catholicism and, 98–99; church-state relations
and, 66; communism versus spiritual-
ism and, 94; displaced persons activism
and, 67; education and, 67; foreign aid
relief and, 115; foreign policy and, 166,
168, 248n10; freedom of religion and,
67; missionary activism and, 98–99; New
Christian Right and, 70; political activism
and, 10, 66–69, 102–3, 128; separationism
and, 10; tax exemptions and, 141. *See also*
NAE; neo-evangelicals; *specific leaders*
orthodox theology, 10, 62–63, 126–27, 195

pacifism: evangelicals and, 12, 86, 105,
164; left-leaning evangelicals and, 6, 15,
163; NAE and, 165, 168, 190, 213;
non-evangelicals and, 169–70
partisan politics: Cold War liberalism and,
195; consensus and, 21, 168, 171, 183, 209;

conservative Protestantism and, 7, 16,
168–69; evangelicals and, 127, 194; New
Christian Right and, 195; New Right and,
17, 194–95; realignment of evangelicals
and, 194, 206; welfare state and, 196–97.
See also Democratic Party; political activism; Republican Party
patriotic conversionism, 88, 90–91, 94–98
Peace, Freedom and Security Studies Program (PFSS), 168–71, 193
Peace Corps, 32, 117, 219n44, 239n157. *See
also* Kennedy, John F.
peacemaking, 30, 31, 70, 90–91, 111–12, 119,
166–71, 193; left-leaning evangelicals and,
170–72
*PEARL (Public Education and Religious Lib-
erty) v. Nyquist* (1973), 50, 223n106
Pentagon, 66, 68, 107–8
Pentecostalism, 64–65, 240n15
PFM (Prison Fellowship Ministries), 16,
178–81, 193
PFSS (Peace, Freedom and Security Studies
Program), 168–71, 193
Pickus, Robert, 169–70
pietism, 3, 12, 62–64, 69, 89, 121, 127, 174,
226n15
POAU (Protestants and Other Americans
United for the Separation of Church
and State), 190–91; overview, 67;
anti-Catholicism and, 117, 134–37;
church-state relations and, 16, 70, 111;
civil religion creed and, 90; displaced
persons activism and, 114; education
and, 67, 148–49, 154; education critique
by, 148, 154; foreign aid relief and,
110–11, 114; health care and, 157; school
voucher system and, 191; separationism
and, 190–91; subsidiarity critique by,
41–42, 111, 143, 145, 185, 221n77; tax
exemptions and, 48, 142; tuition tax
credits and, 191. *See also* AU
political activism: anticommunism and, 93–
97; evangelicals and, 63–64, 94–95, 102–6;
neo-evangelicals and, 128; New Right and,
97; patriotic conversionism and, 88, 90–91,
94–98; religious groups and, 4–5; subsidiarity and, 45–46. *See also* church-state
relations; OPA; partisan politics
postwar neo-evangelical revival. *See*
neo-evangelicals

167, 180, 184–85, 187, 193–96; limited government image and, 199–200, 208–9; NAE and, 70, 149, 166; New Christian Right and, 70; OPA and, 70; right-wing evangelicals and, 16, 174; subsidiarity and, 16, 199–200, 207–8, 210; welfare state and, 196–97, 206, 210. *See also specific presidents*
resurgent evangelicalism. *See* neo-evangelicals; New Christian Right
Right, the. *See* New Right; right-wing evangelicals
right-wing evangelicals: overview, 15, 62, 163–64, 192–93; calibration between anti-statism and state building discussion and, 174–78, 192, 208; conservatism and, 7, 16; consumer capitalism and, 173; foreign policy and, 164–71; moral issues and, 15, 192; morality politics and, 16, 174–77; national security state and, 7; Republican Party and, 16, 174; separationism critique by, 15, 190–92; subsidiarity and, 15, 177–81, 192, 251n52; welfare state and, 171–74. *See also* New Christian Right
Robertson, Floyd, 101, 110, 156
Robertson, Pat, 71, 179, 188
Rockey, Wendell, 116, 118, 239n153
Roe v. Wade (1973), 140, 186
Roman Catholicism. *See* Catholicism

Salamon, Lester H., 4, 24–25, 40, 215n8
salvation. *See* conversionism
Salvation Army, 13, 29, 42–43, 88, 110–12, 158, 178, 218n27
SBC (Southern Baptist Convention), 15, 65, 107, 115, 143, 144, 159. *See also* Southern Baptists
school prayer, 14–15, 124, 126–27, 139–41, 155, 191, 223n105, 245n121
school voucher system: overview of, 195–96; conservatism and, 183–86; G.I. Bill and, 35; left-leaning evangelicals and, 192; NAE and, 14, 159, 184–88, 191; New Right and, 15; OEO and, 155–56; POAU and, 191; Supreme Court decisions and, 50, 212, 223n104. *See also* education; tuition tax credits; voucher system
secondary and primary education, 9, 35–36, 46–50, 154–56, 186, 207, 254n125. *See also* education

Second Vatican Council, 101, 136, 235n76. *See also* ecumenism
secular conservatism. *See* conservatism
secularists and secularization: overview, 3; church-state relations versus, 112, 140–41; communism and, 95; conservative Protestantism's critique of, 15, 97; evangelicals' critique of, 97, 139–41; foreign policy and, 14–15, 50, 55, 95; separationism and, 124; subsidiarity and, 50, 55, 124, 133–34; welfare state critique of, 14, 139–41. *See also* communism and totalitarianism
separationism: anti-Catholicism and, 138; church-state relations and, 149, 185; evangelicals and, 10, 62, 124, 134, 140, 226n15; foreign policy and, 90–91; left-leaning evangelicals and, 6, 16, 192; religious groups and, 190–91; right-wing evangelicals' critique of, 15, 190–92; Southern Baptists and, 138; welfare state and, 130. *See also specific organizations*
Seventh-Day Adventists, 34, 109, 111–12, 116, 119, 157
Sherry, Michael, 23, 76, 228n56
Shriver, Sargent, 41–42, 146, 219n44
Sider, Ron, 167, 170, 192
Sklansky, Jeffrey, 79
Skocpol, Theda, 27
Smith, Steven Rathgeb, 43, 198
social issues. *See specific issues*
social justice: left-leaning evangelicals and, 14–15, 171–73; welfare state and, 70, 80, 129–30. *See also specific issues*
social policy (public policy), 2–3, 215n2. *See also* child care services; education; Great Society; health care; poverty as moral issue; War on Poverty; welfare state
Social Security, 125; Amendments of 1962, 1967, 1974, 23, 37–38, 41–42; race discrimination and, 84, 232n104
social services: overview, 1, 8, 23, 24, 27–28, 37; Catholicism and, 37–38, 45, 222n92; church-state relations and, 29, 39, 48; Cold War state and, 37–38; evangelicals and, 74; Great Society and, 40–45; mainline Protestantism and, 37–38, 56; privatization of, 8, 25, 44; race discrimination and, 41; retrenchment during Cold War state and, 43–45; subsidiarity and, 52–53; Supreme Court decisions and, 49. *See also specific services*

ACKNOWLEDGMENTS

T he question "Why history?" British writer Graham Swift points out in his novel *Waterland*, contains the answer within itself: The demand for an explanation involves us in a process of thinking about the past. Indeed, we are "story-telling animals" who seek to construct coherent stories of a miasma of disconnected events in order to uncover an elusive idea called "origins." A history book is one of the more curious manifestations of this human predilection, reflecting the struggle to carve out a sphere for critical thought between the dead weight of the past and the overwhelming imperiousness of the present. A book of this nature often has a complex genealogy. Presented to the reader encased in front and back cover with a beginning and an end, it constitutes an act of disciplining language and thinking. At the same time this compact outcome reflects more the demands of publishers, the rituals of the academic world, and the aesthetic preferences of the critical reader than the realities of the writing process. In the world of the latter, the book, like the proverbial cat, often has nine lives. It is conceived, abandoned, retrieved, shelved, revised, postponed, reformulated, abandoned again, and then (hopefully) rises from the ashes. At times it is on intellectual life support, at other times it grows wings and flies by itself. Sometimes a detached critique by a more or less sympathetic observer proves more fruitful than weeks of dedicated labor. Sometimes an off-the-cuff remark of a bystander turns out to be more important than rounds of presentations at scholarly conferences. And most remarkably, at the beginning of writing there are a lot of questions and a range of answers; at the end it's the other way around.

In light of this, it is the continuous encouragement and intellectual support from friends and colleagues throughout the long period of designing and writing this book that I am most indebted to and feel most thankful for. Alan Lessoff, Knud Krakau, Hans-Jürgen Grabbe, Michaela Hoenicke Moore, Celeste-Marie Bernier, Paul Boyer, Marcus Graeser, Andrew Preston, Darren Dochuk, Bethany Moreton, and Howard Brick have been a constant source of help and inspiration as I trespassed on their time at various stages of the book's creation. Some read drafts, chapters, or the whole manuscript, others endured patiently while I was harping on about some detail of the project. Likewise, many colleagues in the profession were generous with their time and with sharing their ideas. They include John Dumbrell, Gareth Davies, Kendrick Oliver, Daniel Scroop, Jonathan Bell, Iwan Morgan, Mark Noll, Donald Critchlow, Hugh Wilford, Eileen Luhr, David Swartz, Steven Miller, Daniel Williams, Hans Krabbendam, David Weeks, Brent Nelson, Jim Guth, Frances Fitzgerald, Robert Garson, Martin Crawford, Steve Mills, Richard King, Robert Mason, and Daniel Geary. I am grateful for all their contributions, whether made during heated debates late into the night, in giving practical help in finding resources, or simply in expressing their interest and faith in the project. Moreover, it is to friendship expressed in so many different ways that I owe the fact that I was able to write this book. In this respect I am tremendously grateful to David K. Adams, Thomas Fuchs, Kai Kumpf, Bernd and Kathi Klauer, Petra and Carsten Tismer, Brigitte Fleischer, Judith K. Brown, Marlies Krause, Cora Lindsay, Kartik Mithal, Reza Rajabiun, Don and Peggy Patton, and my extended family.

The excellent assistance of the staff at the archives I visited and the professionalism of the editorial team at the University of Pennsylvania Press warrant more than a special mention. In particular, I want to thank Bob Lockhart for being such a supportive and engaged editor who has steered this project competently through the often arcane publishing process, and Naomi Linzer for preparing the index with her trademark combination of speed, professionalism, acuity and thoughtful engagement with the text. The criticisms and generous feedback by the anonymous readers were vital to this book and are, I hope, properly reflected in the revisions I made to the original manuscript.

Research for this project was facilitated by a David Bruce Centre for American Studies Research Grant, sabbatical leave grants from Keele University, and a research fellowship from the John F. Kennedy Institute of the Free University Berlin. Preliminary findings were first presented in "The Cold War State and the Resurgence of Evangelicalism," *Radical History Review* 99 (2007): 19-50, copyright 2007, MARHO: The Radical Historians Organization, Inc., all rights reserved, reprinted by permission of the publisher, Duke University Press. I am also grateful to Routledge for granting permission to use materials previously published in my essays "What Marx, Lenin, and Stalin needed was…to be 'born again'": U.S. Foreign Policy, Church-State Relations and Evangelicals During the Cold War," in *America's "Special Relationships": Foreign and Domestic Aspects of the Politics of Alliance*, ed. John

Dumbrell and Axel R. Schäfer (London: Routledge, 2009), 223-41, and "Religious Nonprofit Organizations, the Cold War, the State and Resurgent Evangelicalism, 1945-1990," in *The U.S. Government, Citizen Groups and the Cold War: The State-Private Network*, ed. Helen Laville and Hugh Wilford (London: Routledge, 2006), 175-93.

This book is dedicated to my wife Brenda, whose love, strength, and endurance has been an inspiration without which this book would not have come about. Living with a historian is not easy. We are obsessive, niggling, pedantic, pompous, and all-knowing, as well as overly self-reflective and self-questioning. We like to "complexify" and "essentialize" in equal measure, while warning about the dangers of both. It requires a very special person to put up with this. And that she definitely is.